BARAKAMON

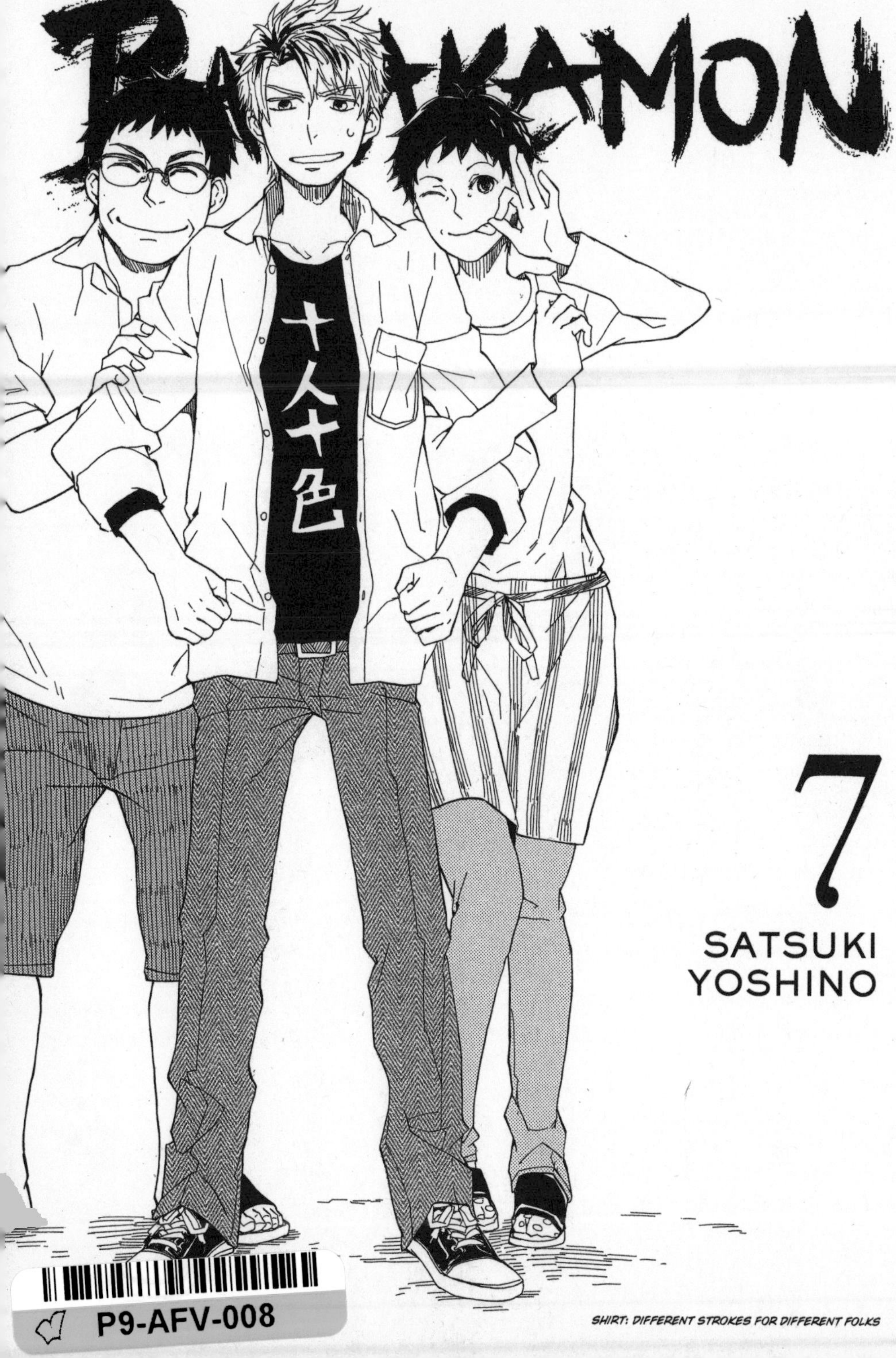
十人十色

7

SATSUKI
YOSHINO

SHIRT: DIFFERENT STROKES FOR DIFFERENT FOLKS

HEADMASTER   POOCH   HANDA-   NARU   TAMA   AKKI
SENSEI

IKU-CHAN   VILLAGE   MA'AM   HINA   HIROSHI   MIWA   MIWA'S DAD
              CHIEF

Contents

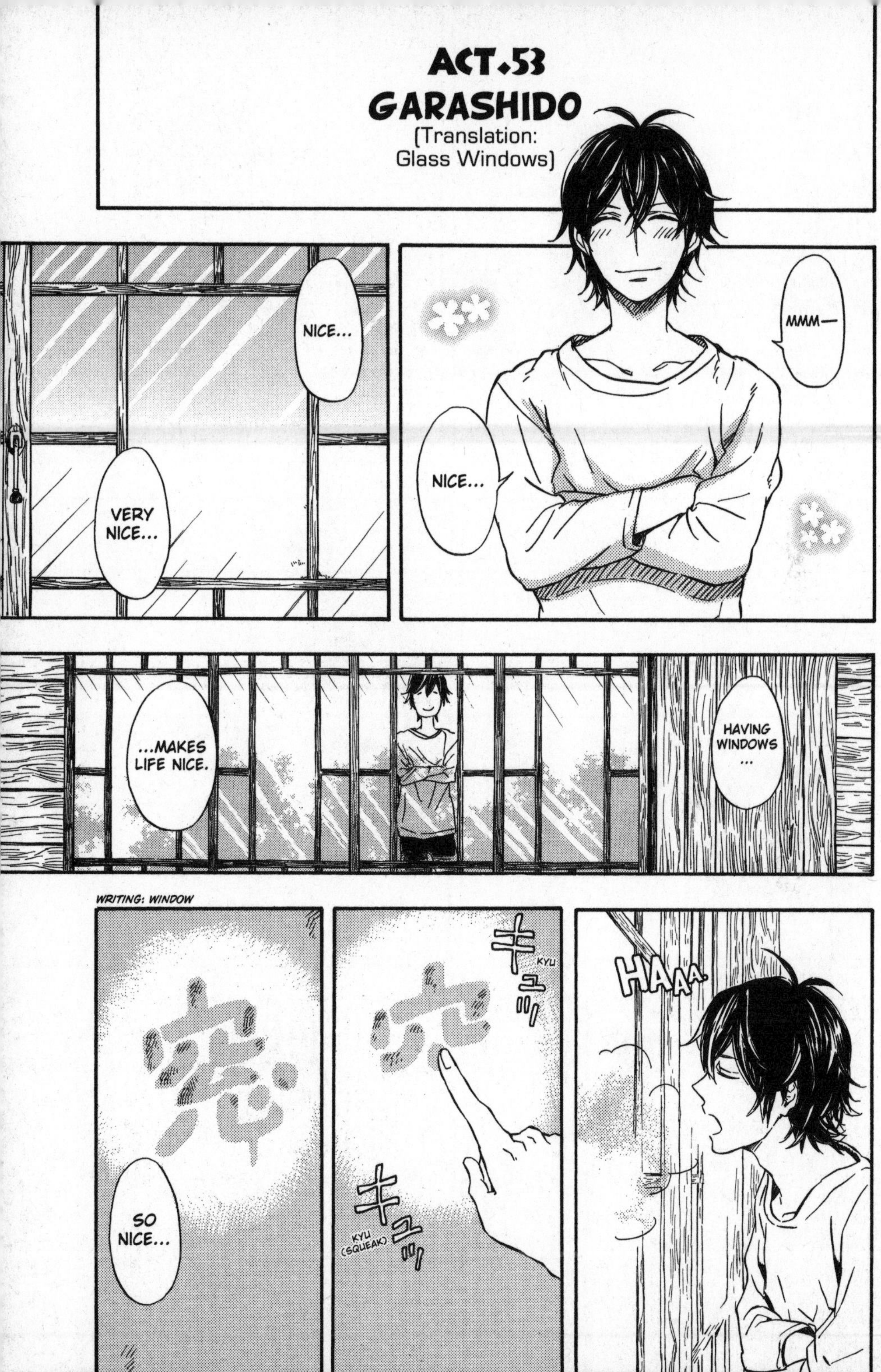
ACT.53
GARASHIDO
(Translation: Glass Windows)
MMM—
NICE...
NICE...
VERY NICE...
HAVING WINDOWS ...
...MAKES LIFE NICE.
HAAA.
KYU
穴
KYU (SQUEAK)
WRITING: WINDOW
窓
SO NICE...

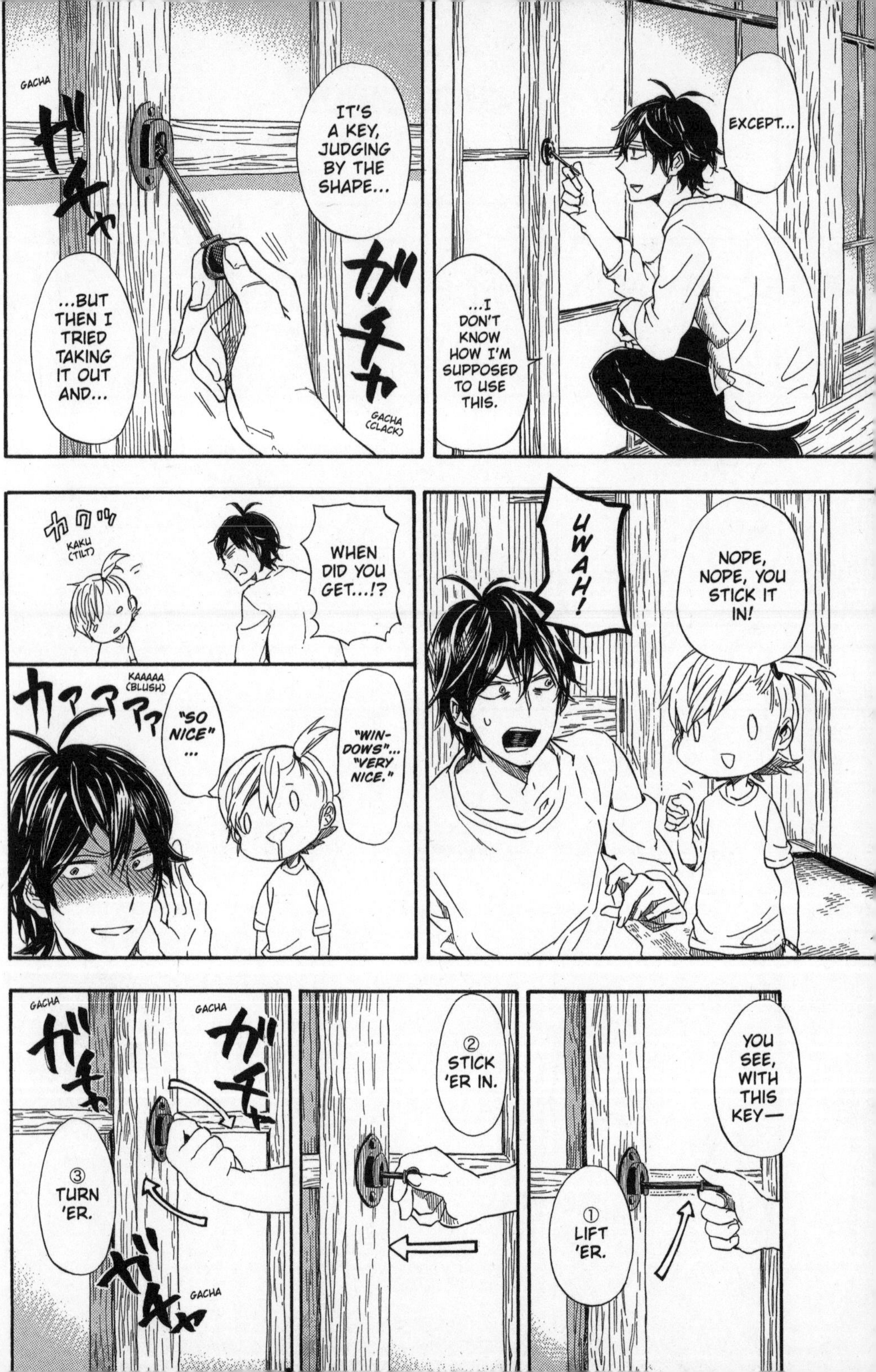
EXCEPT...
...I DON'T KNOW HOW I'M SUPPOSED TO USE THIS.
IT'S A KEY, JUDGING BY THE SHAPE...
ガチャ
GACHA (CLACK)
ガチャ
GACHA
...BUT THEN I TRIED TAKING IT OUT AND...
UWAH!
NOPE, NOPE, YOU STICK IT IN!
WHEN DID YOU GET...!?
カクッ
KAKU (TILT)
"WIN-DOWS"... "VERY NICE."
"SO NICE" ...
カアアアア
KAAAAA (BLUSH)
YOU SEE, WITH THIS KEY—
① LIFT 'ER.
② STICK 'ER IN.
ガチャ
GACHA
ガチャ
GACHA
③ TURN 'ER.
ガチャ
GACHA

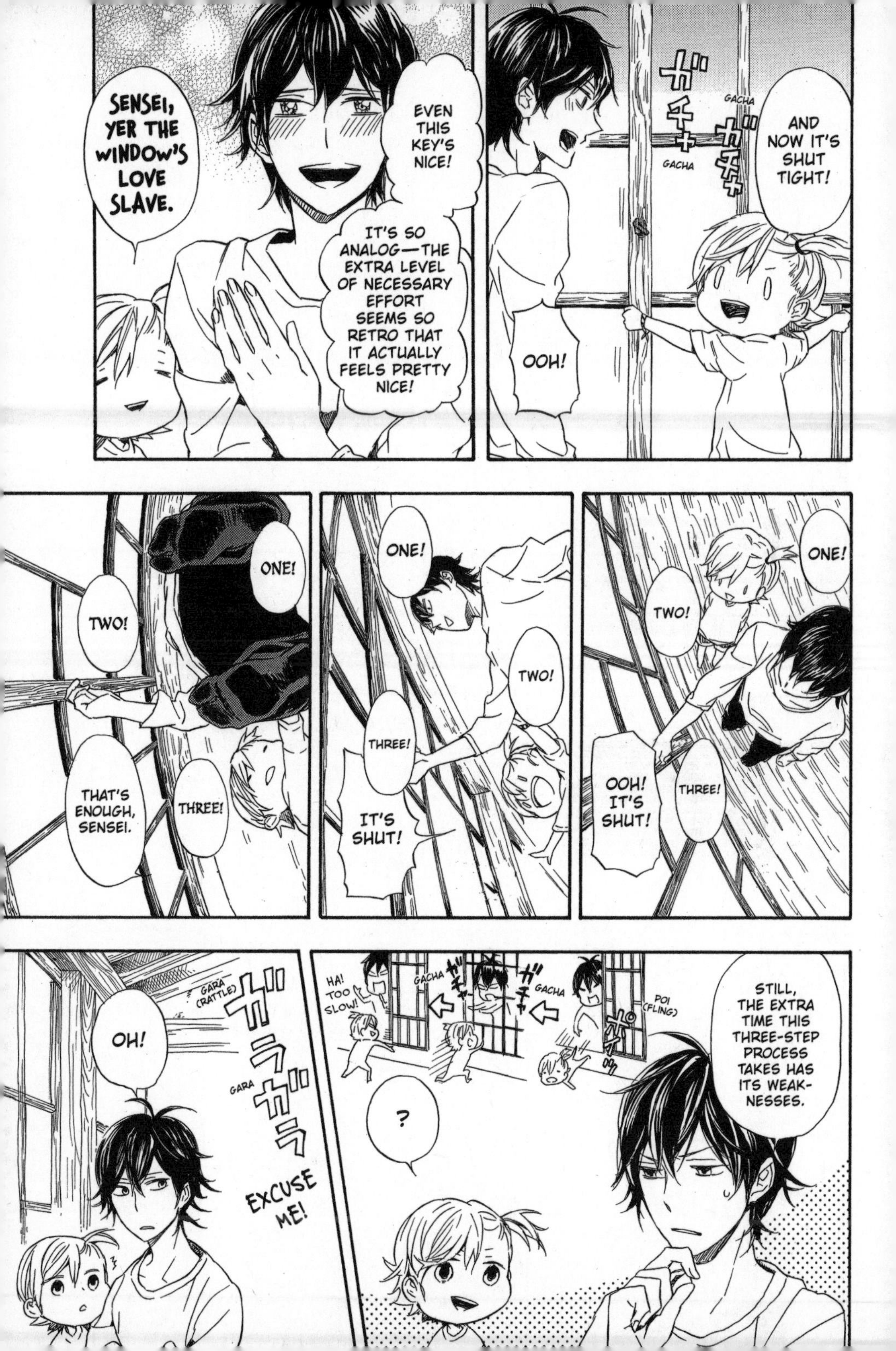
AND NOW IT'S SHUT TIGHT!
GACHA
GACHA
OOH!
EVEN THIS KEY'S NICE!
IT'S SO ANALOG—THE EXTRA LEVEL OF NECESSARY EFFORT SEEMS SO RETRO THAT IT ACTUALLY FEELS PRETTY NICE!
SENSEI, YER THE WINDOW'S LOVE SLAVE.
ONE!
TWO!
THREE!
OOH! IT'S SHUT!
ONE!
TWO!
THREE!
IT'S SHUT!
ONE!
TWO!
THREE!
THAT'S ENOUGH, SENSEI.
STILL, THE EXTRA TIME THIS THREE-STEP PROCESS TAKES HAS ITS WEAK-NESSES.
POI (FLING)
GACHA
GACHA
HA! TOO SLOW!
?
GARA (RATTLE)
GARA
OH!
EXCUSE ME!

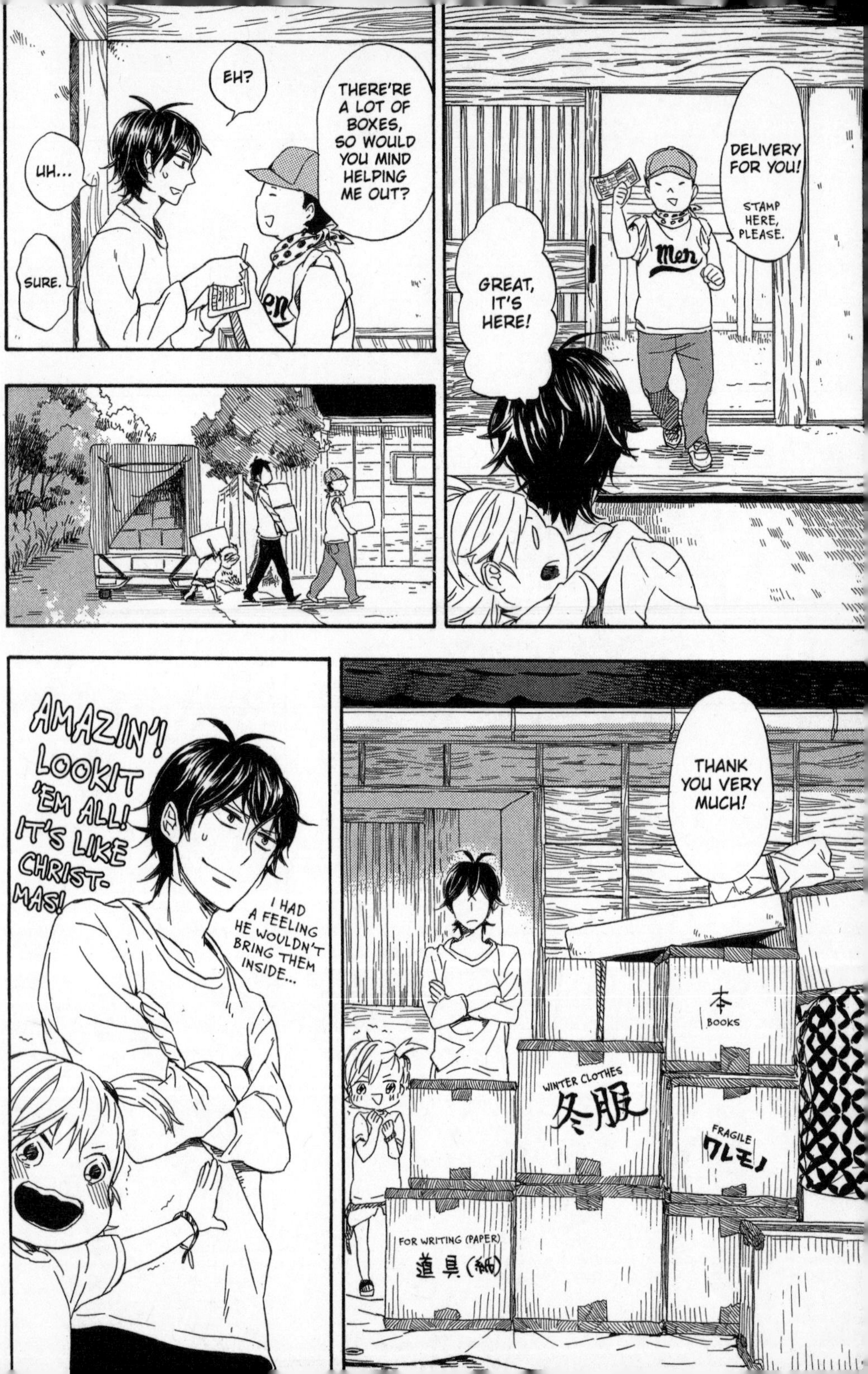
DELIVERY FOR YOU!
STAMP HERE, PLEASE.
GREAT, IT'S HERE!
THERE'RE A LOT OF BOXES, SO WOULD YOU MIND HELPING ME OUT?
EH?
UH...
SURE.
THANK YOU VERY MUCH!
本
BOOKS
WINTER CLOTHES
冬服
FRAGILE
ワレモノ
FOR WRITING (PAPER)
道具(紙)
AMAZIN'! LOOKIT 'EM ALL! IT'S LIKE CHRIST-MAS!
I HAD A FEELING HE WOULDN'T BRING THEM INSIDE...

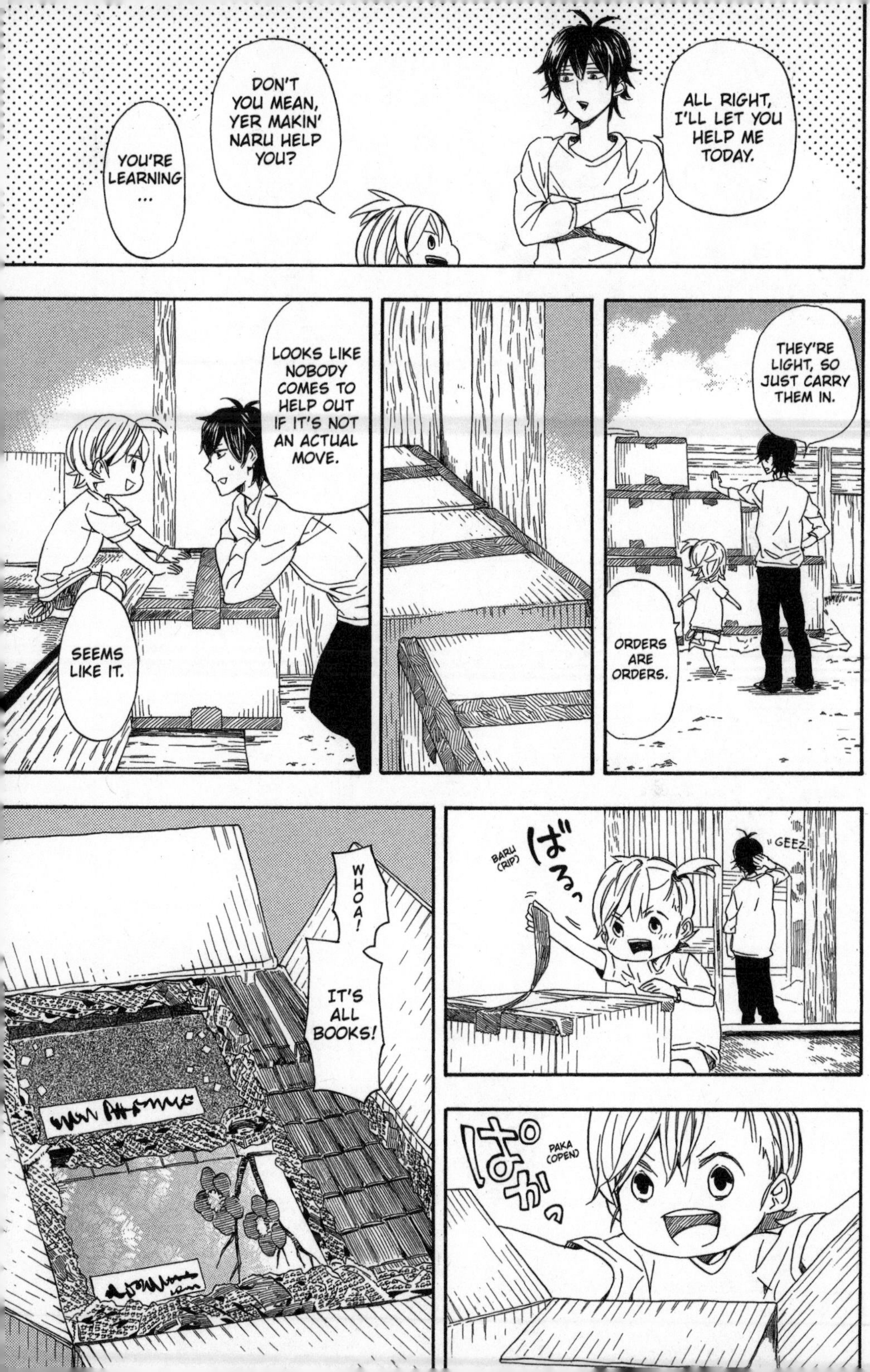
ALL RIGHT, I'LL LET YOU HELP ME TODAY.
DON'T YOU MEAN, YER MAKIN' NARU HELP YOU?
YOU'RE LEARNING ...
THEY'RE LIGHT, SO JUST CARRY THEM IN.
ORDERS ARE ORDERS.
LOOKS LIKE NOBODY COMES TO HELP OUT IF IT'S NOT AN ACTUAL MOVE.
SEEMS LIKE IT.
ばるっ
BARU (RIP)
GEEZ.
ぱかっ
PAKA (OPEN)
WHOA!
IT'S ALL BOOKS!

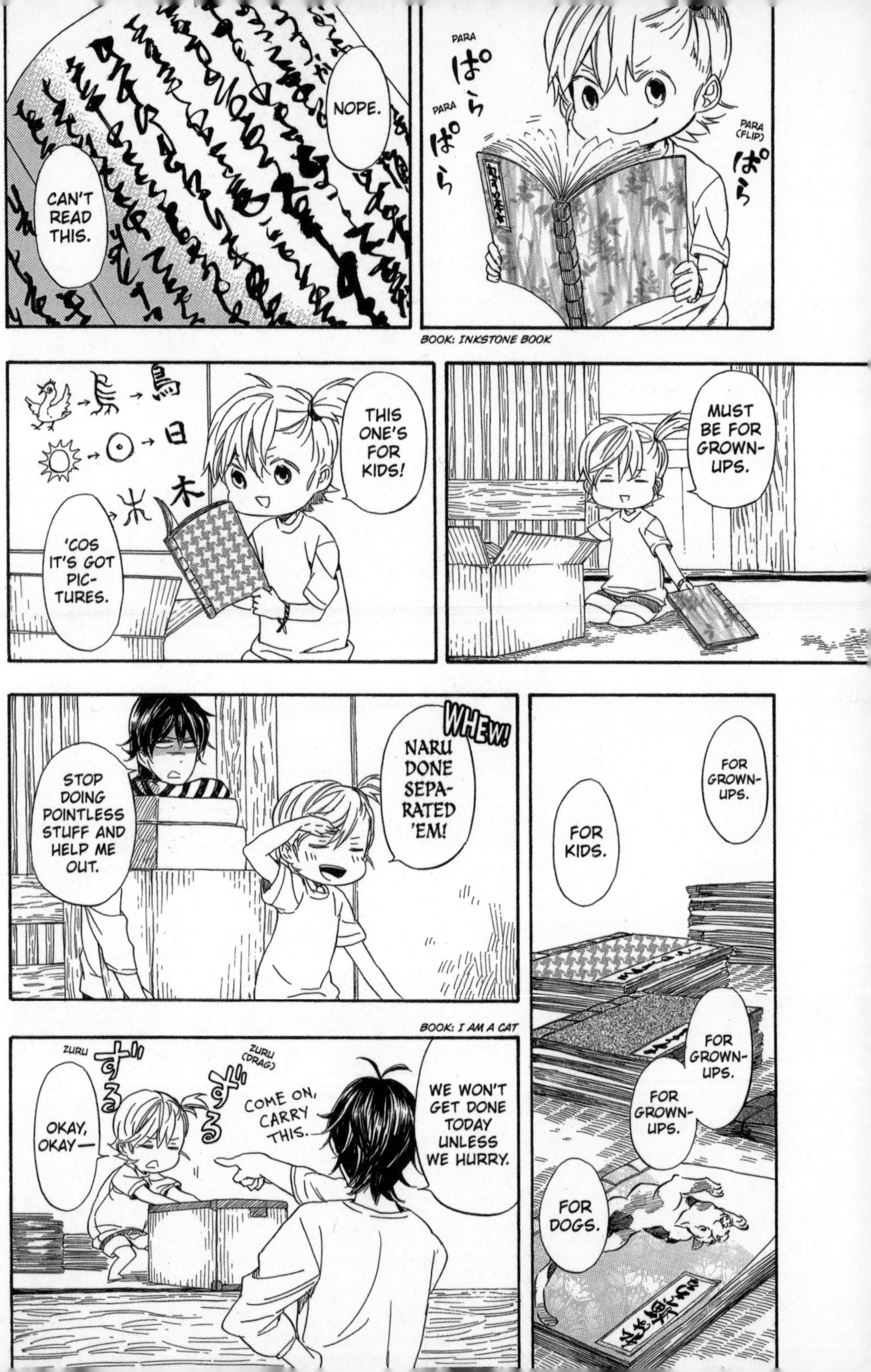
PARA
ぱら
PARA
ぱら
PARA (FLIP)
ぱら
BOOK: INKSTONE BOOK
NOPE.
CAN'T READ THIS.
MUST BE FOR GROWN-UPS.
THIS ONE'S FOR KIDS!
'COS IT'S GOT PIC-TURES.
FOR GROWN-UPS.
FOR KIDS.
FOR GROWN-UPS.
FOR GROWN-UPS.
FOR DOGS.
WHEW!
NARU DONE SEPA-RATED 'EM!
STOP DOING POINTLESS STUFF AND HELP ME OUT.
BOOK: I AM A CAT
WE WON'T GET DONE TODAY UNLESS WE HURRY.
ZURU (DRAG)
ずる
COME ON, CARRY THIS.
ZURU
ずる
OKAY, OKAY—

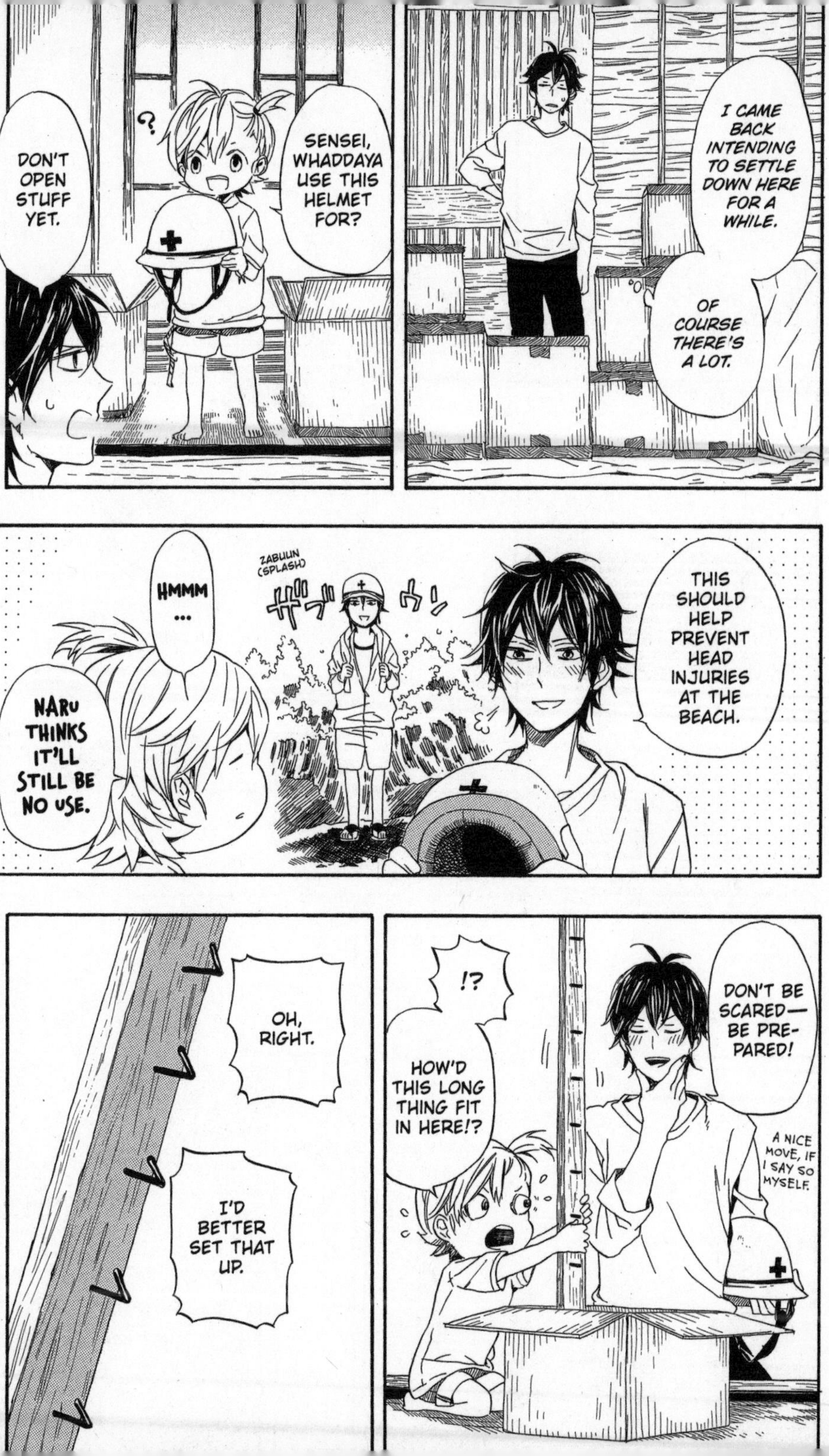
I CAME BACK INTENDING TO SETTLE DOWN HERE FOR A WHILE.
OF COURSE THERE'S A LOT.
SENSEI, WHADDAYA USE THIS HELMET FOR?
?
DON'T OPEN STUFF YET.
THIS SHOULD HELP PREVENT HEAD INJURIES AT THE BEACH.
ZABUUN (SPLASH)
ザブウン
HMMM...
NARU THINKS IT'LL STILL BE NO USE.
DON'T BE SCARED—BE PRE-PARED!
!?
HOW'D THIS LONG THING FIT IN HERE!?
A NICE MOVE, IF I SAY SO MYSELF.
OH, RIGHT.
I'D BETTER SET THAT UP.

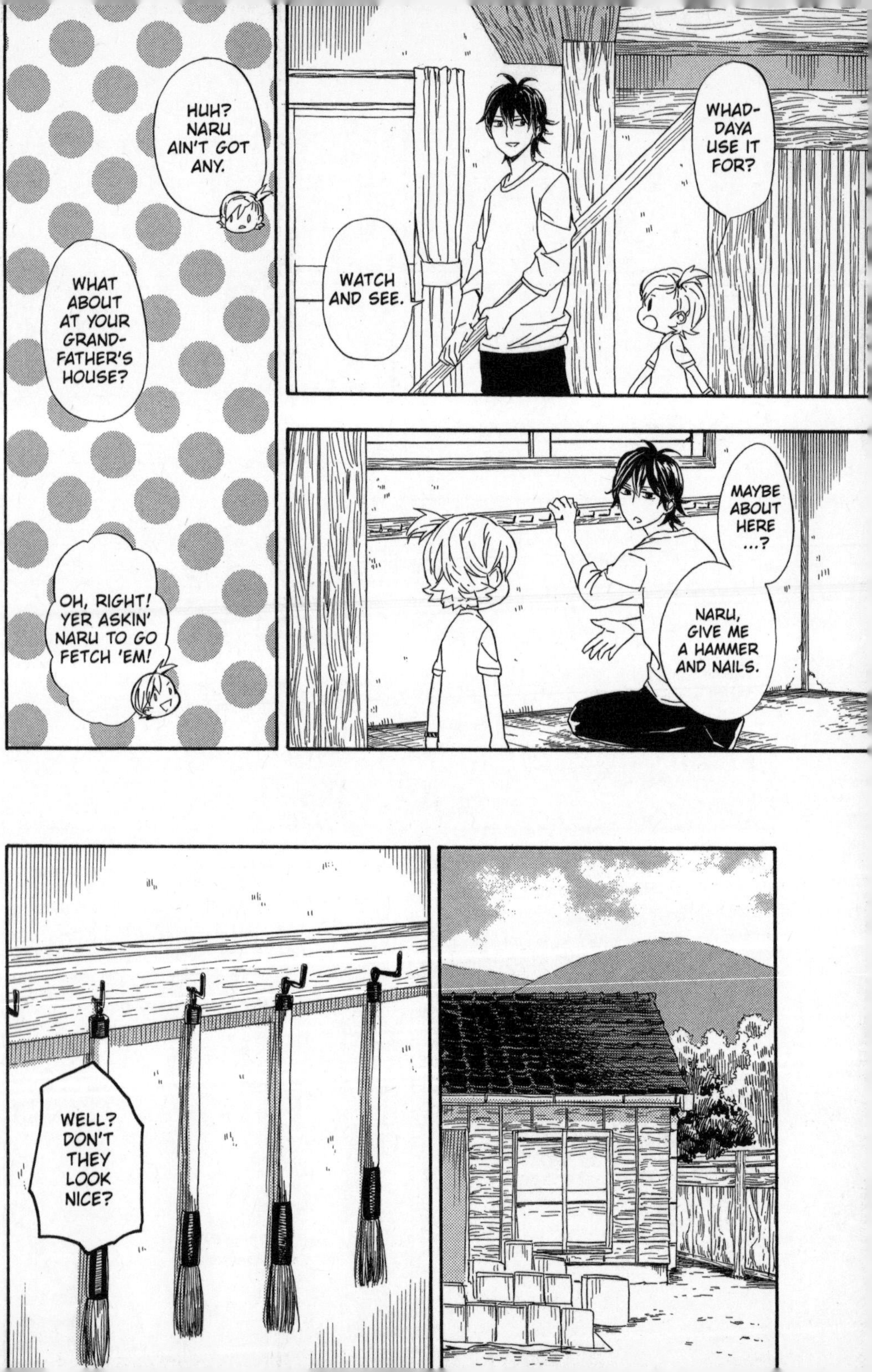
WHAD-DAYA USE IT FOR?
WATCH AND SEE.
MAYBE ABOUT HERE ...?
NARU, GIVE ME A HAMMER AND NAILS.
HUH? NARU AIN'T GOT ANY.
WHAT ABOUT AT YOUR GRAND-FATHER'S HOUSE?
OH, RIGHT! YER ASKIN' NARU TO GO FETCH 'EM!
WELL? DON'T THEY LOOK NICE?

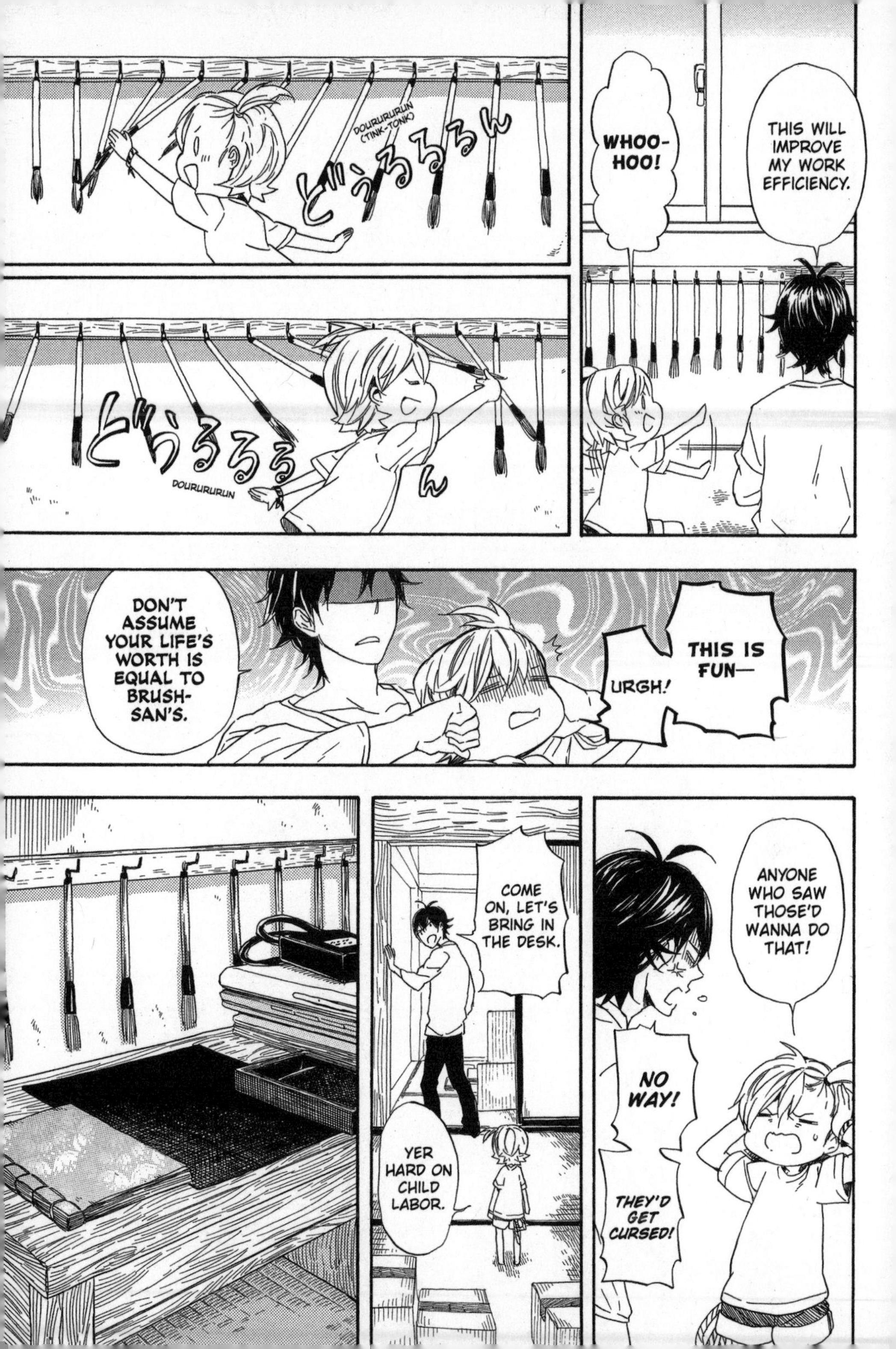
THIS WILL IMPROVE MY WORK EFFICIENCY.
WHOO-HOO!
どぅるるるん
DOURURURUN (TINK-TONK)
どぅるるるん
DOURURURUN
THIS IS FUN—
URGH!
DON'T ASSUME YOUR LIFE'S WORTH IS EQUAL TO BRUSH-SAN'S.
ANYONE WHO SAW THOSE'D WANNA DO THAT!
NO WAY!
THEY'D GET CURSED!
COME ON, LET'S BRING IN THE DESK.
YER HARD ON CHILD LABOR.

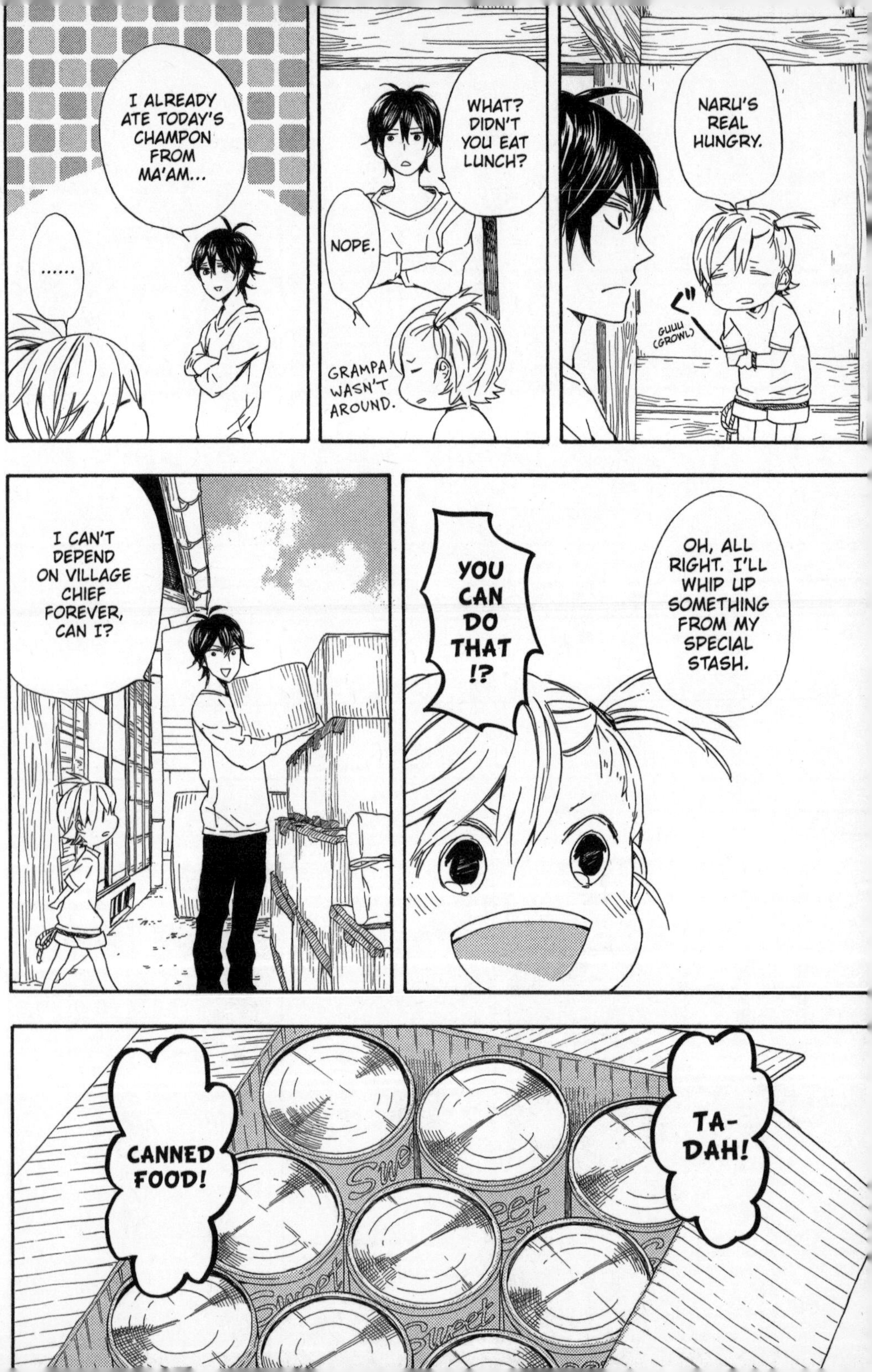
NARU'S REAL HUNGRY.
GUUU (GROWL)
WHAT? DIDN'T YOU EAT LUNCH?
NOPE.
GRAMPA WASN'T AROUND.
I ALREADY ATE TODAY'S CHAMPON FROM MA'AM...
......
OH, ALL RIGHT. I'LL WHIP UP SOMETHING FROM MY SPECIAL STASH.
YOU CAN DO THAT!?
I CAN'T DEPEND ON VILLAGE CHIEF FOREVER, CAN I?
TA-DAH!
CANNED FOOD!

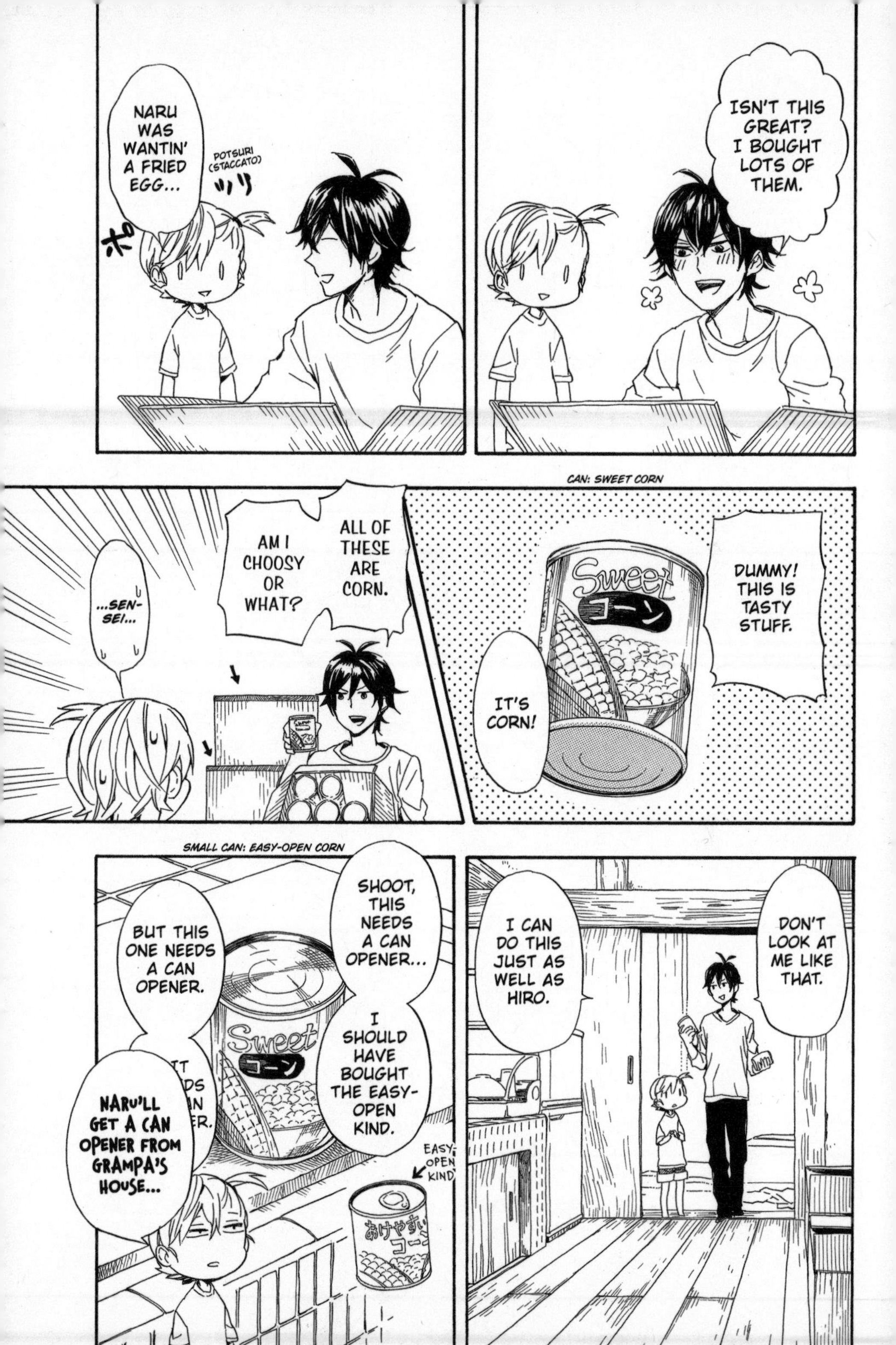
ISN'T THIS GREAT? I BOUGHT LOTS OF THEM.
NARU WAS WANTIN' A FRIED EGG...
POTSURI (STACCATO)
CAN: SWEET CORN
Sweet コーン
DUMMY! THIS IS TASTY STUFF.
IT'S CORN!
ALL OF THESE ARE CORN.
AM I CHOOSY OR WHAT?
...SEN-SEI...
DON'T LOOK AT ME LIKE THAT.
I CAN DO THIS JUST AS WELL AS HIRO.
SMALL CAN: EASY-OPEN CORN
SHOOT, THIS NEEDS A CAN OPENER...
BUT THIS ONE NEEDS A CAN OPENER.
Sweet コーン
I SHOULD HAVE BOUGHT THE EASY-OPEN KIND.
NARU'LL GET A CAN OPENER FROM GRAMPA'S HOUSE...
EASY-OPEN KIND

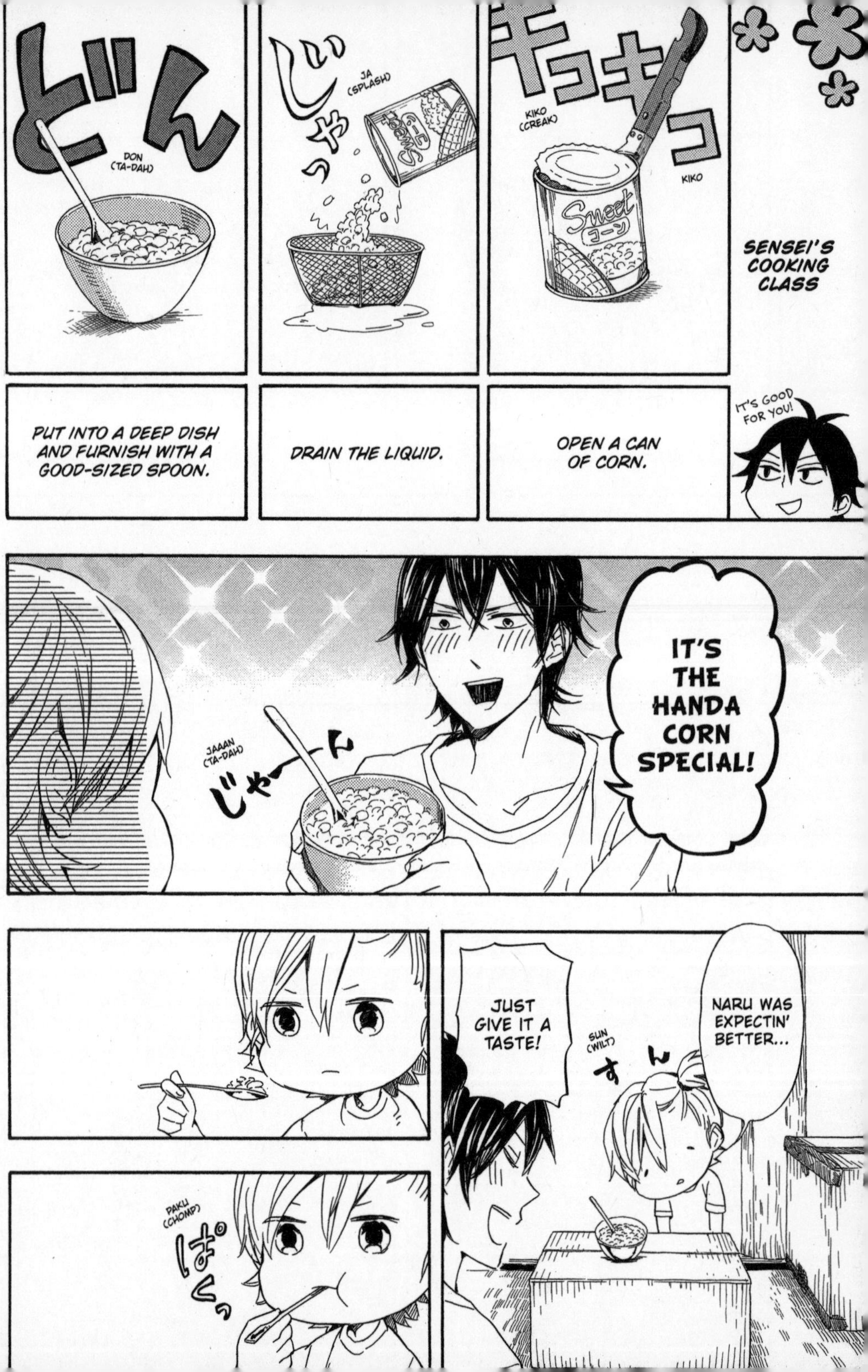
SENSEI'S COOKING CLASS
KIKO (CREAK)
KIKO
JA (SPLASH)
どん
DON (TA-DAH)
IT'S GOOD FOR YOU!
OPEN A CAN OF CORN.
DRAIN THE LIQUID.
PUT INTO A DEEP DISH AND FURNISH WITH A GOOD-SIZED SPOON.
IT'S THE HANDA CORN SPECIAL!
JAAAN (TA-DAH)
NARU WAS EXPECTIN' BETTER...
SUN (WILT)
すん
JUST GIVE IT A TASTE!
PAKU (CHOMP)
ぱくっ

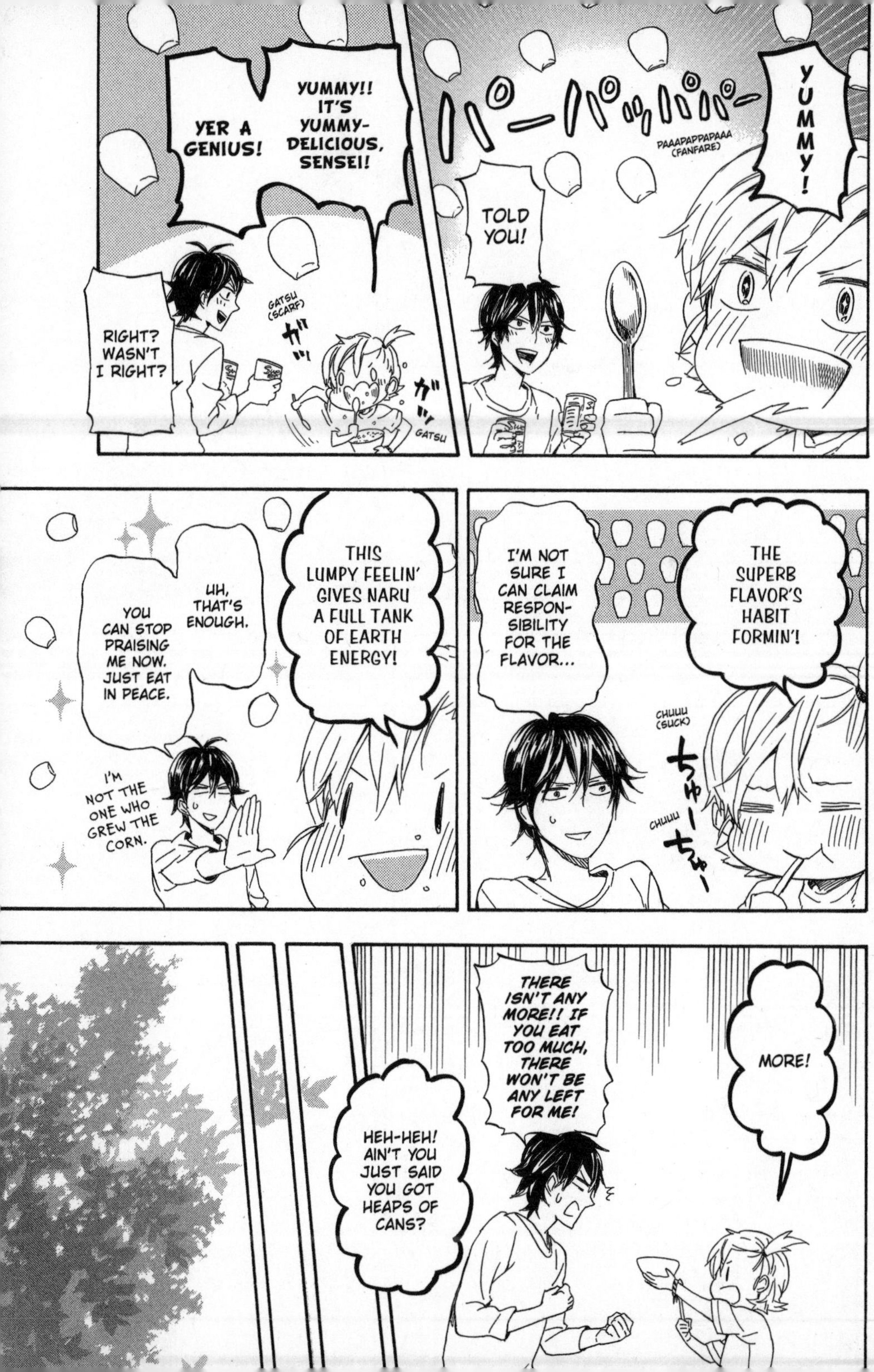
YUMMY!
PAAAPAPPAPAAA (FANFARE)
TOLD YOU!
YUMMY!! IT'S YUMMY-DELICIOUS, SENSEI!
YER A GENIUS!
GATSU (SCARF)
RIGHT? WASN'T I RIGHT?
GATSU
THE SUPERB FLAVOR'S HABIT FORMIN'!
I'M NOT SURE I CAN CLAIM RESPONSIBILITY FOR THE FLAVOR...
CHUUU (SUCK)
CHUUU
THIS LUMPY FEELIN' GIVES NARU A FULL TANK OF EARTH ENERGY!
UH, THAT'S ENOUGH.
YOU CAN STOP PRAISING ME NOW. JUST EAT IN PEACE.
I'M NOT THE ONE WHO GREW THE CORN.
MORE!
THERE ISN'T ANY MORE!! IF YOU EAT TOO MUCH, THERE WON'T BE ANY LEFT FOR ME!
HEH-HEH! AIN'T YOU JUST SAID YOU GOT HEAPS OF CANS?

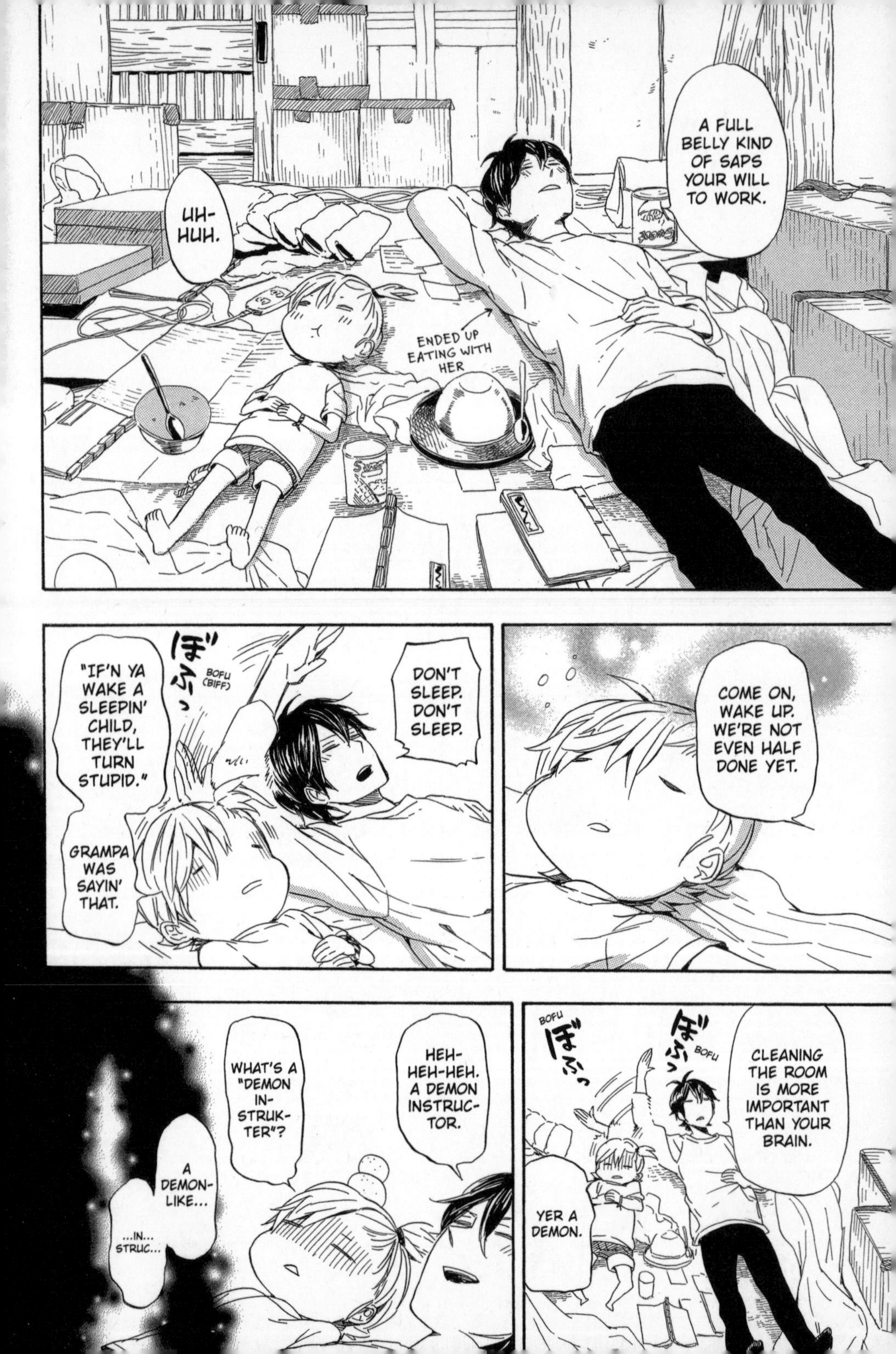
A FULL BELLY KIND OF SAPS YOUR WILL TO WORK.
ENDED UP EATING WITH HER
UH-HUH.
COME ON, WAKE UP. WE'RE NOT EVEN HALF DONE YET.
DON'T SLEEP. DON'T SLEEP.
ぼふっ
BOFU (BIFF)
"IF'N YA WAKE A SLEEPIN' CHILD, THEY'LL TURN STUPID."
GRAMPA WAS SAYIN' THAT.
CLEANING THE ROOM IS MORE IMPORTANT THAN YOUR BRAIN.
ぼふっ
BOFU
ぼふっ
BOFU
YER A DEMON.
HEH-HEH-HEH. A DEMON INSTRUCTOR.
WHAT'S A "DEMON IN-STRUKTER"?
A DEMON-LIKE...
...IN... STRUC...

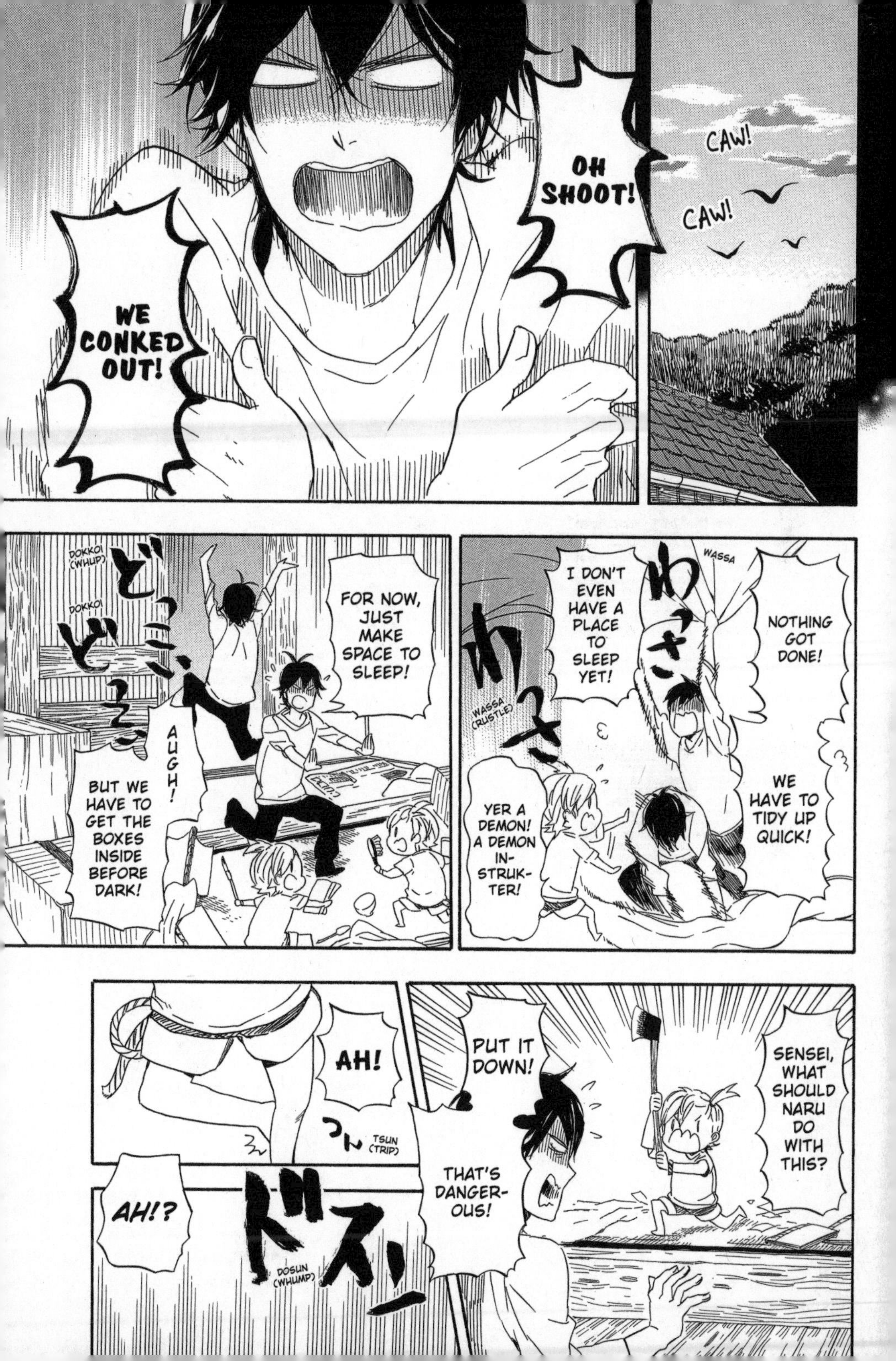
CAW!
CAW!
OH SHOOT!
WE CONKED OUT!
WASSA
NOTHING GOT DONE!
I DON'T EVEN HAVE A PLACE TO SLEEP YET!
WASSA (RUSTLE)
WE HAVE TO TIDY UP QUICK!
YER A DEMON! A DEMON IN-STRUK-TER!
FOR NOW, JUST MAKE SPACE TO SLEEP!
DOKKOI (WHUP)
DOKKOI
AUGH!
BUT WE HAVE TO GET THE BOXES INSIDE BEFORE DARK!
SENSEI, WHAT SHOULD NARU DO WITH THIS?
PUT IT DOWN!
THAT'S DANGER-OUS!
AH!
TSUN (TRIP)
AH!?
DOSUN (WHUMP)

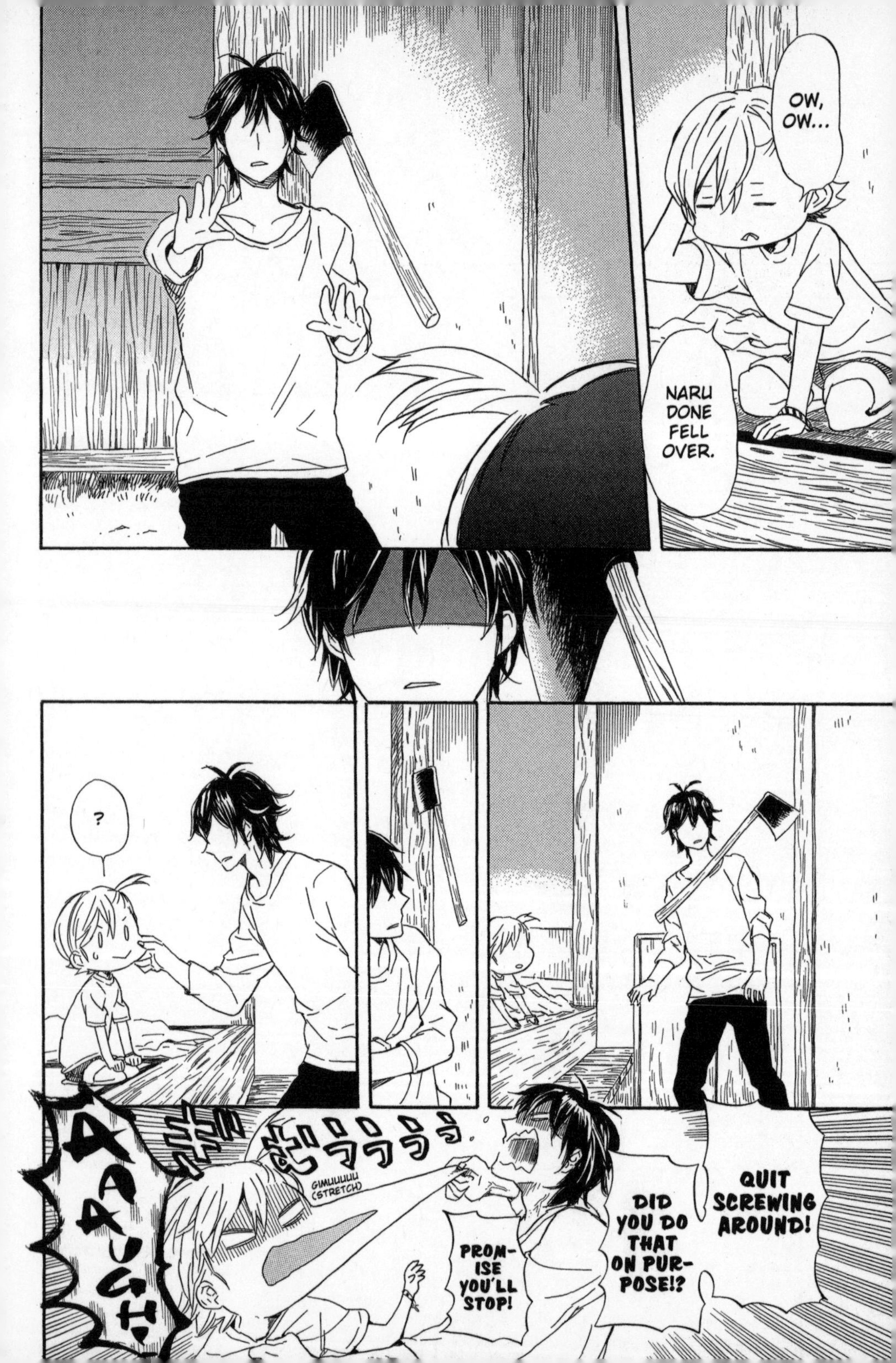
OW, OW...
NARU DONE FELL OVER.
?
QUIT SCREWING AROUND!
DID YOU DO THAT ON PURPOSE!?
PROMISE YOU'LL STOP!
ぎむううううう
GIMUUUUU (STRETCH)
AAAUGH!

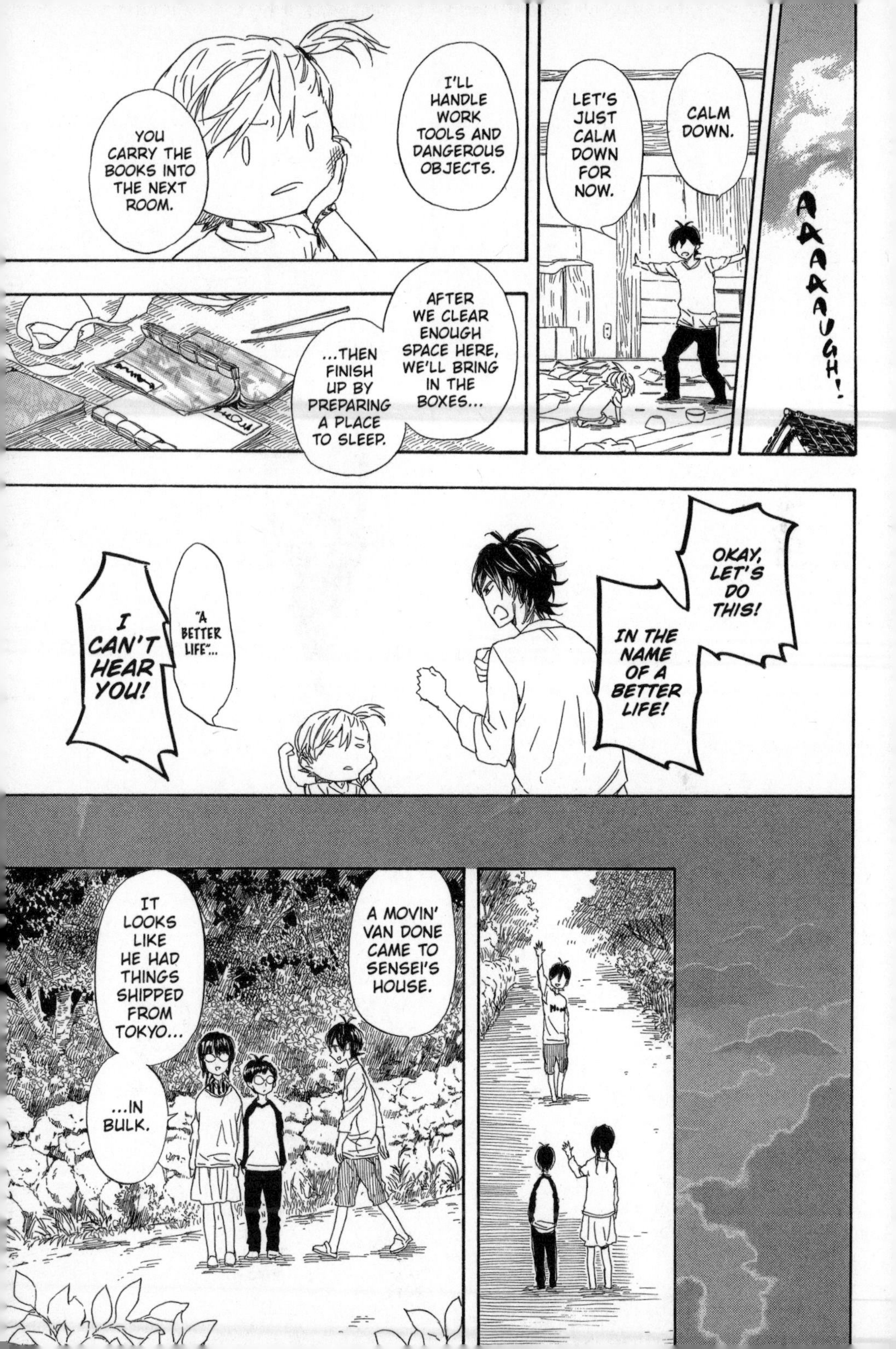
AAAAAAUGH!
CALM DOWN.
LET'S JUST CALM DOWN FOR NOW.
I'LL HANDLE WORK TOOLS AND DANGEROUS OBJECTS.
YOU CARRY THE BOOKS INTO THE NEXT ROOM.
AFTER WE CLEAR ENOUGH SPACE HERE, WE'LL BRING IN THE BOXES...
...THEN FINISH UP BY PREPARING A PLACE TO SLEEP.
OKAY, LET'S DO THIS!
IN THE NAME OF A BETTER LIFE!
"A BETTER LIFE"...
I CAN'T HEAR YOU!
A MOVIN' VAN DONE CAME TO SENSEI'S HOUSE.
IT LOOKS LIKE HE HAD THINGS SHIPPED FROM TOKYO...
...IN BULK.

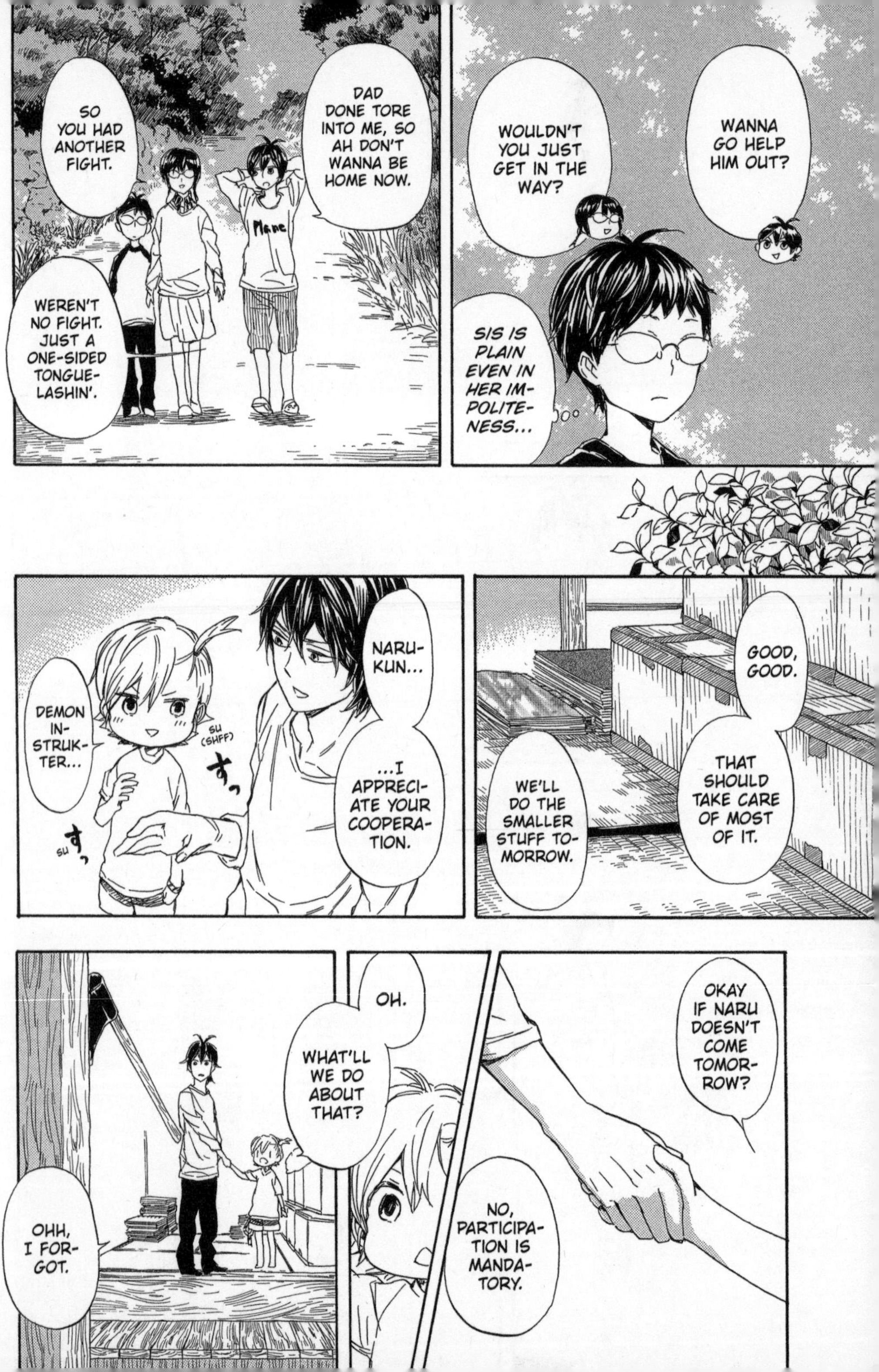
WANNA GO HELP HIM OUT?
WOULDN'T YOU JUST GET IN THE WAY?
SIS IS PLAIN EVEN IN HER IMPOLITENESS...
DAD DONE TORE INTO ME, SO AH DON'T WANNA BE HOME NOW.
Plane
SO YOU HAD ANOTHER FIGHT.
WEREN'T NO FIGHT. JUST A ONE-SIDED TONGUE-LASHIN'.
GOOD, GOOD.
THAT SHOULD TAKE CARE OF MOST OF IT.
WE'LL DO THE SMALLER STUFF TOMORROW.
NARU-KUN...
...I APPRECIATE YOUR COOPERATION.
すっ SU (SHFF)
DEMON INSTRUKTER...
すっ SU
OKAY IF NARU DOESN'T COME TOMORROW?
NO, PARTICIPATION IS MANDATORY.
OH.
WHAT'LL WE DO ABOUT THAT?
OHH, I FORGOT.

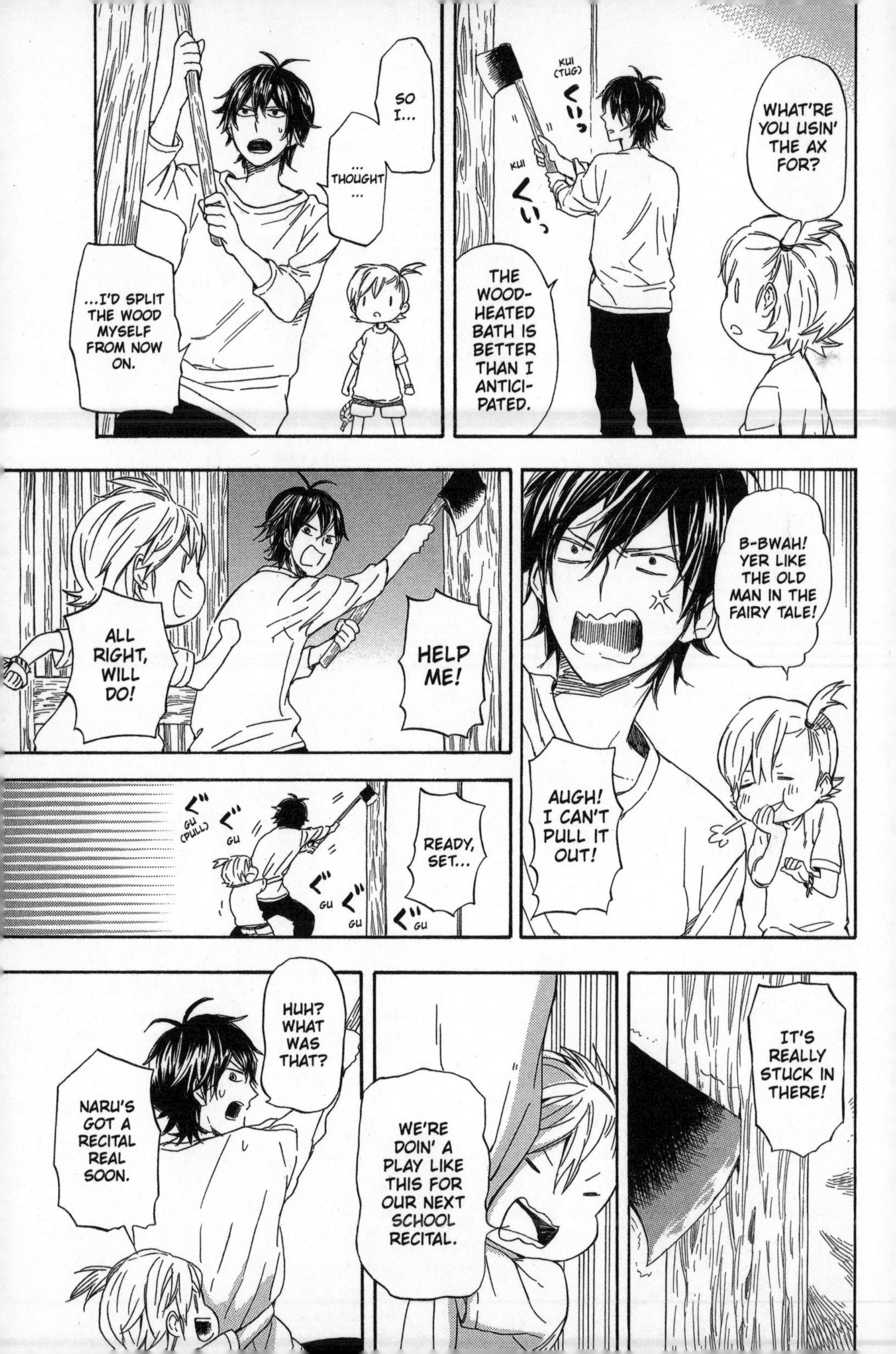
WHAT'RE YOU USIN' THE AX FOR?
KUI (TUG) くいっ
KUI くいっ
THE WOOD-HEATED BATH IS BETTER THAN I ANTICIPATED.
SO I...
...THOUGHT...
...I'D SPLIT THE WOOD MYSELF FROM NOW ON.
B-BWAH! YER LIKE THE OLD MAN IN THE FAIRY TALE!
AUGH! I CAN'T PULL IT OUT!
HELP ME!
ALL RIGHT, WILL DO!
READY, SET...
ぐ GU
ぐ GU
ぐ GU
ぐ GU
ぐ GU (PULL)
IT'S REALLY STUCK IN THERE!
WE'RE DOIN' A PLAY LIKE THIS FOR OUR NEXT SCHOOL RECITAL.
HUH? WHAT WAS THAT?
NARU'S GOT A RECITAL REAL SOON.

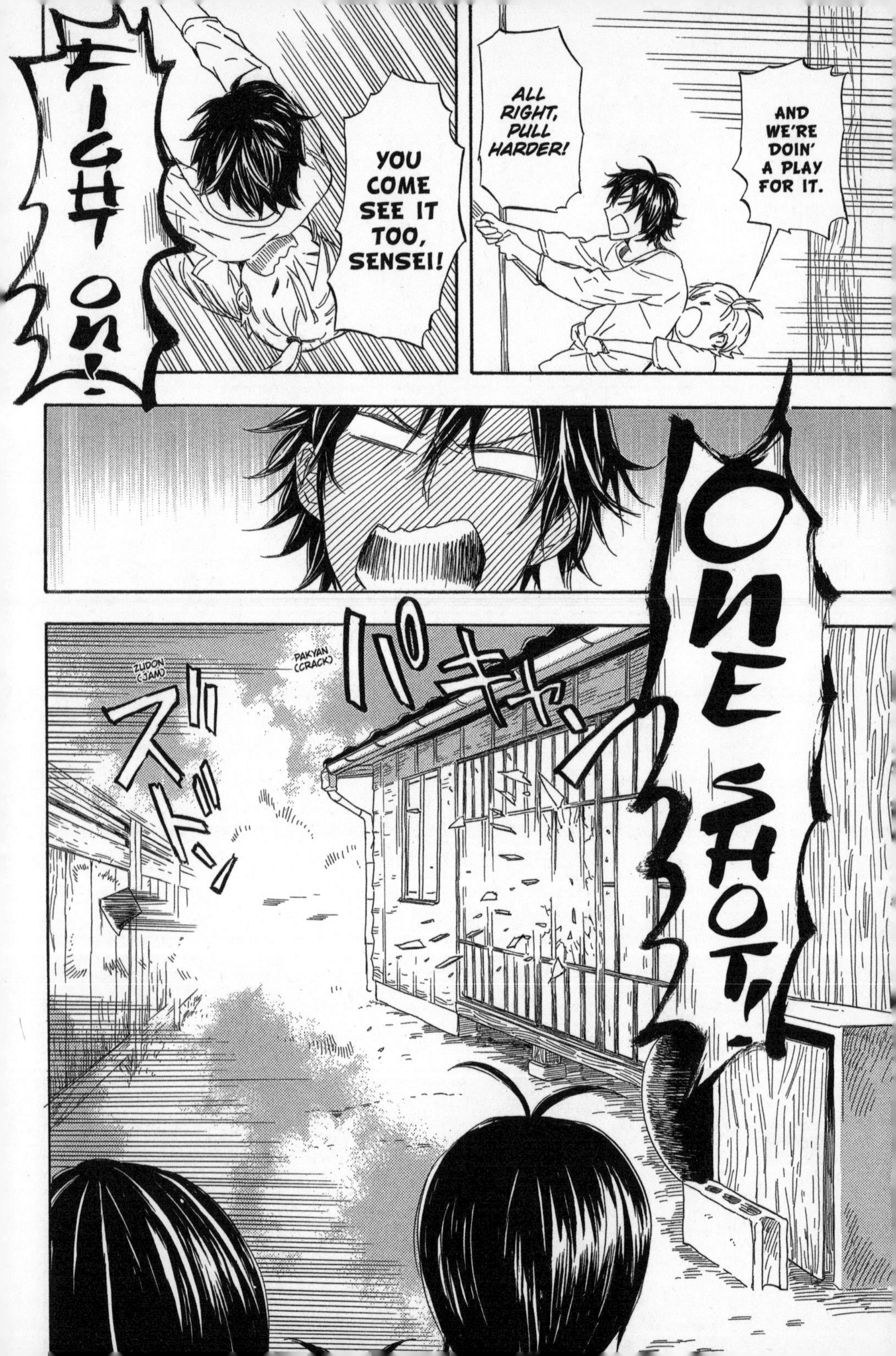
AND WE'RE DOIN' A PLAY FOR IT.
ALL RIGHT, PULL HARDER!
YOU COME SEE IT TOO, SENSEI!
FIGHT ON!
ONE SHOT!
パキャ
PAKYAN (CRACK)
ズドン
ZUDON (JAM)

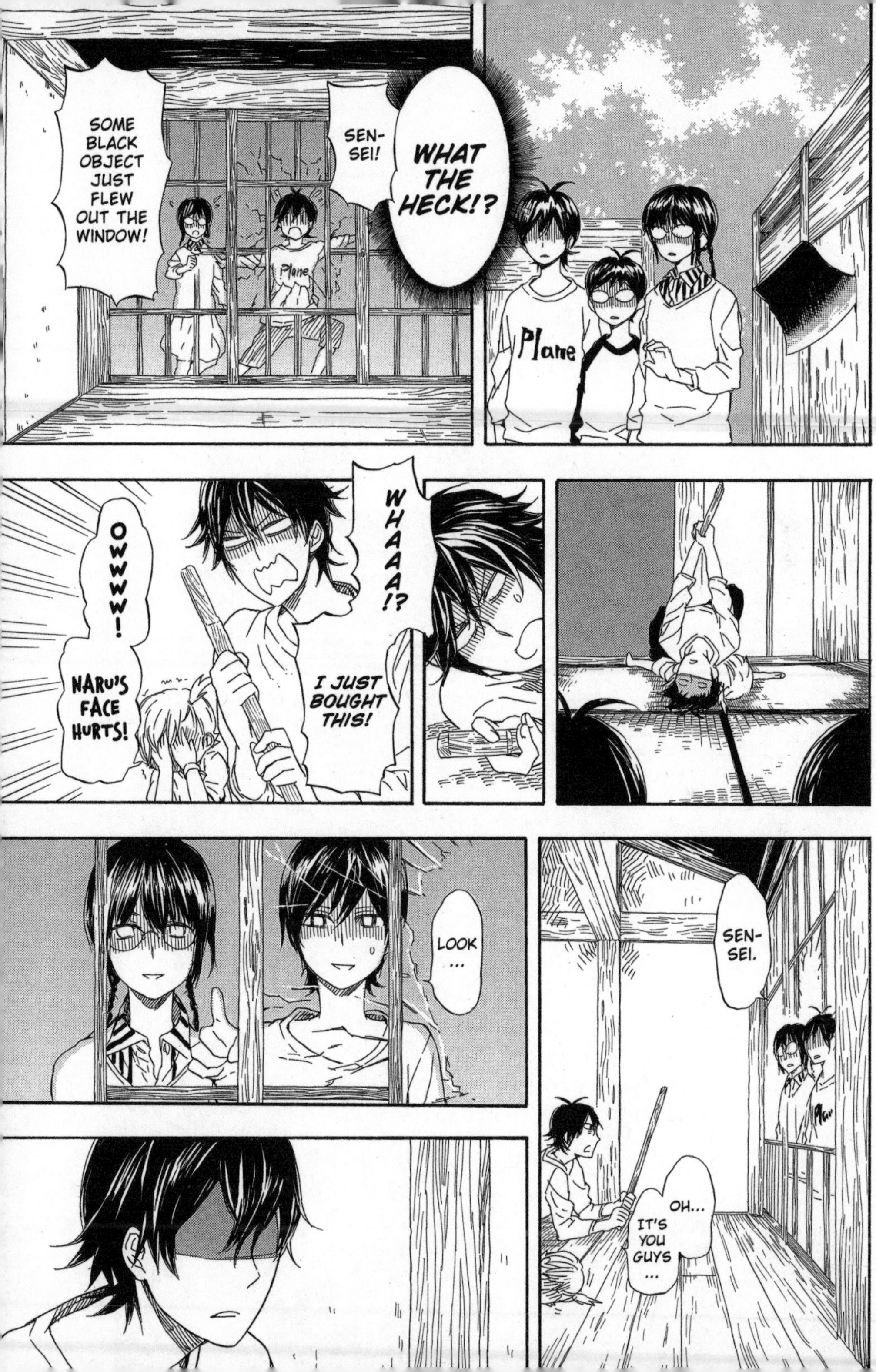
WHAT THE HECK!?
SEN-SEI!
SOME BLACK OBJECT JUST FLEW OUT THE WINDOW!
WHAAAA!?
I JUST BOUGHT THIS!
OWWWWW!
NARU'S FACE HURTS!
SEN-SEI.
OH... IT'S YOU GUYS...
LOOK...

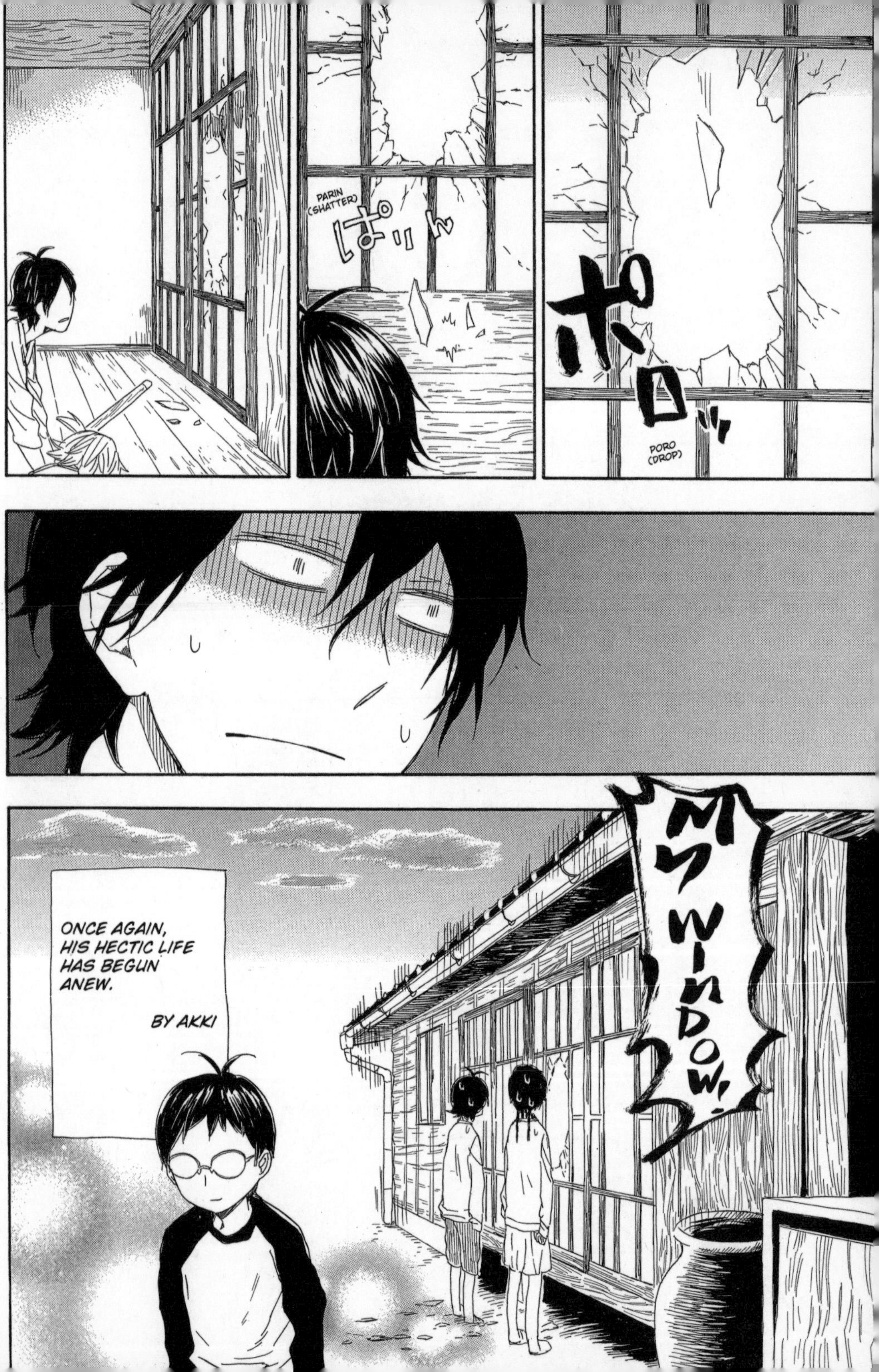
ポロッ
PORO (DROP)
PARIN (SHATTER)
ぱりん
MY WINDOW!
ONCE AGAIN, HIS HECTIC LIFE HAS BEGUN ANEW.
BY AKKI

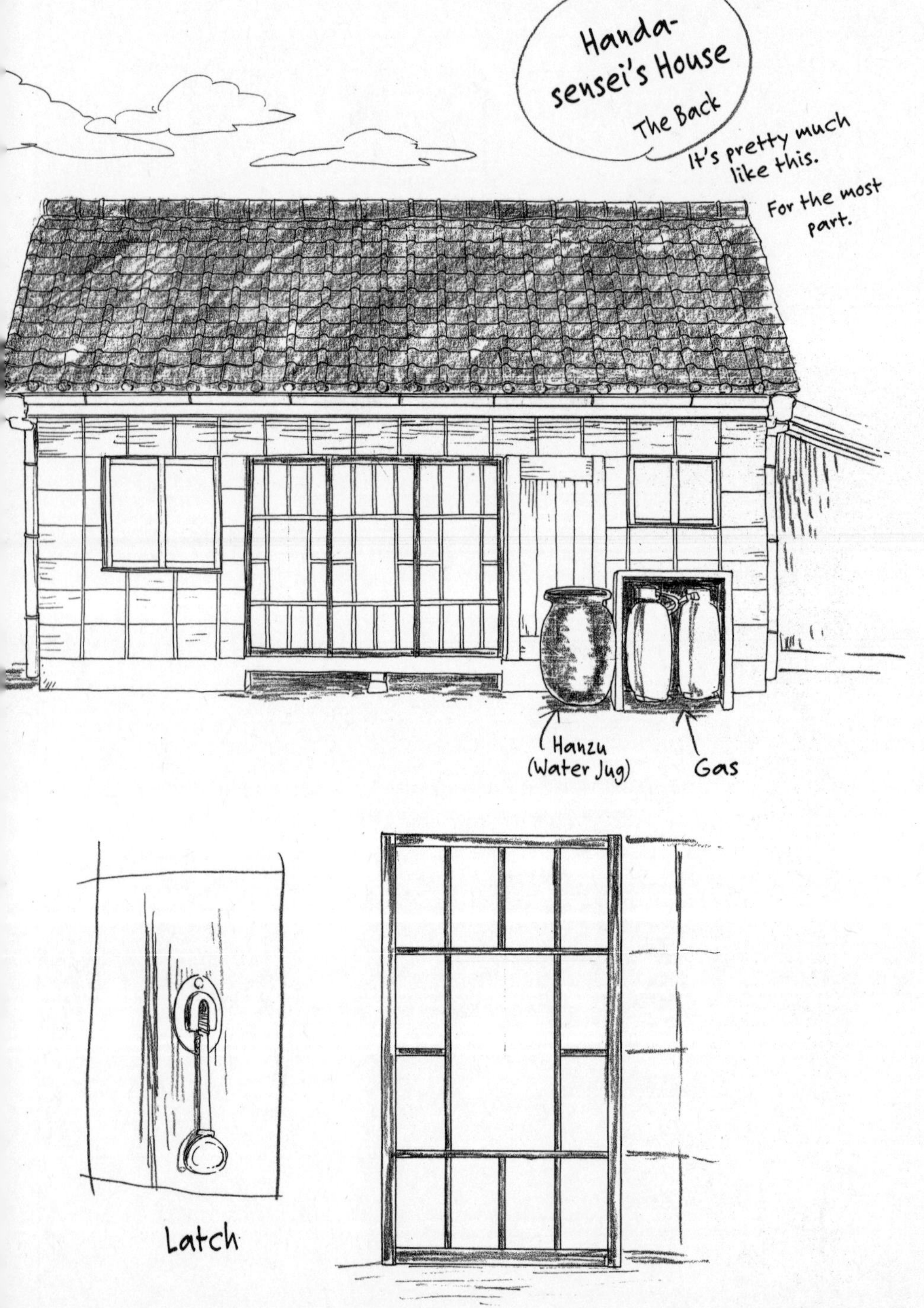
Handa-sensei's House
The Back
It's pretty much like this.
For the most part.
Hanzu (Water Jug)
Gas
Latch

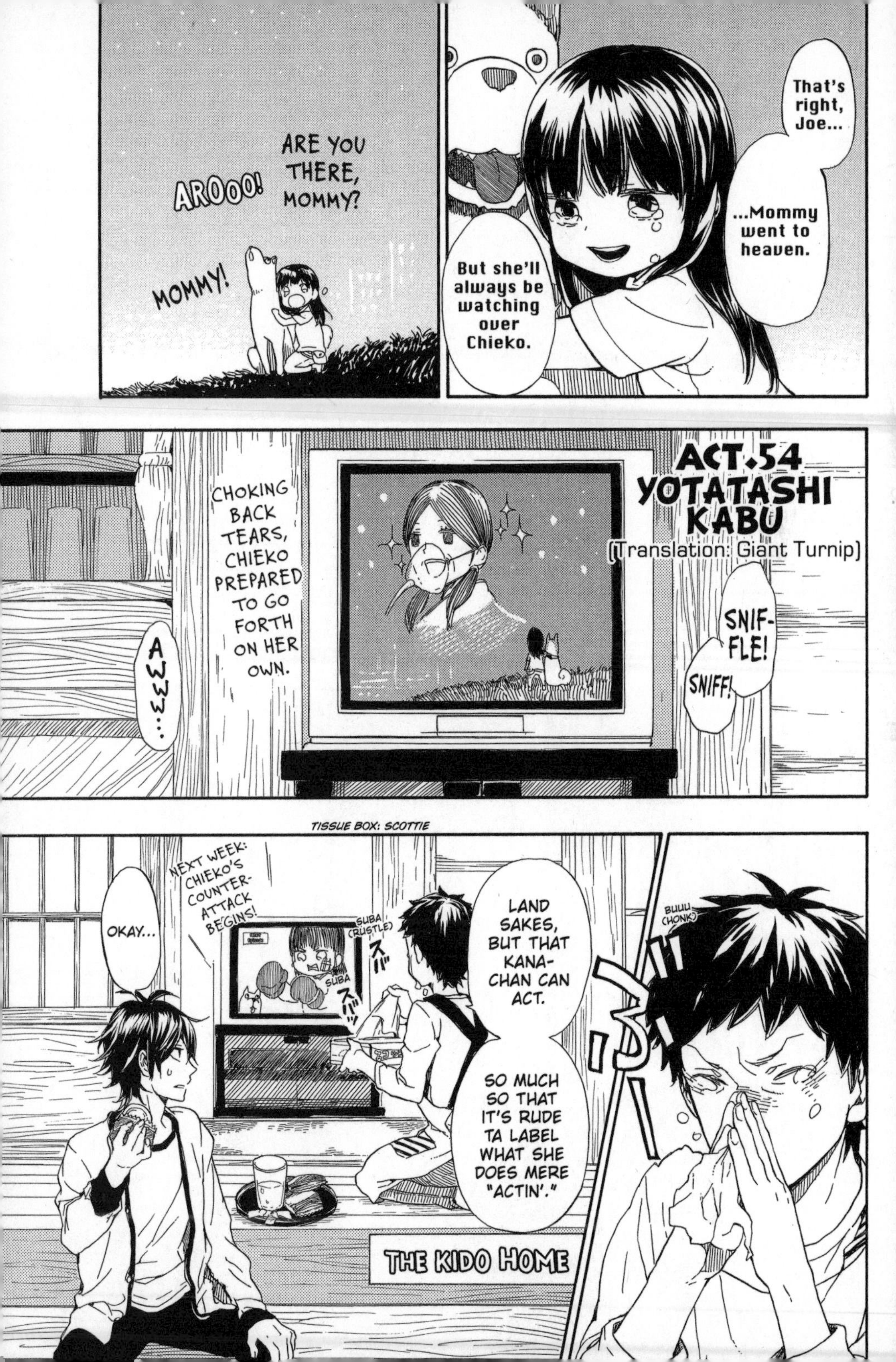
That's right, Joe...
...Mommy went to heaven.
But she'll always be watching over Chieko.
ARE YOU THERE, MOMMY?
AROooo!
MOMMY!
ACT.54 YOTATASHI KABU
(Translation: Giant Turnip)
SNIF-FLE!
SNIFF!
CHOKING BACK TEARS, CHIEKO PREPARED TO GO FORTH ON HER OWN.
AWWW...
TISSUE BOX: SCOTTIE
BUUU (CHONK)
LAND SAKES, BUT THAT KANA-CHAN CAN ACT.
SO MUCH SO THAT IT'S RUDE TA LABEL WHAT SHE DOES MERE "ACTIN'."
THE KIDO HOME
SUBA (RUSTLE)
SUBA
NEXT WEEK: CHIEKO'S COUNTER-ATTACK BEGINS!
OKAY...

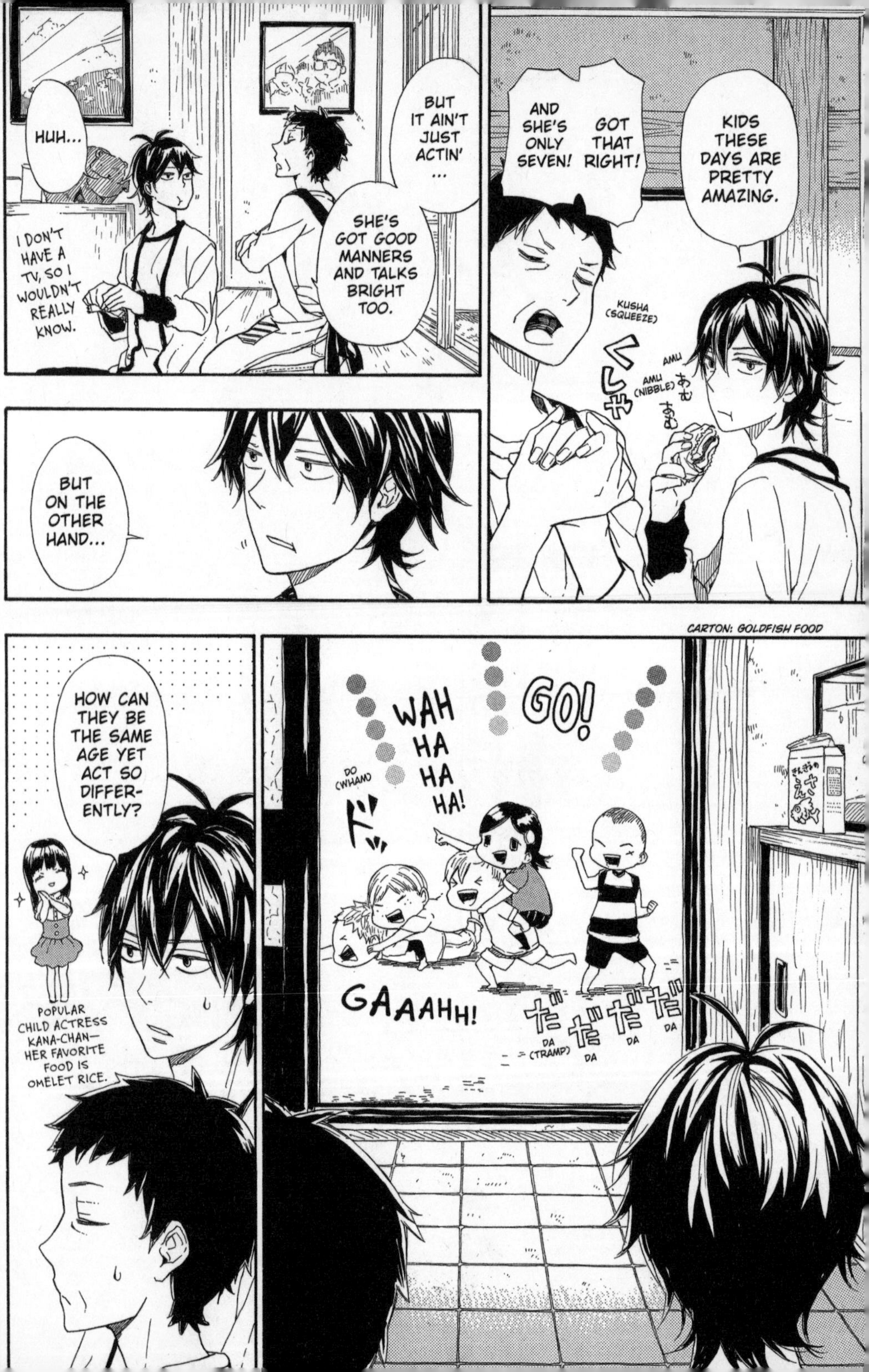
KIDS THESE DAYS ARE PRETTY AMAZING.
GOT THAT RIGHT!
AND SHE'S ONLY SEVEN!
KUSHA (SQUEEZE)
AMU AMU (NIBBLE)
BUT IT AIN'T JUST ACTIN'...
SHE'S GOT GOOD MANNERS AND TALKS BRIGHT TOO.
HUH...
I DON'T HAVE A TV, SO I WOULDN'T REALLY KNOW.
BUT ON THE OTHER HAND...
CARTON: GOLDFISH FOOD
GO!
WAH HA HA HA!
DO (WHAM)
GAAAHH!
DA (TRAMP) DA DA DA
HOW CAN THEY BE THE SAME AGE YET ACT SO DIFFERENTLY?
POPULAR CHILD ACTRESS KANA-CHAN—HER FAVORITE FOOD IS OMELET RICE.

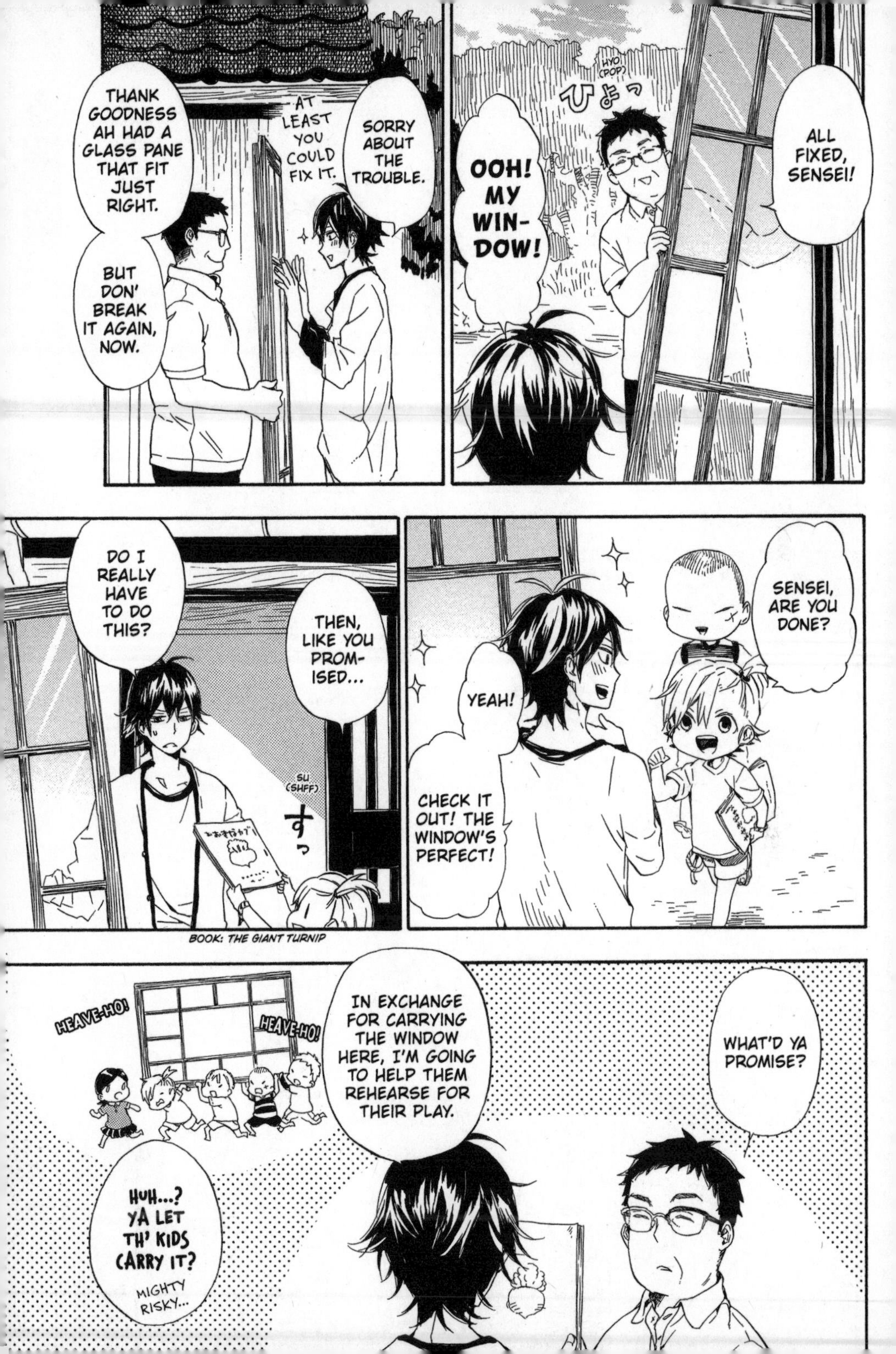
HYO (POP)
ひょっ
ALL FIXED, SENSEI!
OOH! MY WIN-DOW!
SORRY ABOUT THE TROUBLE.
AT LEAST YOU COULD FIX IT.
THANK GOODNESS AH HAD A GLASS PANE THAT FIT JUST RIGHT.
BUT DON' BREAK IT AGAIN, NOW.
SENSEI, ARE YOU DONE?
YEAH!
CHECK IT OUT! THE WINDOW'S PERFECT!
THEN, LIKE YOU PROMISED...
DO I REALLY HAVE TO DO THIS?
SU (SHFF)
すっ
BOOK: THE GIANT TURNIP
WHAT'D YA PROMISE?
IN EXCHANGE FOR CARRYING THE WINDOW HERE, I'M GOING TO HELP THEM REHEARSE FOR THEIR PLAY.
HEAVE-HO!
HEAVE-HO!
HUH...? YA LET TH' KIDS CARRY IT?
MIGHTY RISKY...

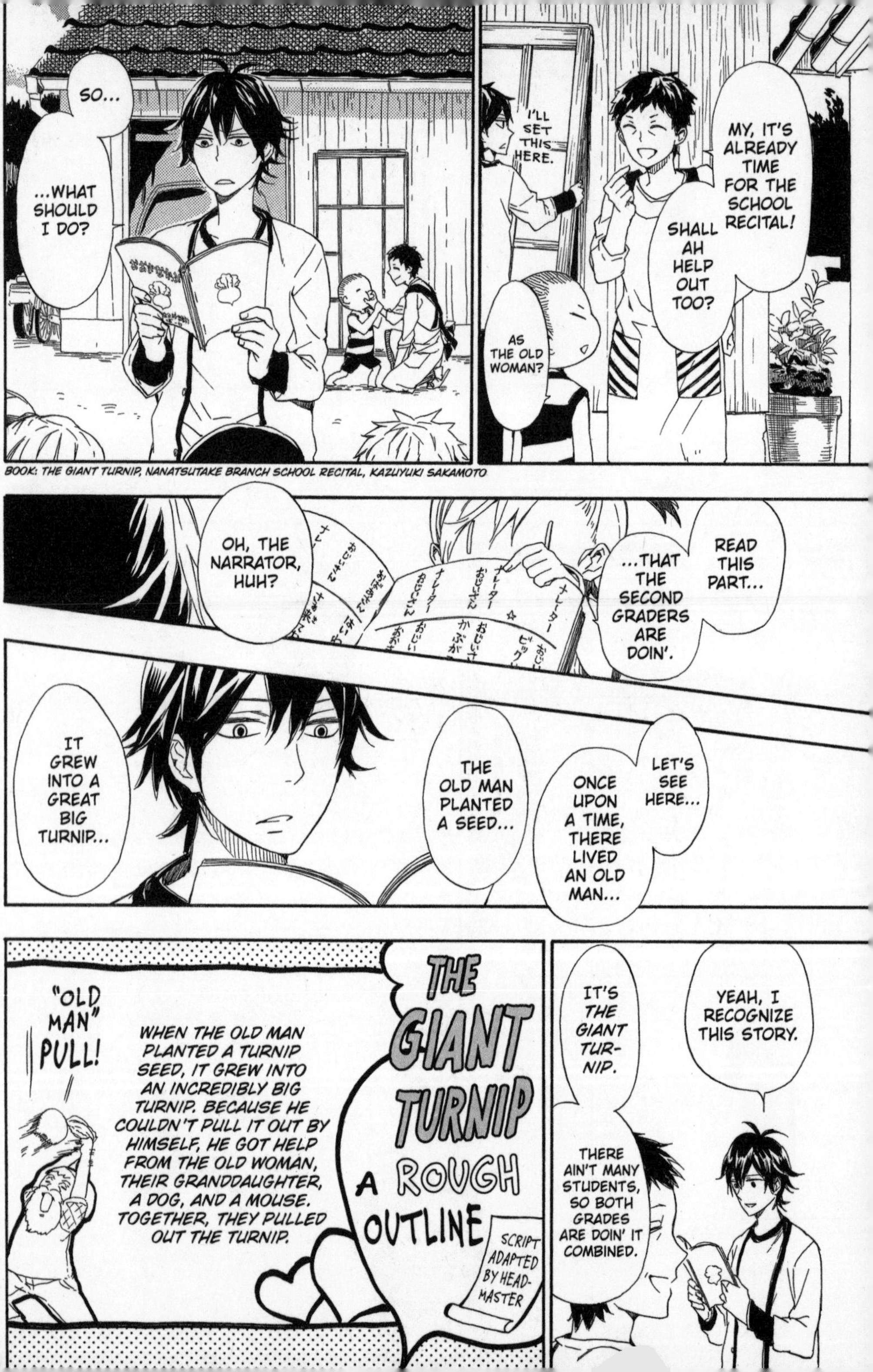
MY, IT'S ALREADY TIME FOR THE SCHOOL RECITAL!
SHALL AH HELP OUT TOO?
AS THE OLD WOMAN?
I'LL SET THIS HERE.
SO...
...WHAT SHOULD I DO?
BOOK: THE GIANT TURNIP, NANATSUTAKE BRANCH SCHOOL RECITAL, KAZUYUKI SAKAMOTO
READ THIS PART...
...THAT THE SECOND GRADERS ARE DOIN'.
OH, THE NARRATOR, HUH?
LET'S SEE HERE...
ONCE UPON A TIME, THERE LIVED AN OLD MAN...
THE OLD MAN PLANTED A SEED...
IT GREW INTO A GREAT BIG TURNIP...
YEAH, I RECOGNIZE THIS STORY.
IT'S THE GIANT TURNIP.
THERE AIN'T MANY STUDENTS, SO BOTH GRADES ARE DOIN' IT COMBINED.
THE GIANT TURNIP A ROUGH OUTLINE
SCRIPT ADAPTED BY HEAD-MASTER
WHEN THE OLD MAN PLANTED A TURNIP SEED, IT GREW INTO AN INCREDIBLY BIG TURNIP. BECAUSE HE COULDN'T PULL IT OUT BY HIMSELF, HE GOT HELP FROM THE OLD WOMAN, THEIR GRANDDAUGHTER, A DOG, AND A MOUSE. TOGETHER, THEY PULLED OUT THE TURNIP.
"OLD MAN" PULL!

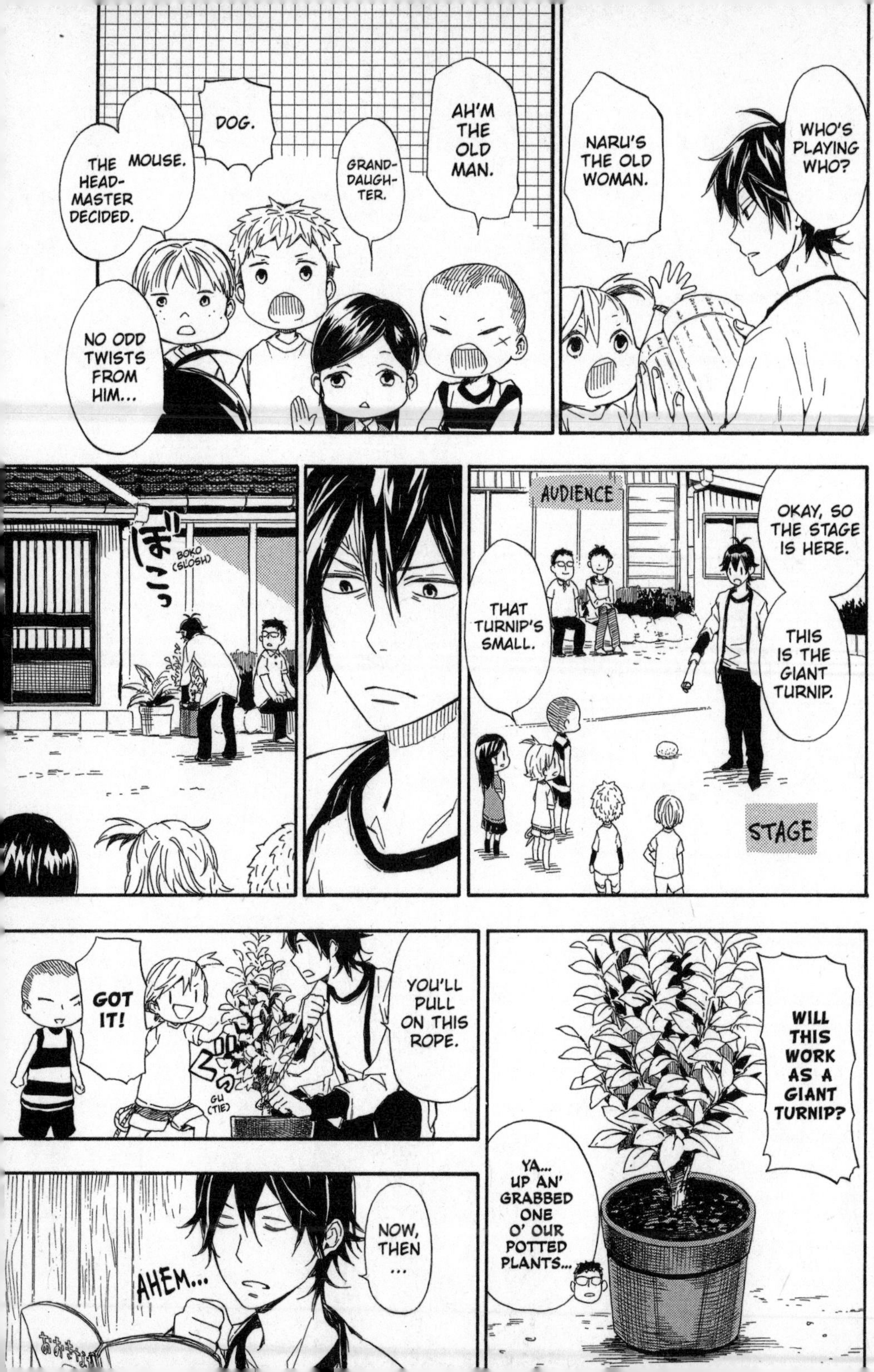
WHO'S PLAYING WHO?
NARU'S THE OLD WOMAN.
AH'M THE OLD MAN.
GRAND-DAUGH-TER.
DOG.
MOUSE.
THE HEAD-MASTER DECIDED.
NO ODD TWISTS FROM HIM...
OKAY, SO THE STAGE IS HERE.
THIS IS THE GIANT TURNIP.
AUDIENCE
STAGE
THAT TURNIP'S SMALL.
ぼこっ
BOKO (SLOSH)
WILL THIS WORK AS A GIANT TURNIP?
YA... UP AN' GRABBED ONE O' OUR POTTED PLANTS...
YOU'LL PULL ON THIS ROPE.
GOT IT!
ぐっ
GU (TIE)
NOW, THEN ...
AHEM...

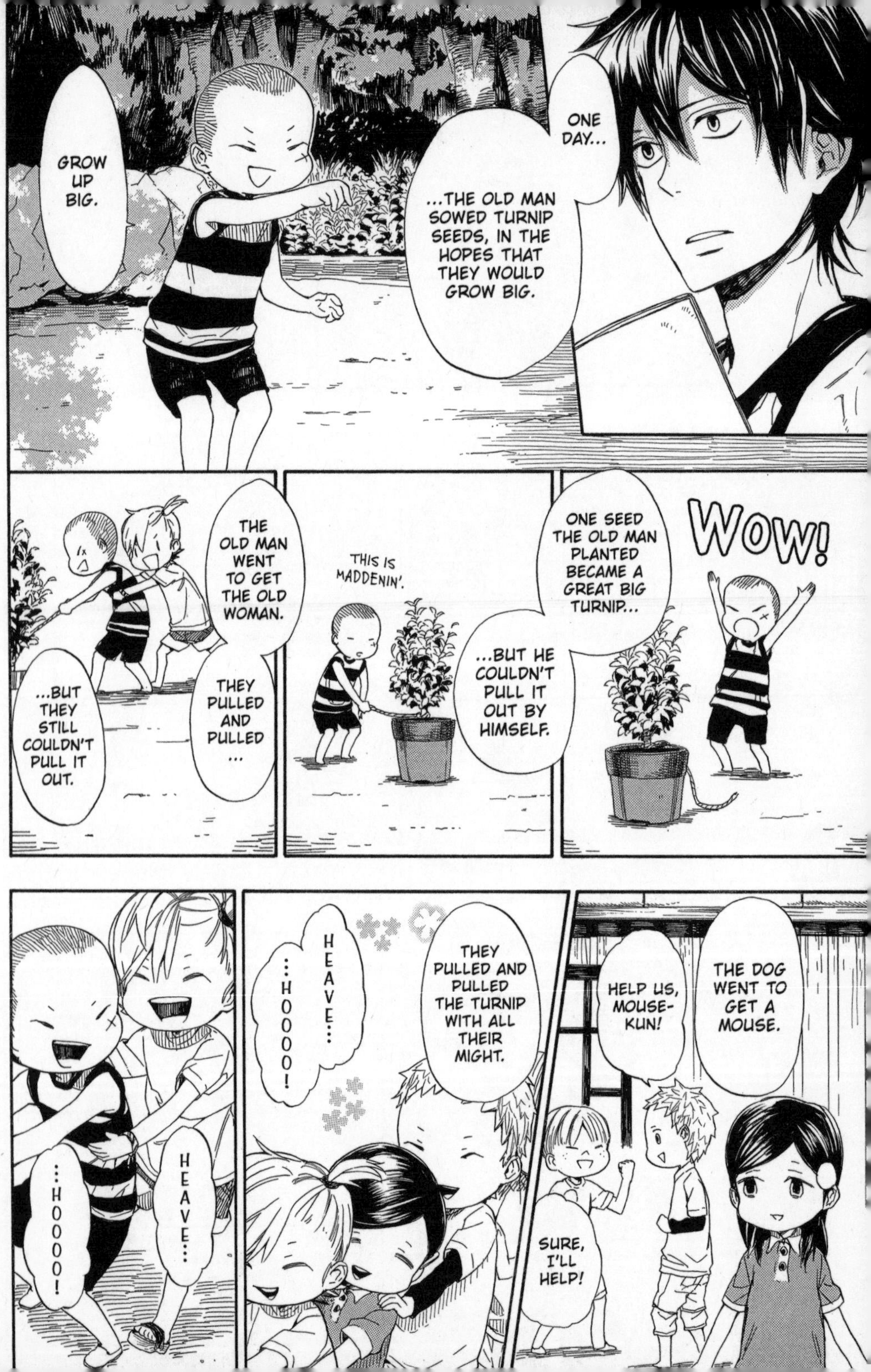

ONE DAY...
...THE OLD MAN SOWED TURNIP SEEDS, IN THE HOPES THAT THEY WOULD GROW BIG.
GROW UP BIG.
WOW!
ONE SEED THE OLD MAN PLANTED BECAME A GREAT BIG TURNIP...
...BUT HE COULDN'T PULL IT OUT BY HIMSELF.
THIS IS MADDENIN'.
THE OLD MAN WENT TO GET THE OLD WOMAN.
THEY PULLED AND PULLED ...
...BUT THEY STILL COULDN'T PULL IT OUT.
THE DOG WENT TO GET A MOUSE.
HELP US, MOUSE-KUN!
SURE, I'LL HELP!
THEY PULLED AND PULLED THE TURNIP WITH ALL THEIR MIGHT.
HEAVE...
...HOOOOO!
HEAVE...
...HOOOOO!

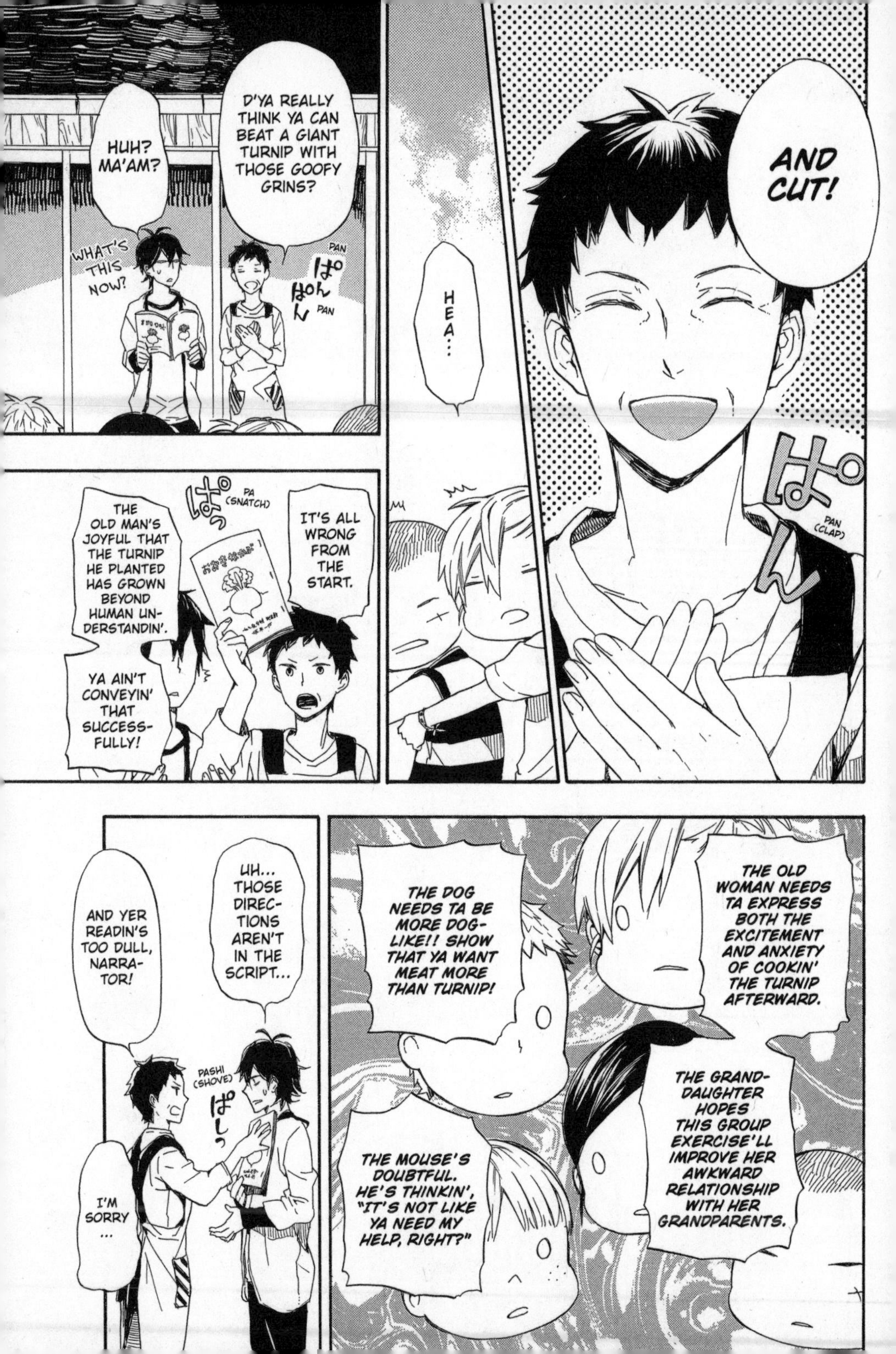
AND CUT!
ぱん
PAN (CLAP)
HEA...
D'YA REALLY THINK YA CAN BEAT A GIANT TURNIP WITH THOSE GOOFY GRINS?
HUH? MA'AM?
PAN
ぱん ぱん
PAN
WHAT'S THIS NOW?
IT'S ALL WRONG FROM THE START.
ぱっ
PA (SNATCH)
おおきなかぶ
THE OLD MAN'S JOYFUL THAT THE TURNIP HE PLANTED HAS GROWN BEYOND HUMAN UNDERSTANDIN'.
YA AIN'T CONVEYIN' THAT SUCCESSFULLY!
THE OLD WOMAN NEEDS TA EXPRESS BOTH THE EXCITEMENT AND ANXIETY OF COOKIN' THE TURNIP AFTERWARD.
THE DOG NEEDS TA BE MORE DOG-LIKE!! SHOW THAT YA WANT MEAT MORE THAN TURNIP!
THE GRANDDAUGHTER HOPES THIS GROUP EXERCISE'LL IMPROVE HER AWKWARD RELATIONSHIP WITH HER GRANDPARENTS.
THE MOUSE'S DOUBTFUL. HE'S THINKIN', "IT'S NOT LIKE YA NEED MY HELP, RIGHT?"
UH... THOSE DIRECTIONS AREN'T IN THE SCRIPT...
AND YER READIN'S TOO DULL, NARRATOR!
PASHI (SHOVE)
ぱしっ
I'M SORRY...

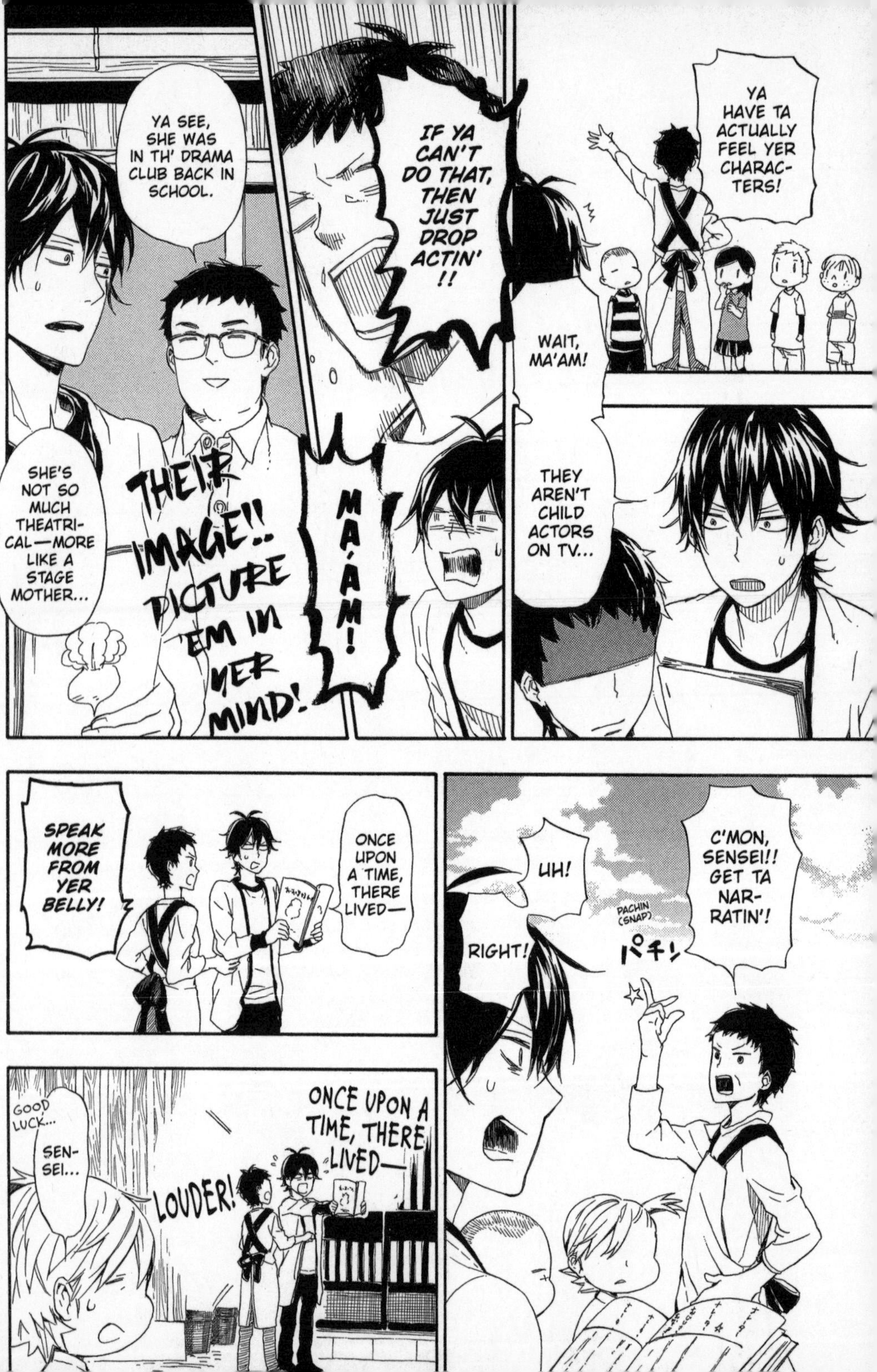
YA HAVE TA ACTUALLY FEEL YER CHARAC-TERS!
WAIT, MA'AM!
THEY AREN'T CHILD ACTORS ON TV...
IF YA CAN'T DO THAT, THEN JUST DROP ACTIN' !!
MA'AM!
THEIR IMAGE!! PICTURE 'EM IN YER MIND!
YA SEE, SHE WAS IN TH' DRAMA CLUB BACK IN SCHOOL.
SHE'S NOT SO MUCH THEATRI-CAL—MORE LIKE A STAGE MOTHER...
C'MON, SENSEI!! GET TA NAR-RATIN'!
PACHIN (SNAP)
パチン
UH!
RIGHT!
ONCE UPON A TIME, THERE LIVED—
SPEAK MORE FROM YER BELLY!
ONCE UPON A TIME, THERE LIVED—
LOUDER!
GOOD LUCK...
SEN-SEI...

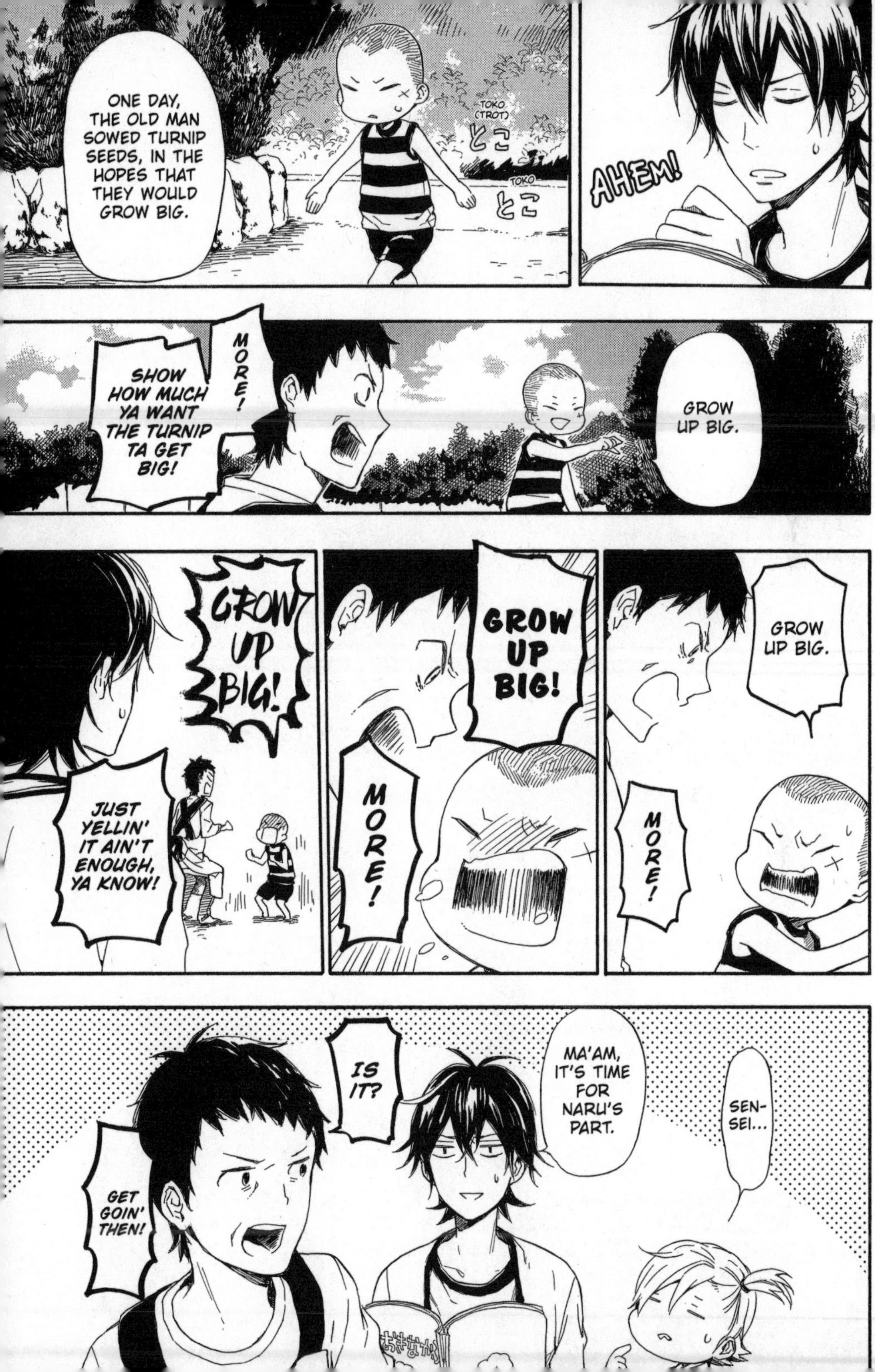
AHEM!
ONE DAY, THE OLD MAN SOWED TURNIP SEEDS, IN THE HOPES THAT THEY WOULD GROW BIG.
TOKO (TROT)
とこ
TOKO
とこ
GROW UP BIG.
MORE!
SHOW HOW MUCH YA WANT THE TURNIP TA GET BIG!
GROW UP BIG.
MORE!
GROW UP BIG!
MORE!
GROW UP BIG!
JUST YELLIN' IT AIN'T ENOUGH, YA KNOW!
SEN-SEI...
MA'AM, IT'S TIME FOR NARU'S PART.
IS IT?
GET GOIN' THEN!

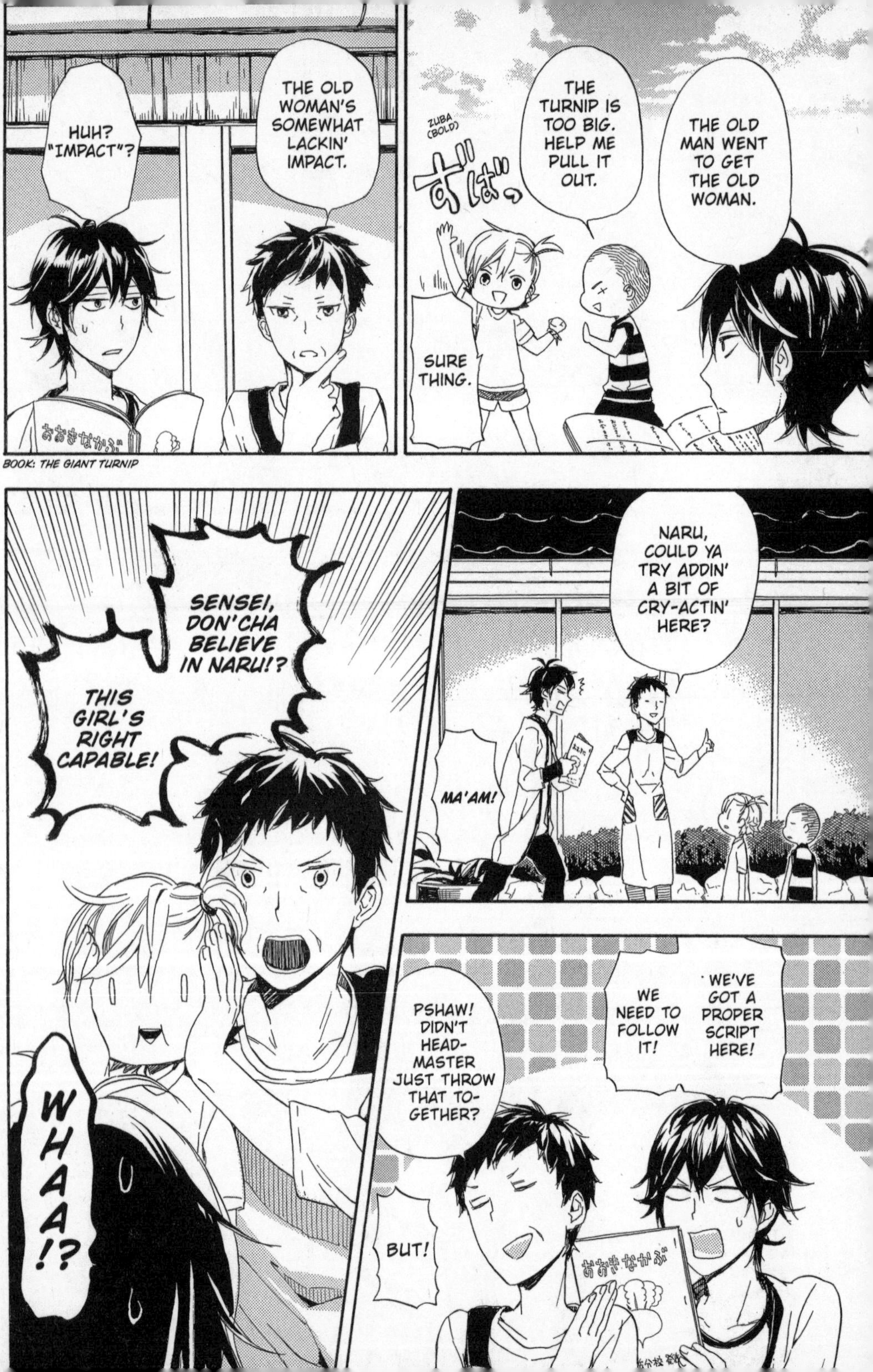
THE OLD MAN WENT TO GET THE OLD WOMAN.
THE TURNIP IS TOO BIG. HELP ME PULL IT OUT.
ZUBA (BOLD)
ずばっ
SURE THING.
THE OLD WOMAN'S SOMEWHAT LACKIN' IMPACT.
HUH? "IMPACT"?
おおきなかぶ
BOOK: THE GIANT TURNIP
NARU, COULD YA TRY ADDIN' A BIT OF CRY-ACTIN' HERE?
MA'AM!
WE'VE GOT A PROPER SCRIPT HERE!
WE NEED TO FOLLOW IT!
PSHAW! DIDN'T HEAD-MASTER JUST THROW THAT TO-GETHER?
BUT!
おおきなかぶ
SENSEI, DON'CHA BELIEVE IN NARU!?
THIS GIRL'S RIGHT CAPABLE!
WHAAA!?

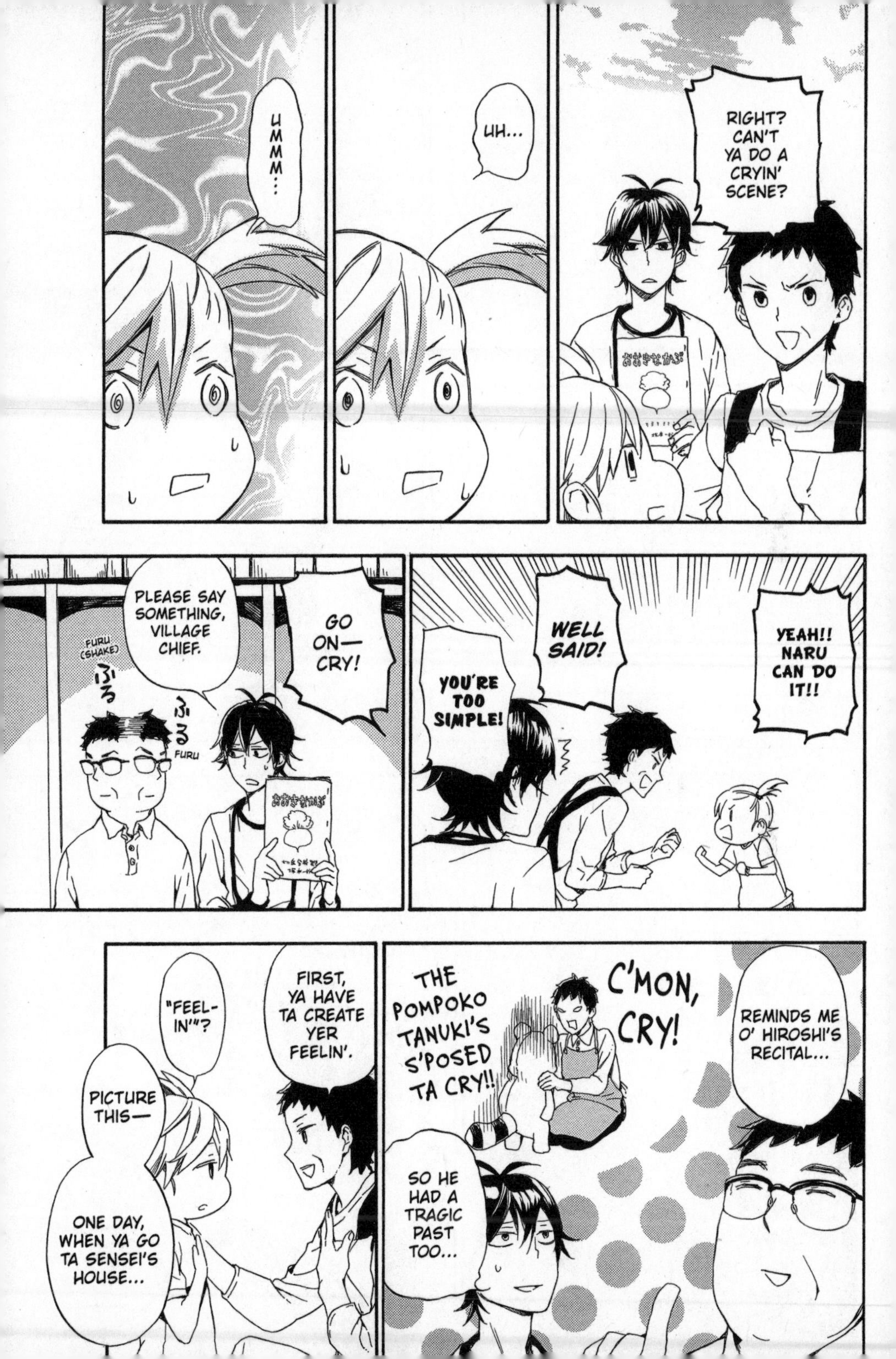
RIGHT? CAN'T YA DO A CRYIN' SCENE?
おおきなかぶ
UH...
UMMM...
YEAH!! NARU CAN DO IT!!
WELL SAID!
YOU'RE TOO SIMPLE!
GO ON— CRY!
PLEASE SAY SOMETHING, VILLAGE CHIEF.
FURU (SHAKE)
ふる
ふる
FURU
REMINDS ME O' HIROSHI'S RECITAL...
C'MON, CRY!
THE POMPOKO TANUKI'S S'POSED TA CRY!!
SO HE HAD A TRAGIC PAST TOO...
FIRST, YA HAVE TA CREATE YER FEELIN'.
"FEEL-IN'"?
PICTURE THIS—
ONE DAY, WHEN YA GO TA SENSEI'S HOUSE...

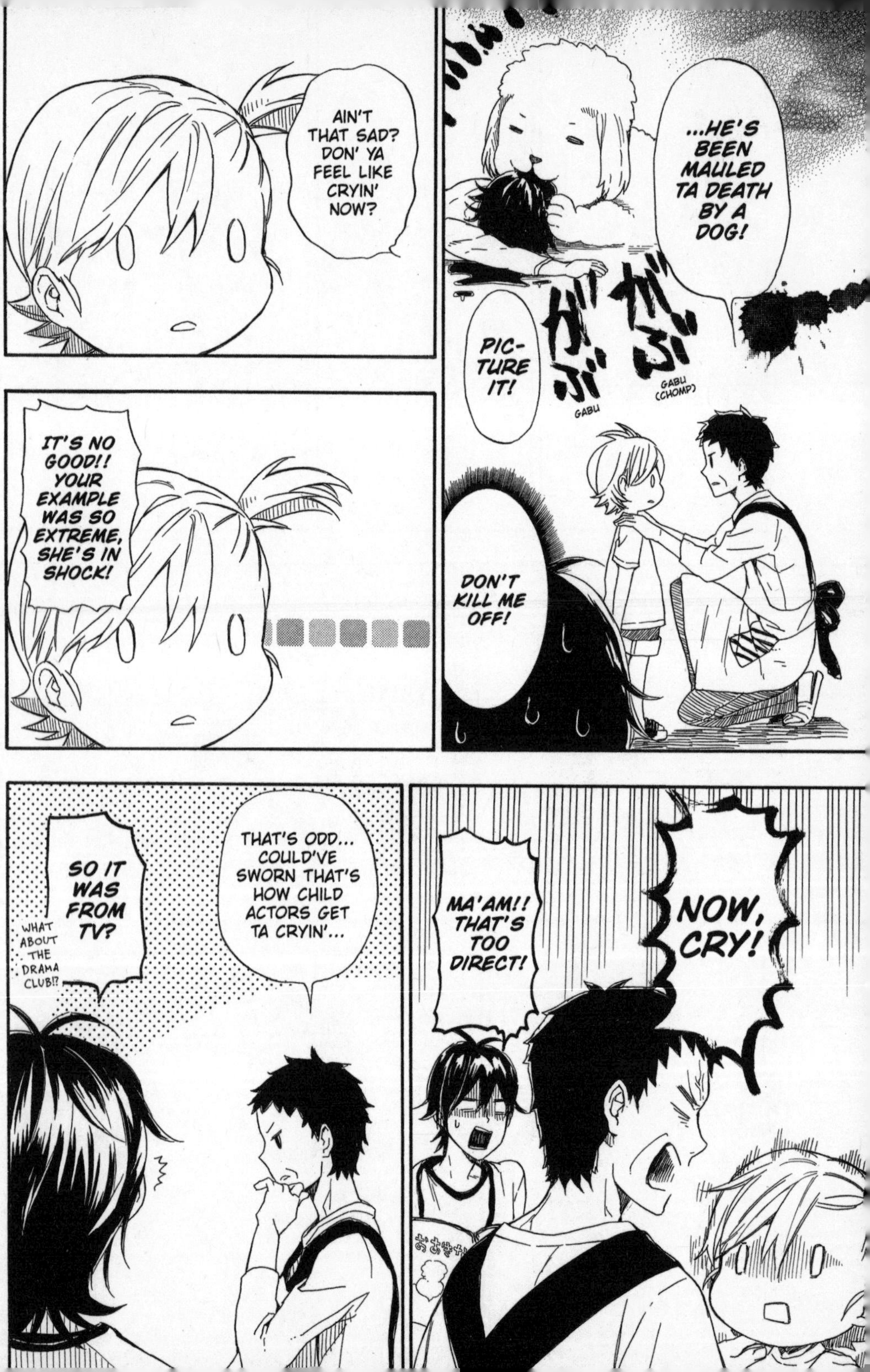
...HE'S BEEN MAULED TA DEATH BY A DOG!
がぶ
GABU (CHOMP)
がぶ
GABU
PIC-TURE IT!
DON'T KILL ME OFF!
AIN'T THAT SAD? DON' YA FEEL LIKE CRYIN' NOW?
IT'S NO GOOD!! YOUR EXAMPLE WAS SO EXTREME, SHE'S IN SHOCK!
NOW, CRY!
MA'AM!! THAT'S TOO DIRECT!
THAT'S ODD... COULD'VE SWORN THAT'S HOW CHILD ACTORS GET TA CRYIN'...
SO IT WAS FROM TV?
WHAT ABOUT THE DRAMA CLUB!?

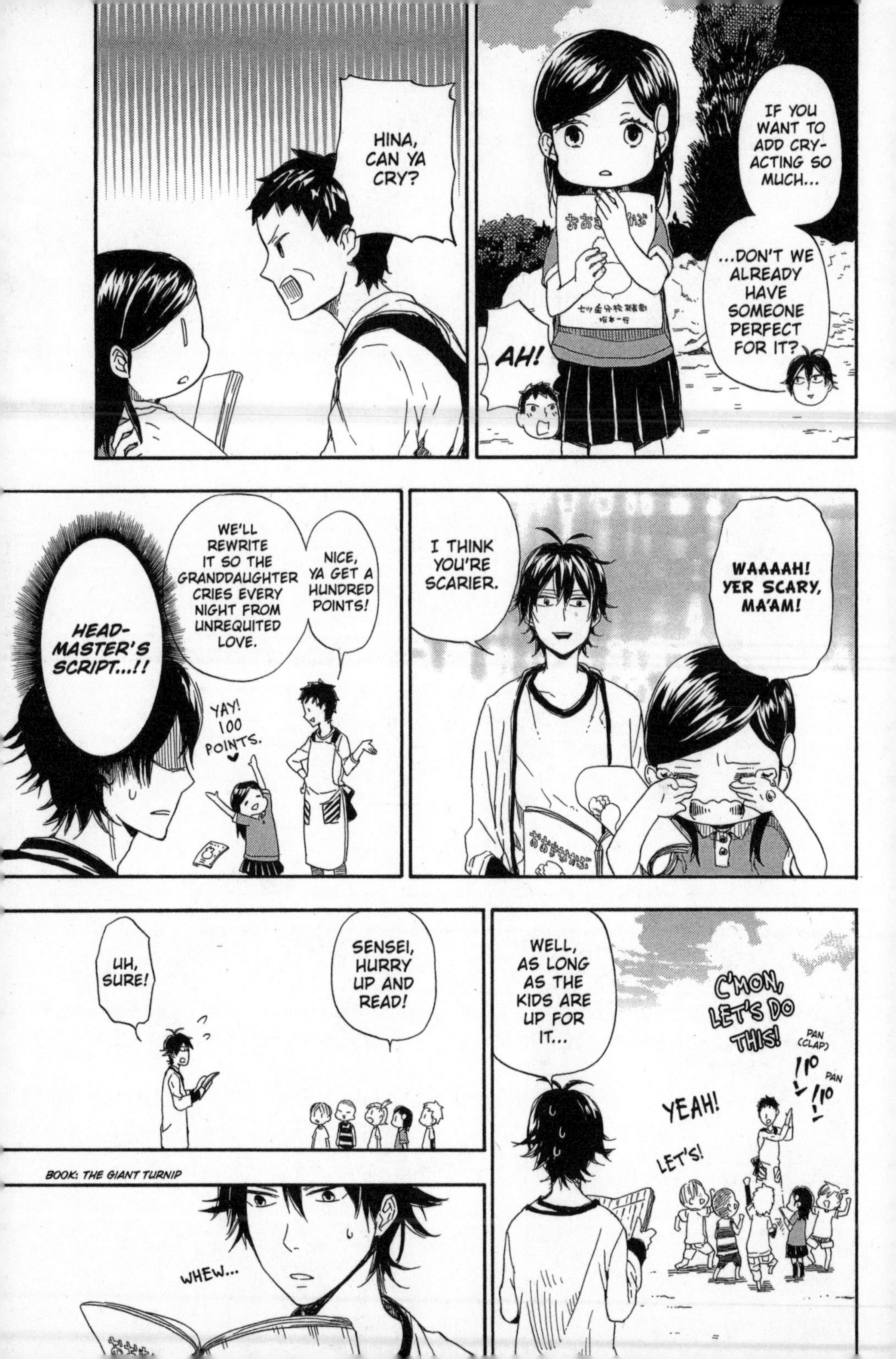
IF YOU WANT TO ADD CRY-ACTING SO MUCH...
...DON'T WE ALREADY HAVE SOMEONE PERFECT FOR IT?
AH!
HINA, CAN YA CRY?
WAAAAH! YER SCARY, MA'AM!
I THINK YOU'RE SCARIER.
NICE, YA GET A HUNDRED POINTS!
WE'LL REWRITE IT SO THE GRANDDAUGHTER CRIES EVERY NIGHT FROM UNREQUITED LOVE.
HEAD-MASTER'S SCRIPT...!!
YAY! 100 POINTS. ♥
WELL, AS LONG AS THE KIDS ARE UP FOR IT...
C'MON, LET'S DO THIS!
PAN (CLAP)
PAN
YEAH!
LET'S!
SENSEI, HURRY UP AND READ!
UH, SURE!
BOOK: THE GIANT TURNIP
WHEW...

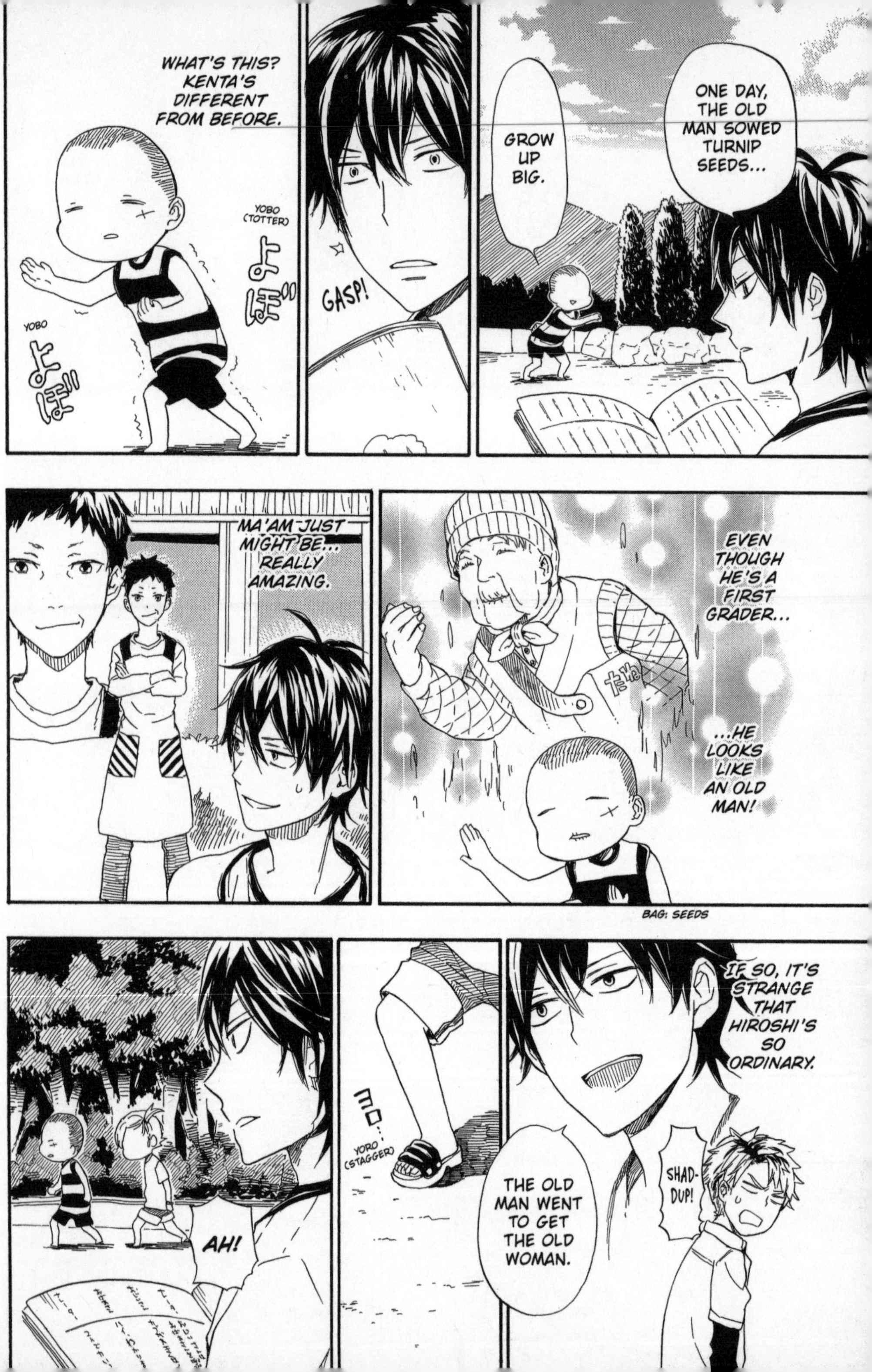
ONE DAY, THE OLD MAN SOWED TURNIP SEEDS...
GROW UP BIG.
GASP!
WHAT'S THIS? KENTA'S DIFFERENT FROM BEFORE.
よぼ
YOBO (TOTTER)
よぼ
YOBO
EVEN THOUGH HE'S A FIRST GRADER...
...HE LOOKS LIKE AN OLD MAN!
BAG: SEEDS
MA'AM JUST MIGHT BE... REALLY AMAZING.
IF SO, IT'S STRANGE THAT HIROSHI'S SO ORDINARY.
SHAD-DUP!
THE OLD MAN WENT TO GET THE OLD WOMAN.
ヨロ…
YORO (STAGGER)
AH!

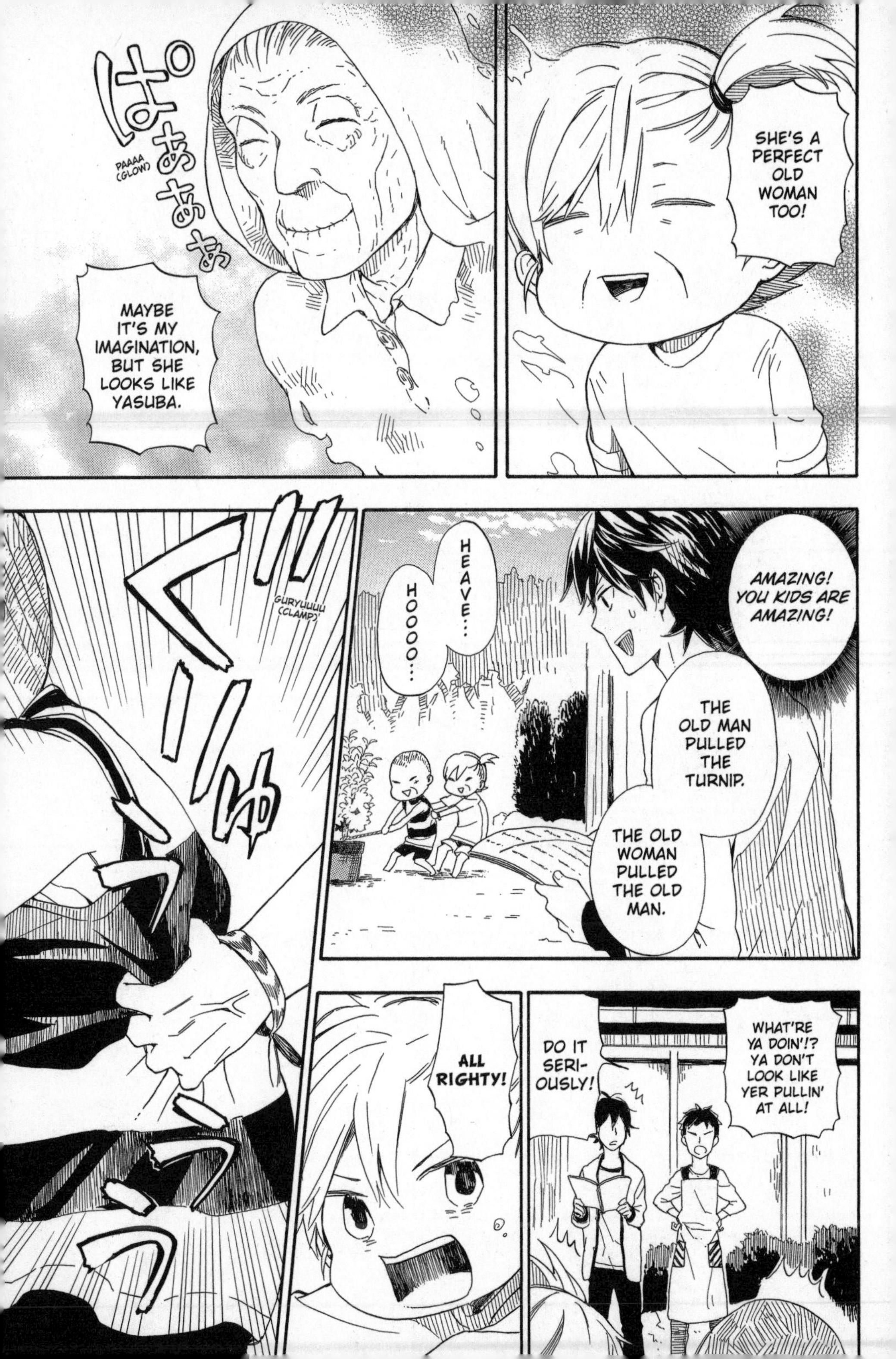
SHE'S A PERFECT OLD WOMAN TOO!
PAAAA (GLOW)
MAYBE IT'S MY IMAGINATION, BUT SHE LOOKS LIKE YASUBA.
AMAZING! YOU KIDS ARE AMAZING!
THE OLD MAN PULLED THE TURNIP.
THE OLD WOMAN PULLED THE OLD MAN.
HEAVE...
HOOOOO...
WHAT'RE YA DOIN'!? YA DON'T LOOK LIKE YER PULLIN' AT ALL!
DO IT SERI-OUSLY!
ALL RIGHTY!
GURYUUUU (CLAMP)

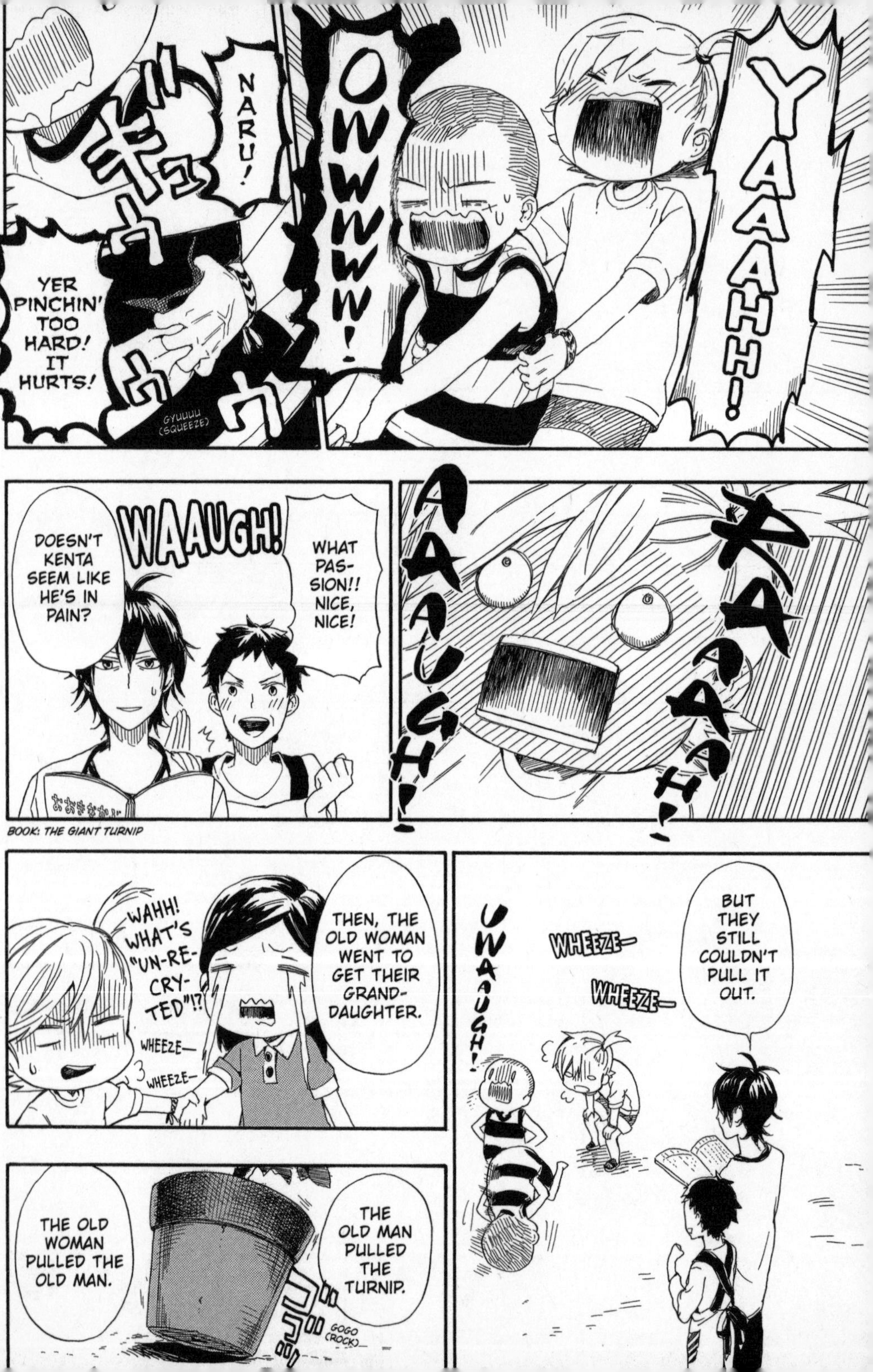
YAAAAHH!
OWWWWWWW!
NARU!
YER PINCHIN' TOO HARD! IT HURTS!
GYUUUU (SQUEEZE)
AAAAH!
AAAUGH!
WHAT PASSION!! NICE, NICE!
WAAUGH!
DOESN'T KENTA SEEM LIKE HE'S IN PAIN?
BUT THEY STILL COULDN'T PULL IT OUT.
WHEEZE—
WHEEZE—
UWAAUGH!
THEN, THE OLD WOMAN WENT TO GET THEIR GRANDDAUGHTER.
WAHH! WHAT'S "UN-RE-CRY-TED"!?
WHEEZE—
WHEEZE—
THE OLD MAN PULLED THE TURNIP.
THE OLD WOMAN PULLED THE OLD MAN.
GOGO (ROCK)
BOOK: THE GIANT TURNIP

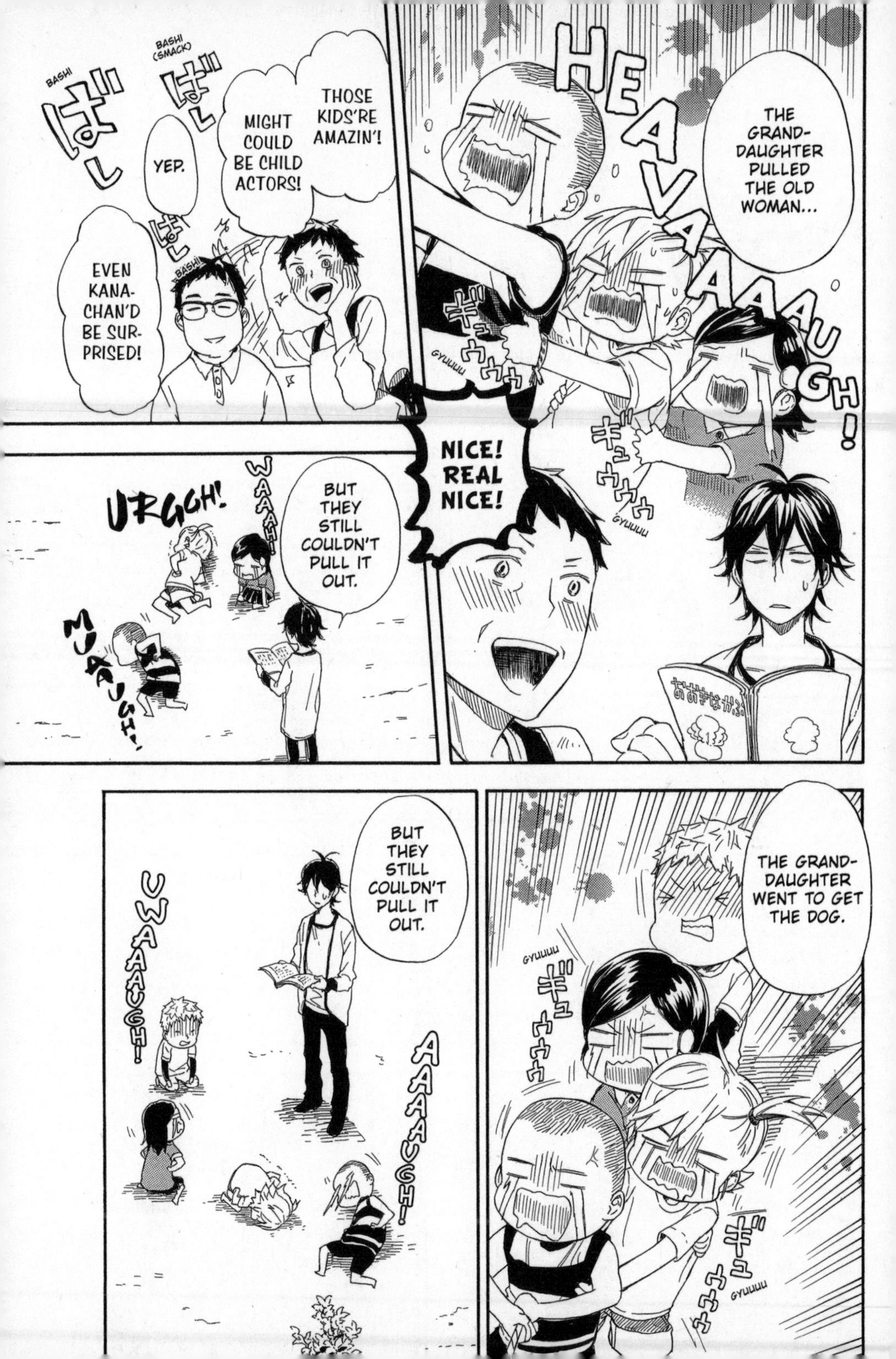
HEAVAAAAAUGH!
THE GRAND-DAUGHTER PULLED THE OLD WOMAN...
GYUUUU
GYUUUU
NICE! REAL NICE!
BASHI (SMACK)
BASHI
THOSE KIDS'RE AMAZIN'!
MIGHT COULD BE CHILD ACTORS!
YEP.
BASHI
EVEN KANA-CHAN'D BE SUR-PRISED!
BUT THEY STILL COULDN'T PULL IT OUT.
WAAAAH!
URGGH!
MUAAUGH!
THE GRAND-DAUGHTER WENT TO GET THE DOG.
GYUUUU
GYUUUU
BUT THEY STILL COULDN'T PULL IT OUT.
AAAAAUGH!
UWAAAAAUGH!

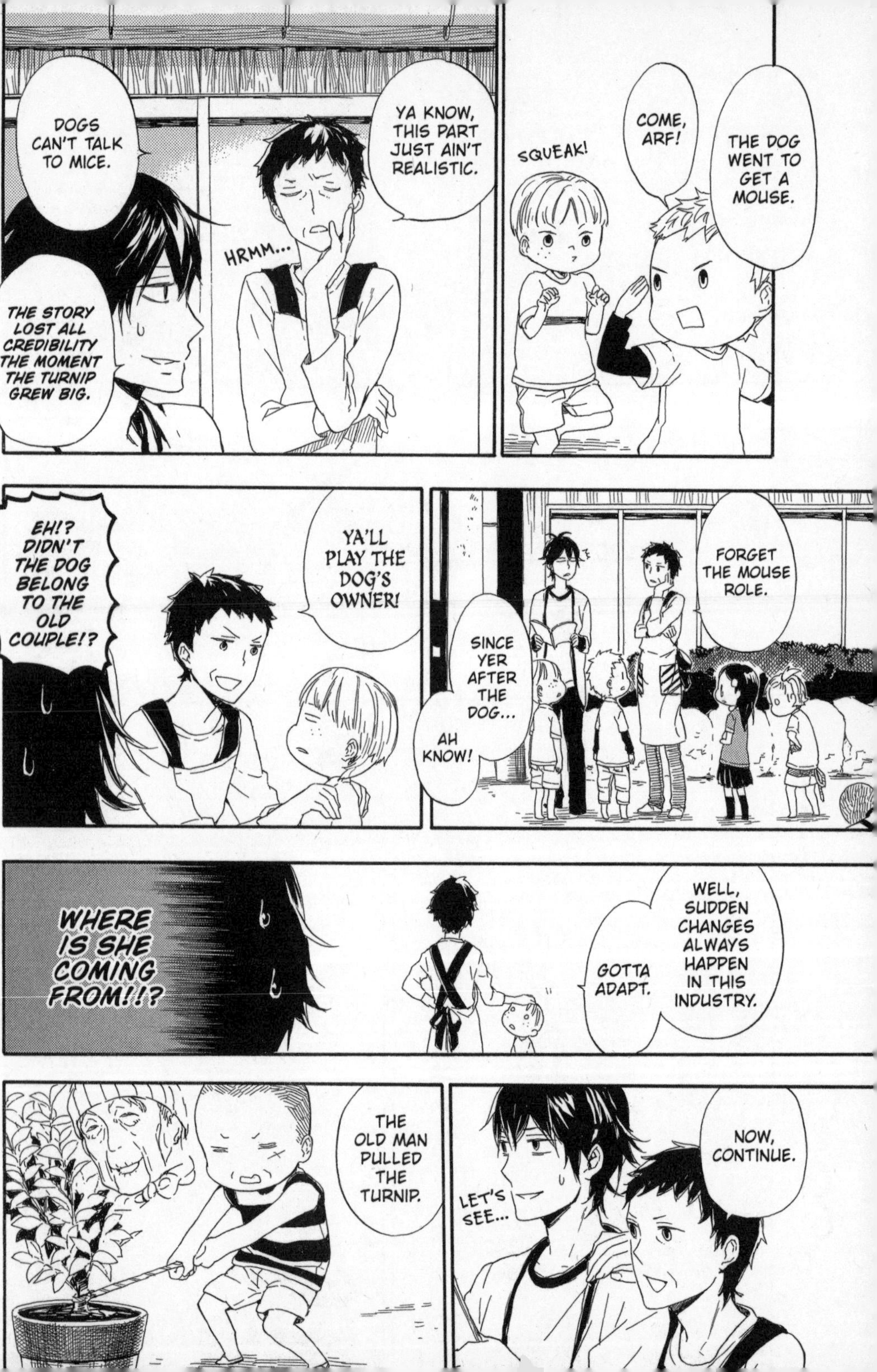
THE DOG WENT TO GET A MOUSE.
COME, ARF!
SQUEAK!
YA KNOW, THIS PART JUST AIN'T REALISTIC.
HRMM...
DOGS CAN'T TALK TO MICE.
THE STORY LOST ALL CREDIBILITY THE MOMENT THE TURNIP GREW BIG.
FORGET THE MOUSE ROLE.
SINCE YER AFTER THE DOG...
AH KNOW!
YA'LL PLAY THE DOG'S OWNER!
EH!? DIDN'T THE DOG BELONG TO THE OLD COUPLE!?
WELL, SUDDEN CHANGES ALWAYS HAPPEN IN THIS INDUSTRY.
GOTTA ADAPT.
WHERE IS SHE COMING FROM!!?
NOW, CONTINUE.
LET'S SEE...
THE OLD MAN PULLED THE TURNIP.

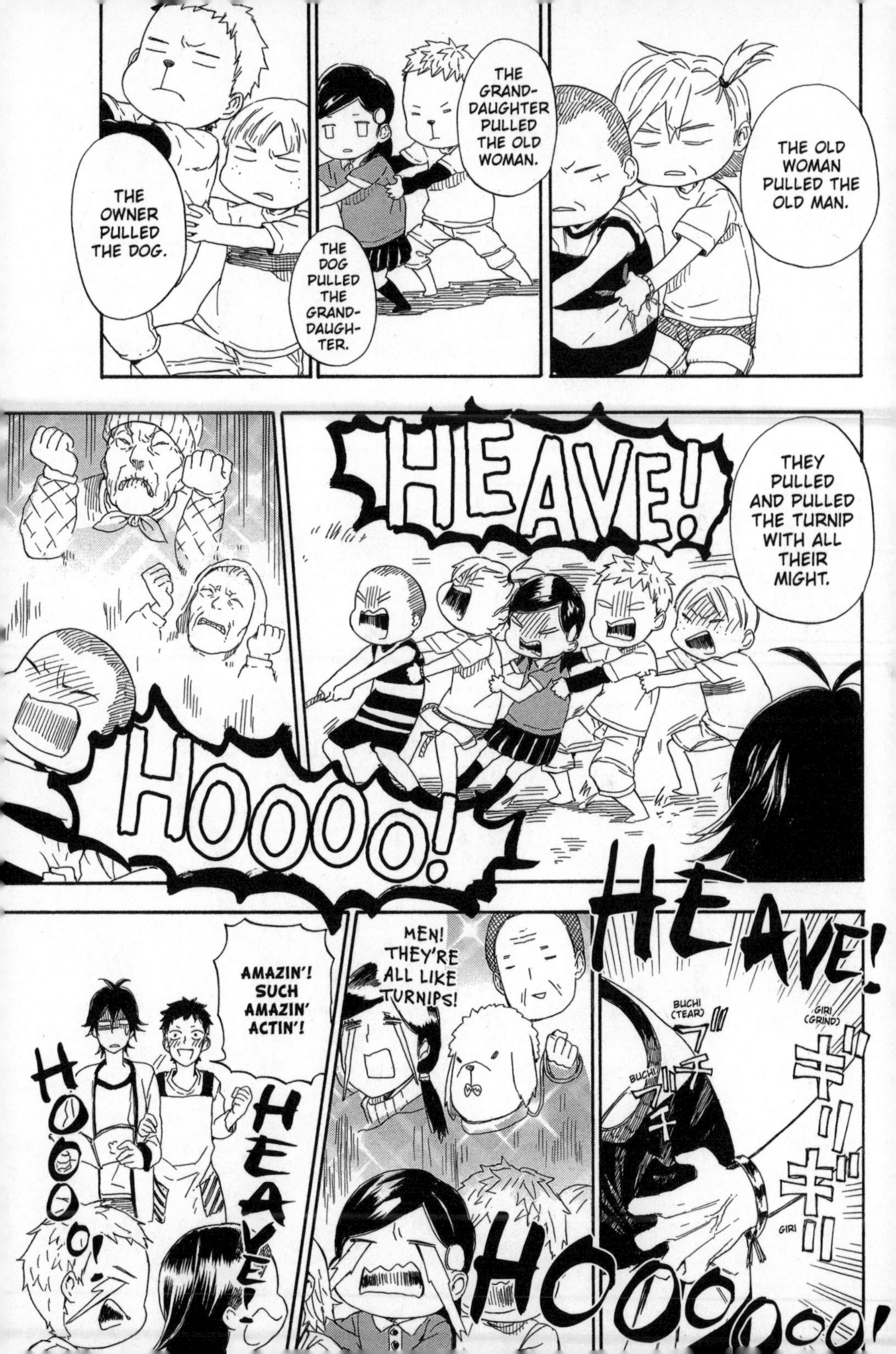

THE OLD WOMAN PULLED THE OLD MAN.
THE GRAND-DAUGHTER PULLED THE OLD WOMAN.
THE DOG PULLED THE GRAND-DAUGH-TER.
THE OWNER PULLED THE DOG.
HEAVE!
THEY PULLED AND PULLED THE TURNIP WITH ALL THEIR MIGHT.
HOOOOO!
HEAVE!
BUCHI (TEAR)
BUCHI
GIRI (GRIND)
GIRI
HOOOOOOOO!
MEN! THEY'RE ALL LIKE TURNIPS!
AMAZIN'! SUCH AMAZIN' ACTIN'!
HEAVE!
HOOOOO!

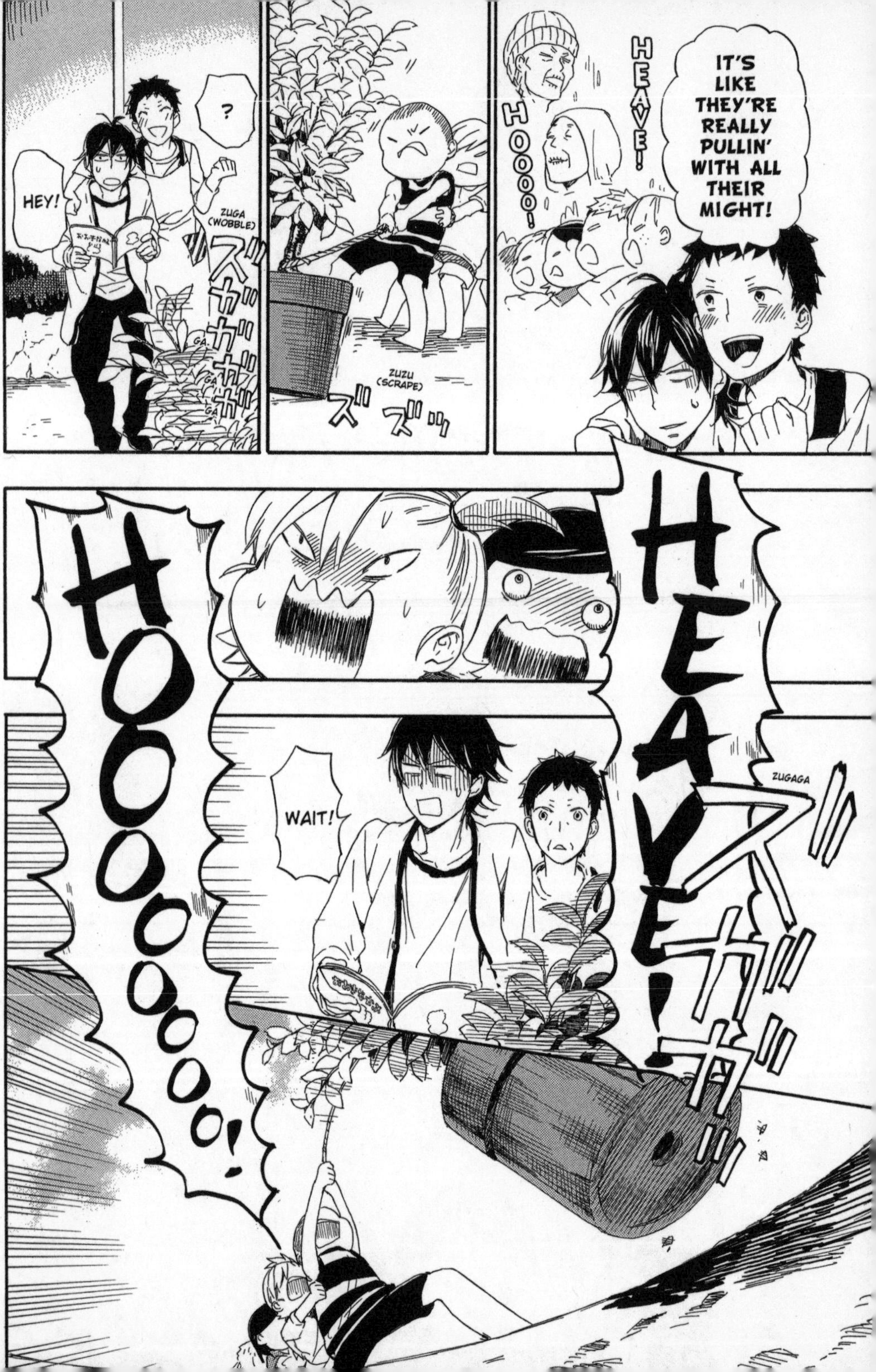

IT'S LIKE THEY'RE REALLY PULLIN' WITH ALL THEIR MIGHT!
HEAVE!
HOOOOO!
ZUZU (SCRAPE)
?
HEY!
ZUGA (WOBBLE)
GA
GA
GA
HEAVE!
HOOOOOOOOO!
ZUGAGA
WAIT!

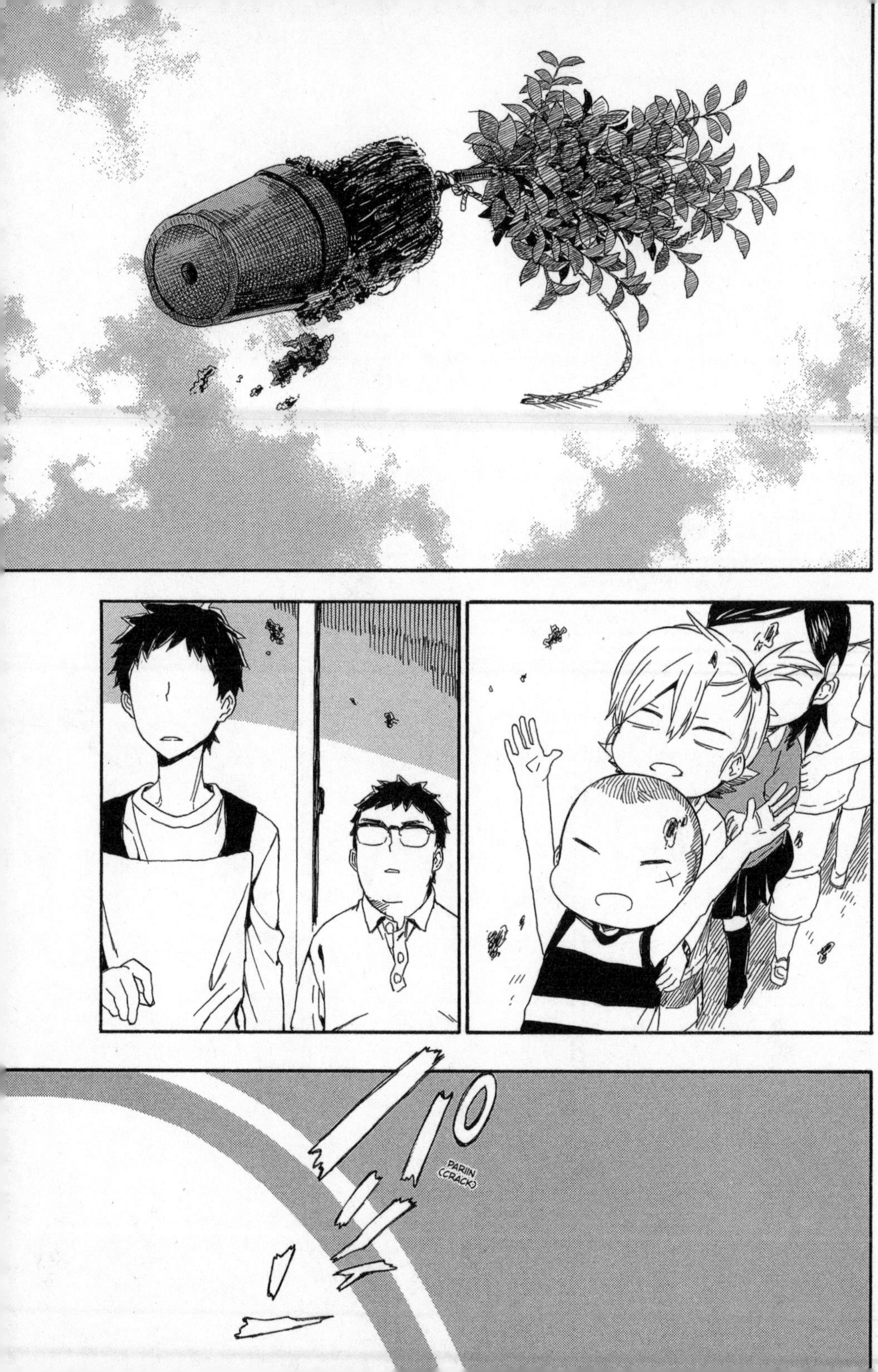
PARIIN
(CRACK)

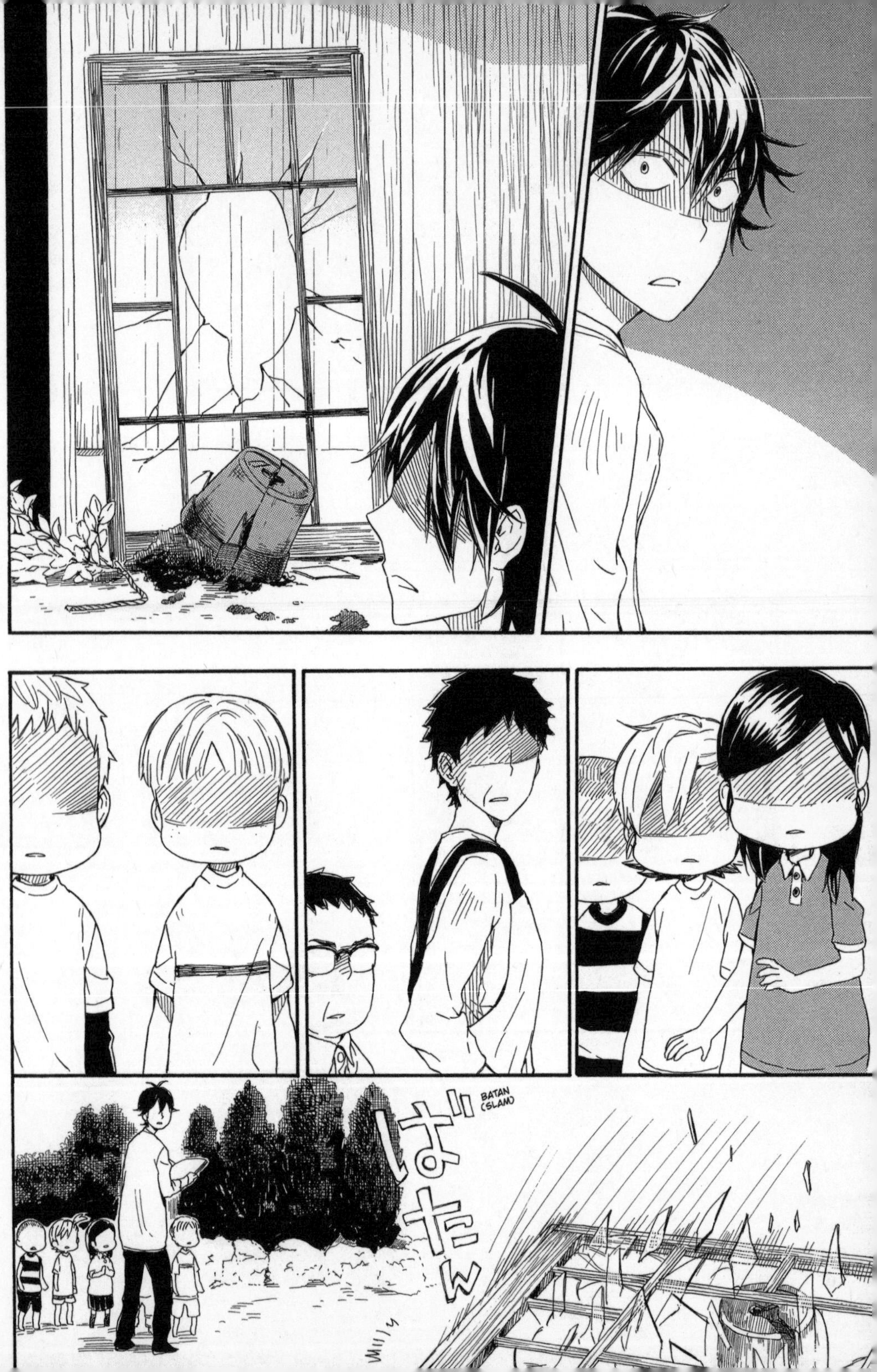
ばたん
BATAN (SLAM)

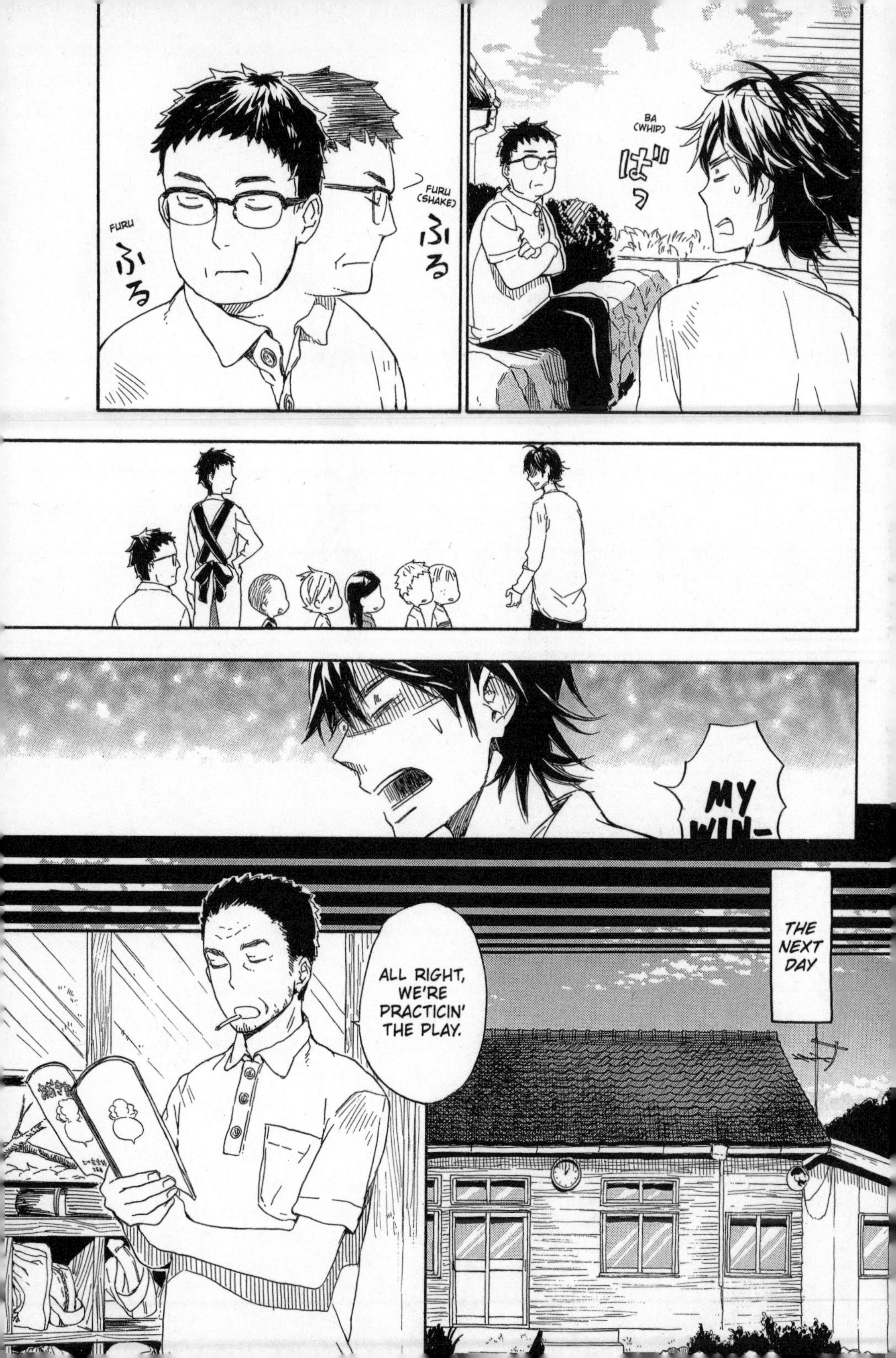
BA (WHIP)
ばッ
FURU (SHAKE)
ふる
FURU
ふる
MY WIN-
THE NEXT DAY
ALL RIGHT, WE'RE PRACTICIN' THE PLAY.

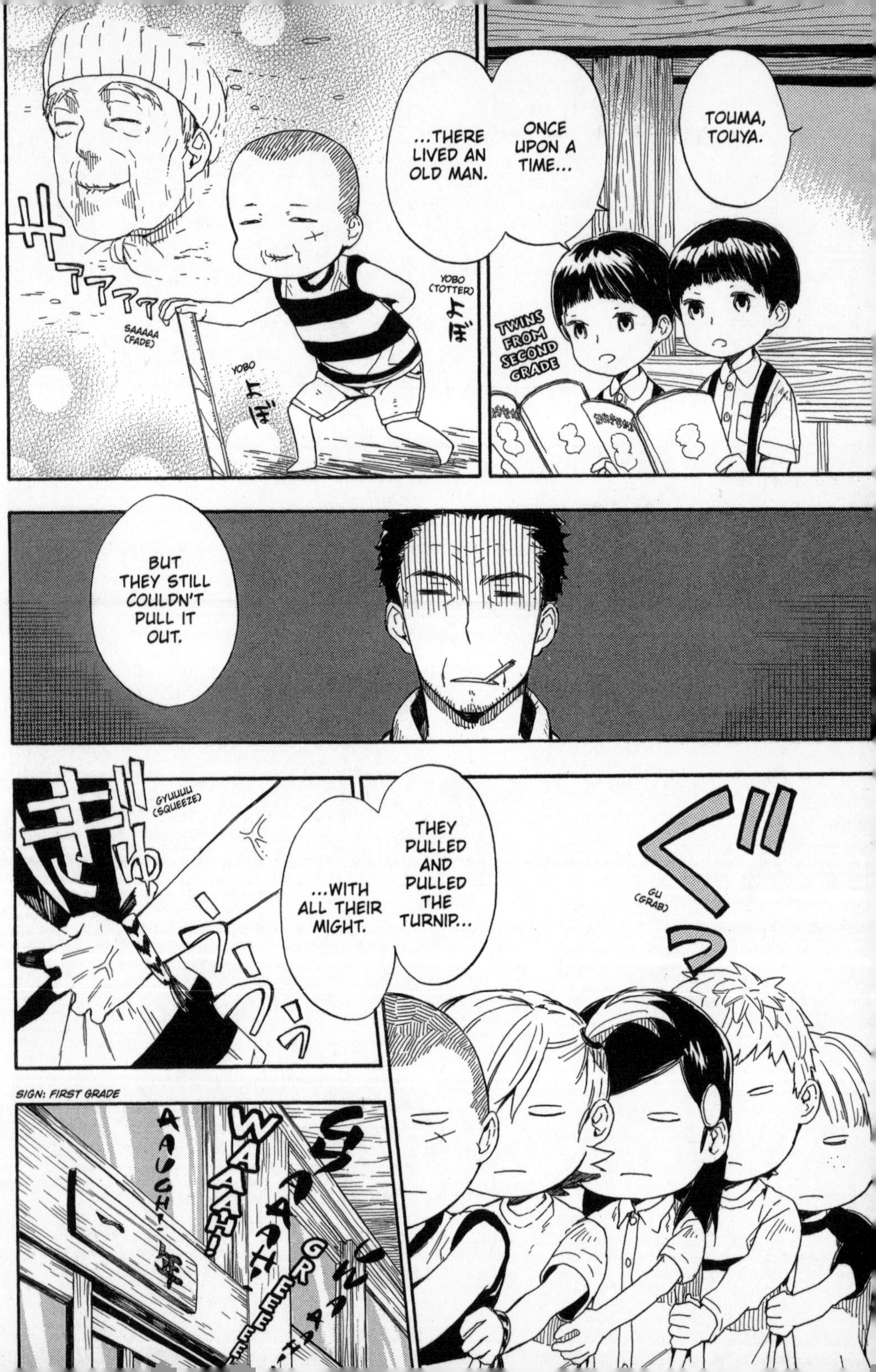
TOUMA, TOUYA.
ONCE UPON A TIME...
...THERE LIVED AN OLD MAN.
TWINS FROM SECOND GRADE
YOBO (TOTTER)
よぼ
YOBO
よぼ
SAAAAA (FADE)
BUT THEY STILL COULDN'T PULL IT OUT.
THEY PULLED AND PULLED THE TURNIP...
...WITH ALL THEIR MIGHT.
GU (GRAB)
GYUUUU (SQUEEZE)
SIGN: FIRST GRADE
WAAAH!
AAUGH!

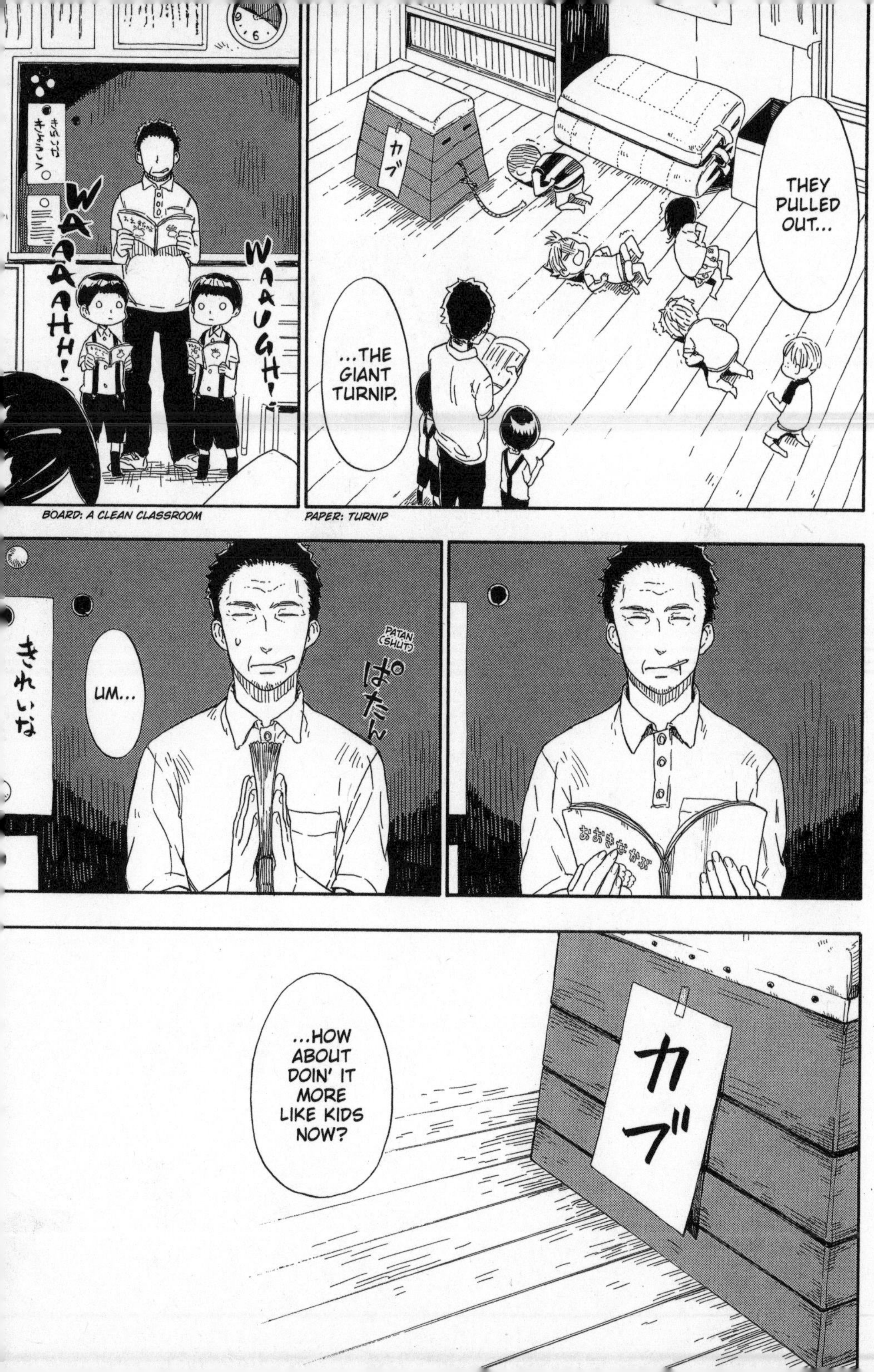
カブ
THEY PULLED OUT...
...THE GIANT TURNIP.
PAPER: TURNIP
WAAUGH!!
WAAAAHH!!
BOARD: A CLEAN CLASSROOM
おおきなかぶ
PATAN (SHUT)
ぱたん
UM...
きれいな
...HOW ABOUT DOIN' IT MORE LIKE KIDS NOW?
カブ

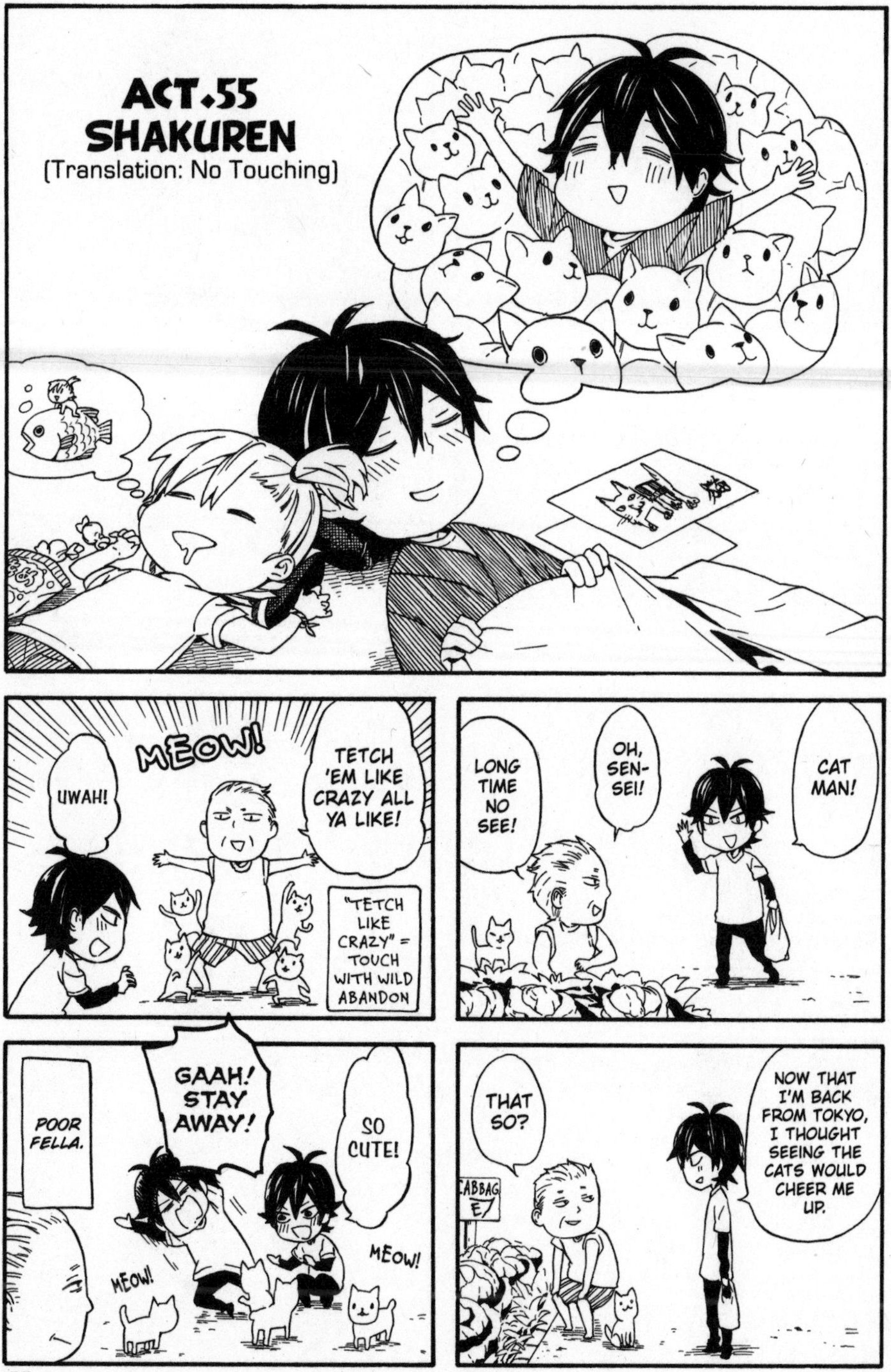
ACT.55
SHAKUREN
(Translation: No Touching)
CAT MAN!
OH, SEN-SEI!
LONG TIME NO SEE!
TETCH 'EM LIKE CRAZY ALL YA LIKE!
MEOW!
UWAH!
"TETCH LIKE CRAZY" = TOUCH WITH WILD ABANDON
NOW THAT I'M BACK FROM TOKYO, I THOUGHT SEEING THE CATS WOULD CHEER ME UP.
THAT SO?
CABBAGE
SO CUTE!
GAAH! STAY AWAY!
MEOW!
MEOW!
POOR FELLA.

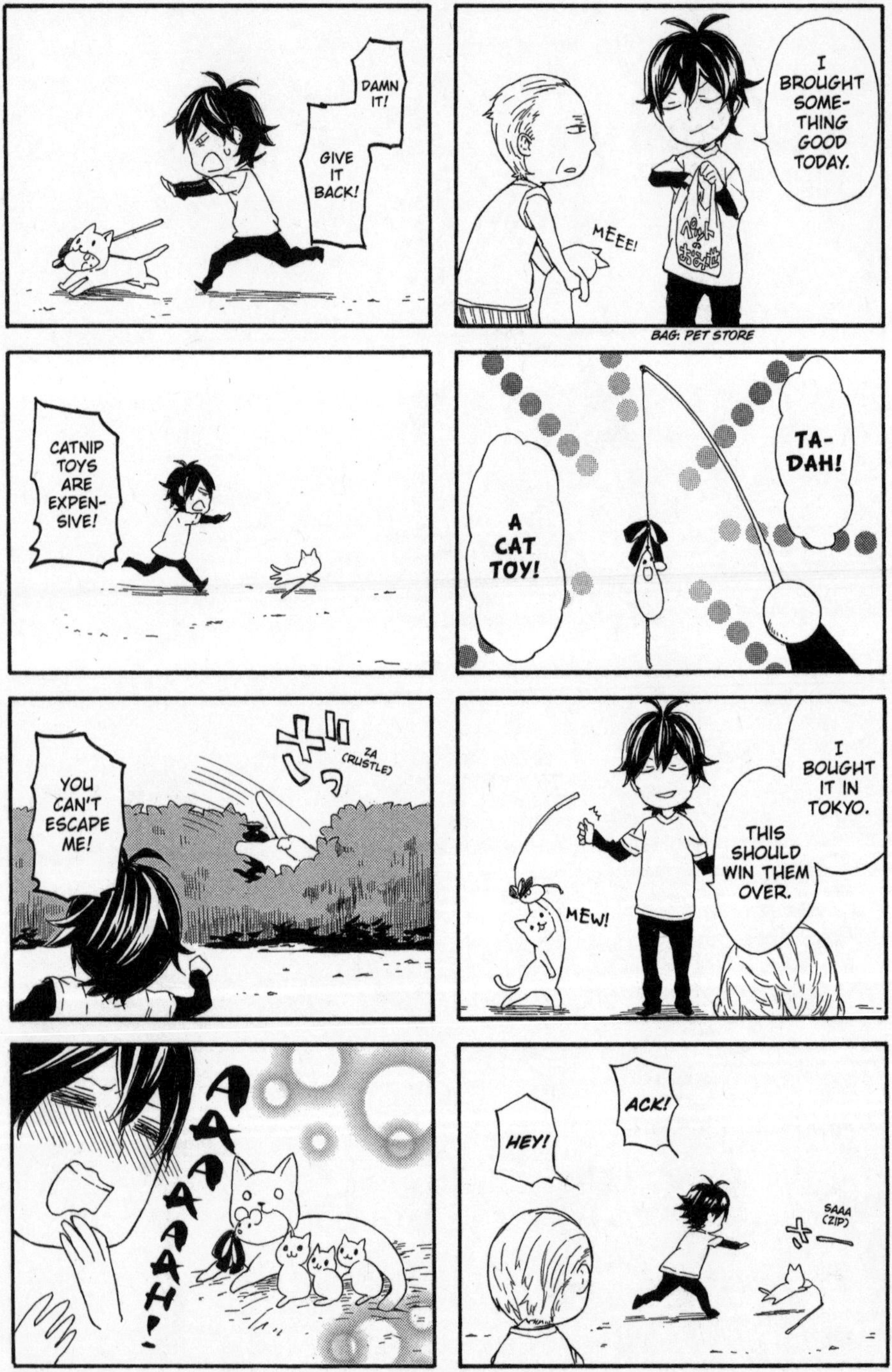
I BROUGHT SOME-THING GOOD TODAY.
MEEE!
BAG: PET STORE
TA-DAH!
A CAT TOY!
I BOUGHT IT IN TOKYO.
THIS SHOULD WIN THEM OVER.
MEW!
ACK!
HEY!
SAAA (ZIP)
DAMN IT!
GIVE IT BACK!
CATNIP TOYS ARE EXPEN-SIVE!
ZA (RUSTLE)
YOU CAN'T ESCAPE ME!
AAAAAAAH!

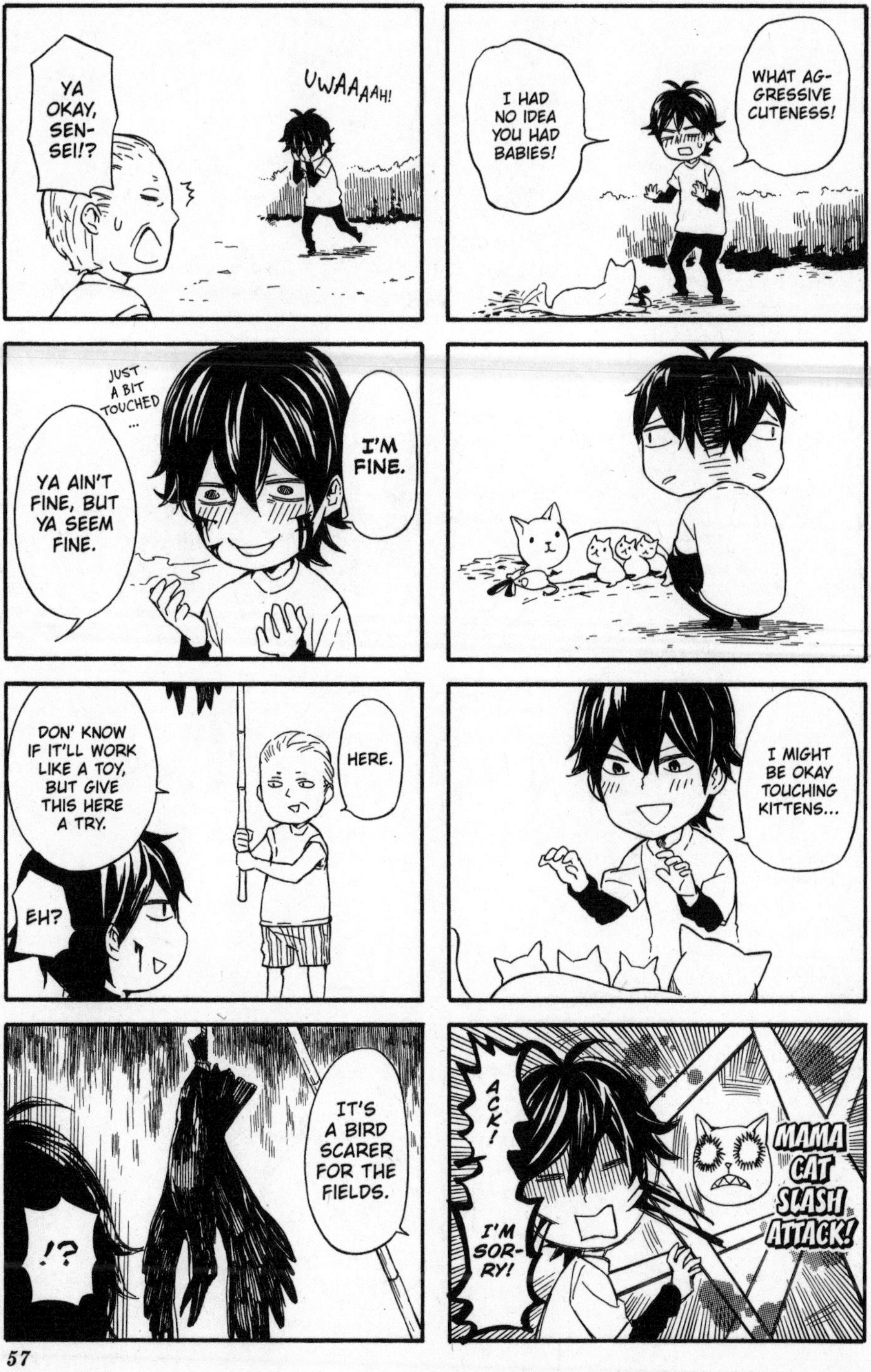
WHAT AGGRESSIVE CUTENESS!
I HAD NO IDEA YOU HAD BABIES!
UWAAAAAH!
YA OKAY, SENSEI!?
I'M FINE.
JUST A BIT TOUCHED...
YA AIN'T FINE, BUT YA SEEM FINE.
I MIGHT BE OKAY TOUCHING KITTENS...
HERE.
DON' KNOW IF IT'LL WORK LIKE A TOY, BUT GIVE THIS HERE A TRY.
EH?
MAMA CAT SLASH ATTACK!
ACK!
I'M SORRY!
IT'S A BIRD SCARER FOR THE FIELDS.
!?

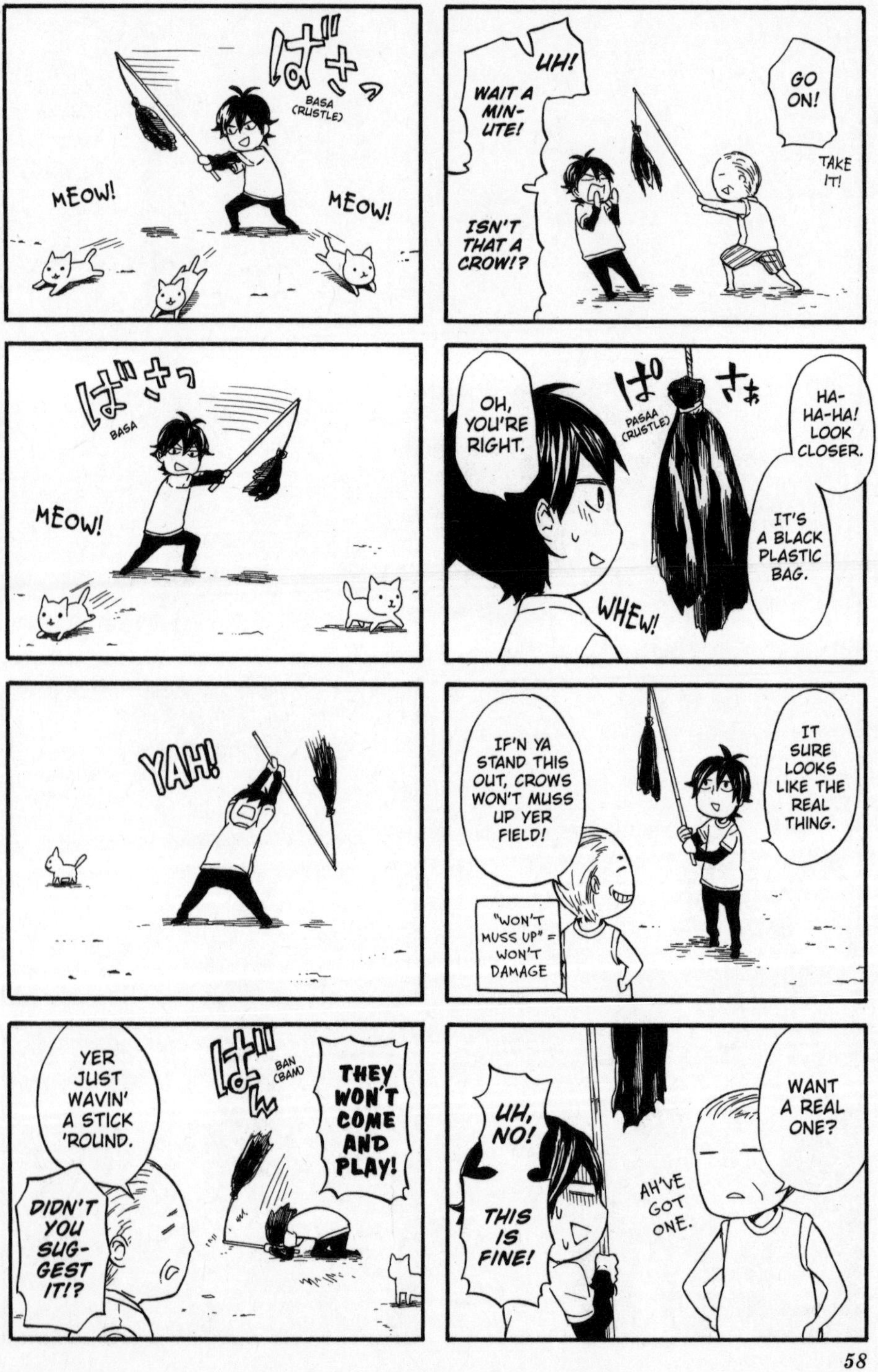
GO ON!
TAKE IT!
UH!
WAIT A MIN-UTE!
ISN'T THAT A CROW!?
ばさっ
BASA (RUSTLE)
MEOW!
MEOW!
HA-HA-HA! LOOK CLOSER.
IT'S A BLACK PLASTIC BAG.
ぱさぁ
PASAA (RUSTLE)
OH, YOU'RE RIGHT.
WHEW!
ばさっ
BASA
MEOW!
IT SURE LOOKS LIKE THE REAL THING.
IF'N YA STAND THIS OUT, CROWS WON'T MUSS UP YER FIELD!
"WON'T MUSS UP" = WON'T DAMAGE
YAH!
WANT A REAL ONE?
AH'VE GOT ONE.
UH, NO!
THIS IS FINE!
THEY WON'T COME AND PLAY!
ばん
BAN (BAM)
YER JUST WAVIN' A STICK 'ROUND.
DIDN'T YOU SUG-GEST IT!?

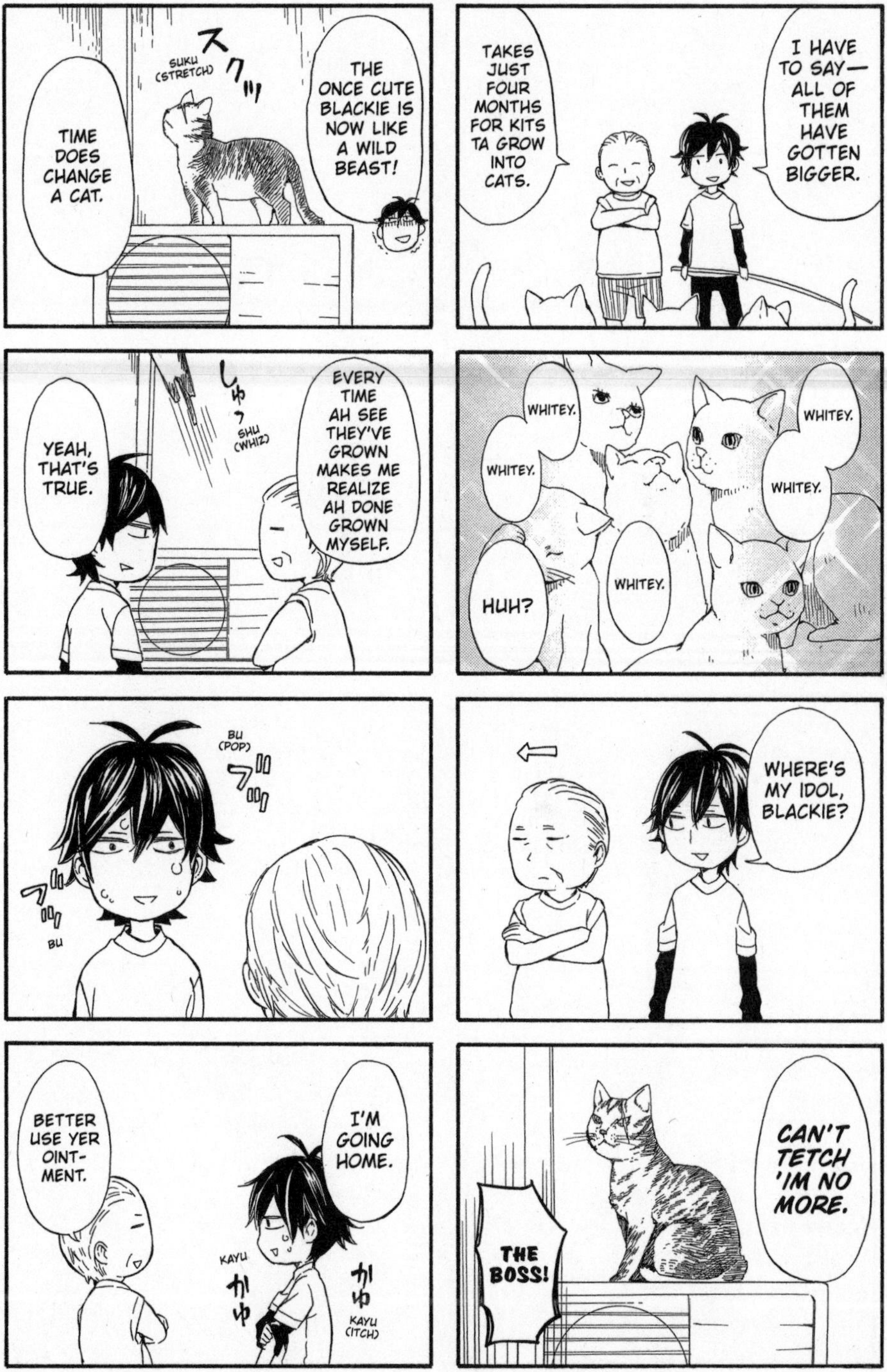
I HAVE TO SAY— ALL OF THEM HAVE GOTTEN BIGGER.
TAKES JUST FOUR MONTHS FOR KITS TA GROW INTO CATS.
THE ONCE CUTE BLACKIE IS NOW LIKE A WILD BEAST!
スクッ
SUKU (STRETCH)
TIME DOES CHANGE A CAT.
WHITEY.
WHITEY.
WHITEY.
WHITEY.
WHITEY.
HUH?
EVERY TIME AH SEE THEY'VE GROWN MAKES ME REALIZE AH DONE GROWN MYSELF.
しゅっ
SHU (WHIZ)
YEAH, THAT'S TRUE.
WHERE'S MY IDOL, BLACKIE?
BU (POP)
ブッ
ブッ
BU
CAN'T TETCH 'IM NO MORE.
THE BOSS!
I'M GOING HOME.
かゆ
KAYU (ITCH)
かゆ
KAYU
BETTER USE YER OINT-MENT.

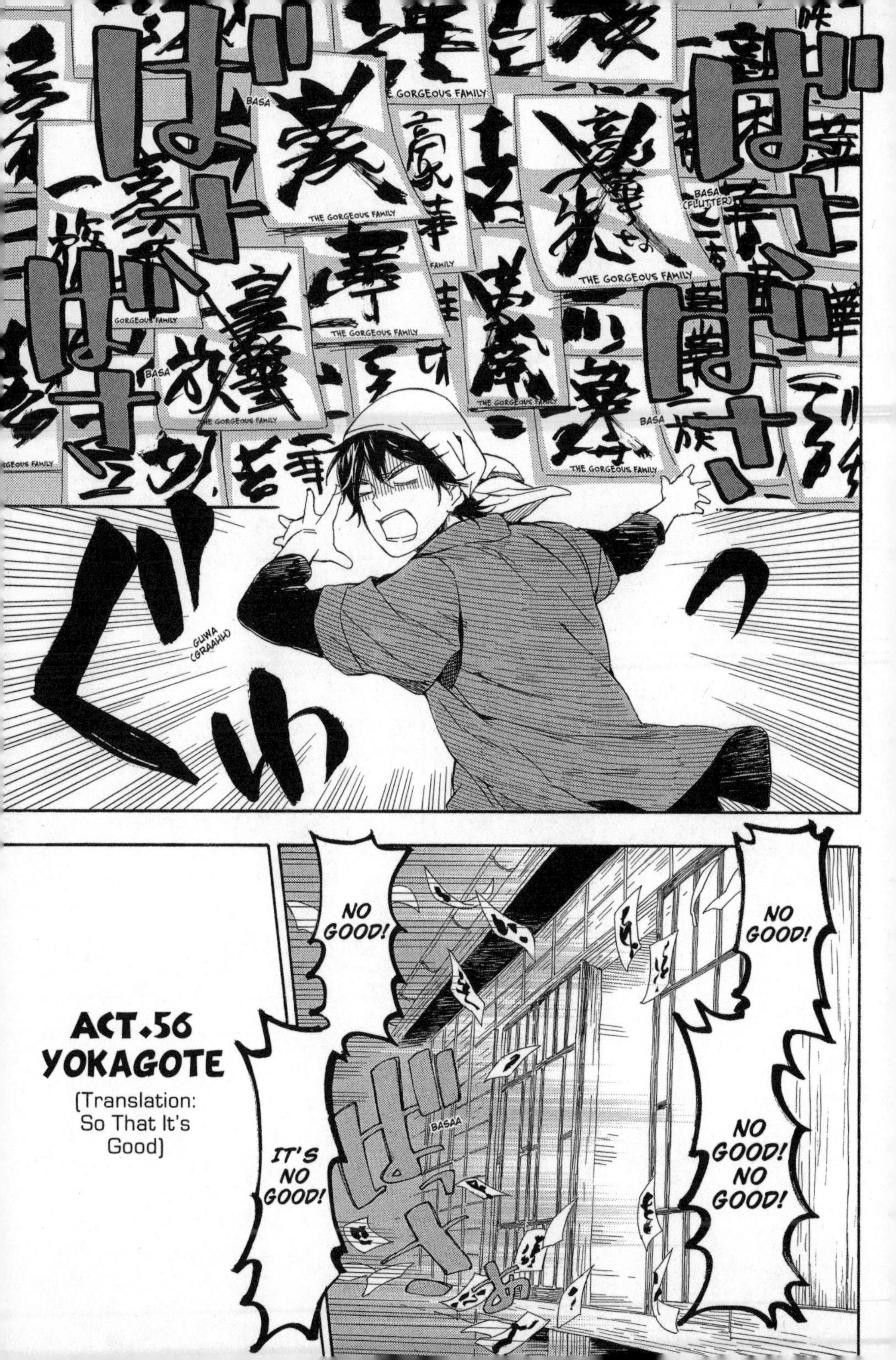
BASA
THE GORGEOUS FAMILY
BASA (FLUTTER)
THE GORGEOUS FAMILY
THE GORGEOUS FAMILY
FAMILY
THE GORGEOUS FAMILY
GORGEOUS FAMILY
BASA
THE GORGEOUS FAMILY
THE GORGEOUS FAMILY
BASA
THE GORGEOUS FAMILY
GORGEOUS FAMILY
GUWA (GRAAHH)
NO GOOD!
NO GOOD! NO GOOD!
NO GOOD!
BASAA
IT'S NO GOOD!
ACT.56 YOKAGOTE
(Translation: So That It's Good)

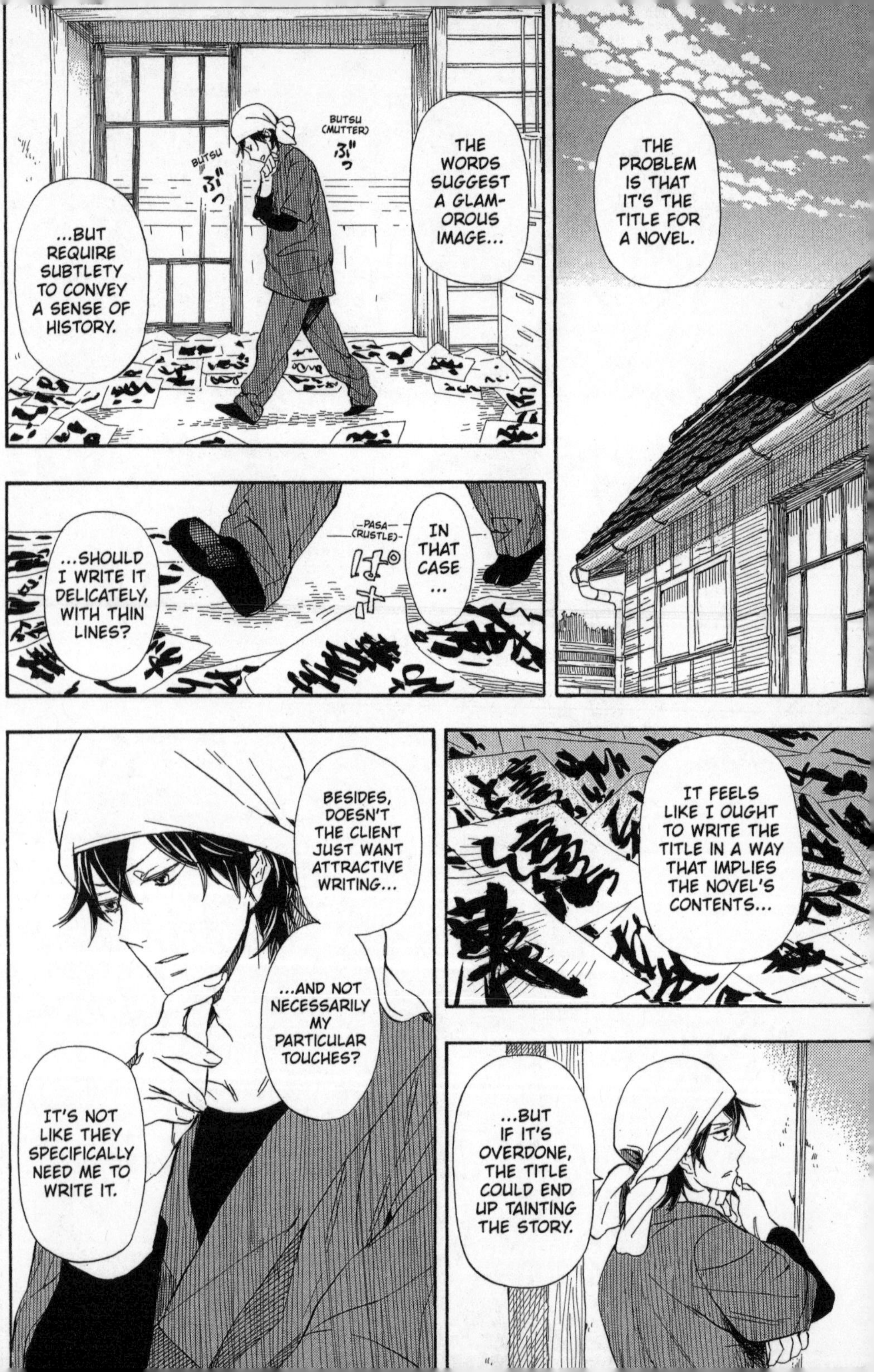
THE PROBLEM IS THAT IT'S THE TITLE FOR A NOVEL.
THE WORDS SUGGEST A GLAMOROUS IMAGE...
BUTSU (MUTTER) ぶつ
BUTSU ぶつ
...BUT REQUIRE SUBTLETY TO CONVEY A SENSE OF HISTORY.
IN THAT CASE...
PASA (RUSTLE) ぱさ
...SHOULD I WRITE IT DELICATELY, WITH THIN LINES?
IT FEELS LIKE I OUGHT TO WRITE THE TITLE IN A WAY THAT IMPLIES THE NOVEL'S CONTENTS...
...BUT IF IT'S OVERDONE, THE TITLE COULD END UP TAINTING THE STORY.
BESIDES, DOESN'T THE CLIENT JUST WANT ATTRACTIVE WRITING...
...AND NOT NECESSARILY MY PARTICULAR TOUCHES?
IT'S NOT LIKE THEY SPECIFICALLY NEED ME TO WRITE IT.

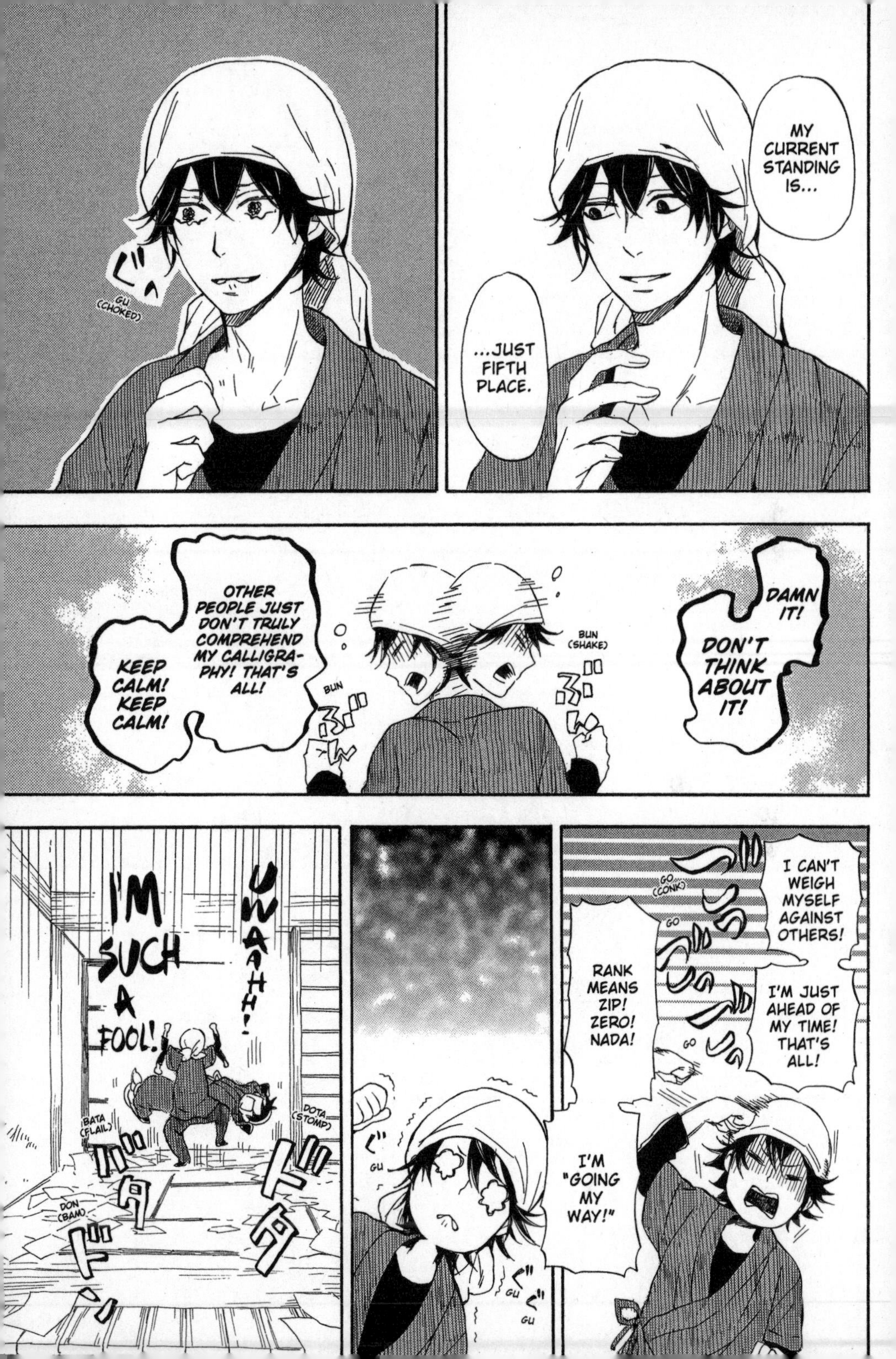
MY CURRENT STANDING IS...
...JUST FIFTH PLACE.
GU (CHOKED)
DAMN IT!
DON'T THINK ABOUT IT!
BUN (SHAKE)
OTHER PEOPLE JUST DON'T TRULY COMPREHEND MY CALLIGRA-PHY! THAT'S ALL!
KEEP CALM! KEEP CALM!
BUN
I CAN'T WEIGH MYSELF AGAINST OTHERS!
GO (CONK)
GO
I'M JUST AHEAD OF MY TIME! THAT'S ALL!
GO
RANK MEANS ZIP! ZERO! NADA!
I'M "GOING MY WAY!"
GU
GU
GU
UWAAHH!
I'M SUCH A FOOL!
DOTA (STOMP)
BATA (FLAIL)
DON (BAM)

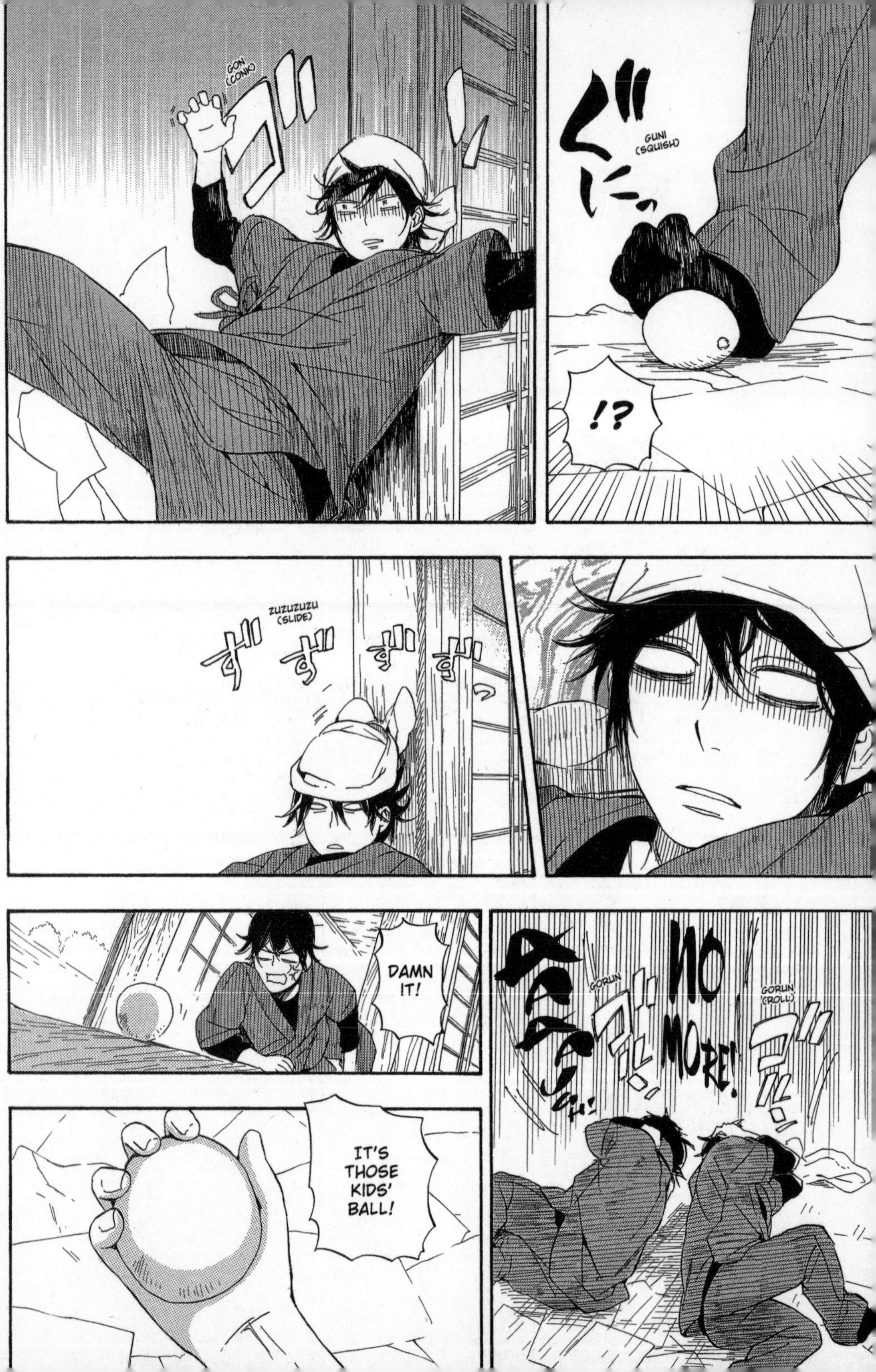
GUNI (SQUISH)
!?
GON (CONK)
ZUZUZUZU (SLIDE)
NO MORE!
GORUN
GORUN (ROLL)
DAMN IT!
IT'S THOSE KIDS' BALL!

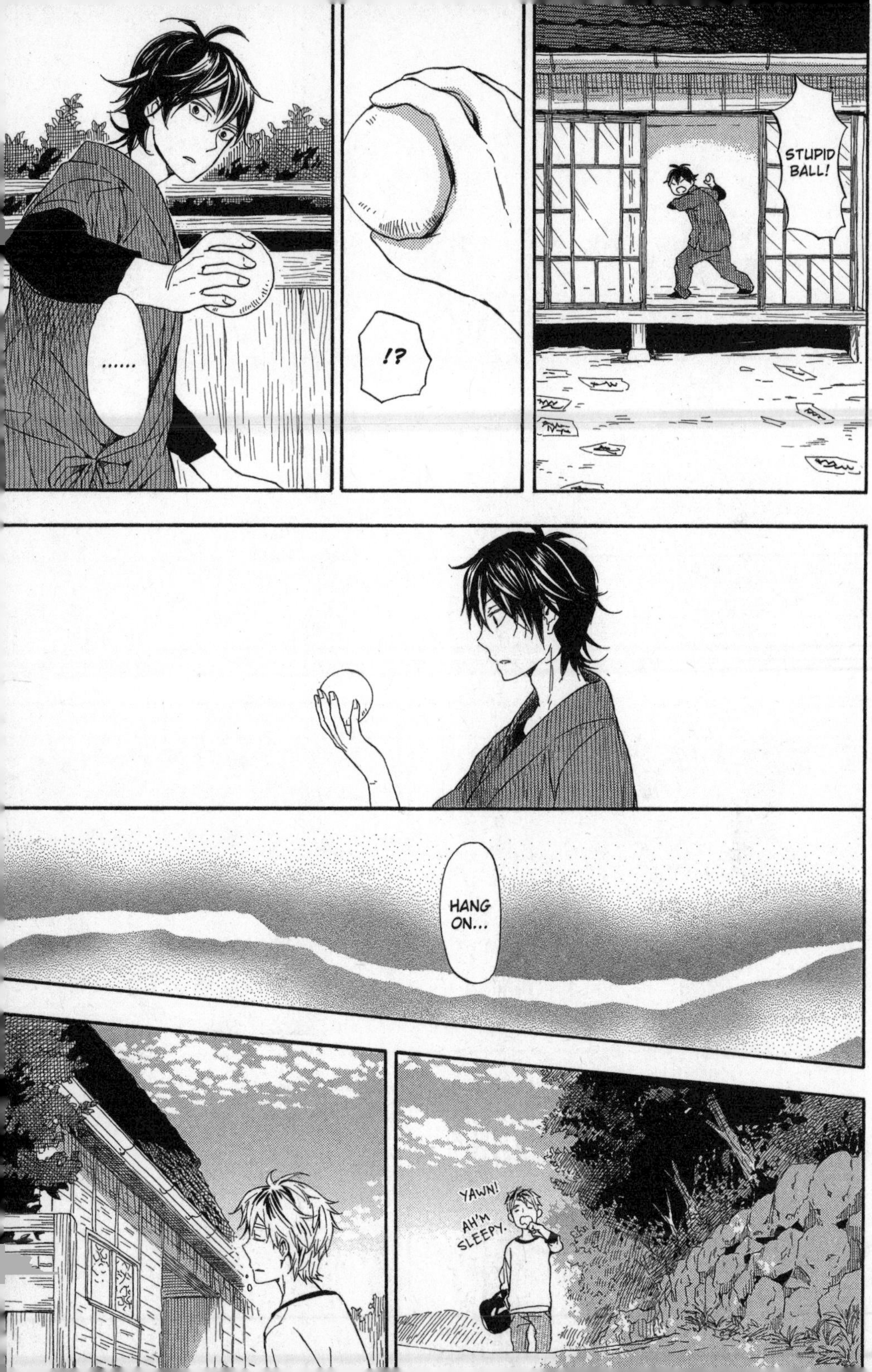
STUPID BALL!
!?
......
HANG ON...
YAWN!
AH'M SLEEPY.

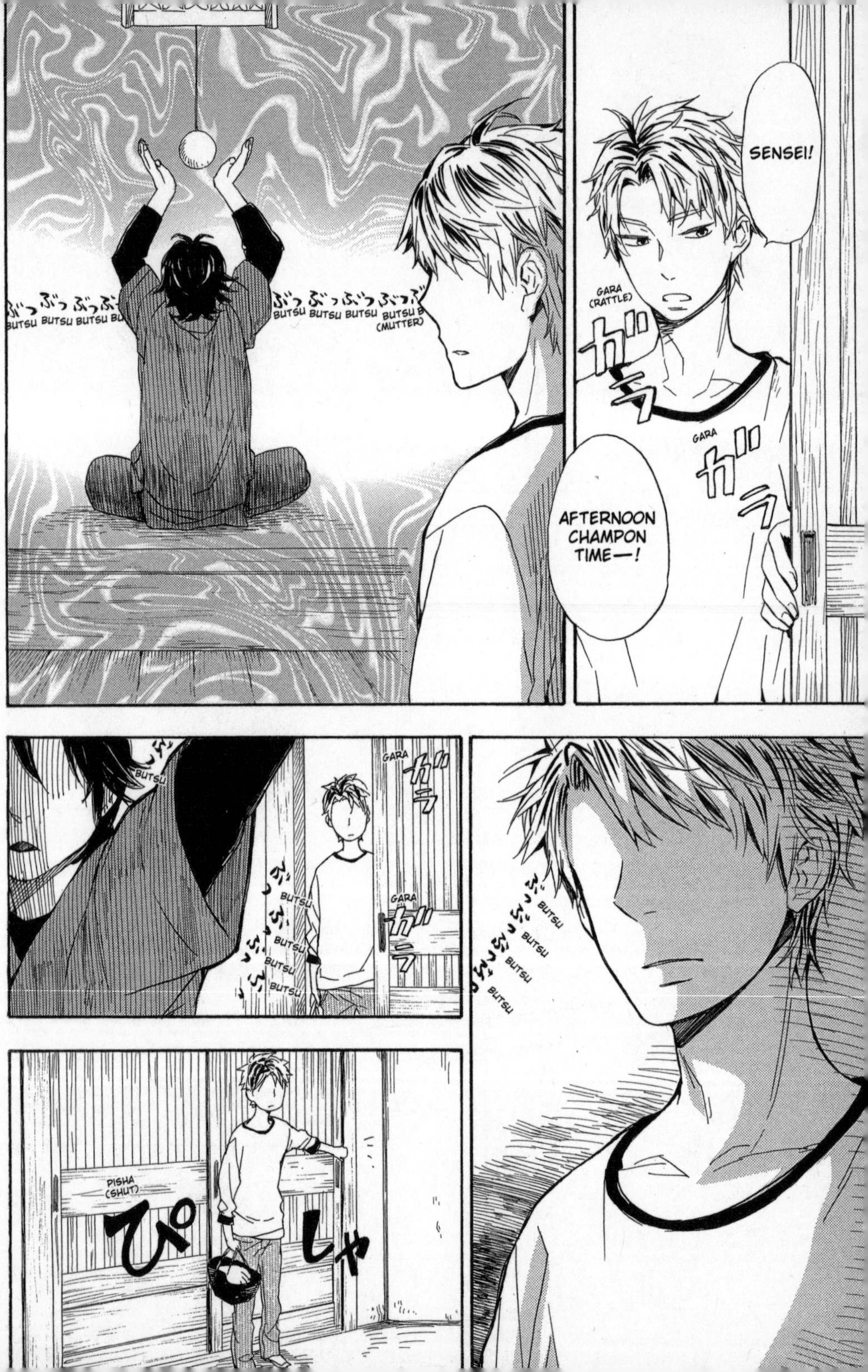
SENSEI!
GARA (RATTLE)
ガラ
GARA
ガラ
AFTERNOON CHAMPON TIME—!
ぶつぶつぶつぶつ
BUTSU BUTSU BUTSU BUTSU (MUTTER)
ぶつぶつぶつぶ
BUTSU BUTSU BUTSU BU
BUTSU BUTSU BUTSU BUTSU
BUTSU
GARA
ガラ
GARA
ガラ
BUTSU BUTSU BUTSU BUTSU
PISHA (SHUT)
ぴしゃ

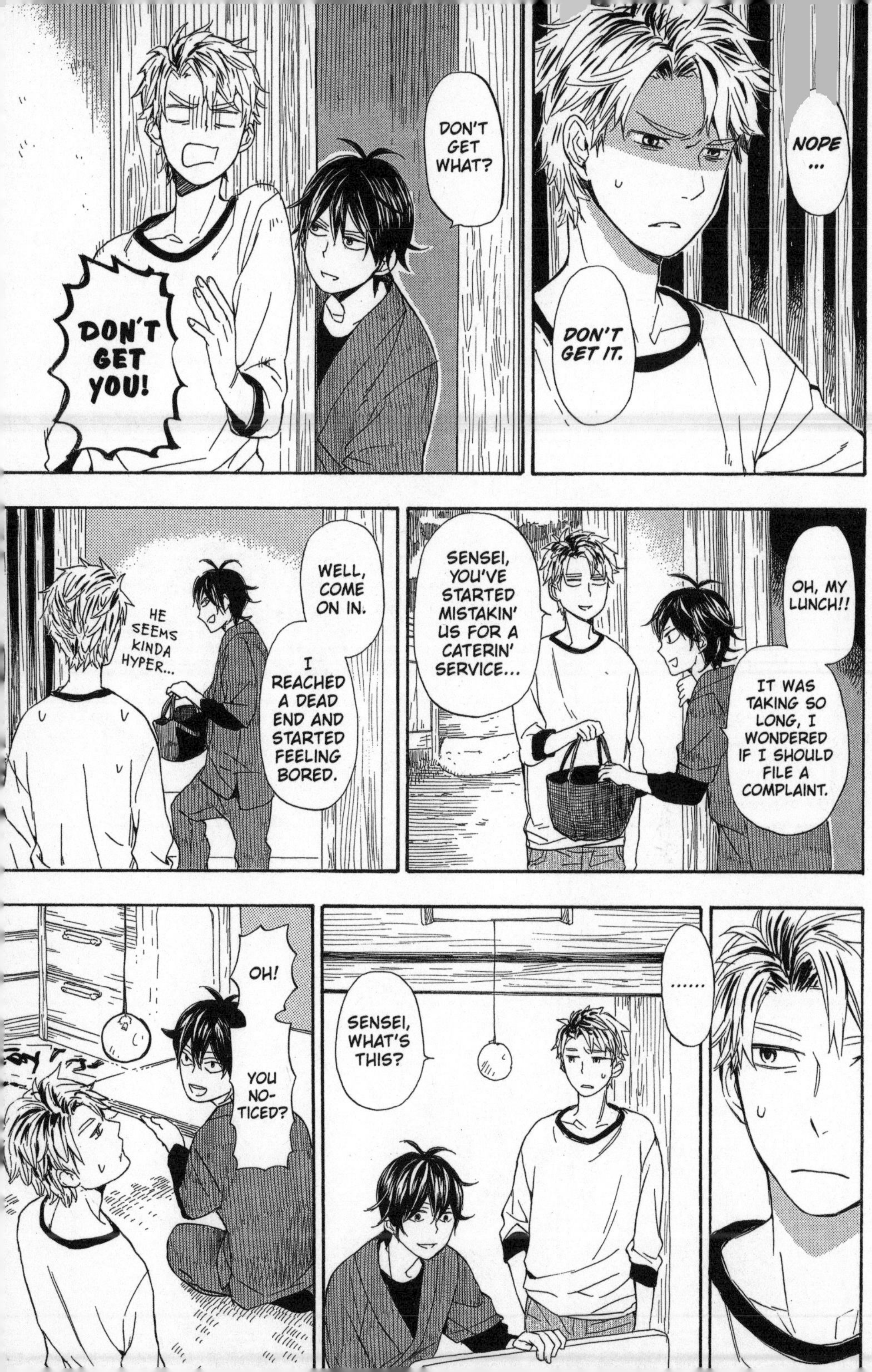
NOPE ...
DON'T GET IT.
DON'T GET WHAT?
DON'T GET YOU!
OH, MY LUNCH!!
SENSEI, YOU'VE STARTED MISTAKIN' US FOR A CATERIN' SERVICE...
IT WAS TAKING SO LONG, I WONDERED IF I SHOULD FILE A COMPLAINT.
WELL, COME ON IN.
I REACHED A DEAD END AND STARTED FEELING BORED.
HE SEEMS KINDA HYPER...
......
SENSEI, WHAT'S THIS?
OH!
YOU NO-TICED?

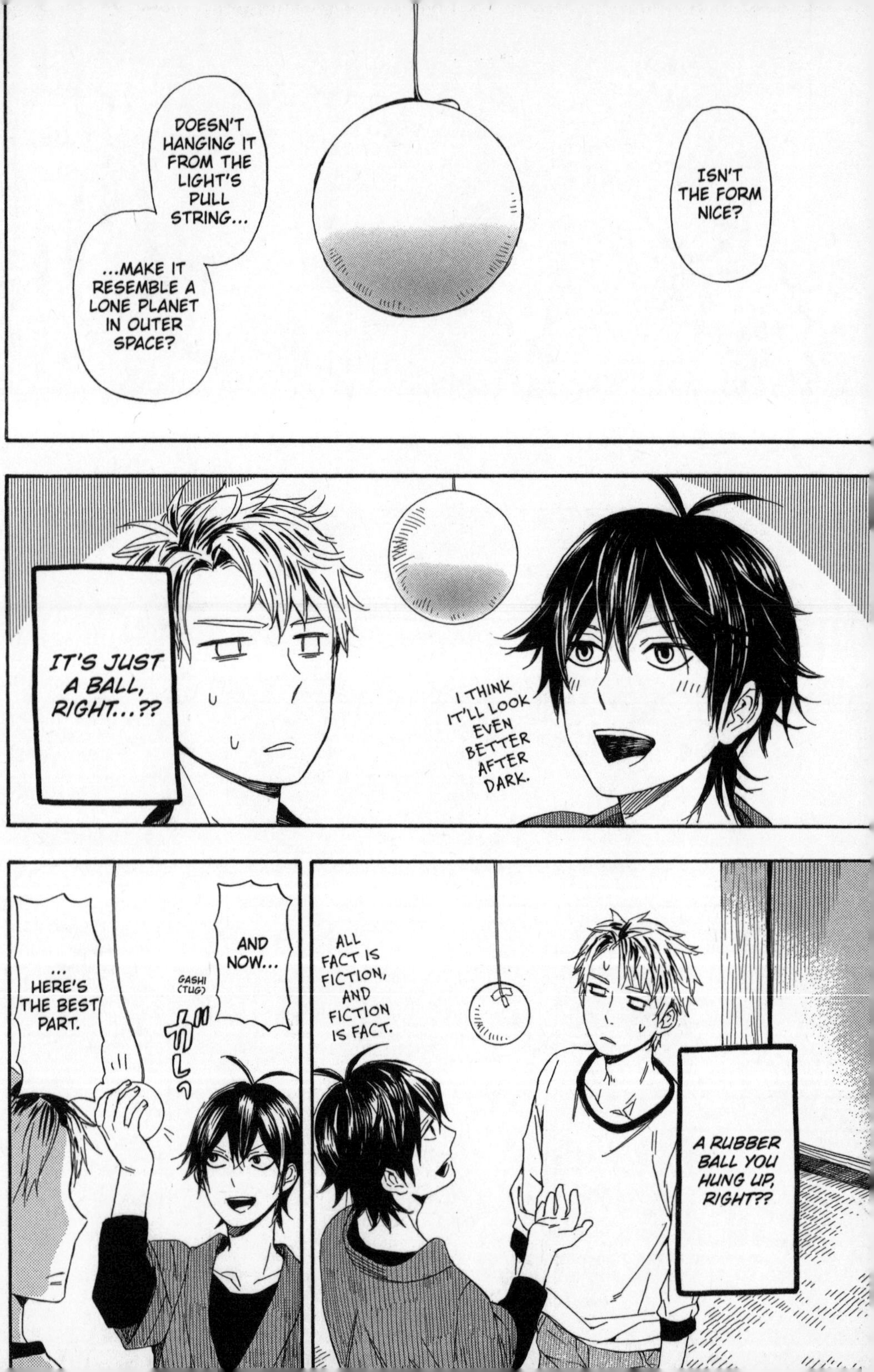
ISN'T THE FORM NICE?
DOESN'T HANGING IT FROM THE LIGHT'S PULL STRING...
...MAKE IT RESEMBLE A LONE PLANET IN OUTER SPACE?
I THINK IT'LL LOOK EVEN BETTER AFTER DARK.
IT'S JUST A BALL, RIGHT...??
A RUBBER BALL YOU HUNG UP, RIGHT??
ALL FACT IS FICTION, AND FICTION IS FACT.
AND NOW...
GASHI (TUG)
ガシッ
...HERE'S THE BEST PART.

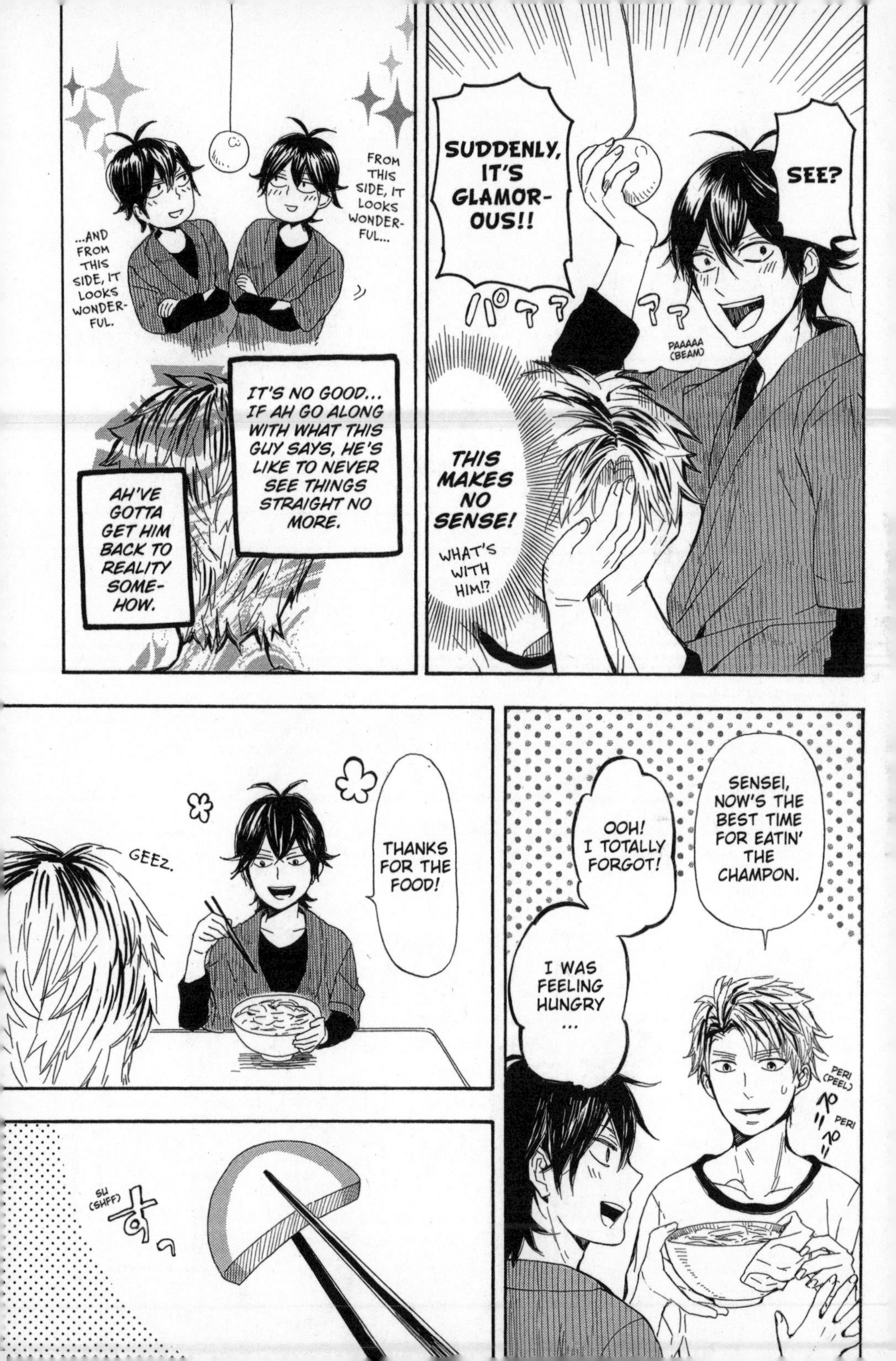
SEE?
SUDDENLY, IT'S GLAMOR-OUS!!
PAAAAA (BEAM)
THIS MAKES NO SENSE!
WHAT'S WITH HIM!?
FROM THIS SIDE, IT LOOKS WONDER-FUL...
...AND FROM THIS SIDE, IT LOOKS WONDER-FUL.
IT'S NO GOOD... IF AH GO ALONG WITH WHAT THIS GUY SAYS, HE'S LIKE TO NEVER SEE THINGS STRAIGHT NO MORE.
AH'VE GOTTA GET HIM BACK TO REALITY SOME-HOW.
SENSEI, NOW'S THE BEST TIME FOR EATIN' THE CHAMPON.
OOH! I TOTALLY FORGOT!
I WAS FEELING HUNGRY ...
PERI (PEEL)
PERI
THANKS FOR THE FOOD!
GEEZ.
SU (SHFF)

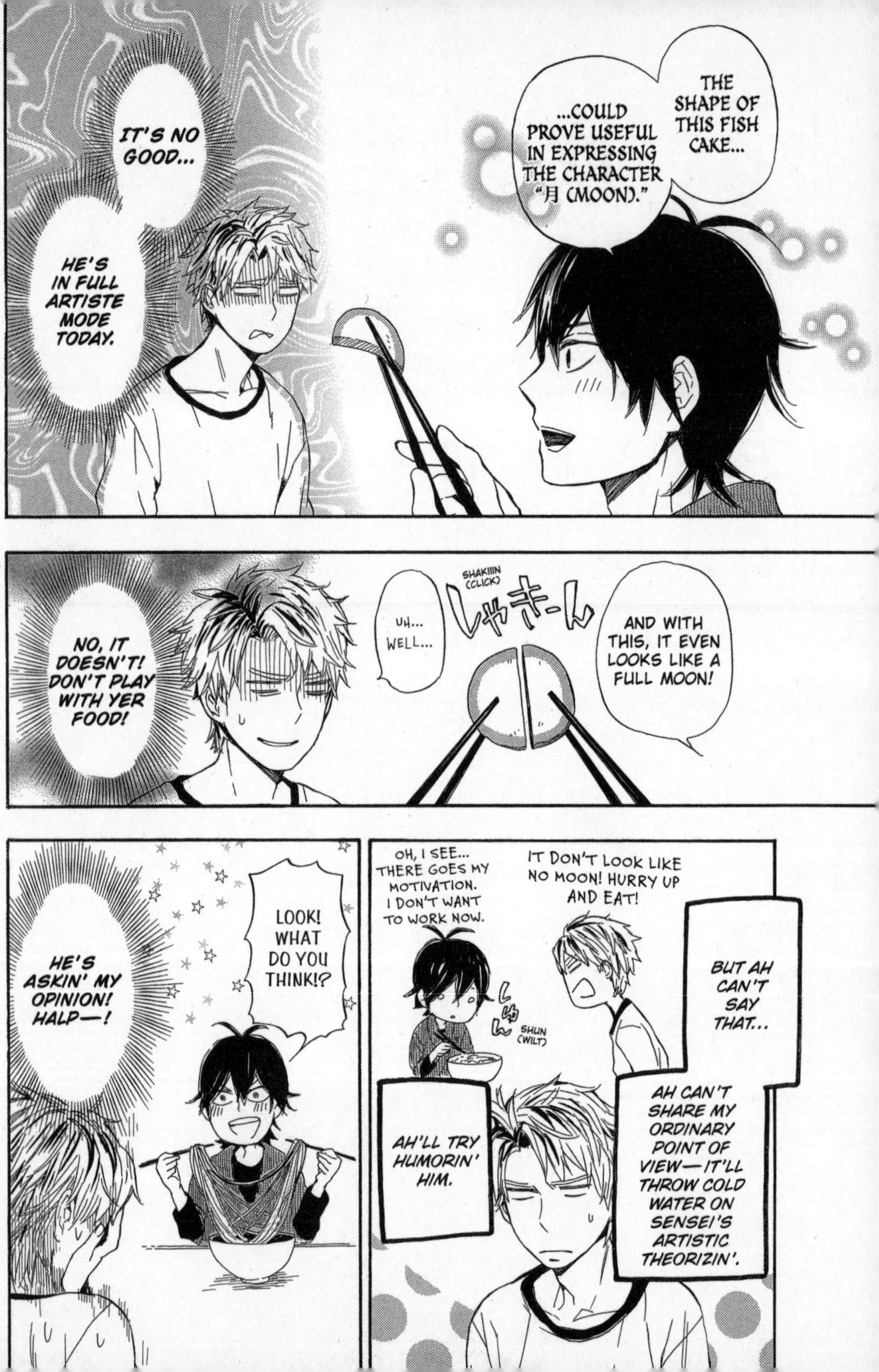
THE SHAPE OF THIS FISH CAKE...
...COULD PROVE USEFUL IN EXPRESSING THE CHARACTER "月 (MOON)."
IT'S NO GOOD...
HE'S IN FULL ARTISTE MODE TODAY.
AND WITH THIS, IT EVEN LOOKS LIKE A FULL MOON!
SHAKIIIN (CLICK)
しゃきーん
UH... WELL...
NO, IT DOESN'T! DON'T PLAY WITH YER FOOD!
IT DON'T LOOK LIKE NO MOON! HURRY UP AND EAT!
OH, I SEE... THERE GOES MY MOTIVATION. I DON'T WANT TO WORK NOW.
しゅん
SHUN (WILT)
BUT AH CAN'T SAY THAT...
AH CAN'T SHARE MY ORDINARY POINT OF VIEW—IT'LL THROW COLD WATER ON SENSEI'S ARTISTIC THEORIZIN'.
AH'LL TRY HUMORIN' HIM.
LOOK! WHAT DO YOU THINK!?
HE'S ASKIN' MY OPINION! HALP—!

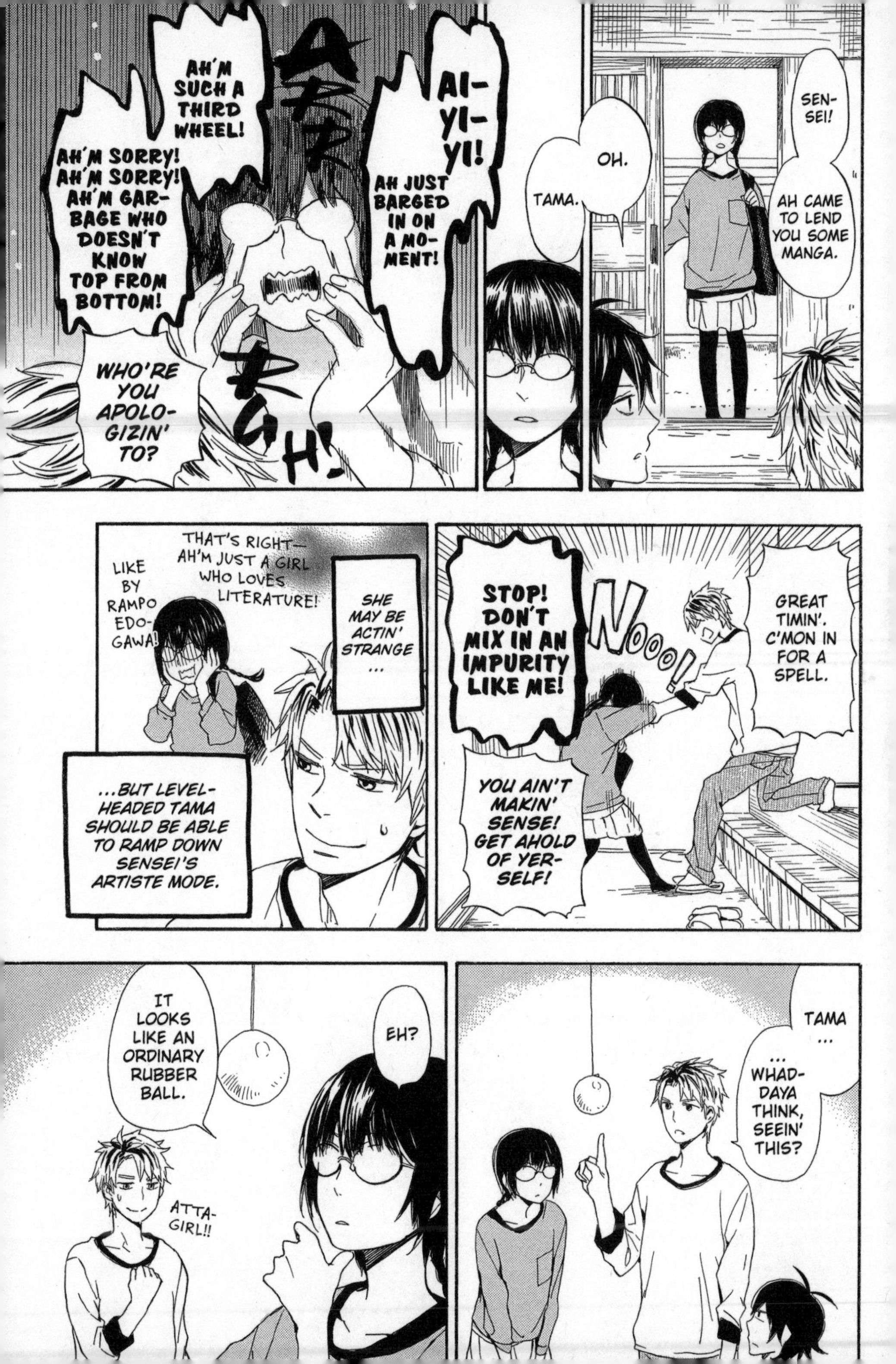
SEN-SEI!
AH CAME TO LEND YOU SOME MANGA.
OH.
TAMA.
AI-YI-YI!
AH JUST BARGED IN ON A MO-MENT!
AH'M SUCH A THIRD WHEEL!
AH'M SORRY! AH'M SORRY! AH'M GAR-BAGE WHO DOESN'T KNOW TOP FROM BOTTOM!
WHO'RE YOU APOLO-GIZIN' TO?
GREAT TIMIN'. C'MON IN FOR A SPELL.
NOOO!
STOP! DON'T MIX IN AN IMPURITY LIKE ME!
YOU AIN'T MAKIN' SENSE! GET AHOLD OF YER-SELF!
THAT'S RIGHT— AH'M JUST A GIRL WHO LOVES LITERATURE!
LIKE BY RAMPO EDO-GAWA!
SHE MAY BE ACTIN' STRANGE ...
...BUT LEVEL-HEADED TAMA SHOULD BE ABLE TO RAMP DOWN SENSEI'S ARTISTE MODE.
TAMA ...
... WHAD-DAYA THINK, SEEIN' THIS?
EH?
IT LOOKS LIKE AN ORDINARY RUBBER BALL.
ATTA-GIRL!!

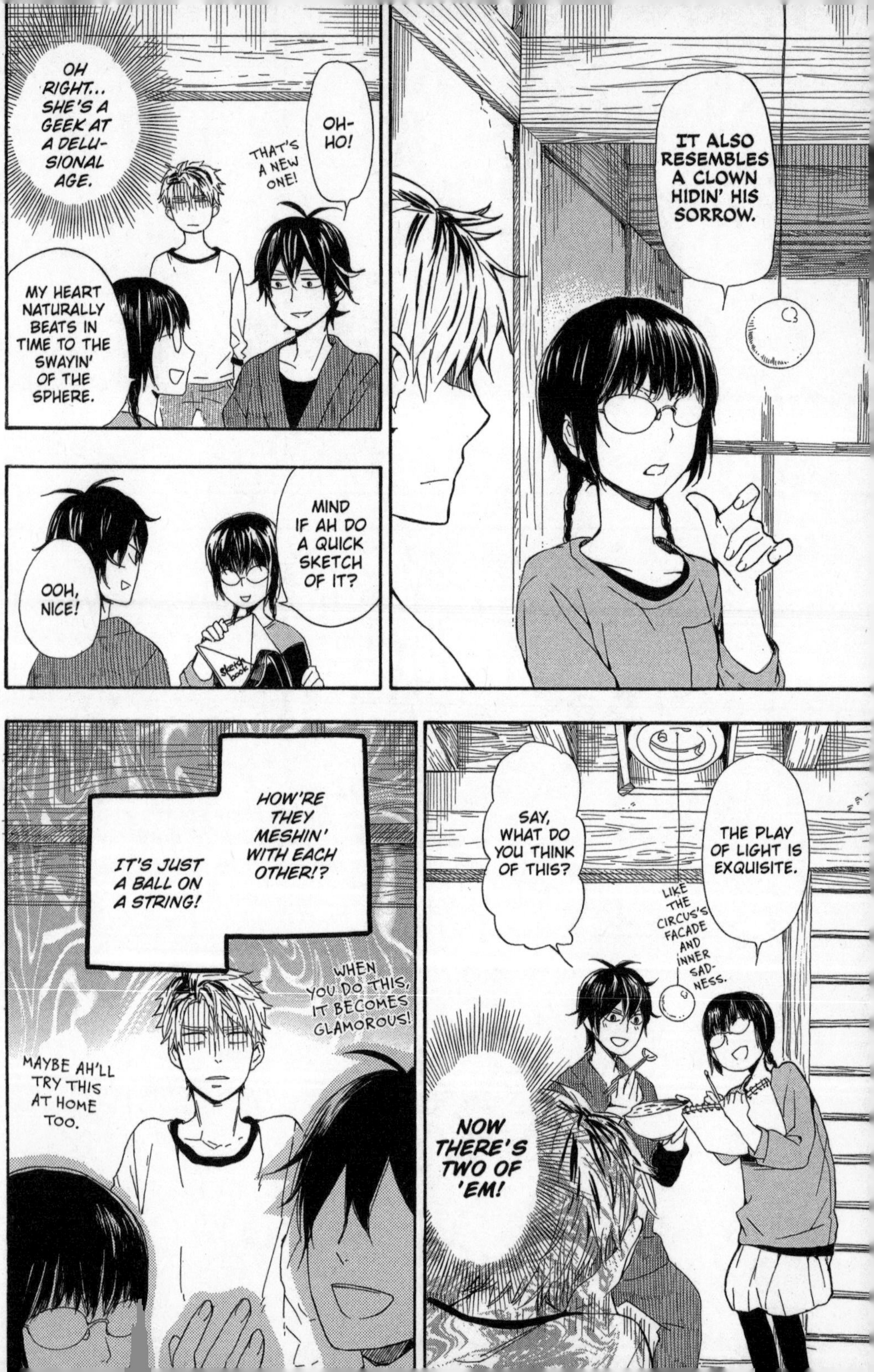
IT ALSO RESEMBLES A CLOWN HIDIN' HIS SORROW.
OH-HO!
THAT'S A NEW ONE!
OH RIGHT... SHE'S A GEEK AT A DELUSIONAL AGE.
MY HEART NATURALLY BEATS IN TIME TO THE SWAYIN' OF THE SPHERE.
MIND IF AH DO A QUICK SKETCH OF IT?
OOH, NICE!
THE PLAY OF LIGHT IS EXQUISITE.
LIKE THE CIRCUS'S FACADE AND INNER SADNESS.
SAY, WHAT DO YOU THINK OF THIS?
NOW THERE'S TWO OF 'EM!
HOW'RE THEY MESHIN' WITH EACH OTHER!?
IT'S JUST A BALL ON A STRING!
WHEN YOU DO THIS, IT BECOMES GLAMOROUS!
MAYBE AH'LL TRY THIS AT HOME TOO.

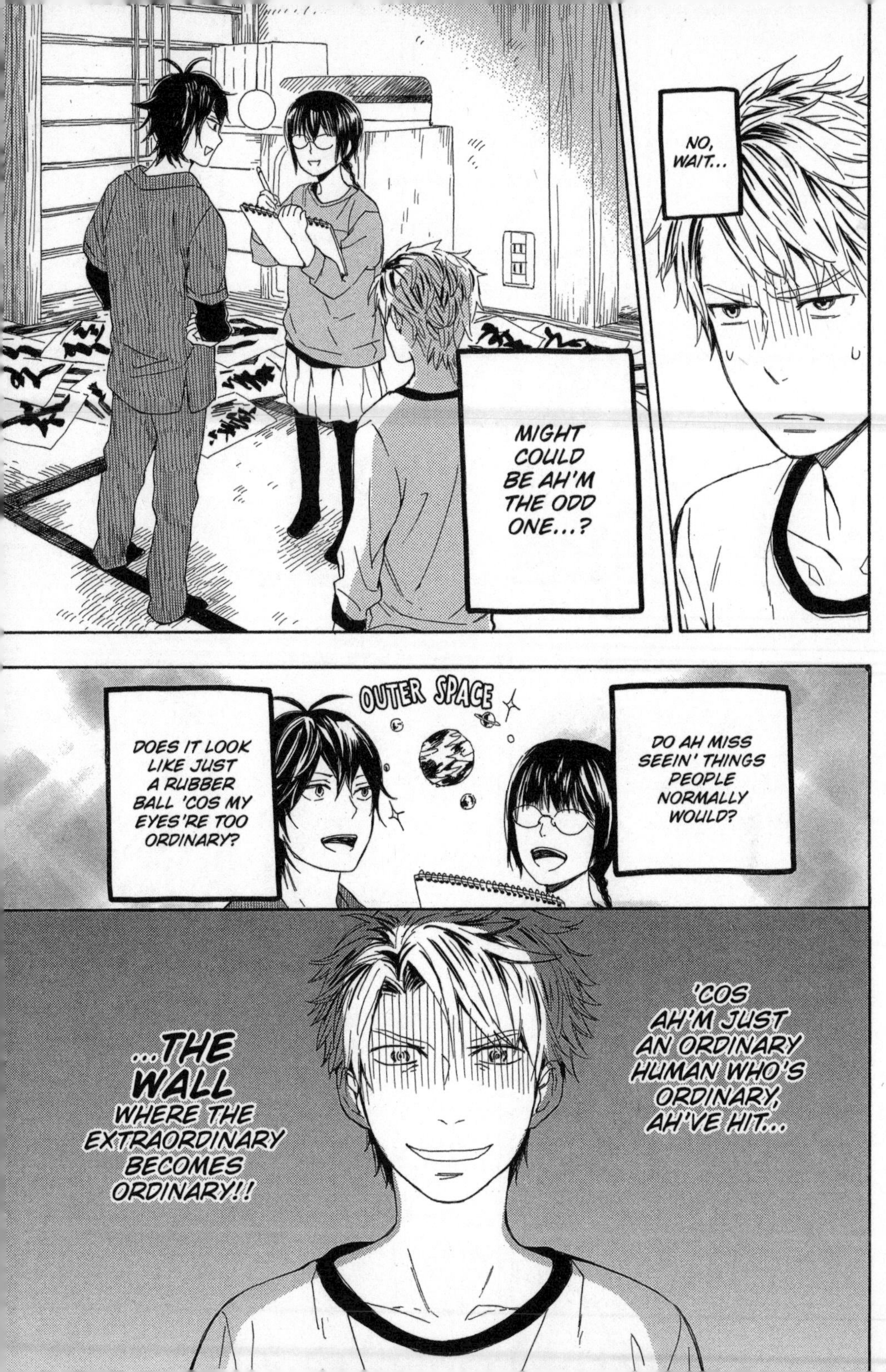
NO, WAIT...
MIGHT COULD BE AH'M THE ODD ONE...?
DO AH MISS SEEIN' THINGS PEOPLE NORMALLY WOULD?
OUTER SPACE
DOES IT LOOK LIKE JUST A RUBBER BALL 'COS MY EYES'RE TOO ORDINARY?
'COS AH'M JUST AN ORDINARY HUMAN WHO'S ORDINARY, AH'VE HIT...
...THE WALL WHERE THE EXTRAORDINARY BECOMES ORDINARY!!

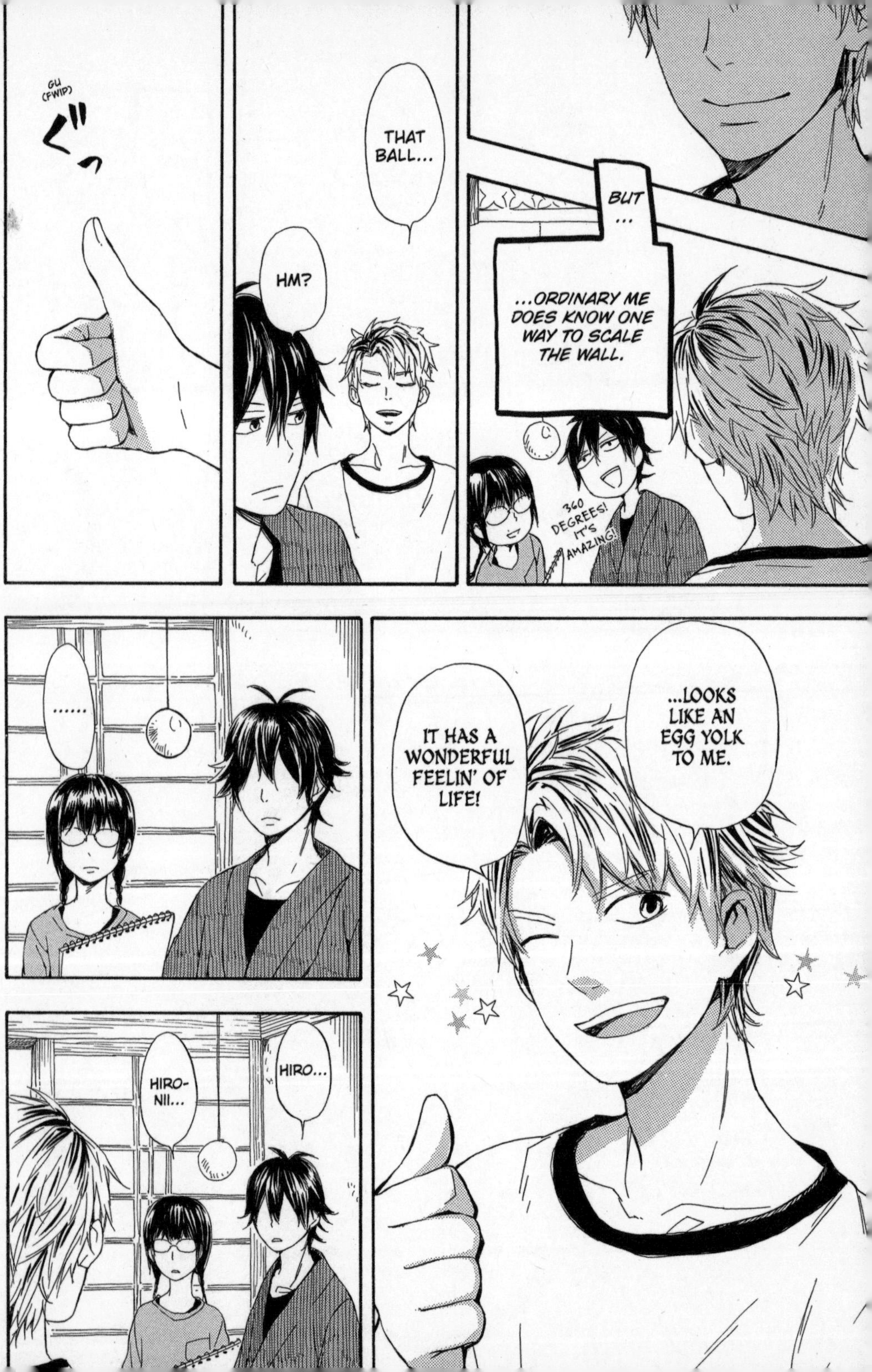
BUT ...
...ORDINARY ME DOES KNOW ONE WAY TO SCALE THE WALL.
360 DEGREES! IT'S AMAZING!
THAT BALL...
HM?
GU (FWIP)
ぐっ
...LOOKS LIKE AN EGG YOLK TO ME.
IT HAS A WONDERFUL FEELIN' OF LIFE!
......
HIRO...
HIRO-NII...

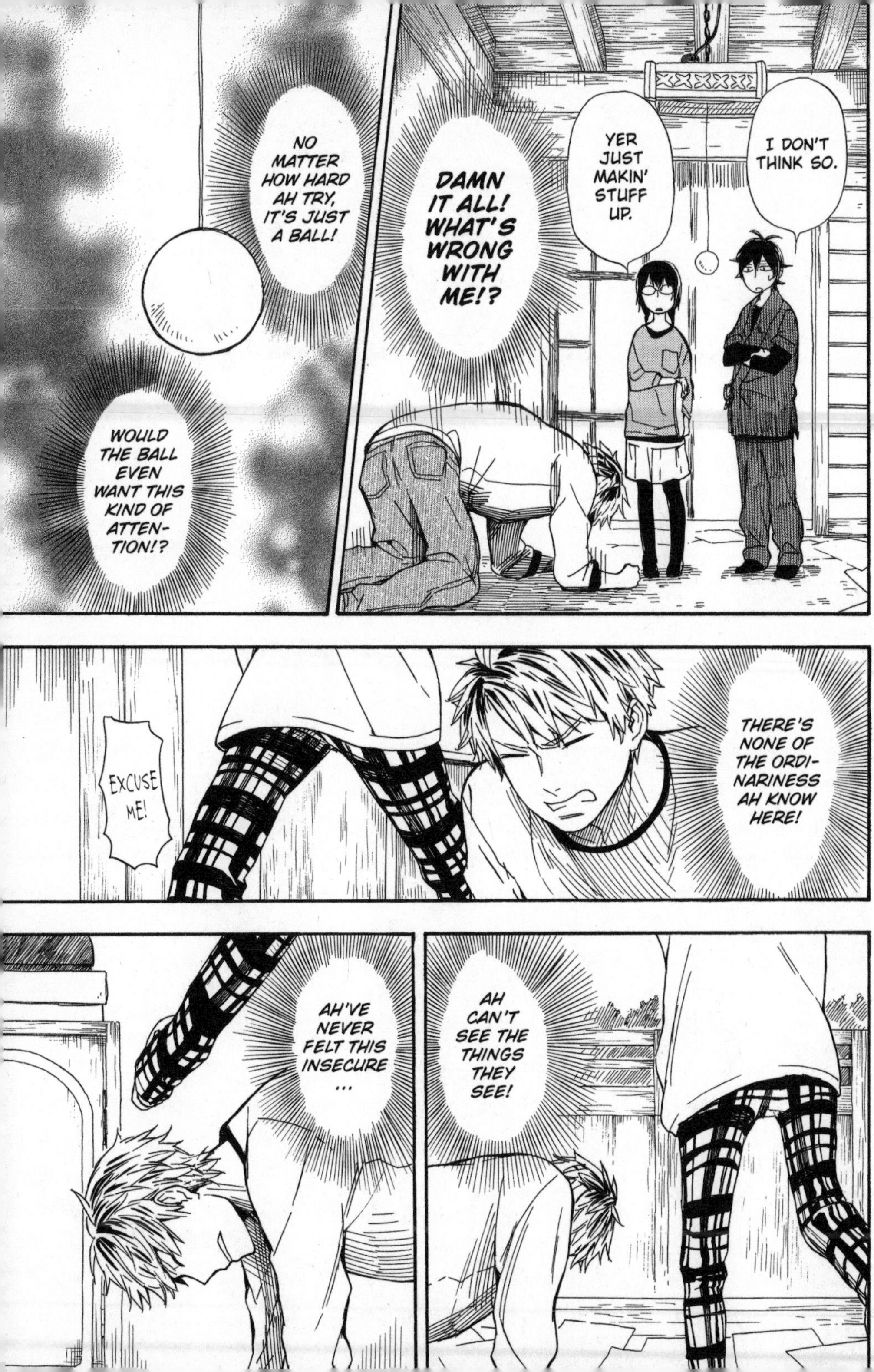
I DON'T THINK SO.
YER JUST MAKIN' STUFF UP.
DAMN IT ALL! WHAT'S WRONG WITH ME!?
NO MATTER HOW HARD AH TRY, IT'S JUST A BALL!
WOULD THE BALL EVEN WANT THIS KIND OF ATTENTION!?
THERE'S NONE OF THE ORDINARINESS AH KNOW HERE!
EXCUSE ME!
AH CAN'T SEE THE THINGS THEY SEE!
AH'VE NEVER FELT THIS INSECURE...

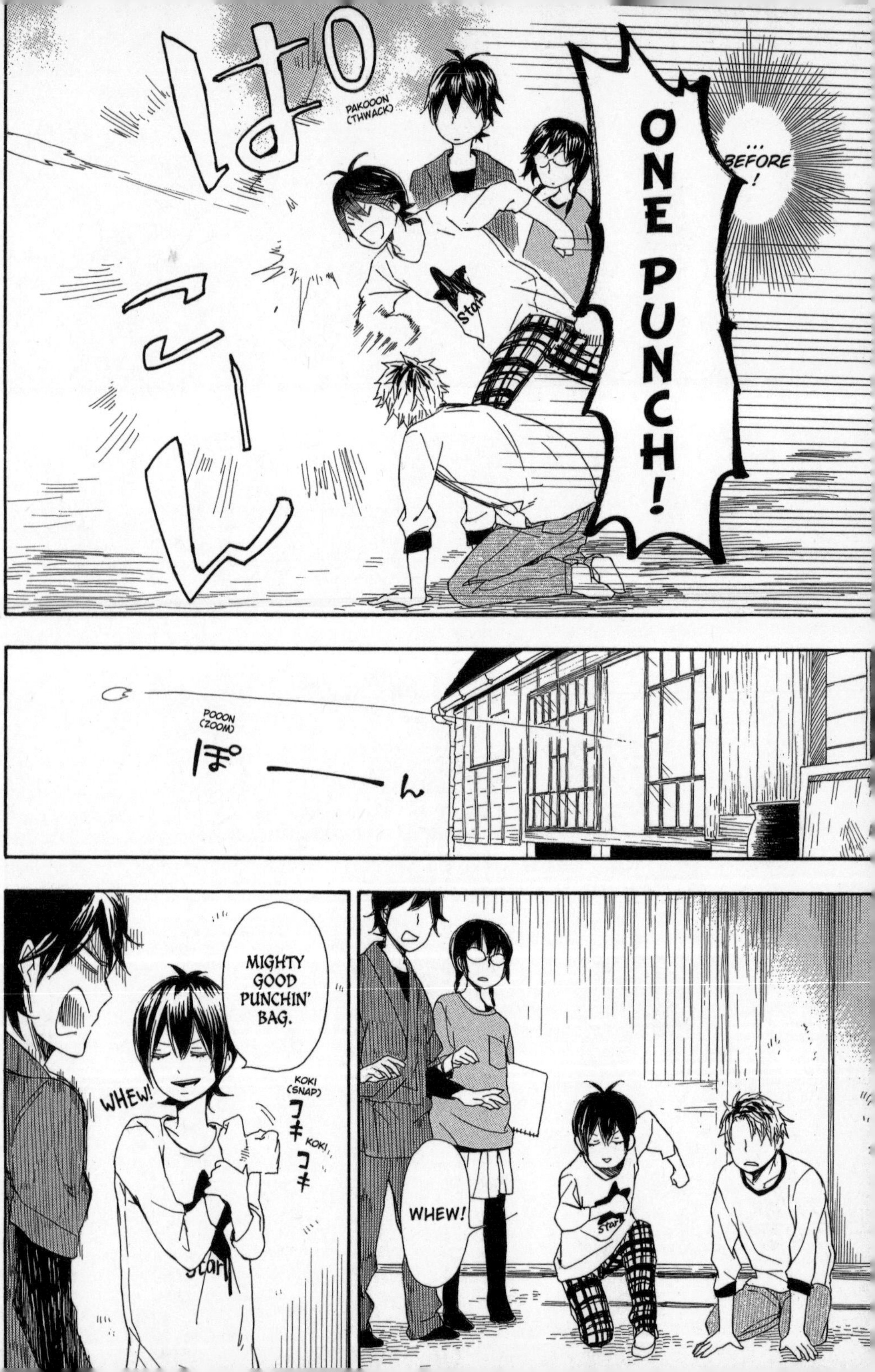
...BEFORE!
ONE PUNCH!
PAKOOON (THWACK)
ぱこーーん
POOON (ZOOM)
ぽーーん
WHEW!
MIGHTY GOOD PUNCHIN' BAG.
KOKI (SNAP)
コキ KOKI コキ
WHEW!

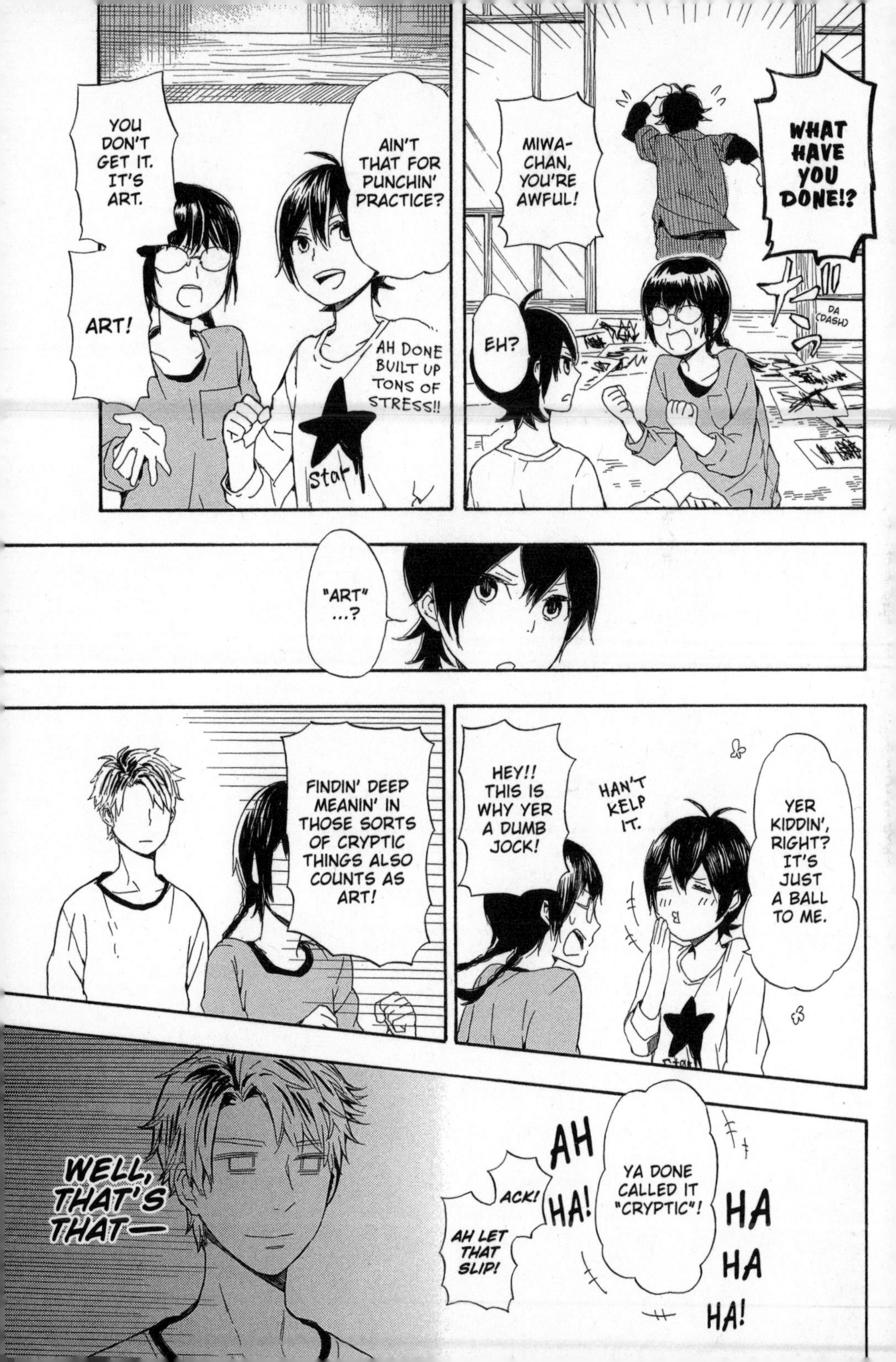
WHAT HAVE YOU DONE!?
MIWA-CHAN, YOU'RE AWFUL!
DA (DASH)
EH?
AIN'T THAT FOR PUNCHIN' PRACTICE?
YOU DON'T GET IT. IT'S ART.
ART!
AH DONE BUILT UP TONS OF STRESS!!
Star
"ART" ...?
YER KIDDIN', RIGHT? IT'S JUST A BALL TO ME.
HAN'T KELP IT.
HEY!! THIS IS WHY YER A DUMB JOCK!
FINDIN' DEEP MEANIN' IN THOSE SORTS OF CRYPTIC THINGS ALSO COUNTS AS ART!
HA HA HA!
YA DONE CALLED IT "CRYPTIC"!
AH HA!
ACK!
AH LET THAT SLIP!
WELL, THAT'S THAT—

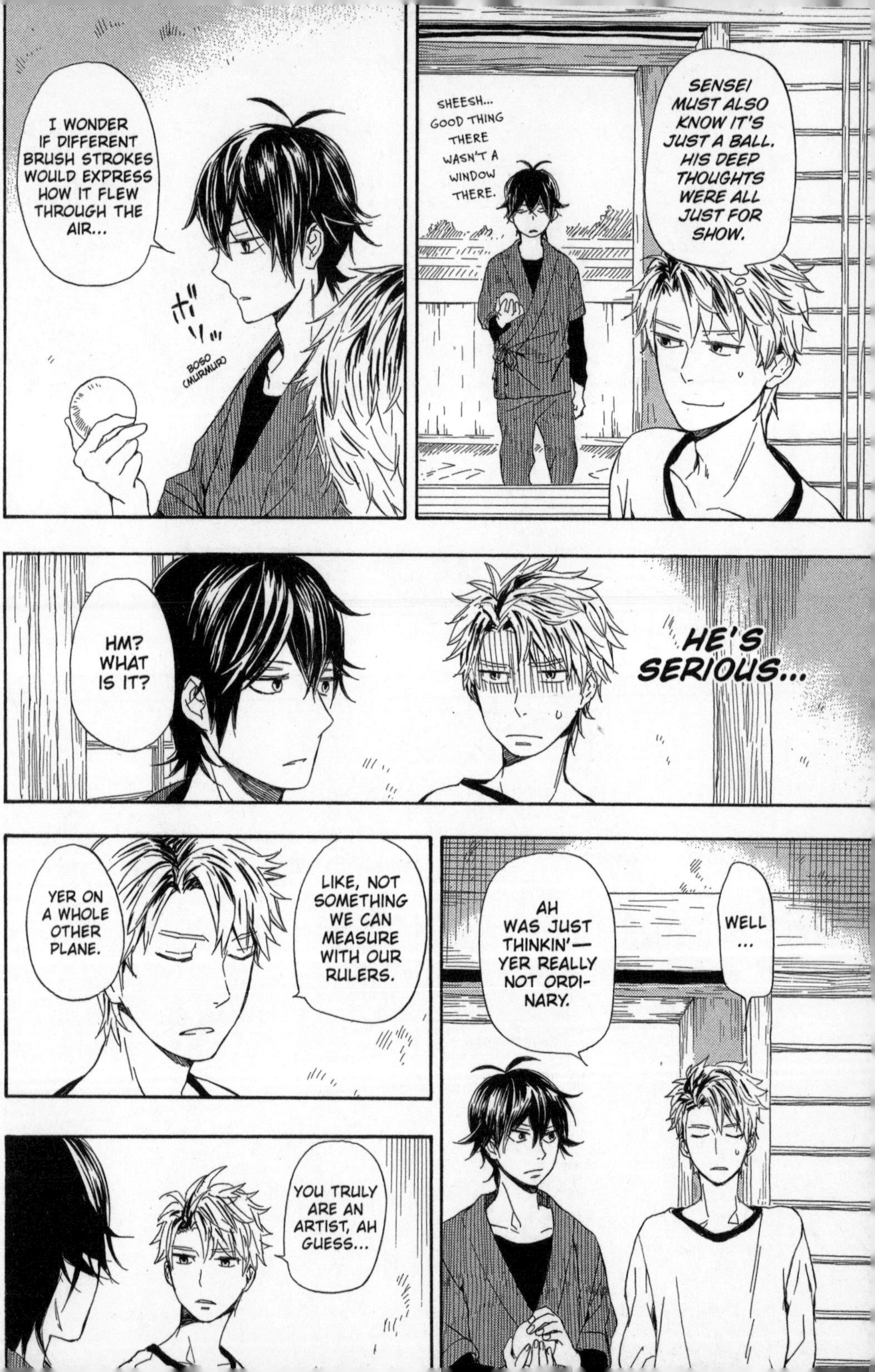
SENSEI MUST ALSO KNOW IT'S JUST A BALL. HIS DEEP THOUGHTS WERE ALL JUST FOR SHOW.
SHEESH... GOOD THING THERE WASN'T A WINDOW THERE.
I WONDER IF DIFFERENT BRUSH STROKES WOULD EXPRESS HOW IT FLEW THROUGH THE AIR...
BOSO (MURMUR)
HE'S SERIOUS...
HM? WHAT IS IT?
WELL ...
AH WAS JUST THINKIN'— YER REALLY NOT ORDI- NARY.
LIKE, NOT SOMETHING WE CAN MEASURE WITH OUR RULERS.
YER ON A WHOLE OTHER PLANE.
YOU TRULY ARE AN ARTIST, AH GUESS...

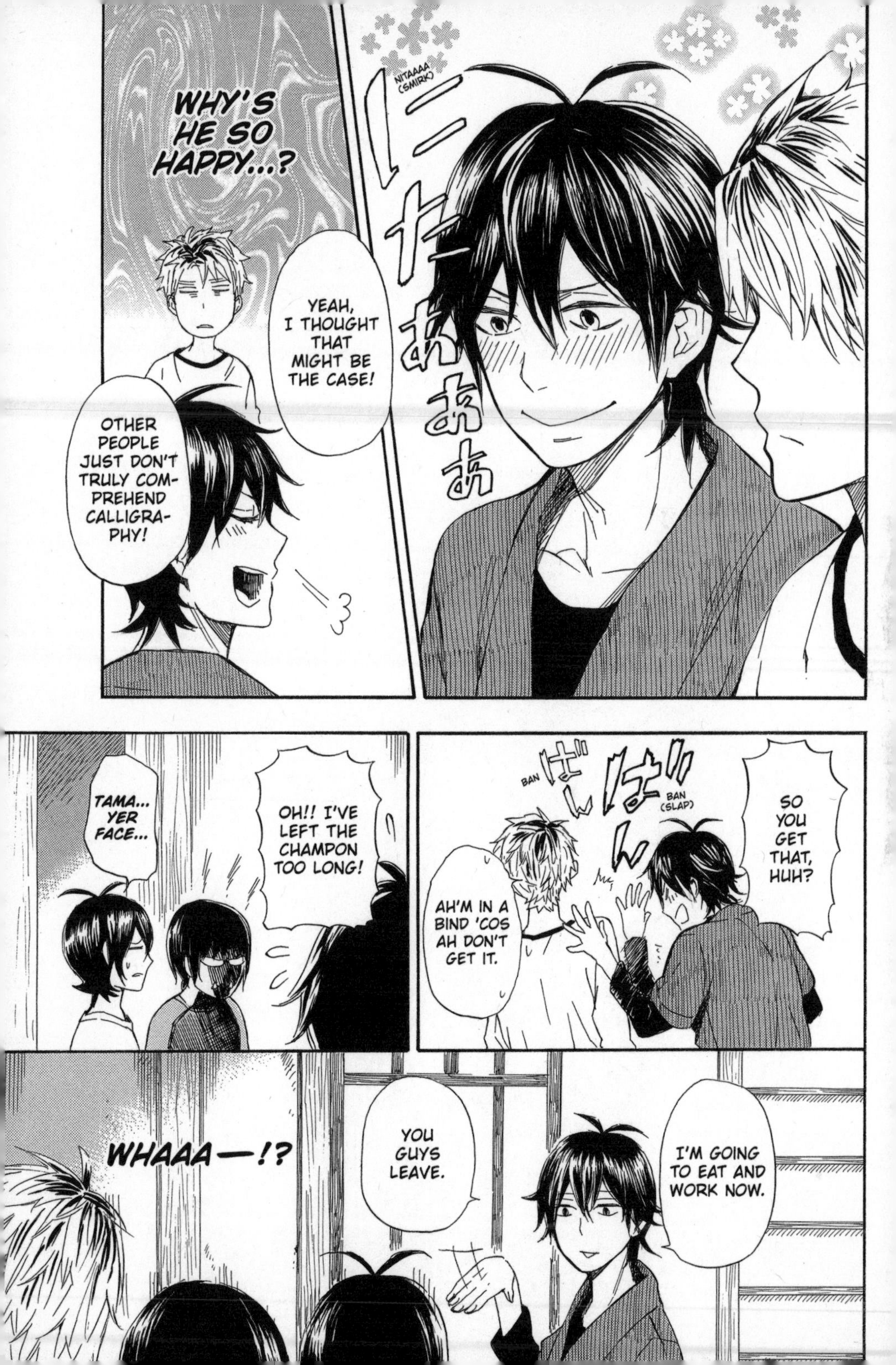
NITAAAA (SMIRK)
にたあああ
YEAH, I THOUGHT THAT MIGHT BE THE CASE!
OTHER PEOPLE JUST DON'T TRULY COMPREHEND CALLIGRAPHY!
WHY'S HE SO HAPPY...?
BAN
ばん
BAN (SLAP)
SO YOU GET THAT, HUH?
AH'M IN A BIND 'COS AH DON'T GET IT.
OH!! I'VE LEFT THE CHAMPON TOO LONG!
TAMA... YER FACE...
I'M GOING TO EAT AND WORK NOW.
YOU GUYS LEAVE.
WHAAA—!?

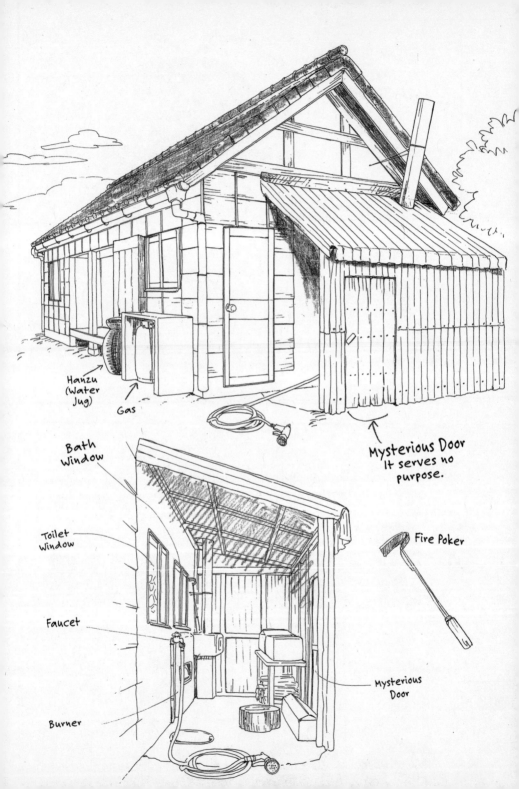

Hanzu
(Water
Jug)

Gas

Mysterious Door
It serves no
purpose.

Bath
Window

Toilet
Window

Fire Poker

Faucet

Burner

Mysterious
Door

ACT.57
TAKUMON WARU
(Translation: Splitting Firewood)

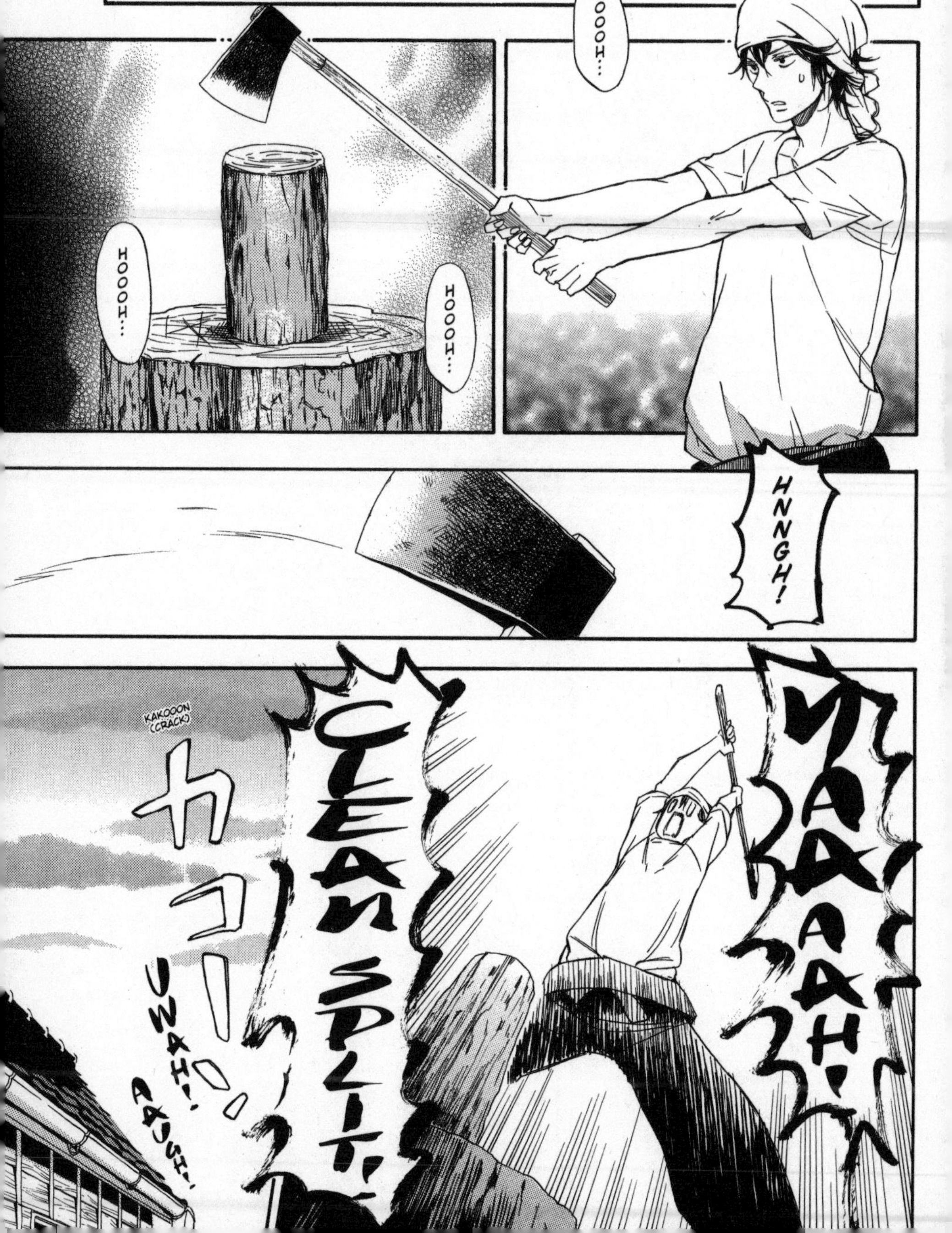
HOOOH...
HOOOH...
HOOOH...
HNNGH!
WAAAAAH!
CLEAN SPLIT!
KAKOOON (CRACK)
カコーン
UWAH! AAUGH!

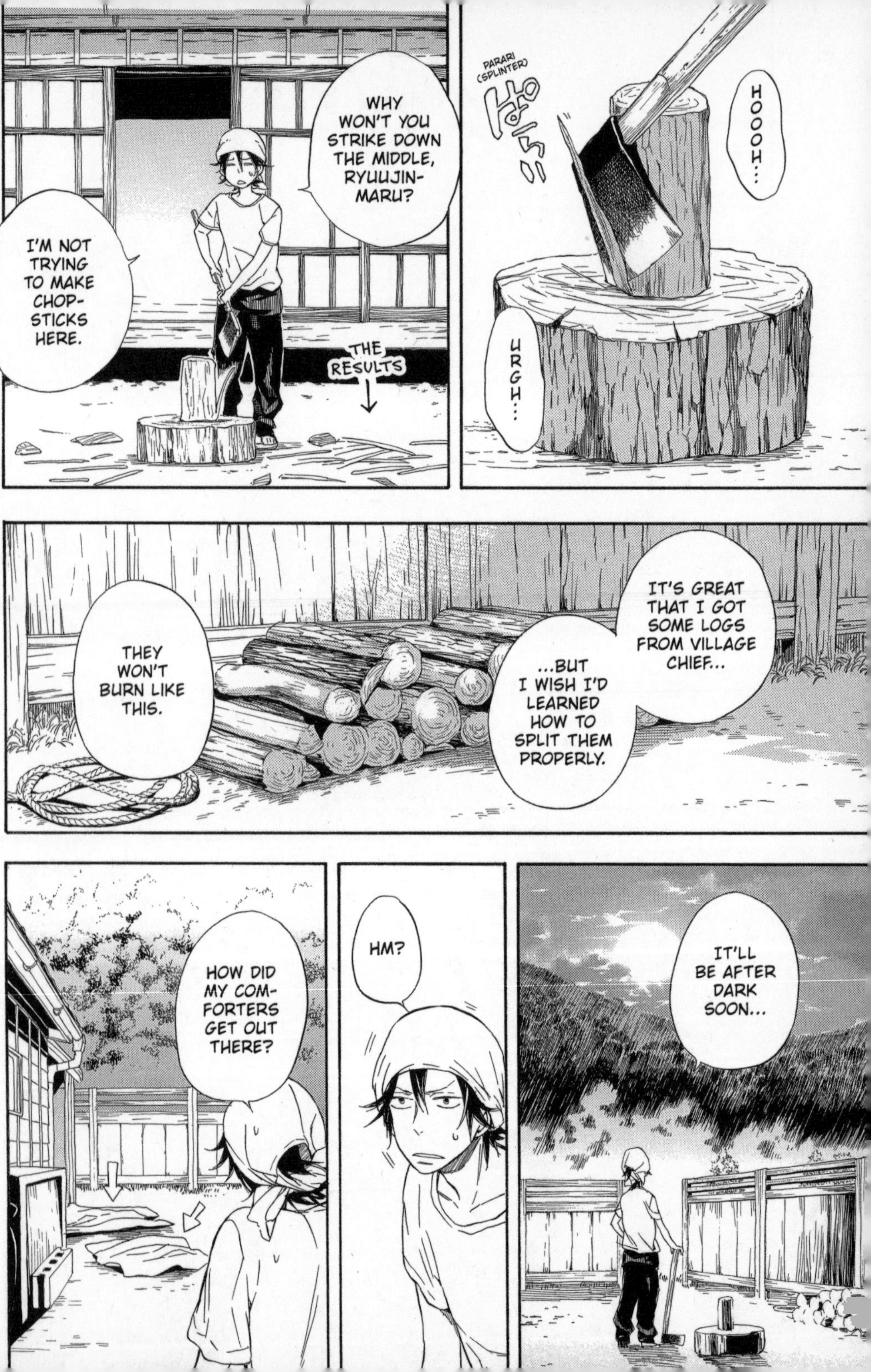
HOOOH...
PARARI (SPLINTER)
URGH...
WHY WON'T YOU STRIKE DOWN THE MIDDLE, RYUUJIN-MARU?
I'M NOT TRYING TO MAKE CHOP-STICKS HERE.
THE RESULTS
IT'S GREAT THAT I GOT SOME LOGS FROM VILLAGE CHIEF...
...BUT I WISH I'D LEARNED HOW TO SPLIT THEM PROPERLY.
THEY WON'T BURN LIKE THIS.
IT'LL BE AFTER DARK SOON...
HM?
HOW DID MY COM-FORTERS GET OUT THERE?

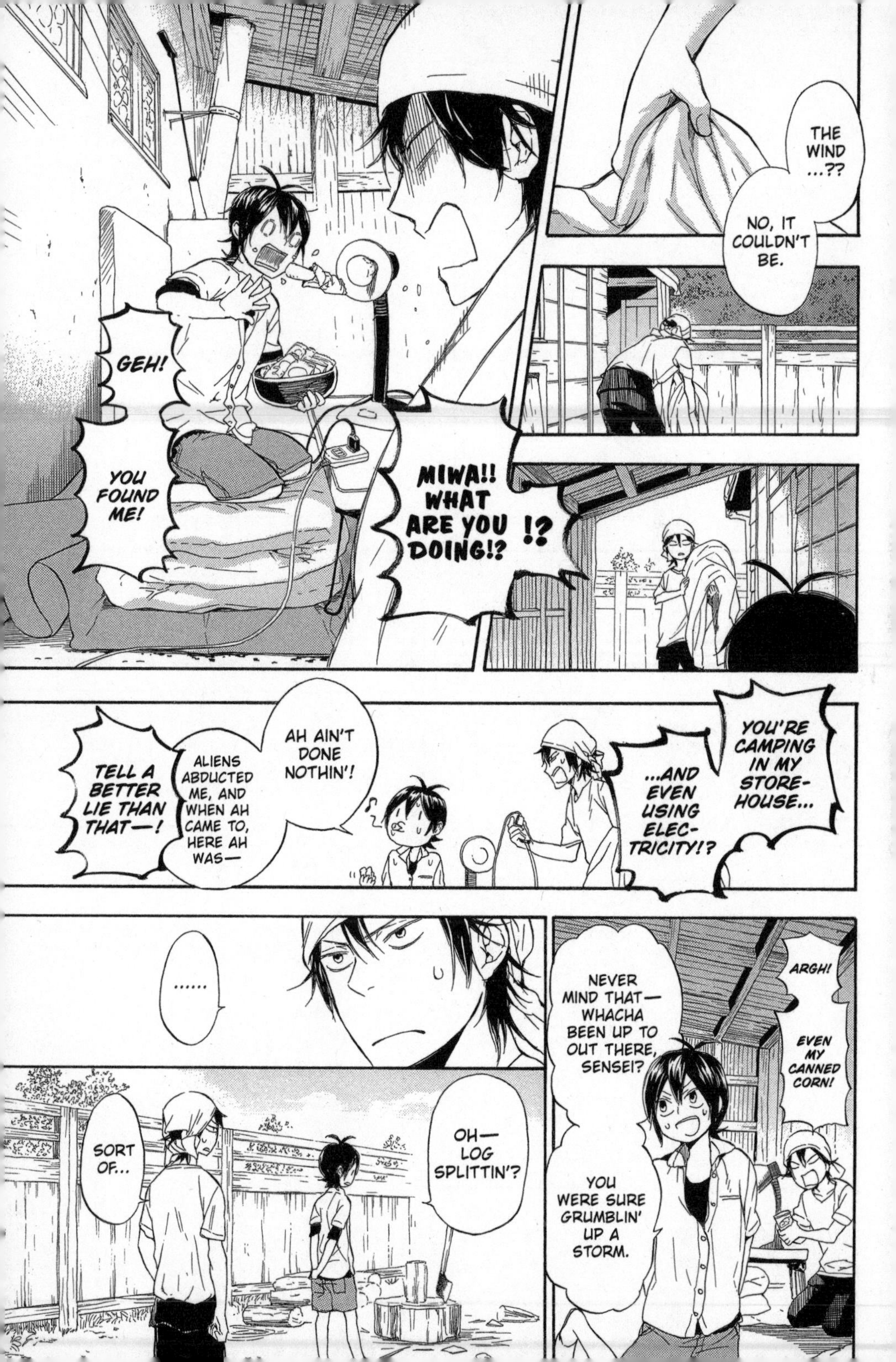
THE WIND ...??
NO, IT COULDN'T BE.
MIWA!! WHAT ARE YOU DOING!?
!?
GEH!
YOU FOUND ME!
YOU'RE CAMPING IN MY STORE-HOUSE...
...AND EVEN USING ELEC-TRICITY!?
AH AIN'T DONE NOTHIN'!
ALIENS ABDUCTED ME, AND WHEN AH CAME TO, HERE AH WAS—
TELL A BETTER LIE THAN THAT—!
ARGH!
EVEN MY CANNED CORN!
NEVER MIND THAT— WHACHA BEEN UP TO OUT THERE, SENSEI?
YOU WERE SURE GRUMBLIN' UP A STORM.
......
OH— LOG SPLITTIN'?
SORT OF...

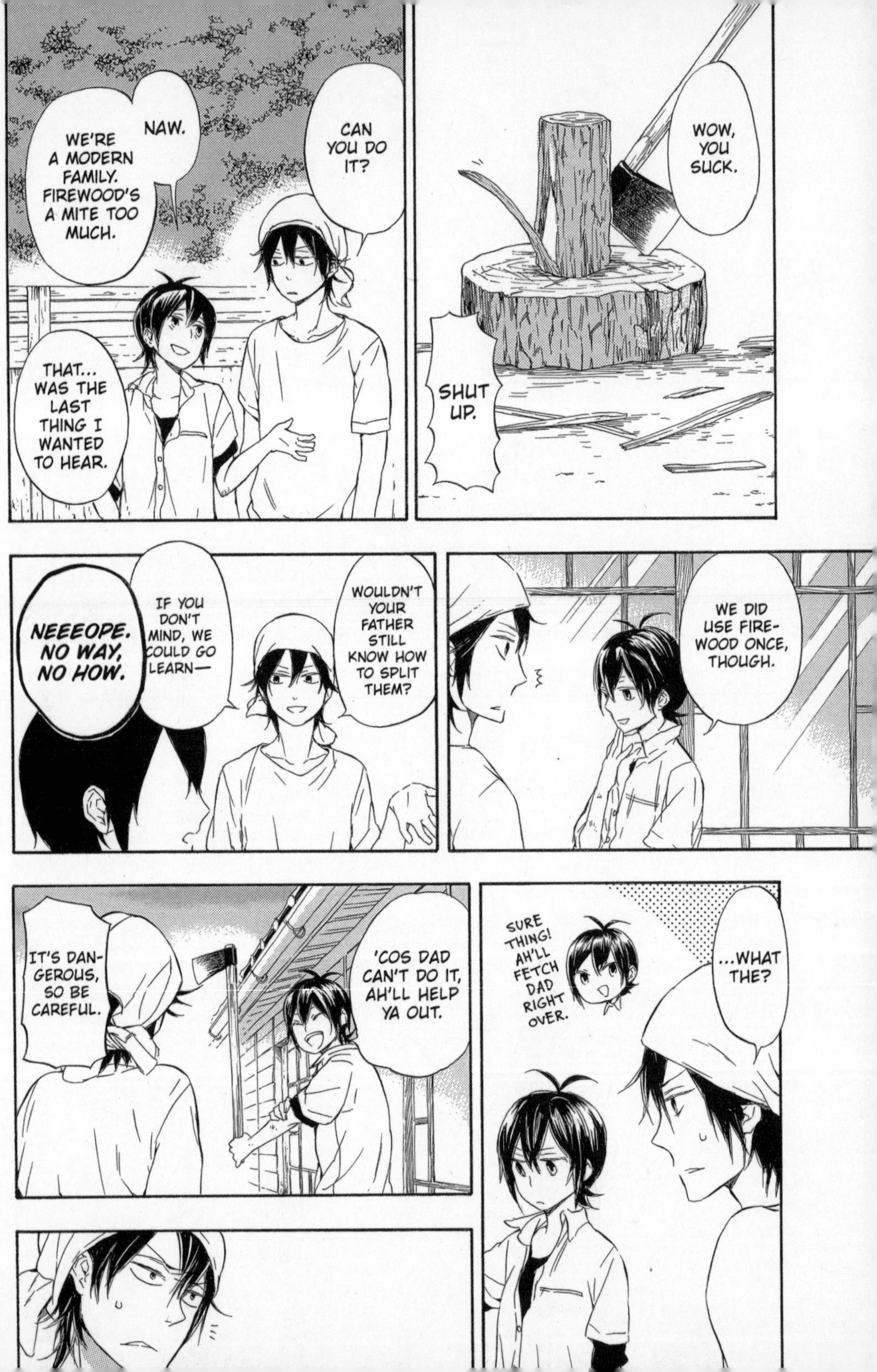
WOW, YOU SUCK.
SHUT UP.
CAN YOU DO IT?
NAW.
WE'RE A MODERN FAMILY. FIREWOOD'S A MITE TOO MUCH.
THAT... WAS THE LAST THING I WANTED TO HEAR.
WE DID USE FIRE-WOOD ONCE, THOUGH.
WOULDN'T YOUR FATHER STILL KNOW HOW TO SPLIT THEM?
IF YOU DON'T MIND, WE COULD GO LEARN—
NEEEOPE. NO WAY, NO HOW.
...WHAT THE?
SURE THING! AH'LL FETCH DAD RIGHT OVER.
'COS DAD CAN'T DO IT, AH'LL HELP YA OUT.
IT'S DAN-GEROUS, SO BE CAREFUL.

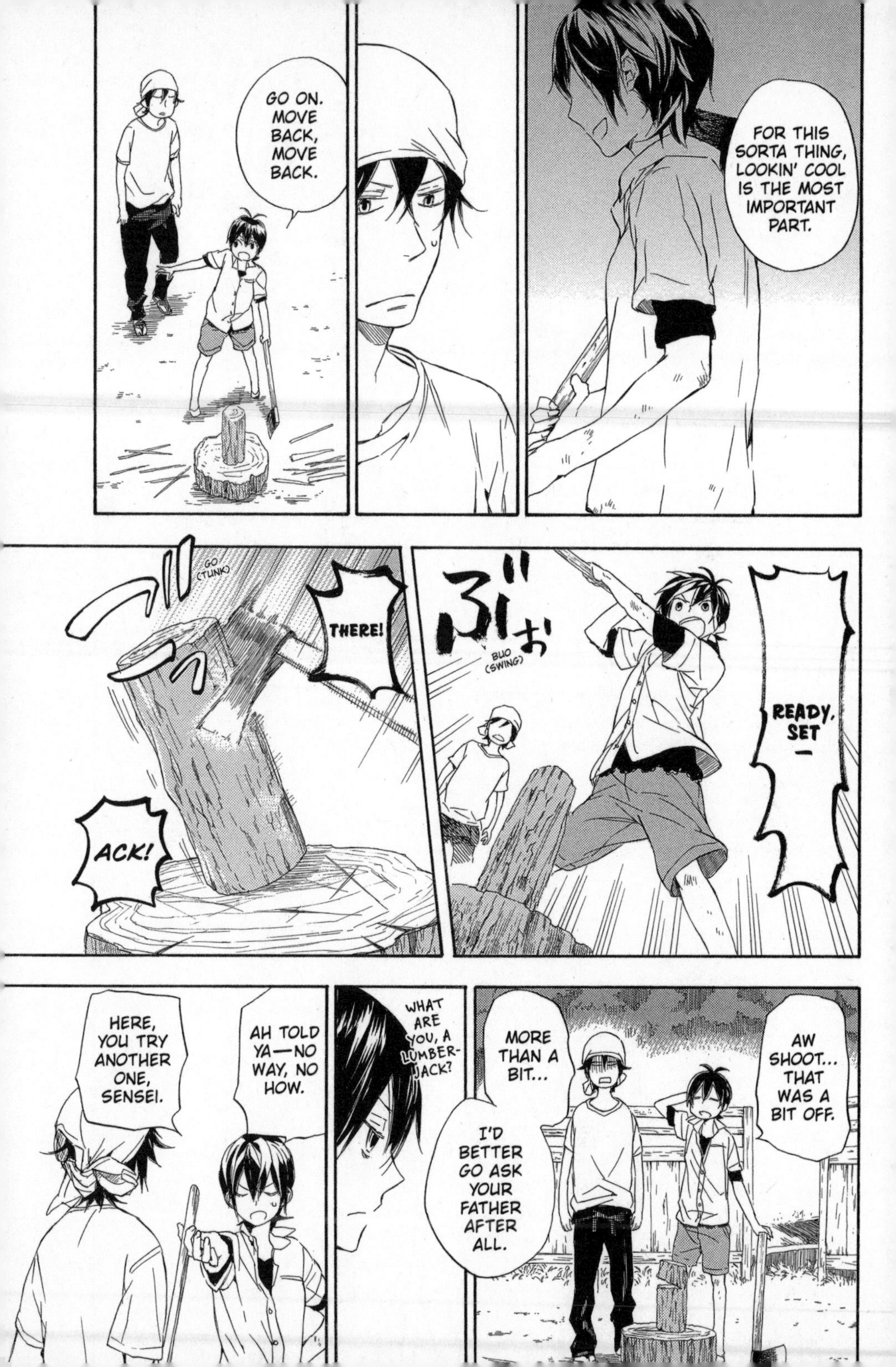
FOR THIS SORTA THING, LOOKIN' COOL IS THE MOST IMPORTANT PART.
GO ON. MOVE BACK, MOVE BACK.
READY, SET—
ぶお
BUO (SWING)
GO (TUNK)
THERE!
ACK!
AW SHOOT... THAT WAS A BIT OFF.
MORE THAN A BIT...
I'D BETTER GO ASK YOUR FATHER AFTER ALL.
WHAT ARE YOU, A LUMBERJACK?
HERE, YOU TRY ANOTHER ONE, SENSEI.
AH TOLD YA—NO WAY, NO HOW.

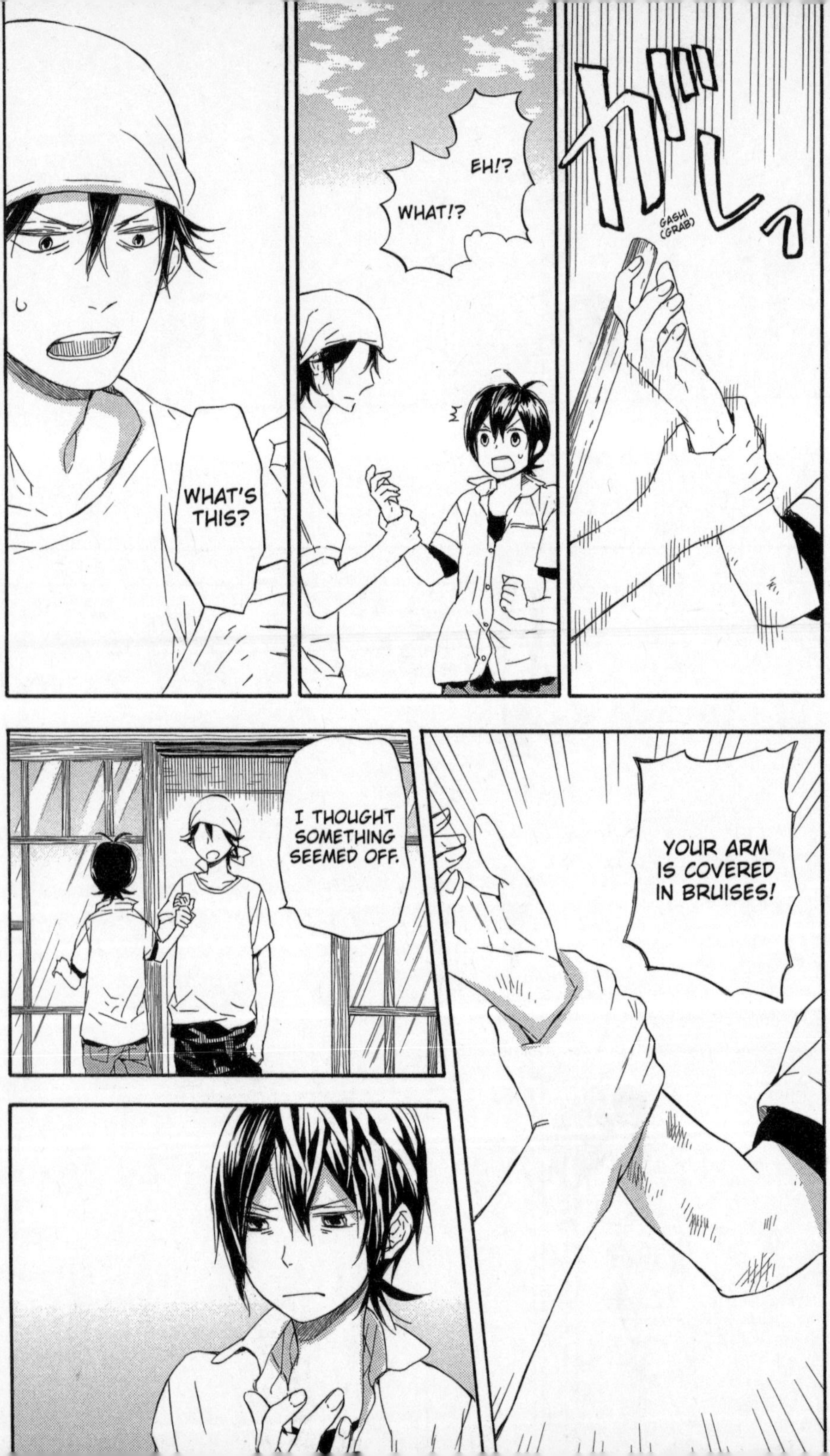
がしっ
GASHI (GRAB)
EH!?
WHAT!?
WHAT'S THIS?
YOUR ARM IS COVERED IN BRUISES!
I THOUGHT SOMETHING SEEMED OFF.

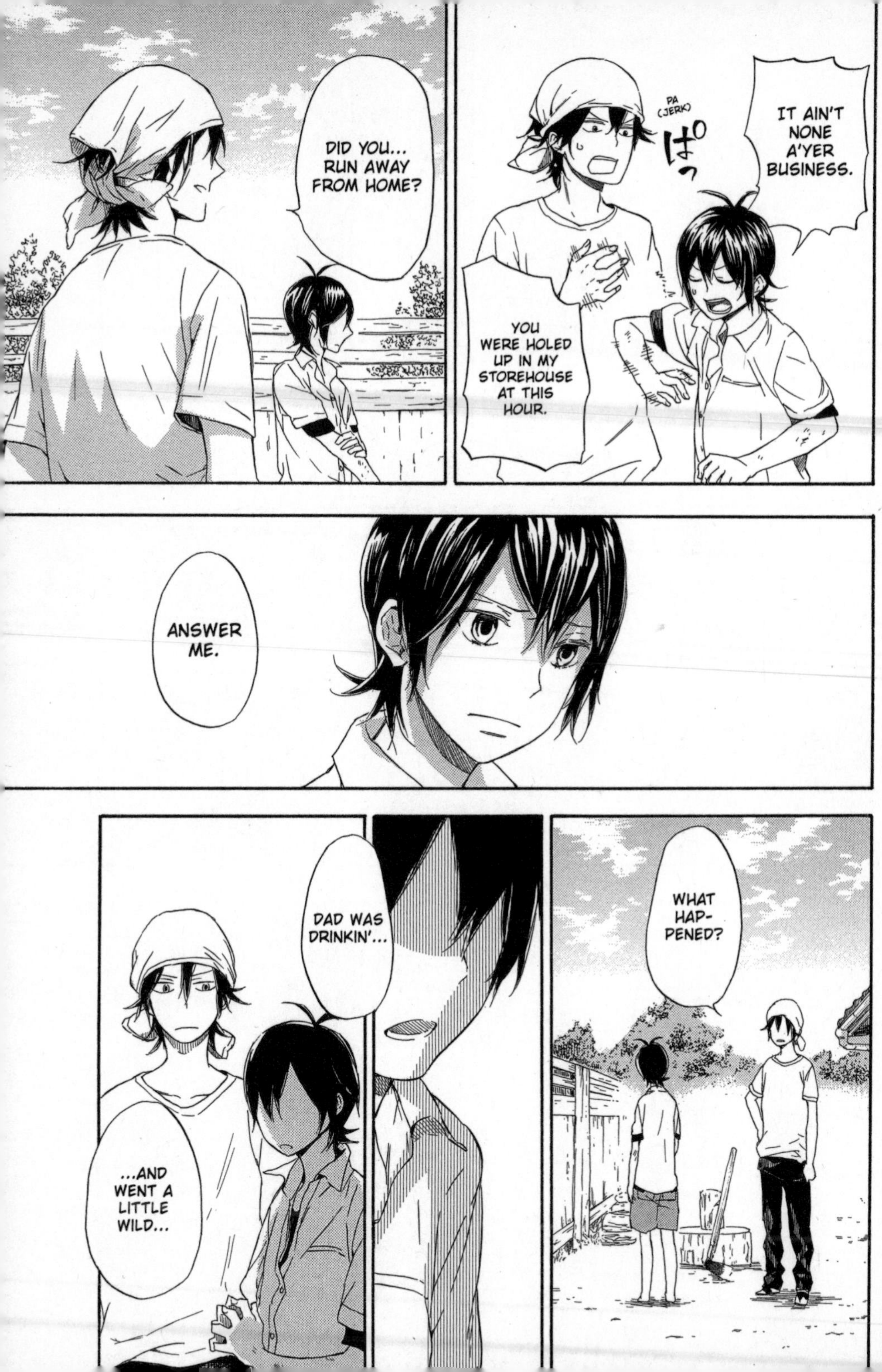
IT AIN'T NONE A'YER BUSINESS.
PA (JERK)
ぱっ
YOU WERE HOLED UP IN MY STOREHOUSE AT THIS HOUR.
DID YOU... RUN AWAY FROM HOME?
ANSWER ME.
WHAT HAP-PENED?
DAD WAS DRINKIN'...
...AND WENT A LITTLE WILD...

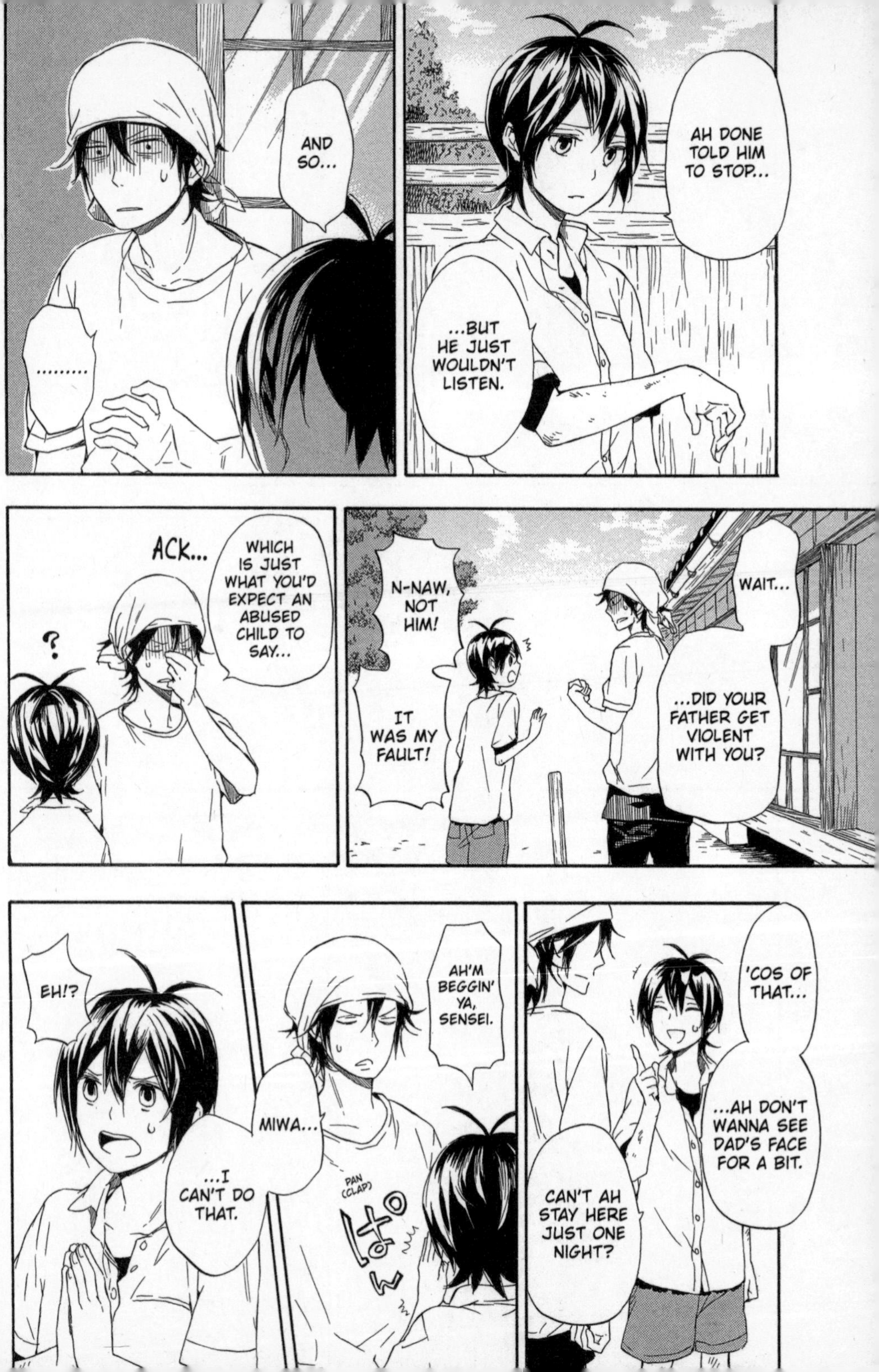
AH DONE TOLD HIM TO STOP...
...BUT HE JUST WOULDN'T LISTEN.
AND SO...
....
WAIT...
...DID YOUR FATHER GET VIOLENT WITH YOU?
N-NAW, NOT HIM!
IT WAS MY FAULT!
WHICH IS JUST WHAT YOU'D EXPECT AN ABUSED CHILD TO SAY...
ACK...
?
'COS OF THAT...
...AH DON'T WANNA SEE DAD'S FACE FOR A BIT.
CAN'T AH STAY HERE JUST ONE NIGHT?
AH'M BEGGIN' YA, SENSEI.
MIWA...
PAN (CLAP)
ぱん
EH!?
...I CAN'T DO THAT.

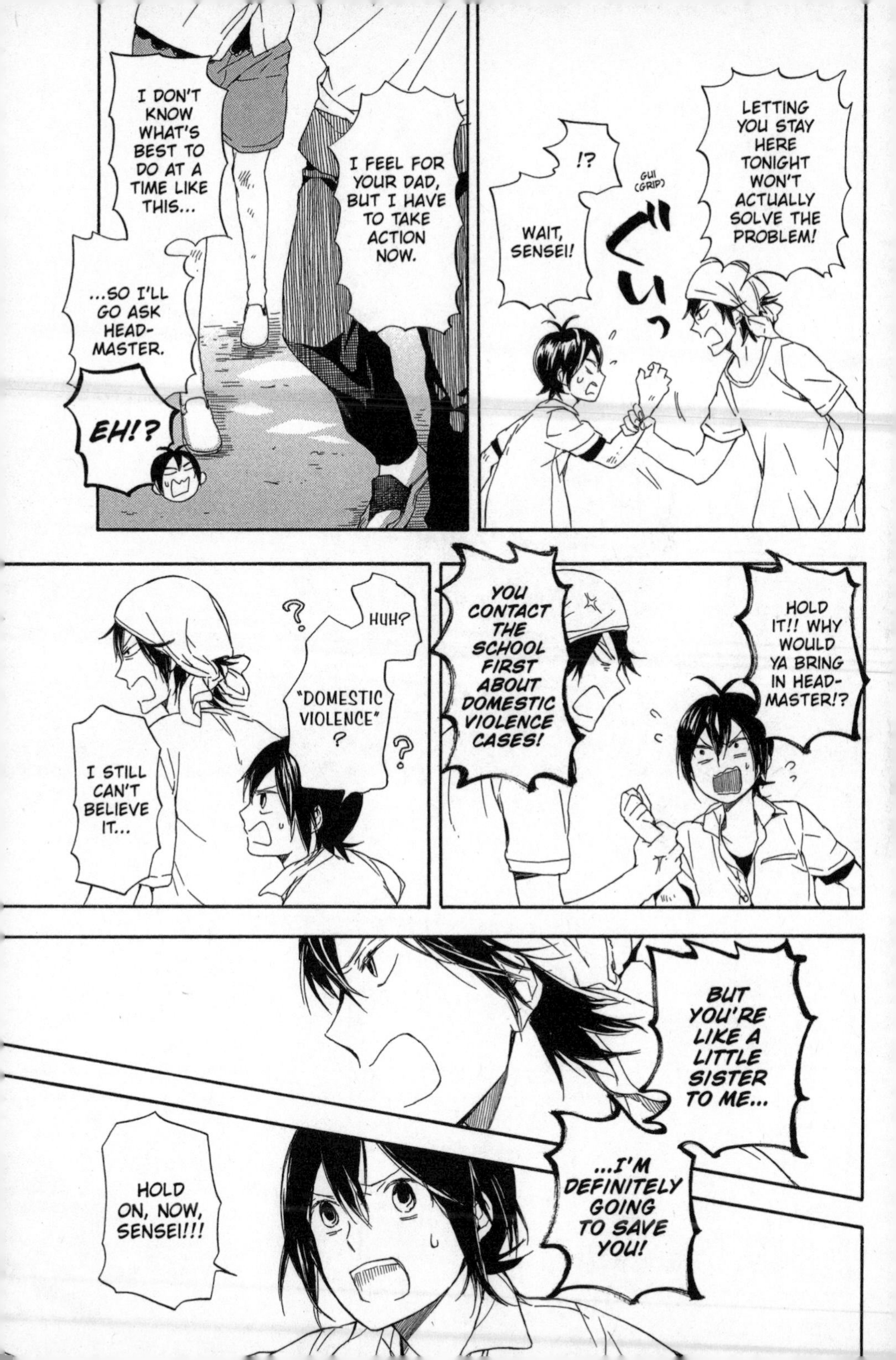

LETTING YOU STAY HERE TONIGHT WON'T ACTUALLY SOLVE THE PROBLEM!
GUI (GRIP)
ぐいっ
!?
WAIT, SENSEI!
I FEEL FOR YOUR DAD, BUT I HAVE TO TAKE ACTION NOW.
I DON'T KNOW WHAT'S BEST TO DO AT A TIME LIKE THIS...
...SO I'LL GO ASK HEAD-MASTER.
EH!?
HOLD IT!! WHY WOULD YA BRING IN HEAD-MASTER!?
YOU CONTACT THE SCHOOL FIRST ABOUT DOMESTIC VIOLENCE CASES!
HUH?
"DOMESTIC VIOLENCE"?
I STILL CAN'T BELIEVE IT...
BUT YOU'RE LIKE A LITTLE SISTER TO ME...
...I'M DEFINITELY GOING TO SAVE YOU!
HOLD ON, NOW, SENSEI!!!

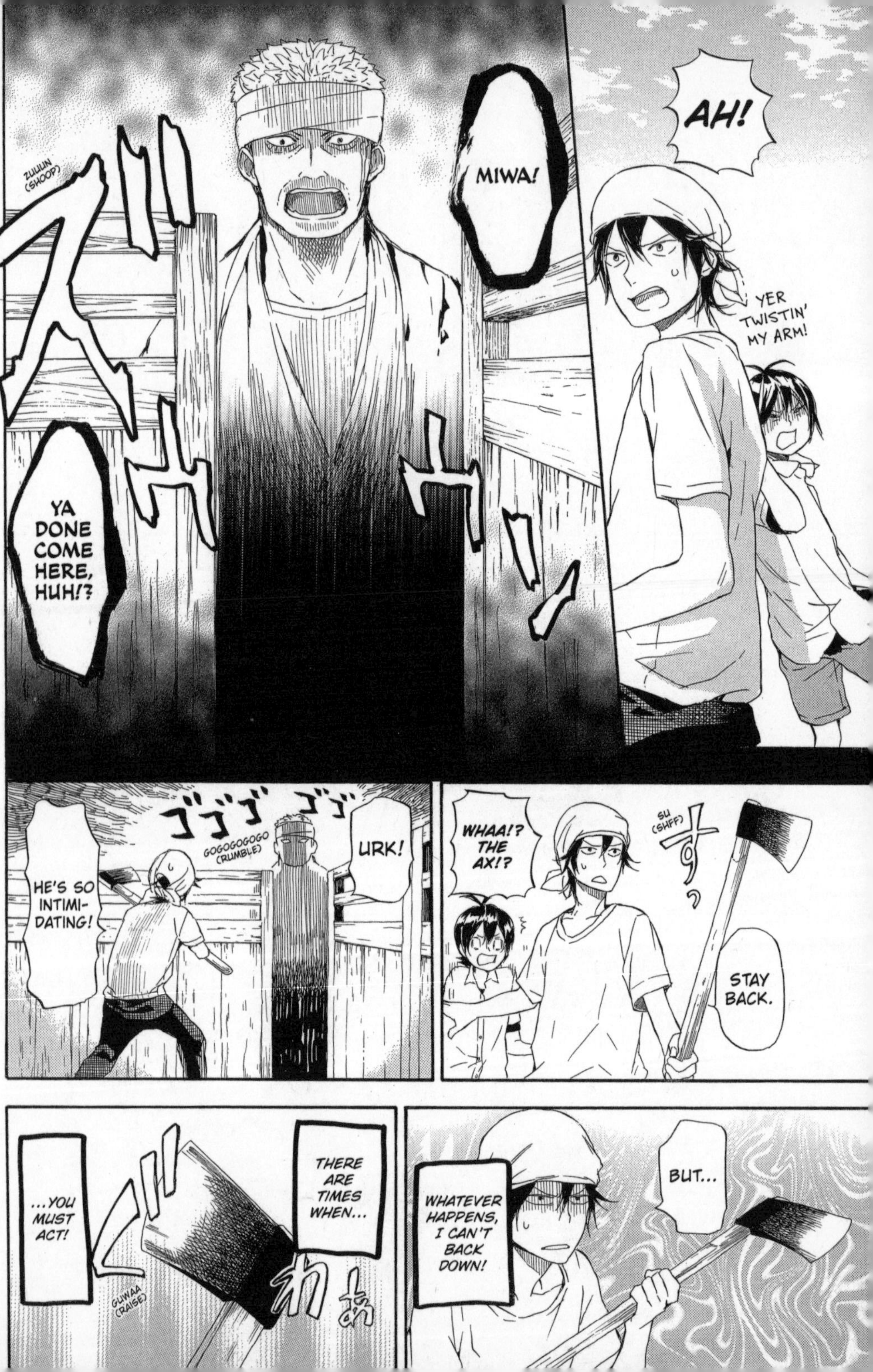
AH!
YER TWISTIN' MY ARM!
MIWA!
ZUUUN (SHOOP)
YA DONE COME HERE, HUH!?
SU (SHFF)
WHAA!? THE AX!?
STAY BACK.
URK!
GOGOGOGOGO (RUMBLE)
HE'S SO INTIMI-DATING!
BUT...
WHATEVER HAPPENS, I CAN'T BACK DOWN!
THERE ARE TIMES WHEN...
...YOU MUST ACT!
GUWAA (RAISE)

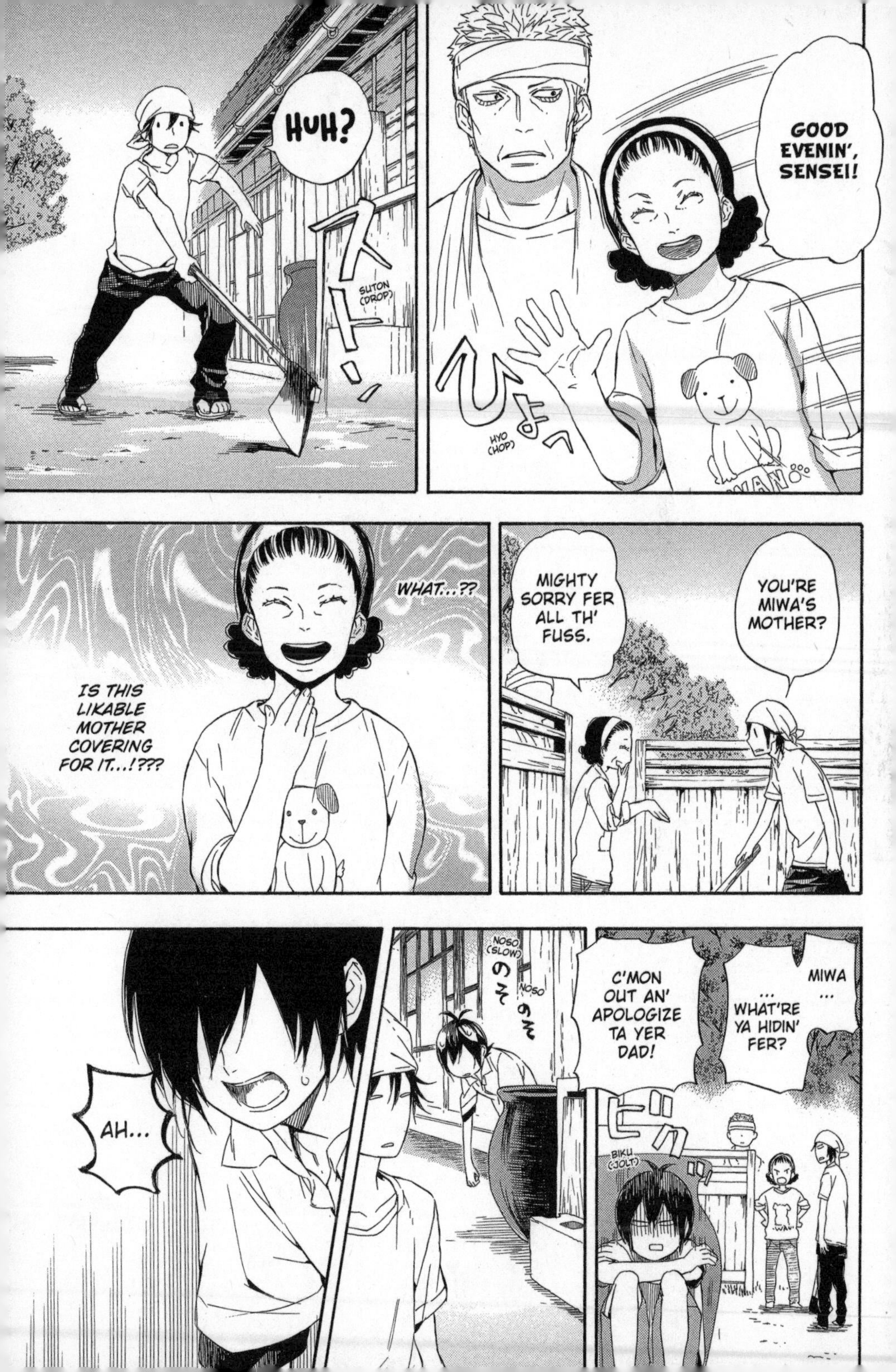
GOOD EVENIN', SENSEI!
HYO (HOP)
HUH?
SUTON (DROP)
YOU'RE MIWA'S MOTHER?
MIGHTY SORRY FER ALL TH' FUSS.
WHAT...??
IS THIS LIKABLE MOTHER COVERING FOR IT...!???
MIWA... WHAT'RE YA HIDIN' FER?
C'MON OUT AN' APOLOGIZE TA YER DAD!
BIKU (JOLT)
NOSO (SLOW)
NOSO
AH...

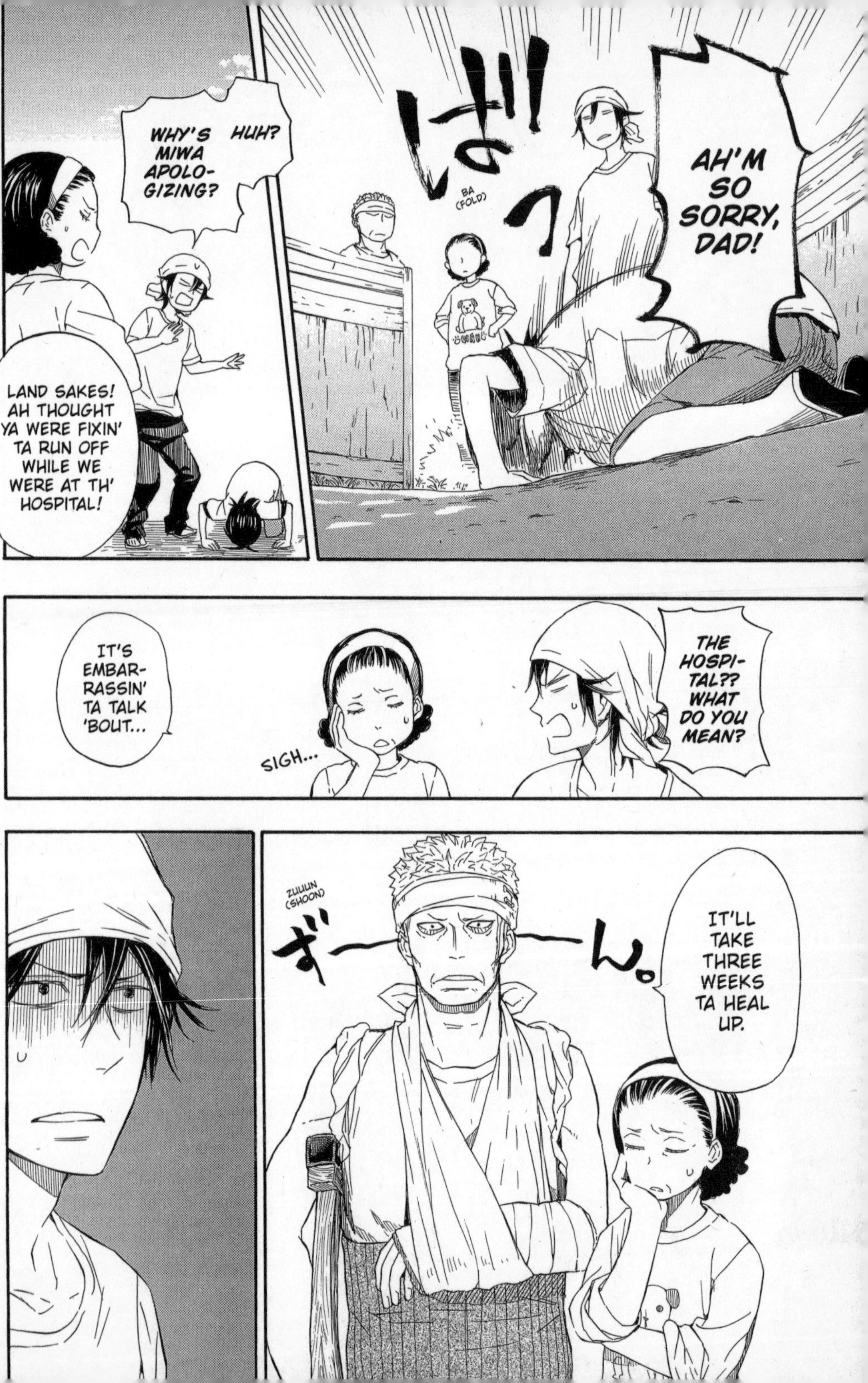
ばっ
BA (FOLD)
AH'M SO SORRY, DAD!
HUH?
WHY'S MIWA APOLOGIZING?
LAND SAKES! AH THOUGHT YA WERE FIXIN' TA RUN OFF WHILE WE WERE AT TH' HOSPITAL!
THE HOSPITAL?? WHAT DO YOU MEAN?
IT'S EMBARRASSIN' TA TALK 'BOUT...
SIGH...
IT'LL TAKE THREE WEEKS TA HEAL UP.
ずーーん。
ZUUUN (SHOON)

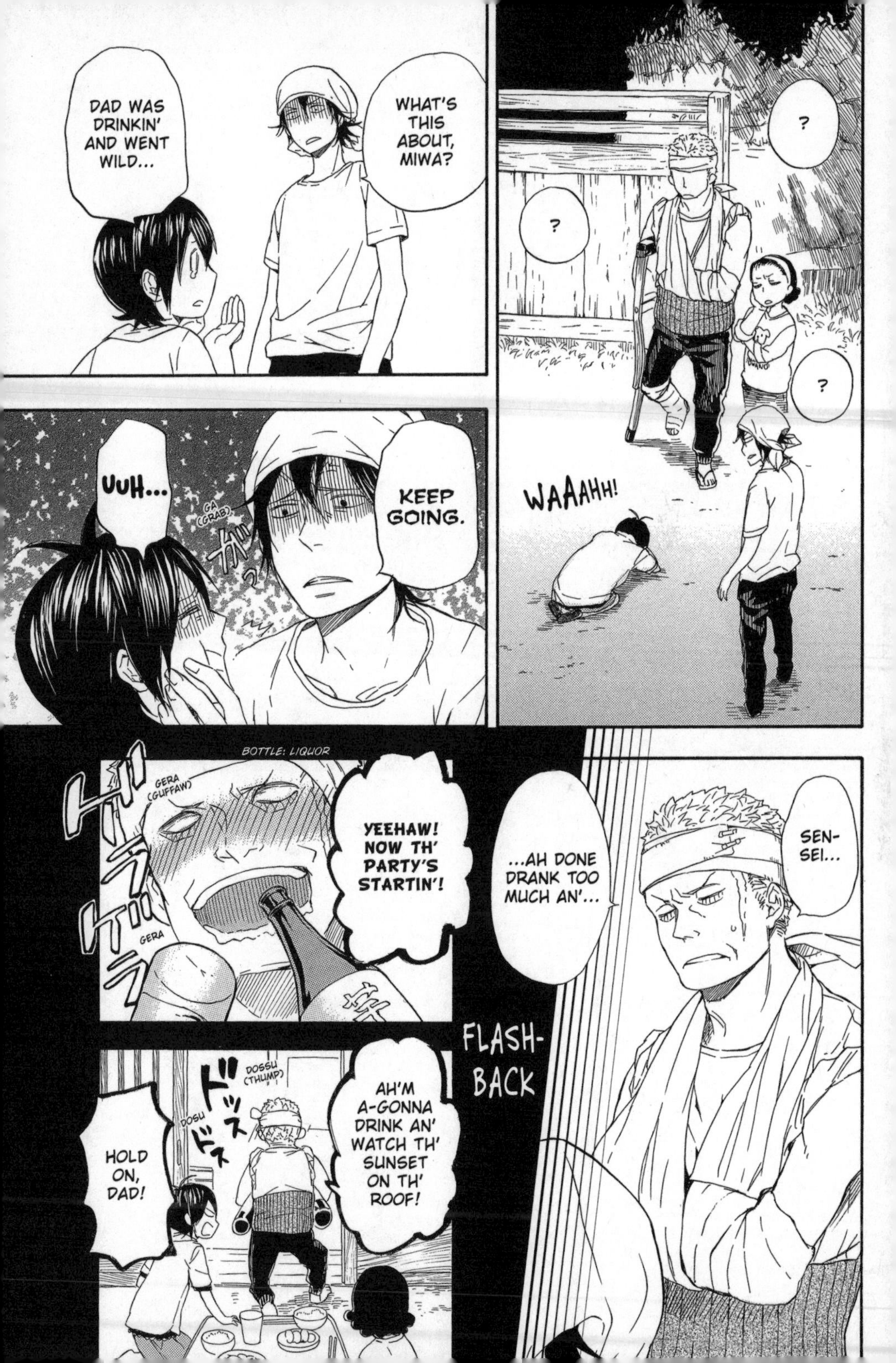
?
?
?
WAAAHH!
WHAT'S THIS ABOUT, MIWA?
DAD WAS DRINKIN' AND WENT WILD...
KEEP GOING.
GA (GRAB)
UUH...
SEN-SEI...
...AH DONE DRANK TOO MUCH AN'...
FLASH-BACK
BOTTLE: LIQUOR
YEEHAW! NOW TH' PARTY'S STARTIN'!
GERA (GUFFAW)
GERA
AH'M A-GONNA DRINK AN' WATCH TH' SUNSET ON TH' ROOF!
DOSSU (THUMP)
DOSU
HOLD ON, DAD!

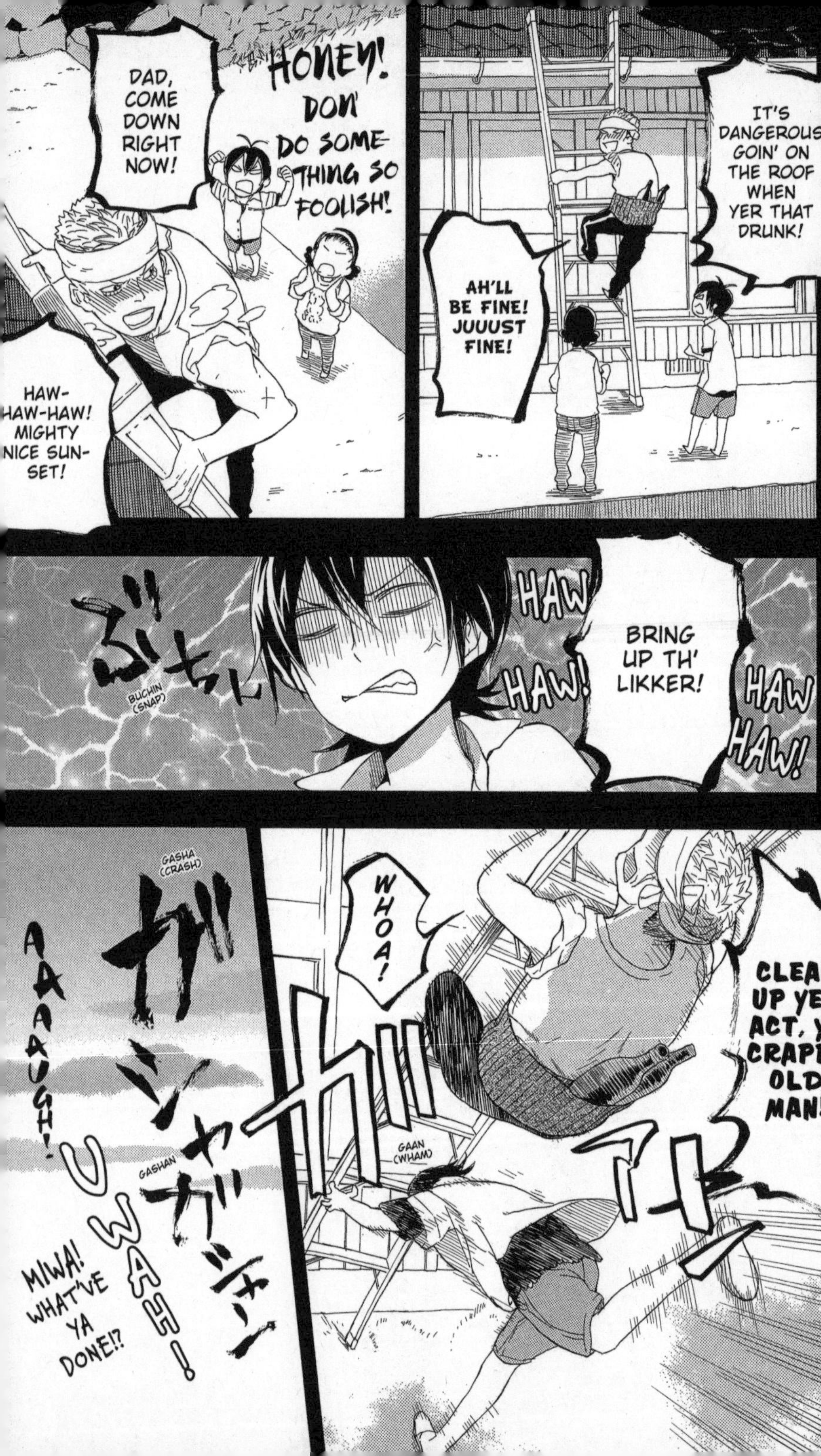
IT'S DANGEROUS GOIN' ON THE ROOF WHEN YER THAT DRUNK!
AH'LL BE FINE! JUUUST FINE!
DAD, COME DOWN RIGHT NOW!
HONEY! DON' DO SOME-THING SO FOOLISH!
HAW-HAW-HAW! MIGHTY NICE SUN-SET!
HAW HAW!
BRING UP TH' LIKKER!
HAW HAW!
ぶちん
BUCHIN (SNAP)
CLEAN UP YER ACT, YA CRAPPY OLD MAN!
WHOA!
GAAN (WHAM)
GASHA (CRASH)
GASHAN
AAAAUGH!
UWAH!
MIWA! WHAT'VE YA DONE!?

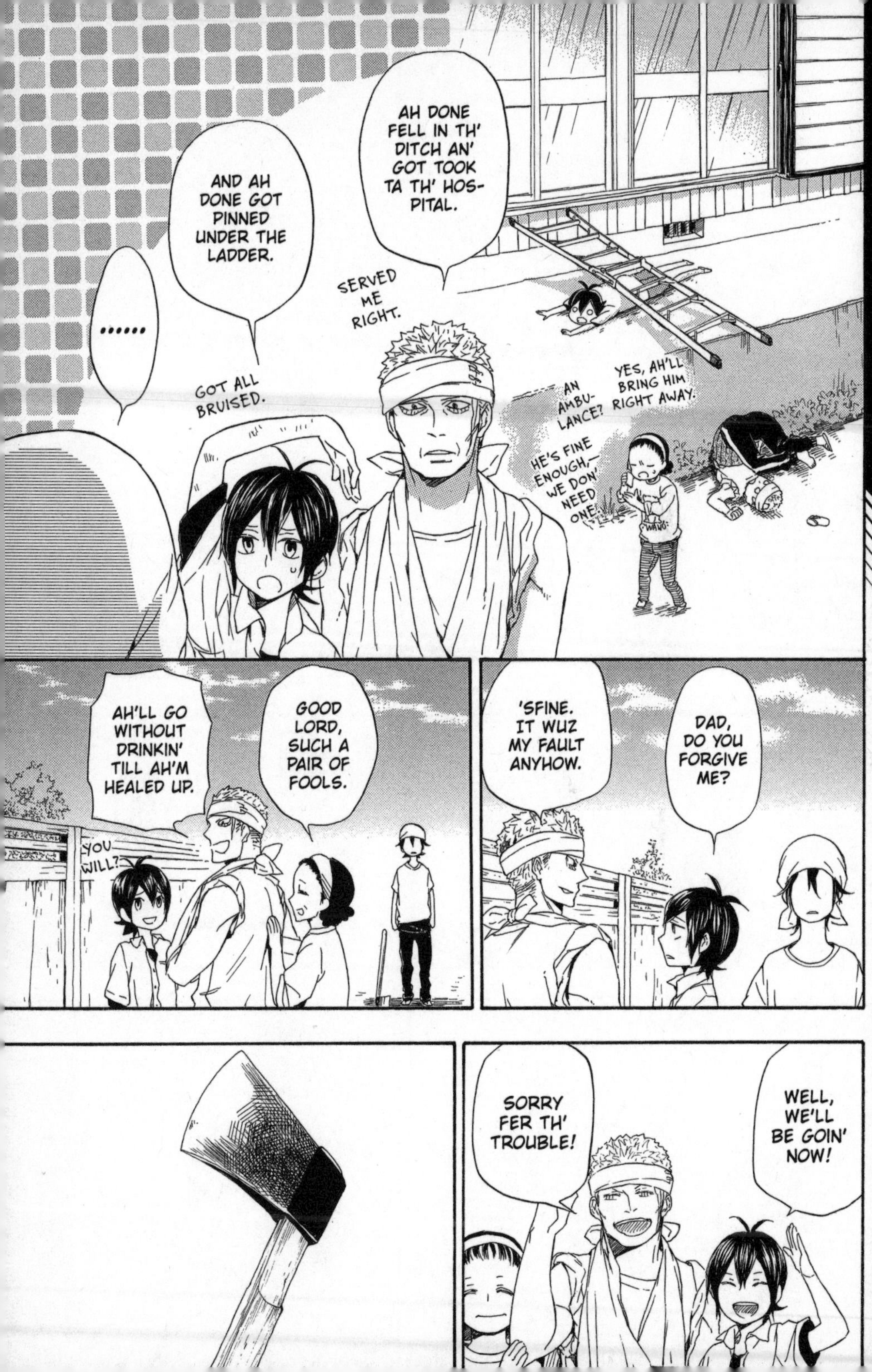
AH DONE FELL IN TH' DITCH AN' GOT TOOK TA TH' HOS-PITAL.
SERVED ME RIGHT.
AND AH DONE GOT PINNED UNDER THE LADDER.
GOT ALL BRUISED.
......
YES, AH'LL BRING HIM RIGHT AWAY.
AN AMBU-LANCE?
HE'S FINE ENOUGH,— WE DON' NEED ONE.
WANG
DAD, DO YOU FORGIVE ME?
'SFINE. IT WUZ MY FAULT ANYHOW.
GOOD LORD, SUCH A PAIR OF FOOLS.
AH'LL GO WITHOUT DRINKIN' TILL AH'M HEALED UP.
YOU WILL?
WELL, WE'LL BE GOIN' NOW!
SORRY FER TH' TROUBLE!

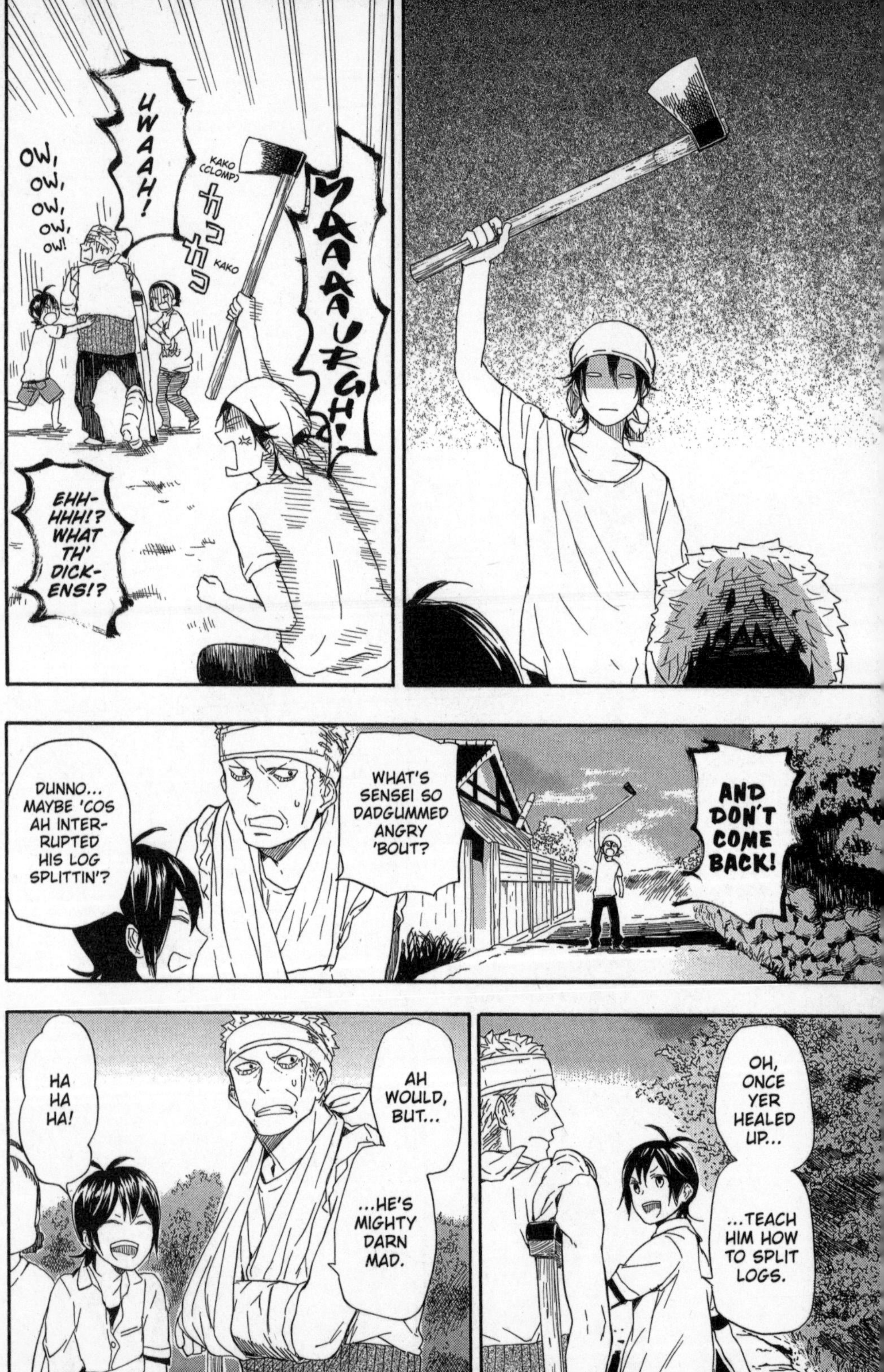
MAAAAURGH!
KAKO (CLOMP)
カッカッ
KAKO
UWAAAH!
OW, OW, OW, OW, OW!
EHHHHH!? WHAT TH' DICKENS!?
AND DON'T COME BACK!
WHAT'S SENSEI SO DADGUMMED ANGRY 'BOUT?
DUNNO... MAYBE 'COS AH INTER-RUPTED HIS LOG SPLITTIN'?
OH, ONCE YER HEALED UP...
...TEACH HIM HOW TO SPLIT LOGS.
AH WOULD, BUT...
...HE'S MIGHTY DARN MAD.
HA HA HA!

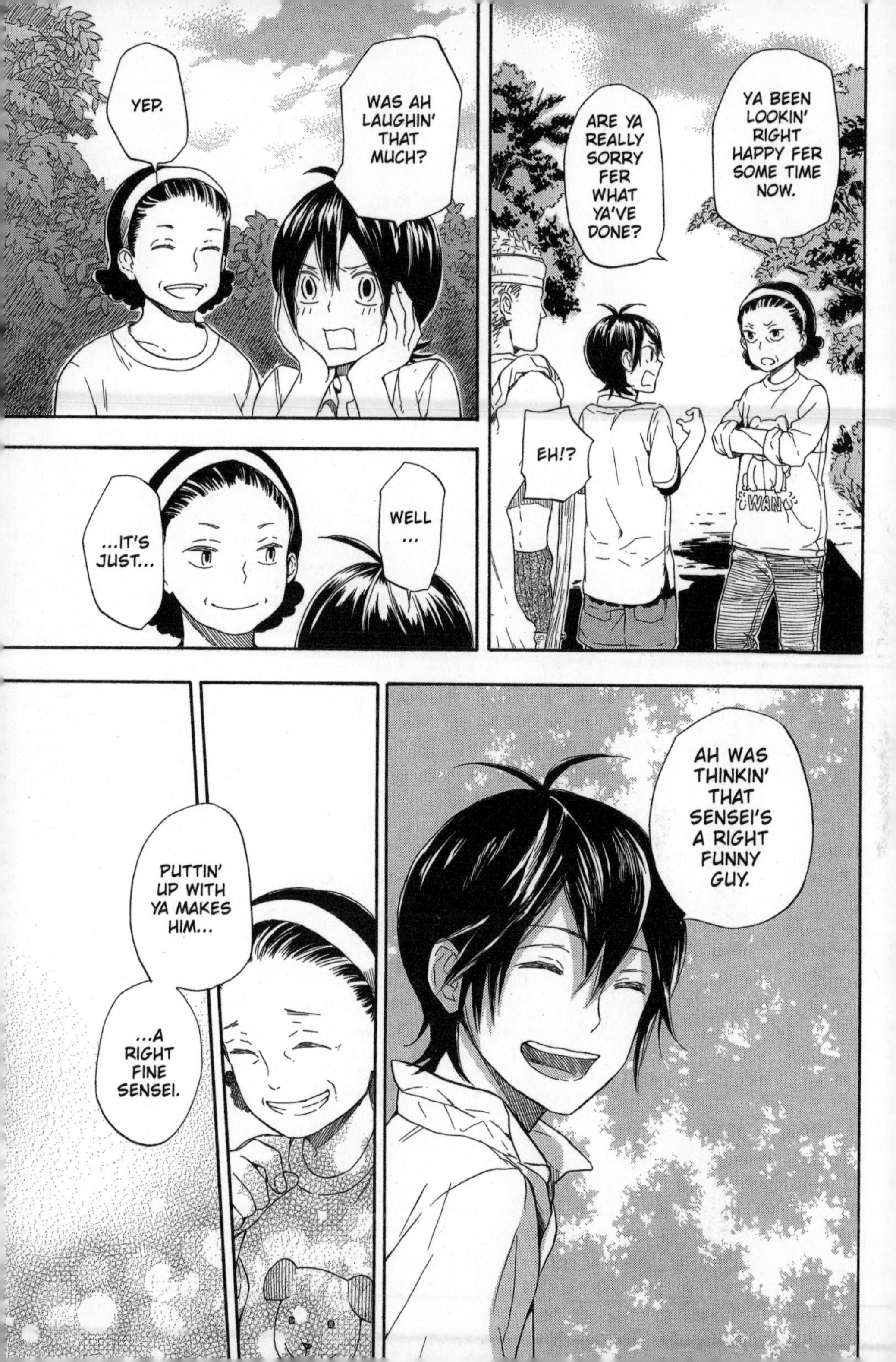
YA BEEN LOOKIN' RIGHT HAPPY FER SOME TIME NOW.
ARE YA REALLY SORRY FER WHAT YA'VE DONE?
EH!?
WAN
WAS AH LAUGHIN' THAT MUCH?
YEP.
WELL ...
...IT'S JUST...
AH WAS THINKIN' THAT SENSEI'S A RIGHT FUNNY GUY.
PUTTIN' UP WITH YA MAKES HIM...
...A RIGHT FINE SENSEI.

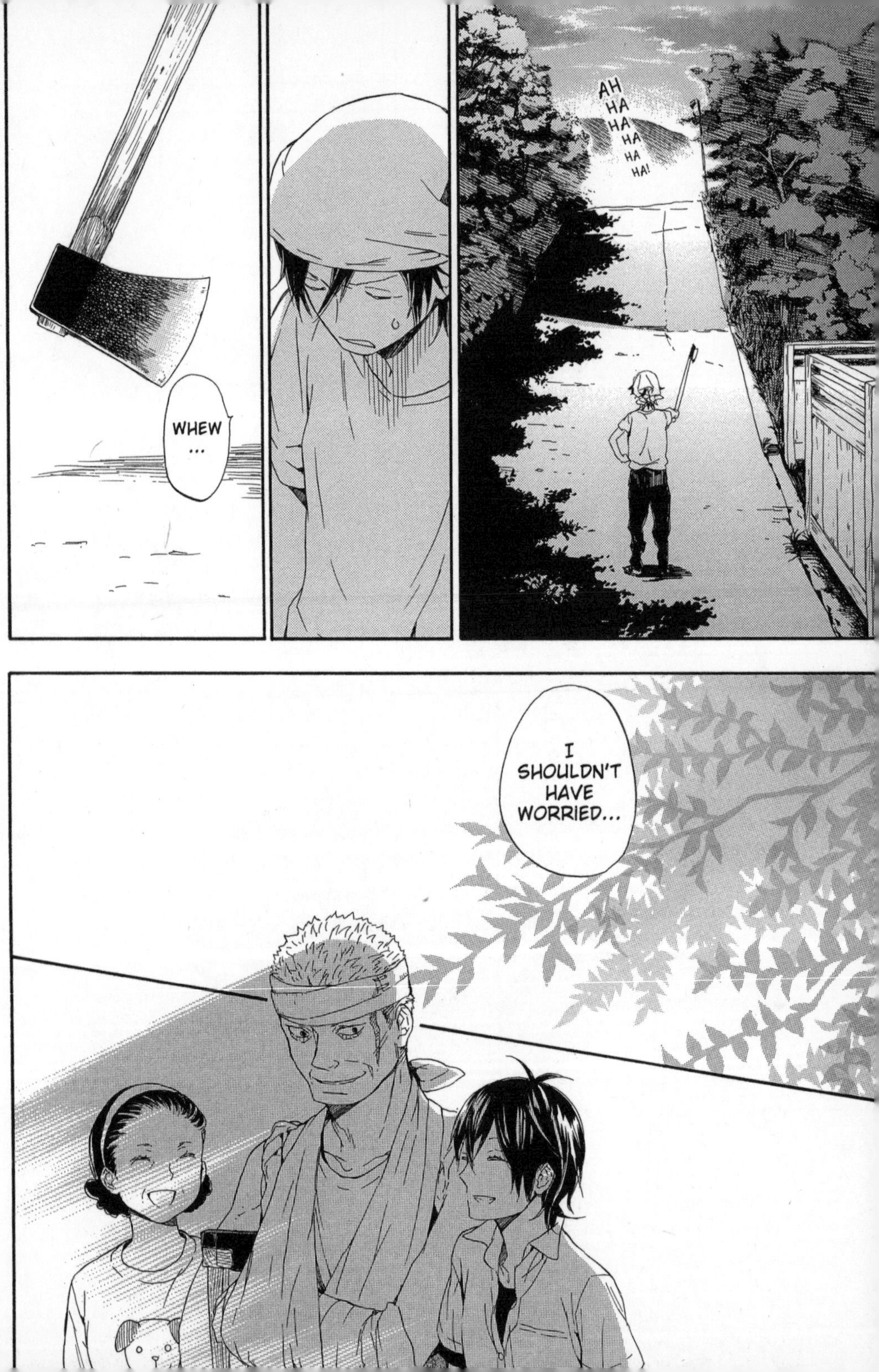
AH HA HA HA HA HA!
WHEW...
I SHOULDN'T HAVE WORRIED...

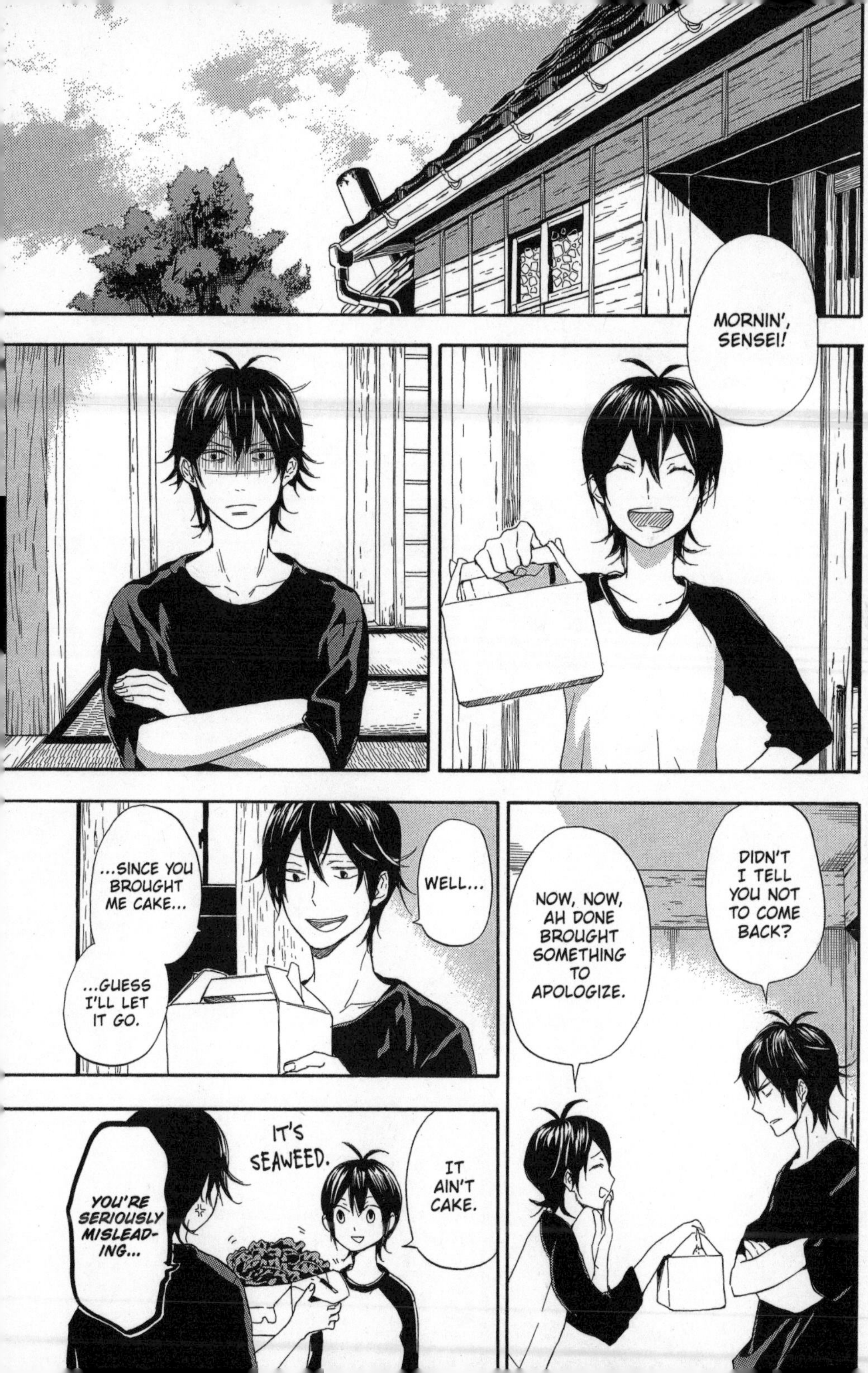
MORNIN', SENSEI!
DIDN'T I TELL YOU NOT TO COME BACK?
NOW, NOW, AH DONE BROUGHT SOMETHING TO APOLOGIZE.
WELL...
...SINCE YOU BROUGHT ME CAKE...
...GUESS I'LL LET IT GO.
IT AIN'T CAKE.
IT'S SEAWEED.
YOU'RE SERIOUSLY MISLEAD-ING...

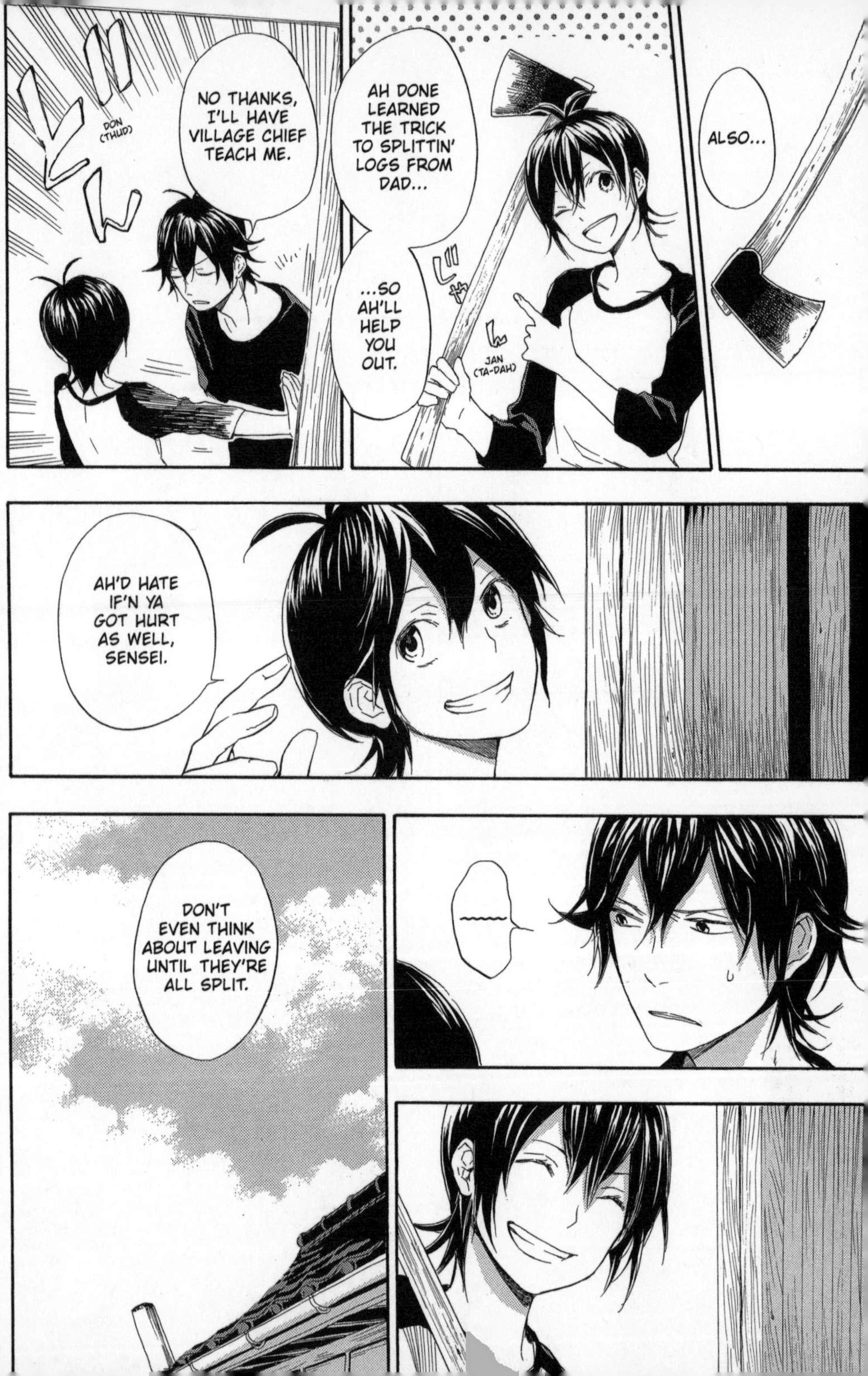
ALSO...
AH DONE LEARNED THE TRICK TO SPLITTIN' LOGS FROM DAD...
...SO AH'LL HELP YOU OUT.
JAN (TA-DAH)
NO THANKS, I'LL HAVE VILLAGE CHIEF TEACH ME.
DON (THUD)
AH'D HATE IF'N YA GOT HURT AS WELL, SENSEI.
......
DON'T EVEN THINK ABOUT LEAVING UNTIL THEY'RE ALL SPLIT.

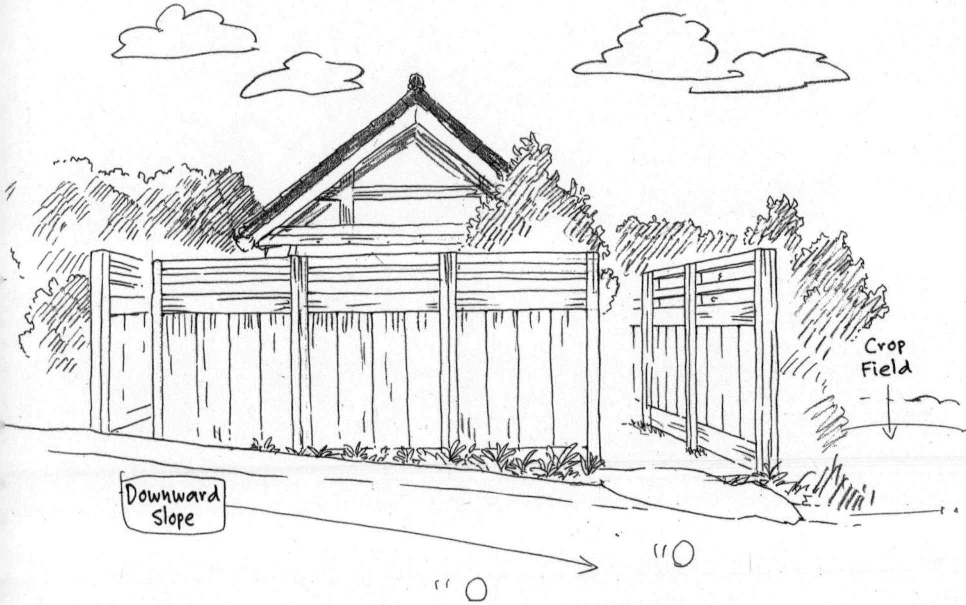
Crop Field
Downward Slope

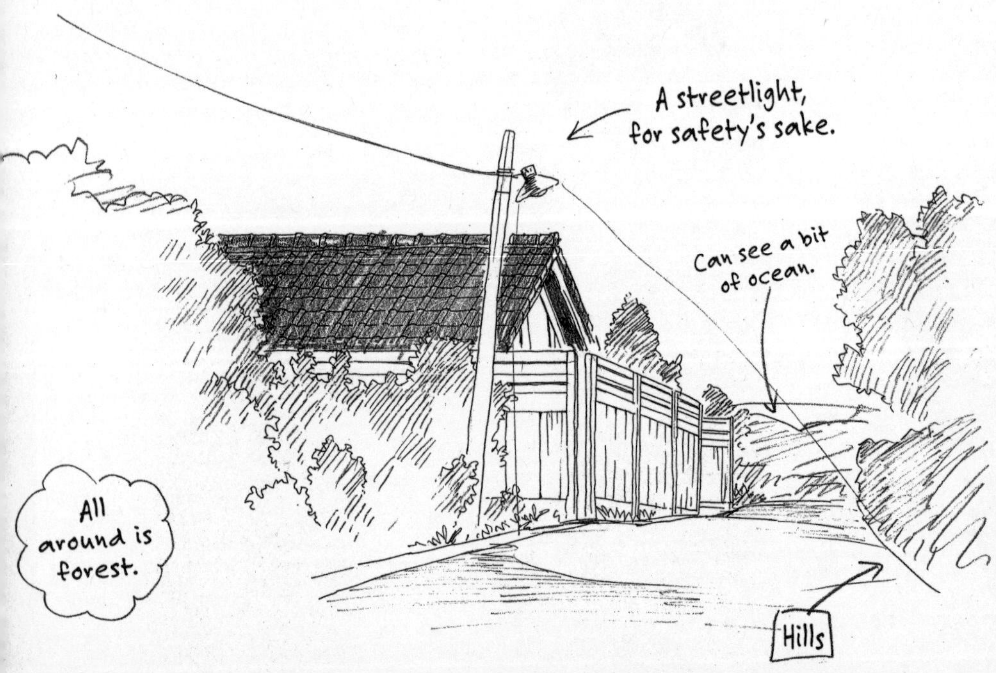
A streetlight, for safety's sake.
Can see a bit of ocean.
All around is forest.
Hills

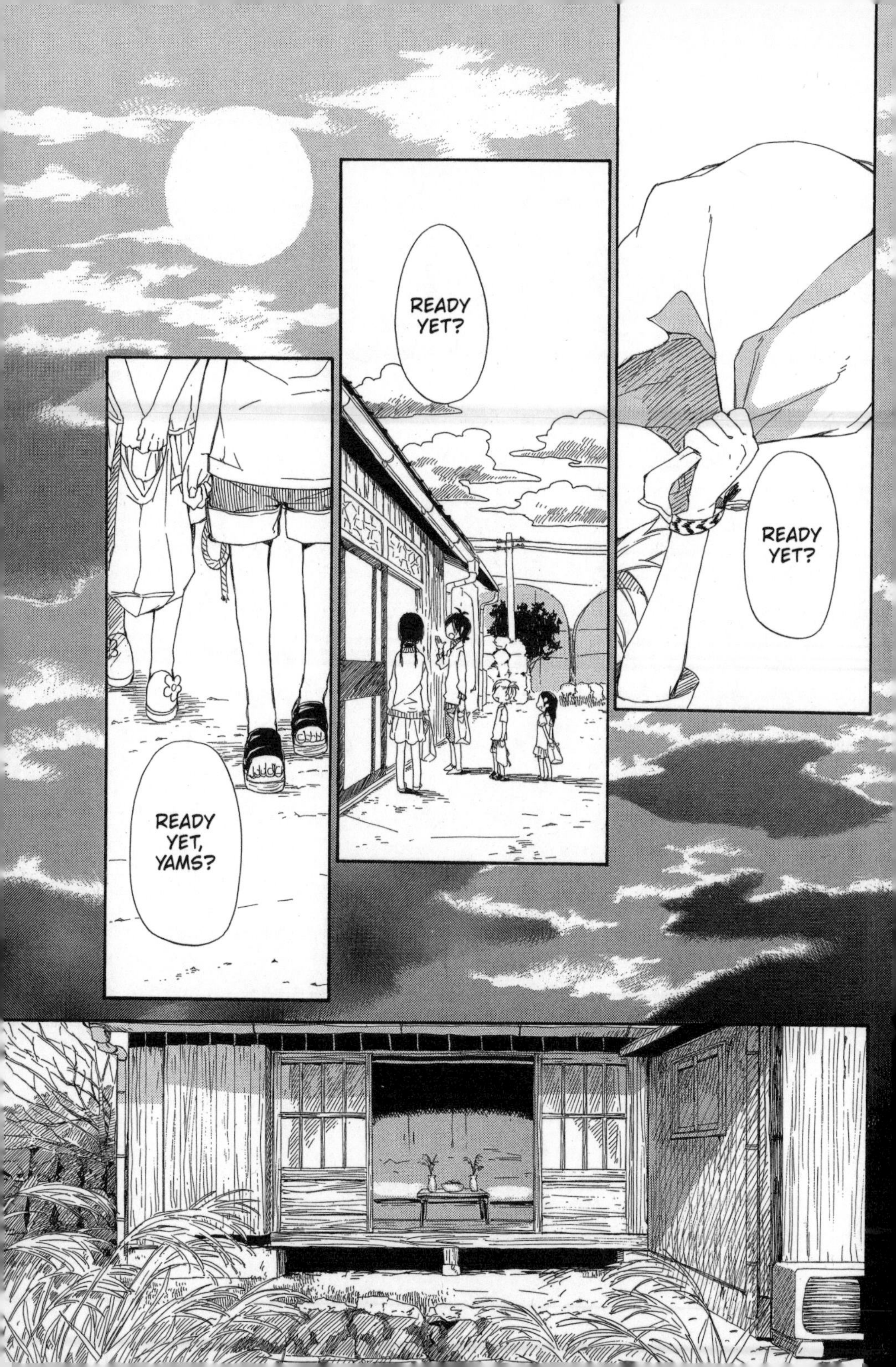
READY YET?
READY YET?
READY YET, YAMS?

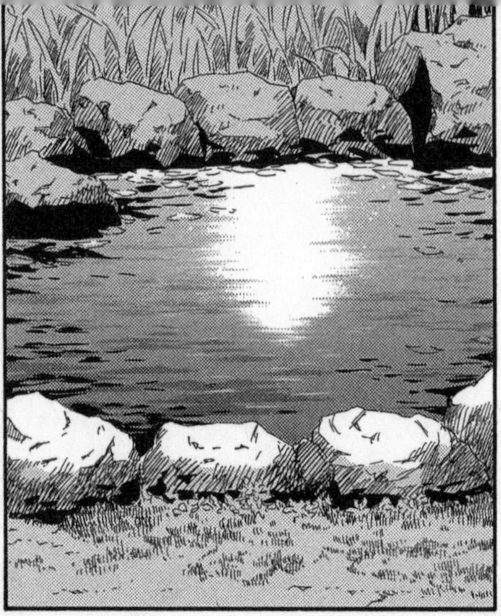
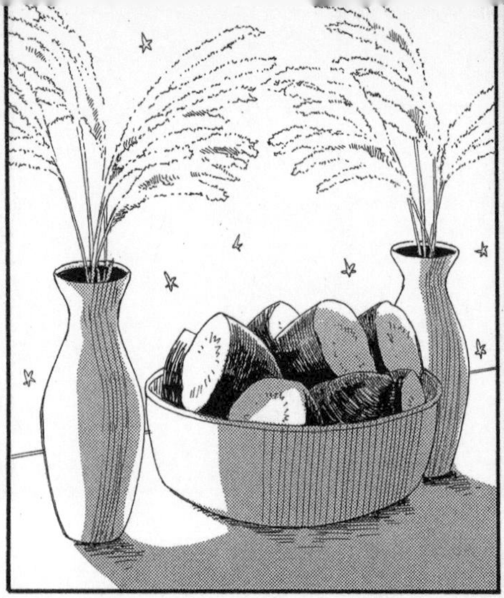
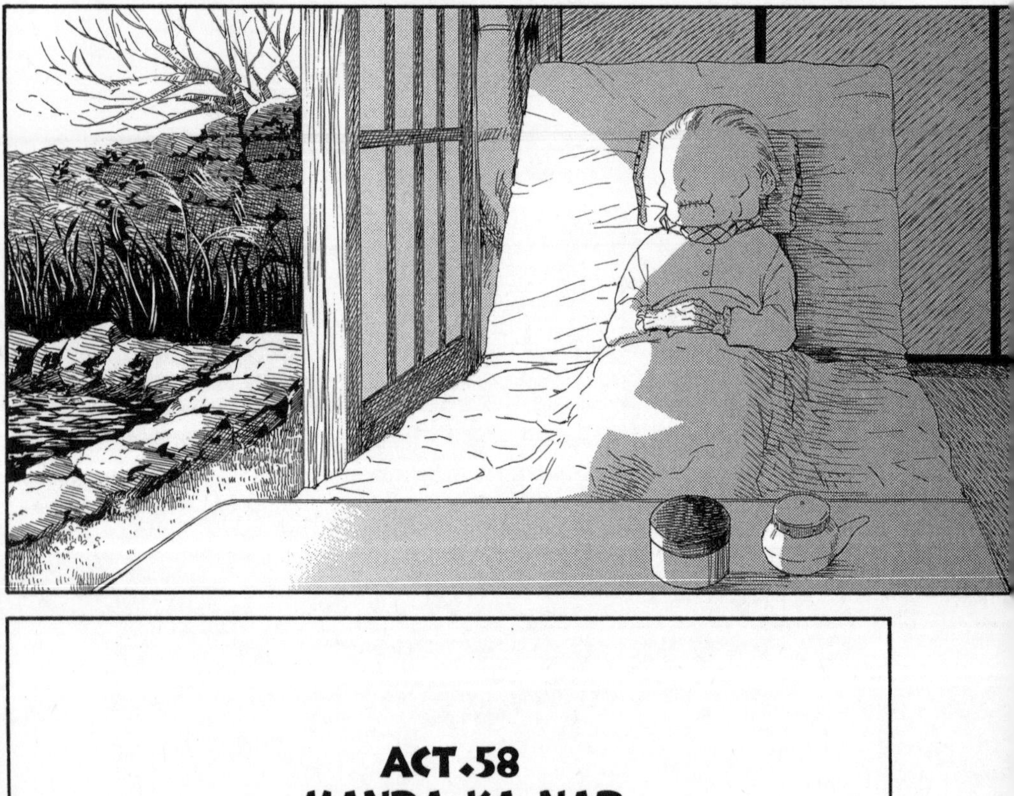

ACT.58
MANDA KA NA?
(Translation: Ready Yet?)

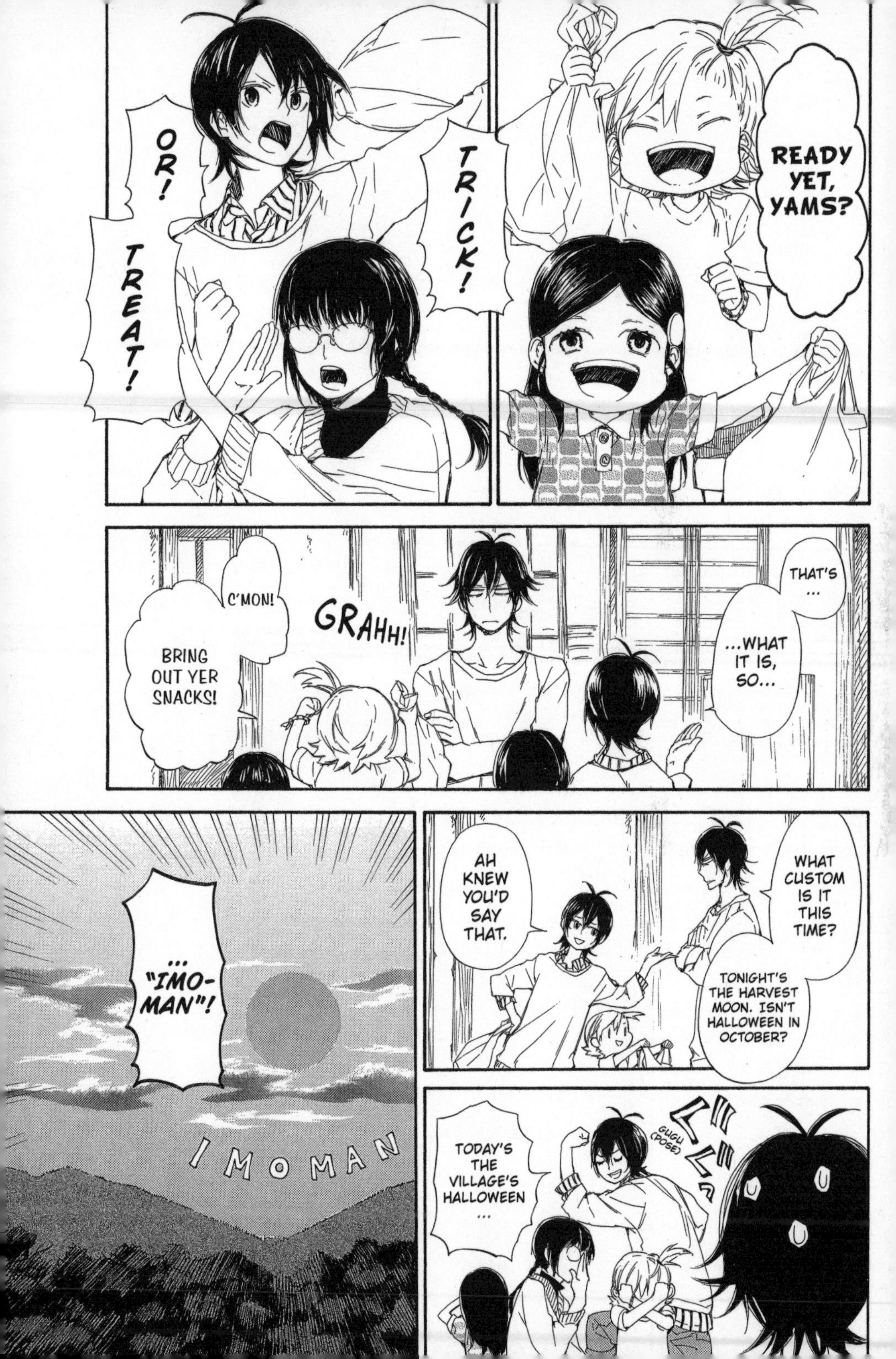
READY YET, YAMS?
TRICK!
OR!
TREAT!
THAT'S ...
...WHAT IT IS, SO...
GRAHH!
C'MON!
BRING OUT YER SNACKS!
WHAT CUSTOM IS IT THIS TIME?
TONIGHT'S THE HARVEST MOON. ISN'T HALLOWEEN IN OCTOBER?
AH KNEW YOU'D SAY THAT.
GUGU (POSE)
TODAY'S THE VILLAGE'S HALLOWEEN ...
... "IMO-MAN"!
IMOMAN

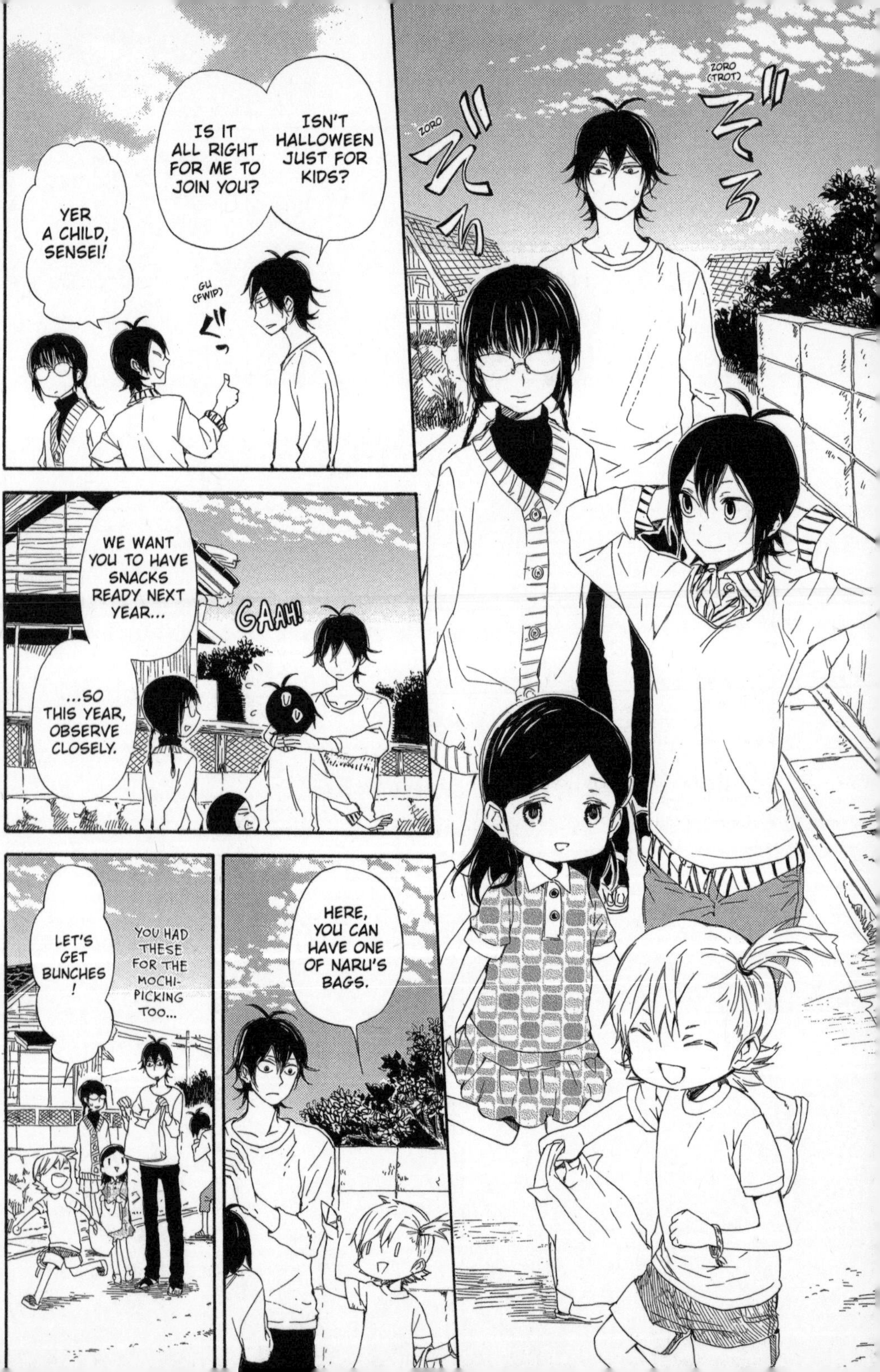
ZORO (TROT)
ZORO
ISN'T HALLOWEEN JUST FOR KIDS?
IS IT ALL RIGHT FOR ME TO JOIN YOU?
GU (FWIP)
YER A CHILD, SENSEI!
WE WANT YOU TO HAVE SNACKS READY NEXT YEAR...
GAAH!
...SO THIS YEAR, OBSERVE CLOSELY.
HERE, YOU CAN HAVE ONE OF NARU'S BAGS.
YOU HAD THESE FOR THE MOCHI-PICKING TOO...
LET'S GET BUNCHES!

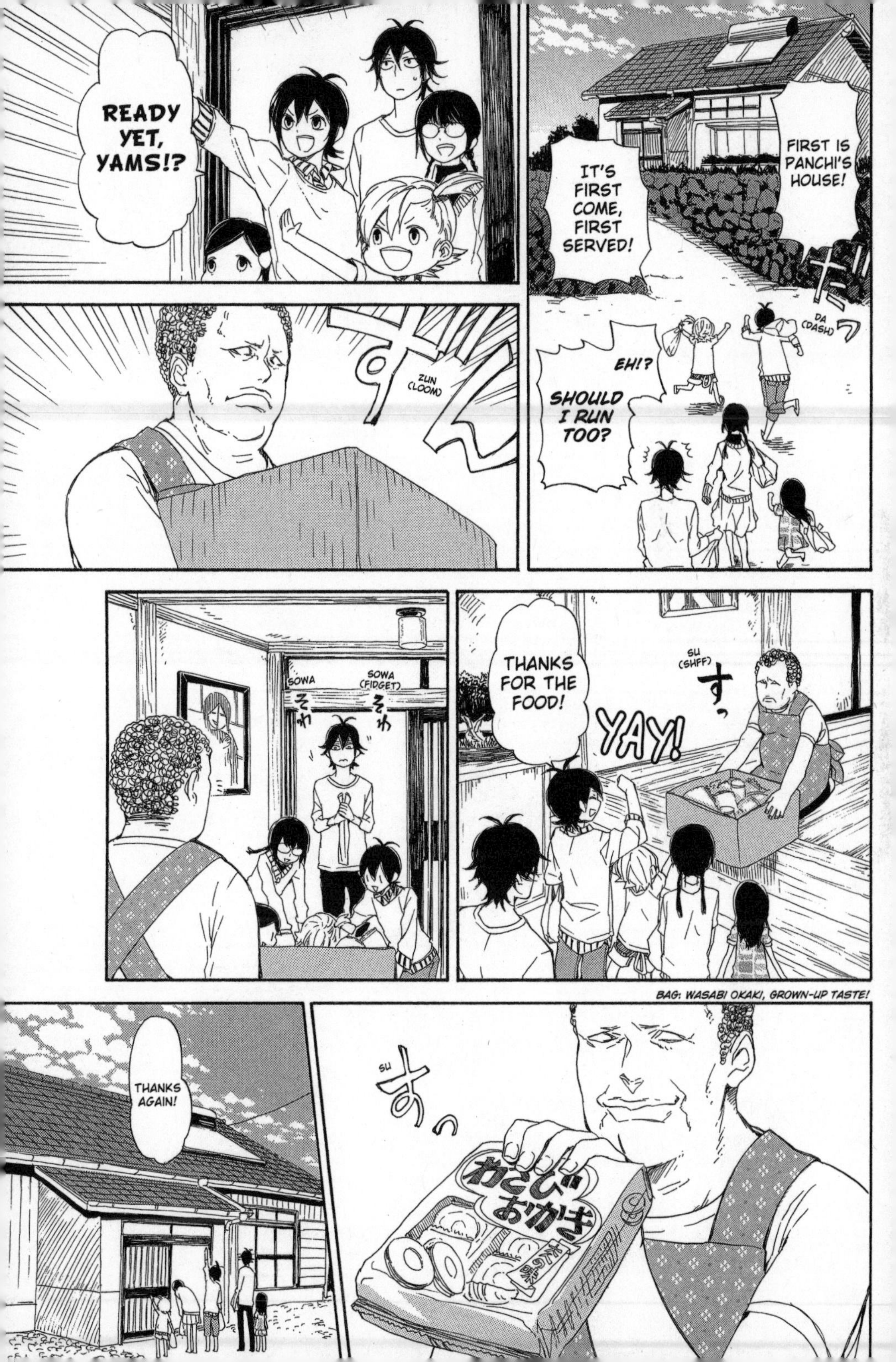
FIRST IS PANCHI'S HOUSE!
IT'S FIRST COME, FIRST SERVED!
DA (DASH)
EH!?
SHOULD I RUN TOO?
READY YET, YAMS!?
ZUN (LOOM)
THANKS FOR THE FOOD!
SU (SHFF)
すっ
YAY!
SOWA (FIDGET)
SOWA
BAG: WASABI OKAKI, GROWN-UP TASTE!
SU
すっ
わさびおかき
THANKS AGAIN!

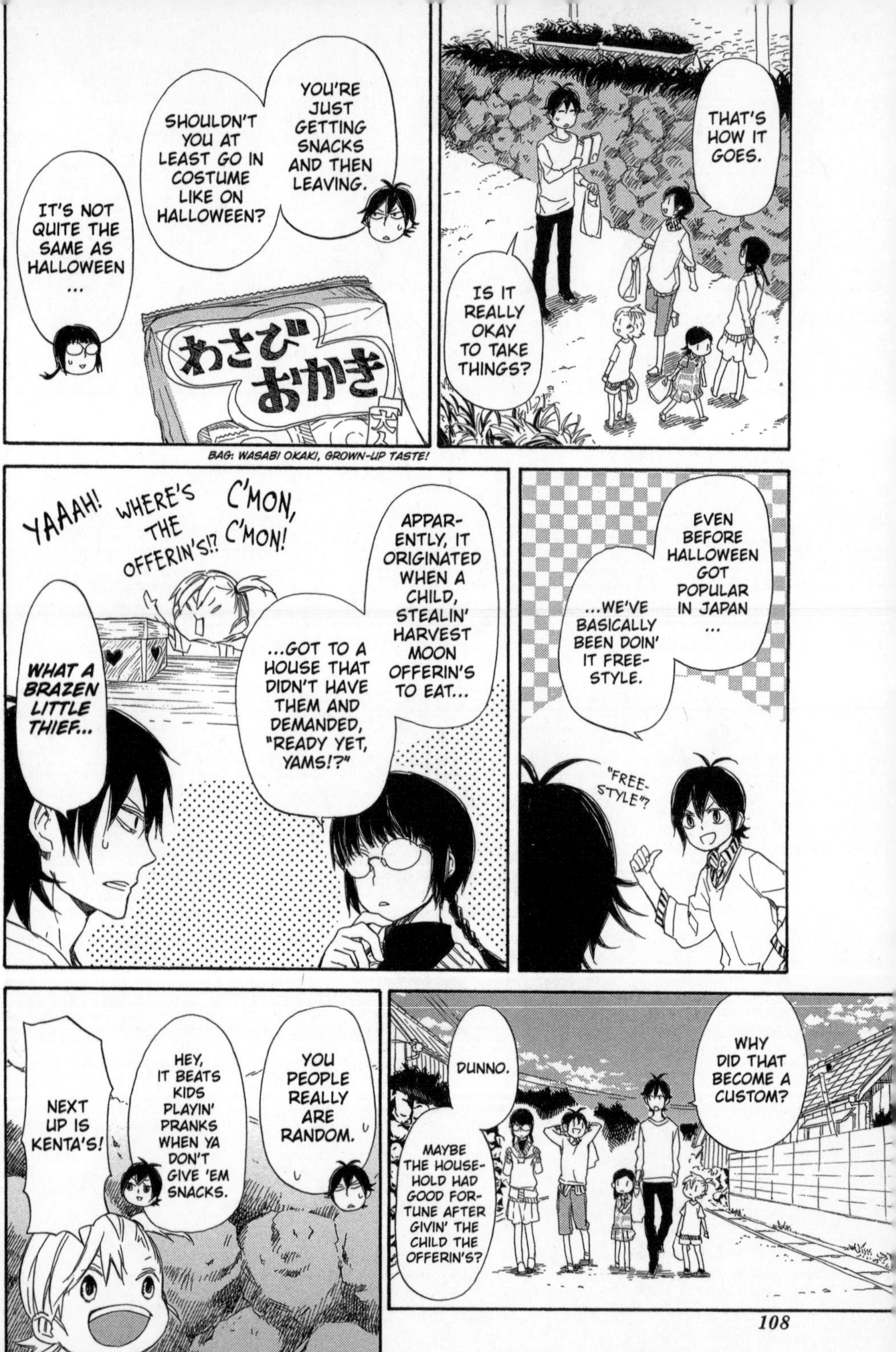
THAT'S HOW IT GOES.
IS IT REALLY OKAY TO TAKE THINGS?
YOU'RE JUST GETTING SNACKS AND THEN LEAVING.
SHOULDN'T YOU AT LEAST GO IN COSTUME LIKE ON HALLOWEEN?
IT'S NOT QUITE THE SAME AS HALLOWEEN ...
わさび おかき
EVEN BEFORE HALLOWEEN GOT POPULAR IN JAPAN ...
...WE'VE BASICALLY BEEN DOIN' IT FREE-STYLE.
"FREE-STYLE"?
APPARENTLY, IT ORIGINATED WHEN A CHILD, STEALIN' HARVEST MOON OFFERIN'S TO EAT...
...GOT TO A HOUSE THAT DIDN'T HAVE THEM AND DEMANDED, "READY YET, YAMS!?"
C'MON, C'MON!
WHERE'S THE OFFERIN'S!?
YAAAH!
WHAT A BRAZEN LITTLE THIEF...
WHY DID THAT BECOME A CUSTOM?
DUNNO.
MAYBE THE HOUSEHOLD HAD GOOD FORTUNE AFTER GIVIN' THE CHILD THE OFFERIN'S?
YOU PEOPLE REALLY ARE RANDOM.
HEY, IT BEATS KIDS PLAYIN' PRANKS WHEN YA DON'T GIVE 'EM SNACKS.
NEXT UP IS KENTA'S!

BAG: WASABI OKAKI, GROWN-UP TASTE!

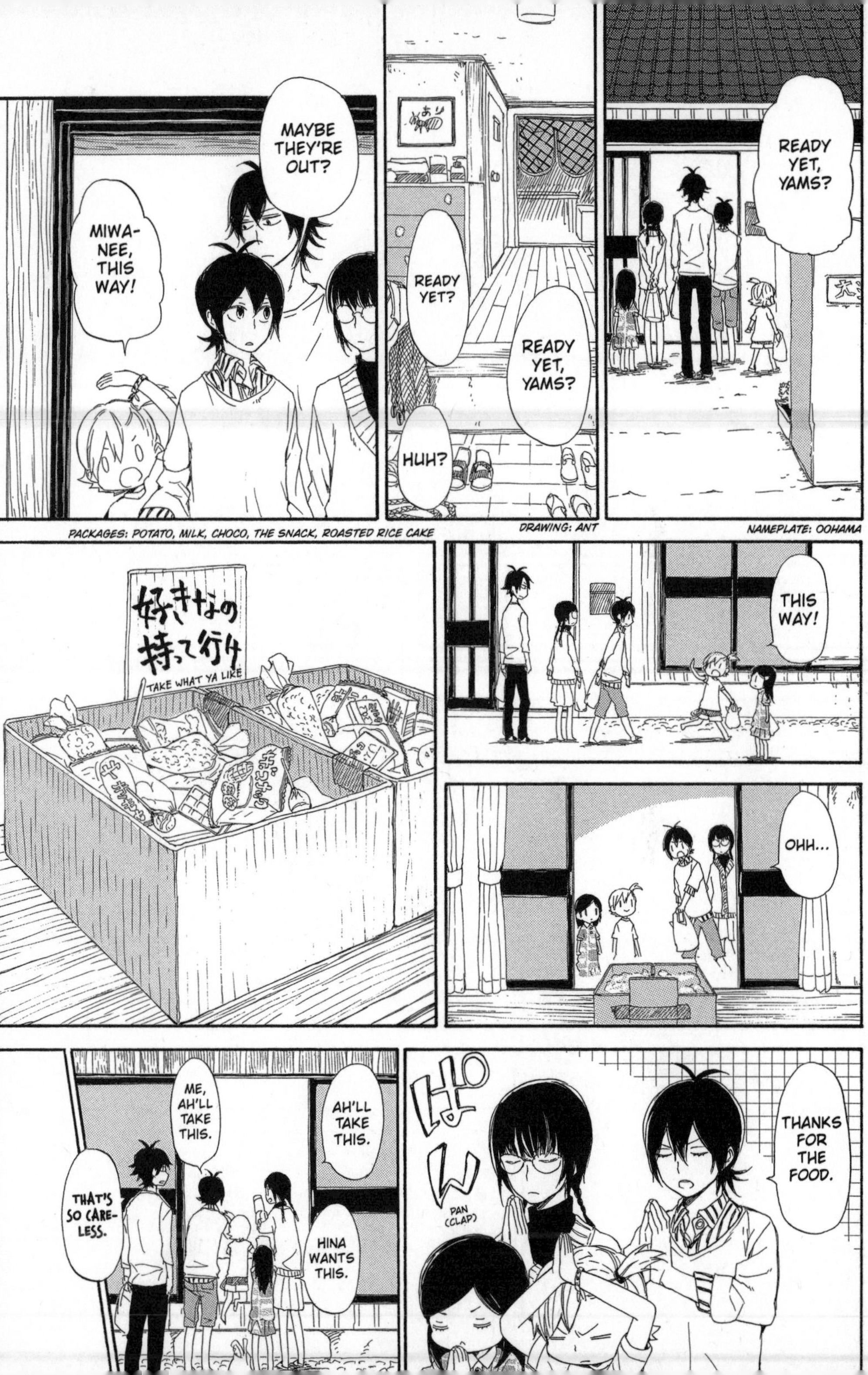
READY YET, YAMS?
READY YET, YAMS?
READY YET?
HUH?
MAYBE THEY'RE OUT?
MIWA-NEE, THIS WAY!
NAMEPLATE: OOHAMA
DRAWING: ANT
PACKAGES: POTATO, MILK, CHOCO, THE SNACK, ROASTED RICE CAKE
THIS WAY!
OHH...
好きなの持って行け
TAKE WHAT YA LIKE
THANKS FOR THE FOOD.
ぱん
PAN (CLAP)
AH'LL TAKE THIS.
ME, AH'LL TAKE THIS.
HINA WANTS THIS.
THAT'S SO CARE-LESS.

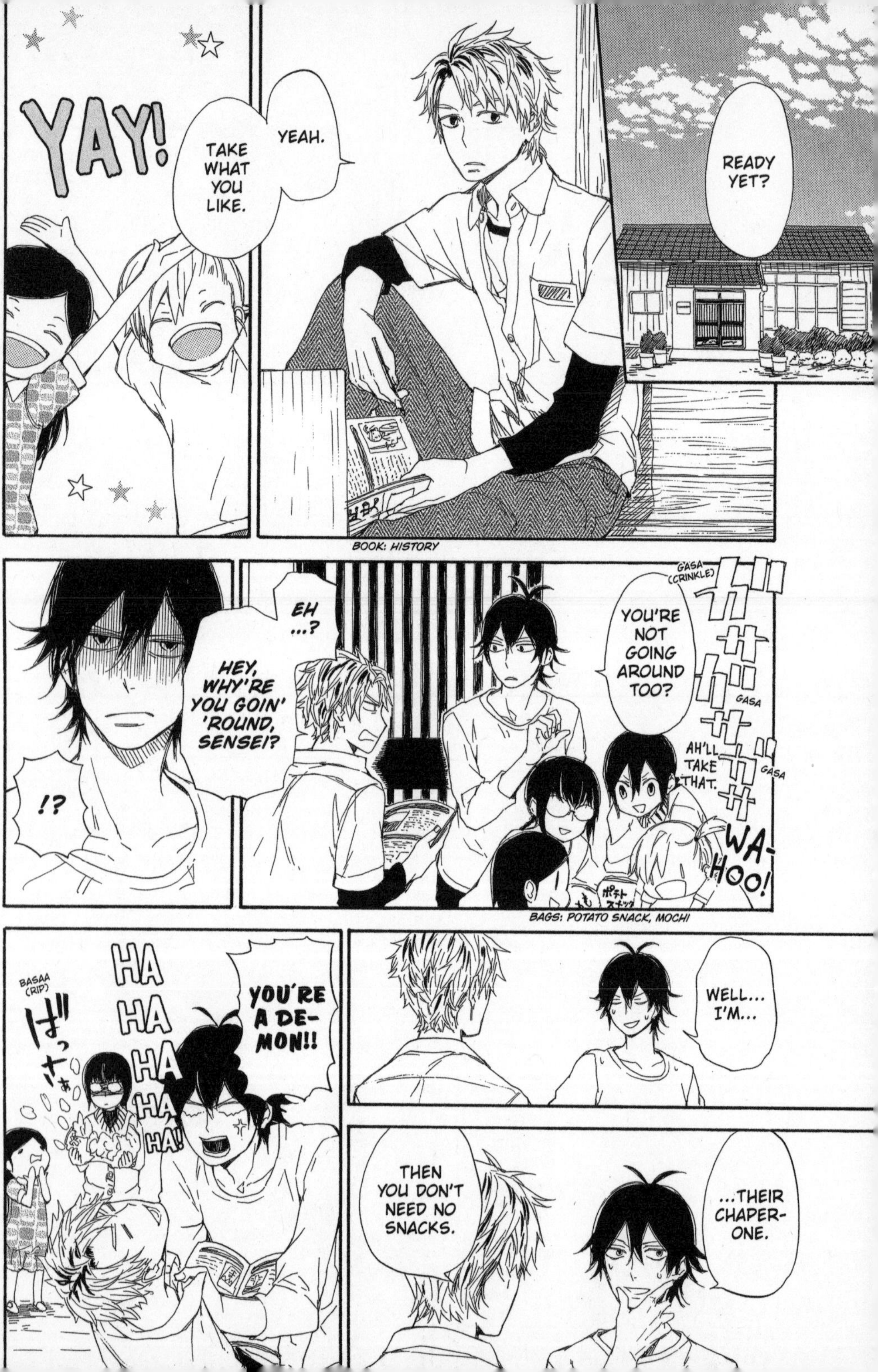
READY YET?
YEAH.
TAKE WHAT YOU LIKE.
YAY!
BOOK: HISTORY
GASA (CRINKLE)
YOU'RE NOT GOING AROUND TOO?
GASA
GASA
AH'LL TAKE THAT.
WA-HOO!
EH ...?
HEY, WHY'RE YOU GOIN' 'ROUND, SENSEI?
BAGS: POTATO SNACK, MOCHI
!?
WELL... I'M...
...THEIR CHAPER-ONE.
THEN YOU DON'T NEED NO SNACKS.
YOU'RE A DE-MON!!
HA HA HA HA HA!
BASAA (RIP)

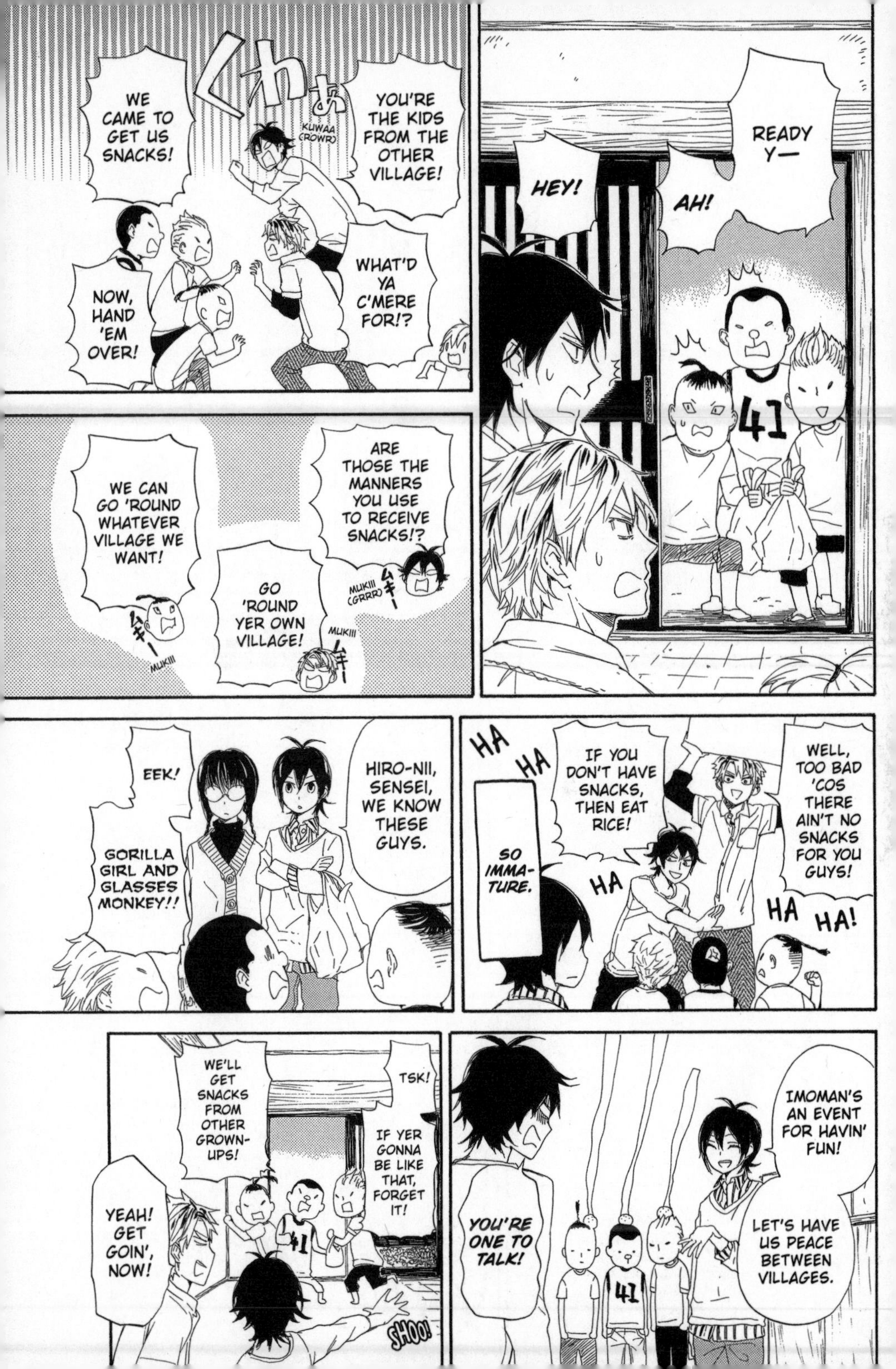
READY Y—
AH!
HEY!
YOU'RE THE KIDS FROM THE OTHER VILLAGE!
くわぁ
KUWAA (ROWR)
WE CAME TO GET US SNACKS!
WHAT'D YA C'MERE FOR!?
NOW, HAND 'EM OVER!
ARE THOSE THE MANNERS YOU USE TO RECEIVE SNACKS!?
ムキー
MUKIII (GRRR)
GO 'ROUND YER OWN VILLAGE!
ムキー
MUKIII
WE CAN GO 'ROUND WHATEVER VILLAGE WE WANT!
ムキー
MUKIII
WELL, TOO BAD 'COS THERE AIN'T NO SNACKS FOR YOU GUYS!
IF YOU DON'T HAVE SNACKS, THEN EAT RICE!
HA HA
SO IMMATURE.
HA
HA HA!
HIRO-NII, SENSEI, WE KNOW THESE GUYS.
EEK!
GORILLA GIRL AND GLASSES MONKEY!!
IMOMAN'S AN EVENT FOR HAVIN' FUN!
LET'S HAVE US PEACE BETWEEN VILLAGES.
YOU'RE ONE TO TALK!
TSK!
IF YER GONNA BE LIKE THAT, FORGET IT!
WE'LL GET SNACKS FROM OTHER GROWN-UPS!
YEAH! GET GOIN', NOW!
SHOO!

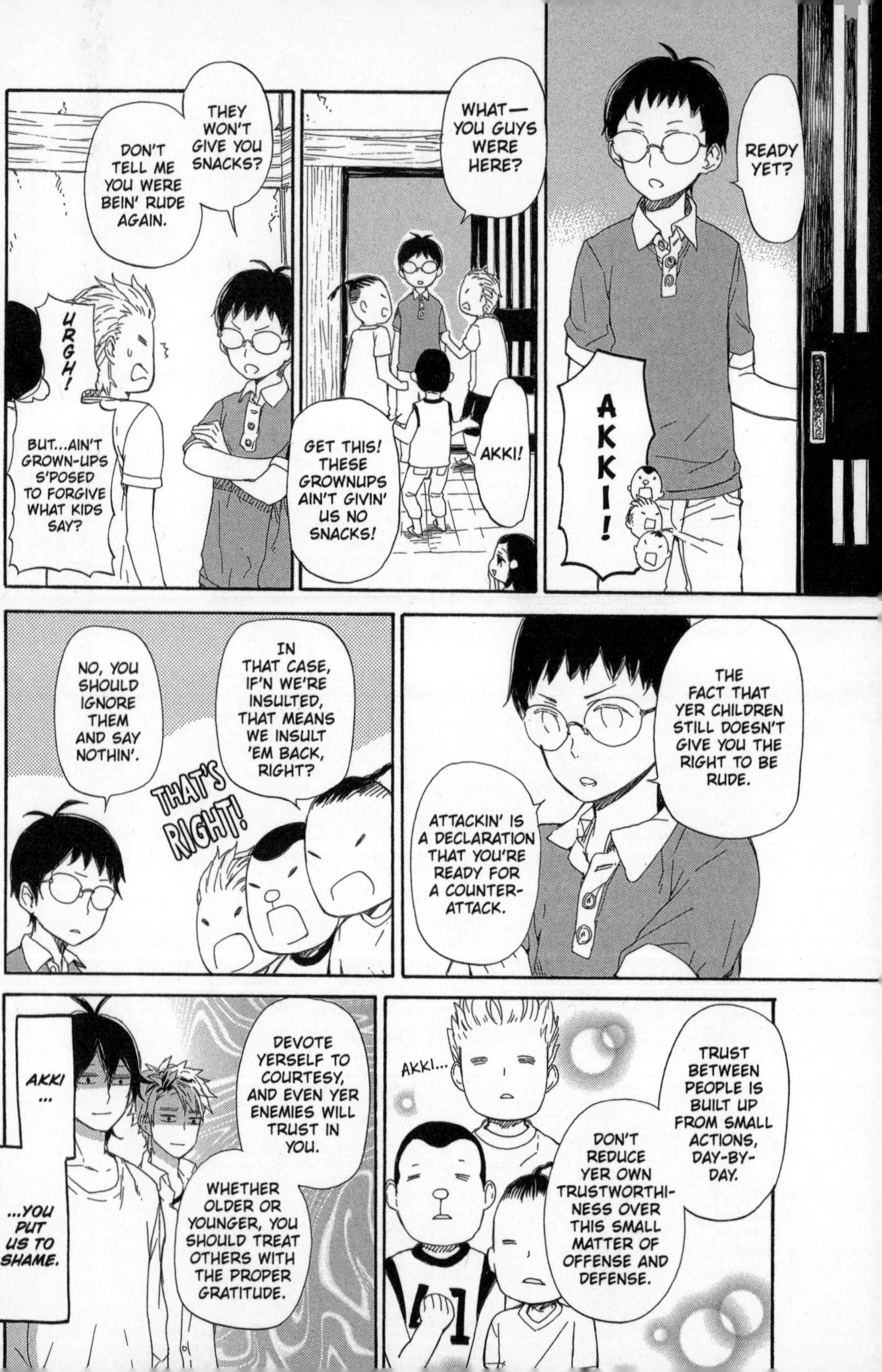
READY YET?
AKKI!
WHAT— YOU GUYS WERE HERE?
AKKI!
GET THIS! THESE GROWNUPS AIN'T GIVIN' US NO SNACKS!
THEY WON'T GIVE YOU SNACKS?
DON'T TELL ME YOU WERE BEIN' RUDE AGAIN.
URGH!
BUT...AIN'T GROWN-UPS S'POSED TO FORGIVE WHAT KIDS SAY?
THE FACT THAT YER CHILDREN STILL DOESN'T GIVE YOU THE RIGHT TO BE RUDE.
ATTACKIN' IS A DECLARATION THAT YOU'RE READY FOR A COUNTER-ATTACK.
IN THAT CASE, IF'N WE'RE INSULTED, THAT MEANS WE INSULT 'EM BACK, RIGHT?
THAT'S RIGHT!
NO, YOU SHOULD IGNORE THEM AND SAY NOTHIN'.
TRUST BETWEEN PEOPLE IS BUILT UP FROM SMALL ACTIONS, DAY-BY-DAY.
DON'T REDUCE YER OWN TRUSTWORTHINESS OVER THIS SMALL MATTER OF OFFENSE AND DEFENSE.
AKKI...
DEVOTE YERSELF TO COURTESY, AND EVEN YER ENEMIES WILL TRUST IN YOU.
WHETHER OLDER OR YOUNGER, YOU SHOULD TREAT OTHERS WITH THE PROPER GRATITUDE.
AKKI...
...YOU PUT US TO SHAME.

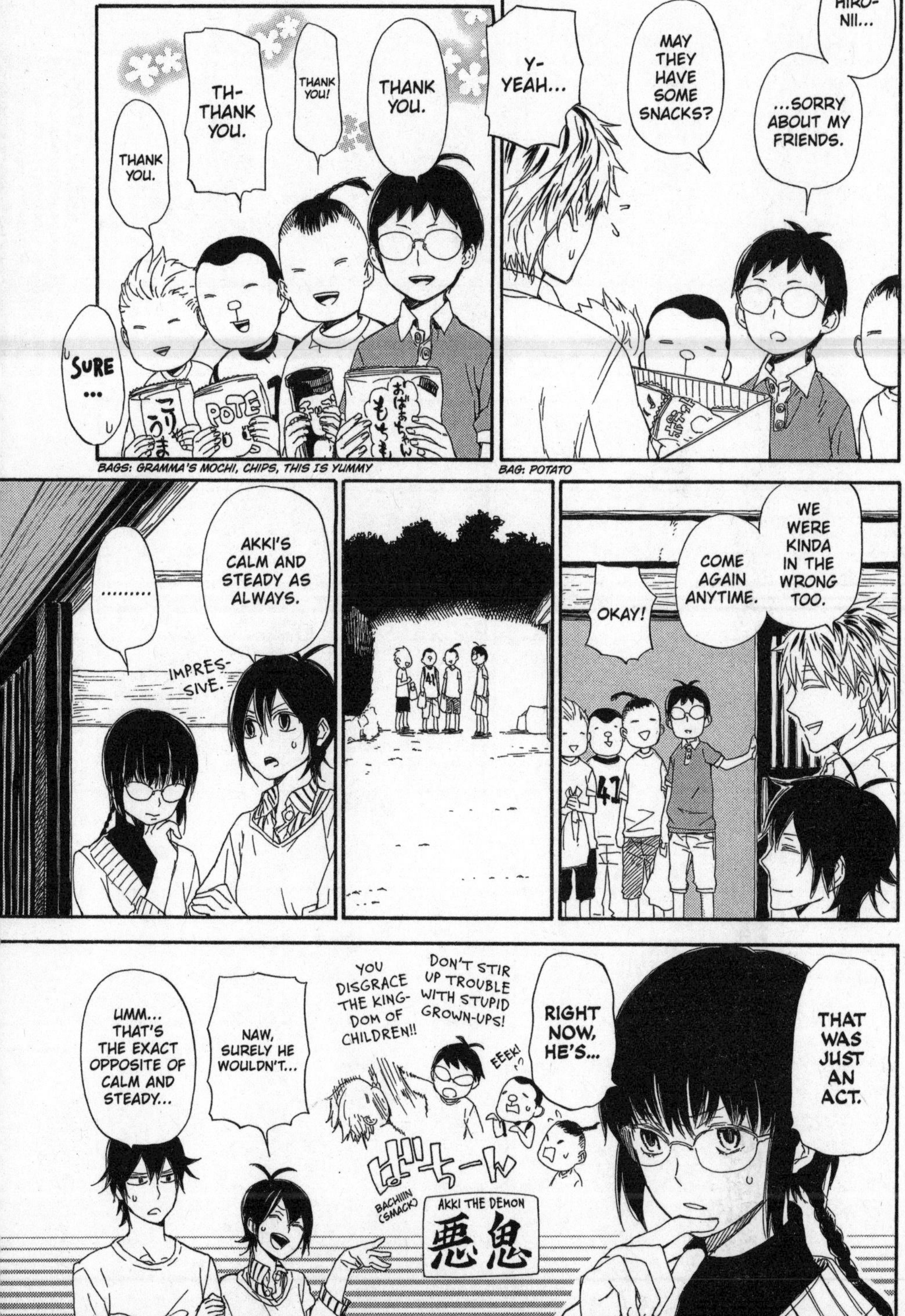
HIRO-NII...
...SORRY ABOUT MY FRIENDS.
MAY THEY HAVE SOME SNACKS?
Y-YEAH...
BAG: POTATO
THANK YOU.
THANK YOU!
TH-THANK YOU.
THANK YOU.
SURE...
POTE
BAGS: GRAMMA'S MOCHI, CHIPS, THIS IS YUMMY
WE WERE KINDA IN THE WRONG TOO.
COME AGAIN ANYTIME.
OKAY!
AKKI'S CALM AND STEADY AS ALWAYS.
IMPRESSIVE.
....
THAT WAS JUST AN ACT.
RIGHT NOW, HE'S...
DON'T STIR UP TROUBLE WITH STUPID GROWN-UPS!
YOU DISGRACE THE KINGDOM OF CHILDREN!!
EEEK!
ぱちーん
BACHIIIN (SMACK)
AKKI THE DEMON
悪鬼
NAW, SURELY HE WOULDN'T...
UMM... THAT'S THE EXACT OPPOSITE OF CALM AND STEADY...

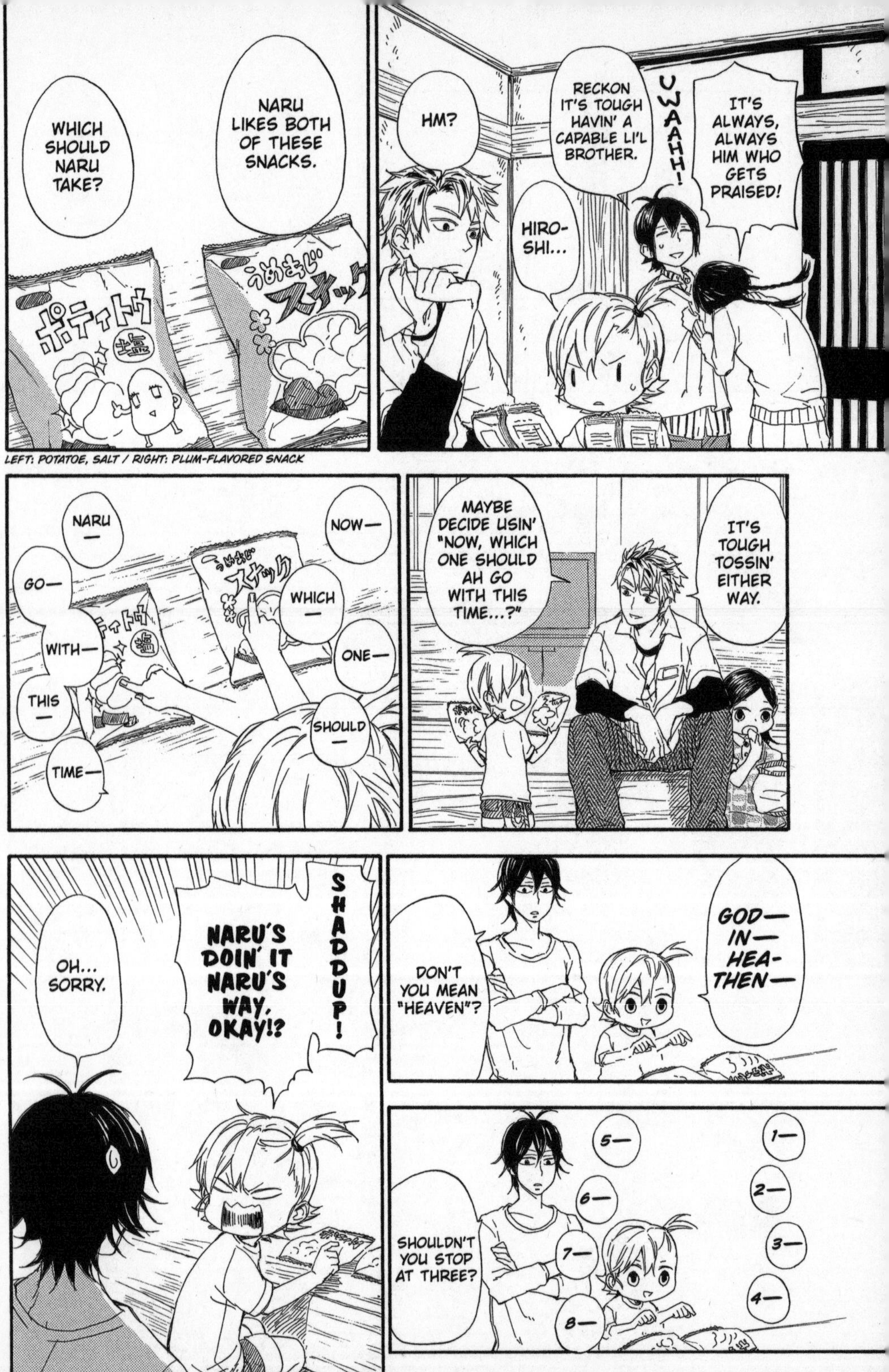
IT'S ALWAYS, ALWAYS HIM WHO GETS PRAISED!
UWAAHH!
RECKON IT'S TOUGH HAVIN' A CAPABLE LI'L BROTHER.
HIRO-SHI...
HM?
NARU LIKES BOTH OF THESE SNACKS.
WHICH SHOULD NARU TAKE?
LEFT: POTATOE, SALT / RIGHT: PLUM-FLAVORED SNACK
IT'S TOUGH TOSSIN' EITHER WAY.
MAYBE DECIDE USIN' "NOW, WHICH ONE SHOULD AH GO WITH THIS TIME...?"
NOW—
WHICH—
ONE—
SHOULD—
NARU—
GO—
WITH—
THIS—
TIME—
GOD—IN—HEA-THEN—
DON'T YOU MEAN "HEAVEN"?
1—
2—
3—
4—
5—
6—
7—
8—
SHOULDN'T YOU STOP AT THREE?
SHADDUP!
NARU'S DOIN' IT NARU'S WAY, OKAY!?
OH... SORRY.

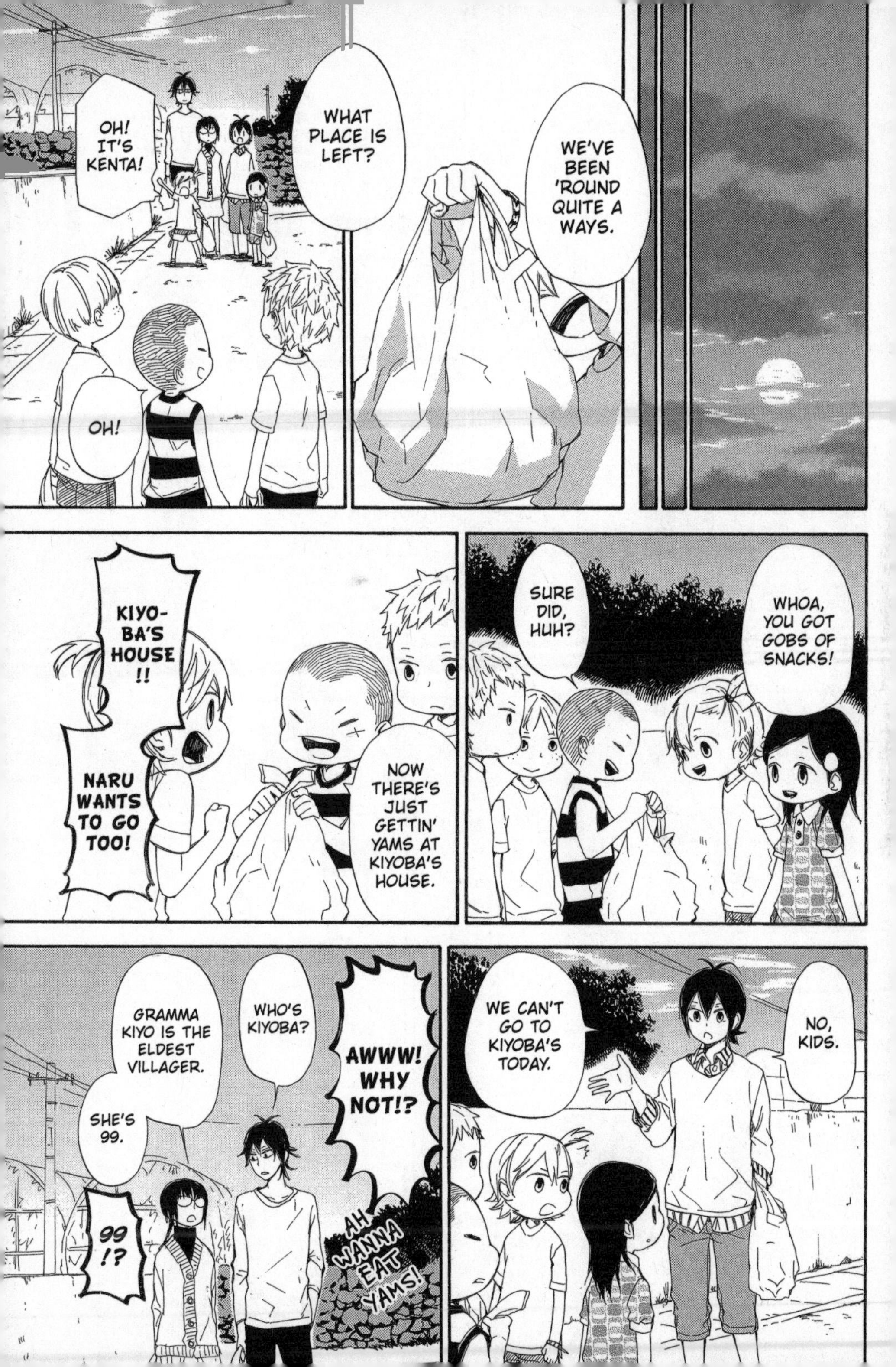
WE'VE BEEN 'ROUND QUITE A WAYS.
WHAT PLACE IS LEFT?
OH! IT'S KENTA!
OH!
WHOA, YOU GOT GOBS OF SNACKS!
SURE DID, HUH?
NOW THERE'S JUST GETTIN' YAMS AT KIYOBA'S HOUSE.
KIYOBA'S HOUSE!!
NARU WANTS TO GO TOO!
NO, KIDS.
WE CAN'T GO TO KIYOBA'S TODAY.
AWWW! WHY NOT!?
AH WANNA EAT YAMS!
WHO'S KIYOBA?
GRAMMA KIYO IS THE ELDEST VILLAGER.
SHE'S 99.
99!?

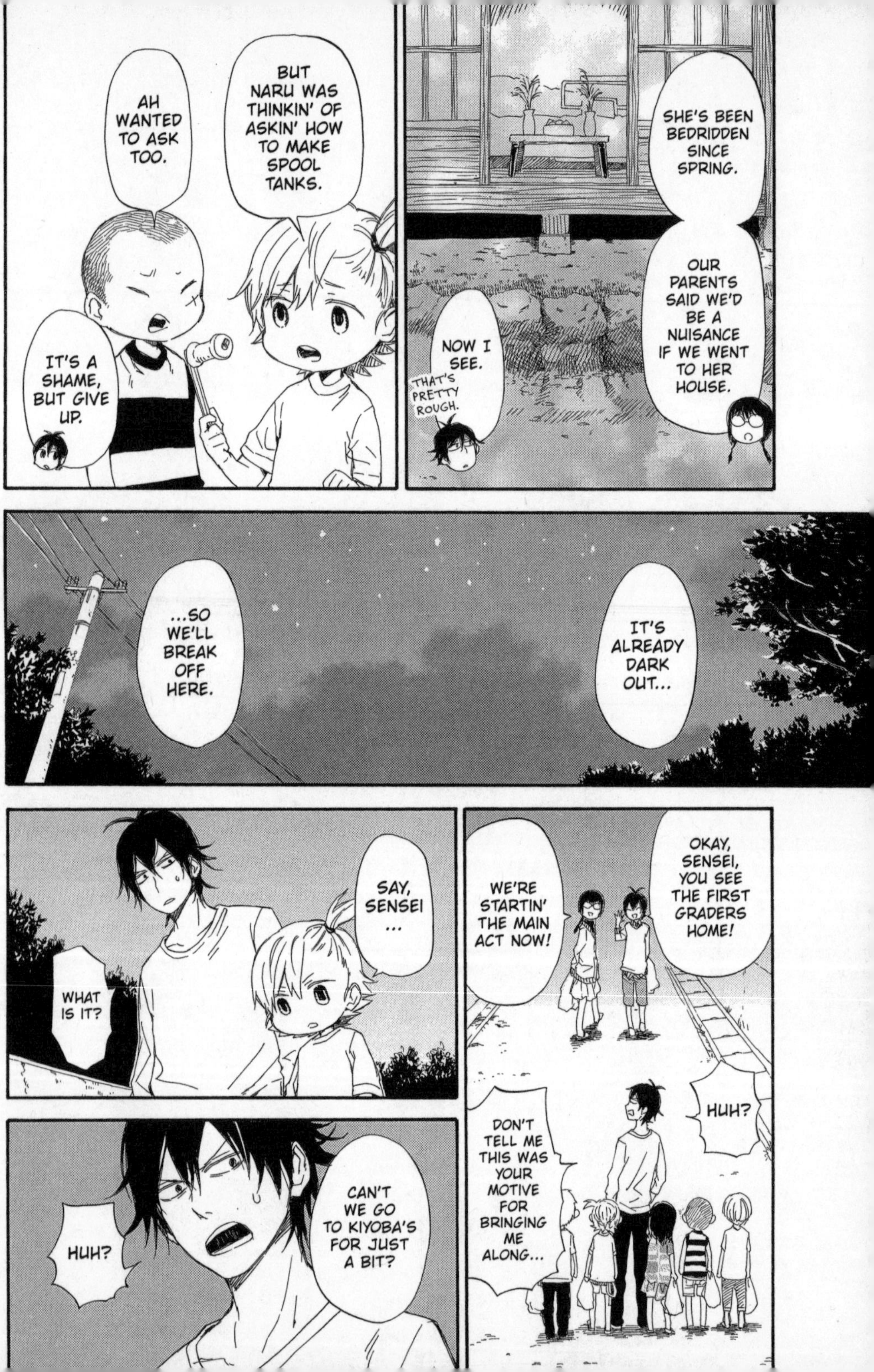
SHE'S BEEN BEDRIDDEN SINCE SPRING.
OUR PARENTS SAID WE'D BE A NUISANCE IF WE WENT TO HER HOUSE.
NOW I SEE.
THAT'S PRETTY ROUGH.
BUT NARU WAS THINKIN' OF ASKIN' HOW TO MAKE SPOOL TANKS.
AH WANTED TO ASK TOO.
IT'S A SHAME, BUT GIVE UP.
IT'S ALREADY DARK OUT...
...SO WE'LL BREAK OFF HERE.
OKAY, SENSEI, YOU SEE THE FIRST GRADERS HOME!
WE'RE STARTIN' THE MAIN ACT NOW!
HUH?
DON'T TELL ME THIS WAS YOUR MOTIVE FOR BRINGING ME ALONG...
SAY, SENSEI...
WHAT IS IT?
CAN'T WE GO TO KIYOBA'S FOR JUST A BIT?
HUH?

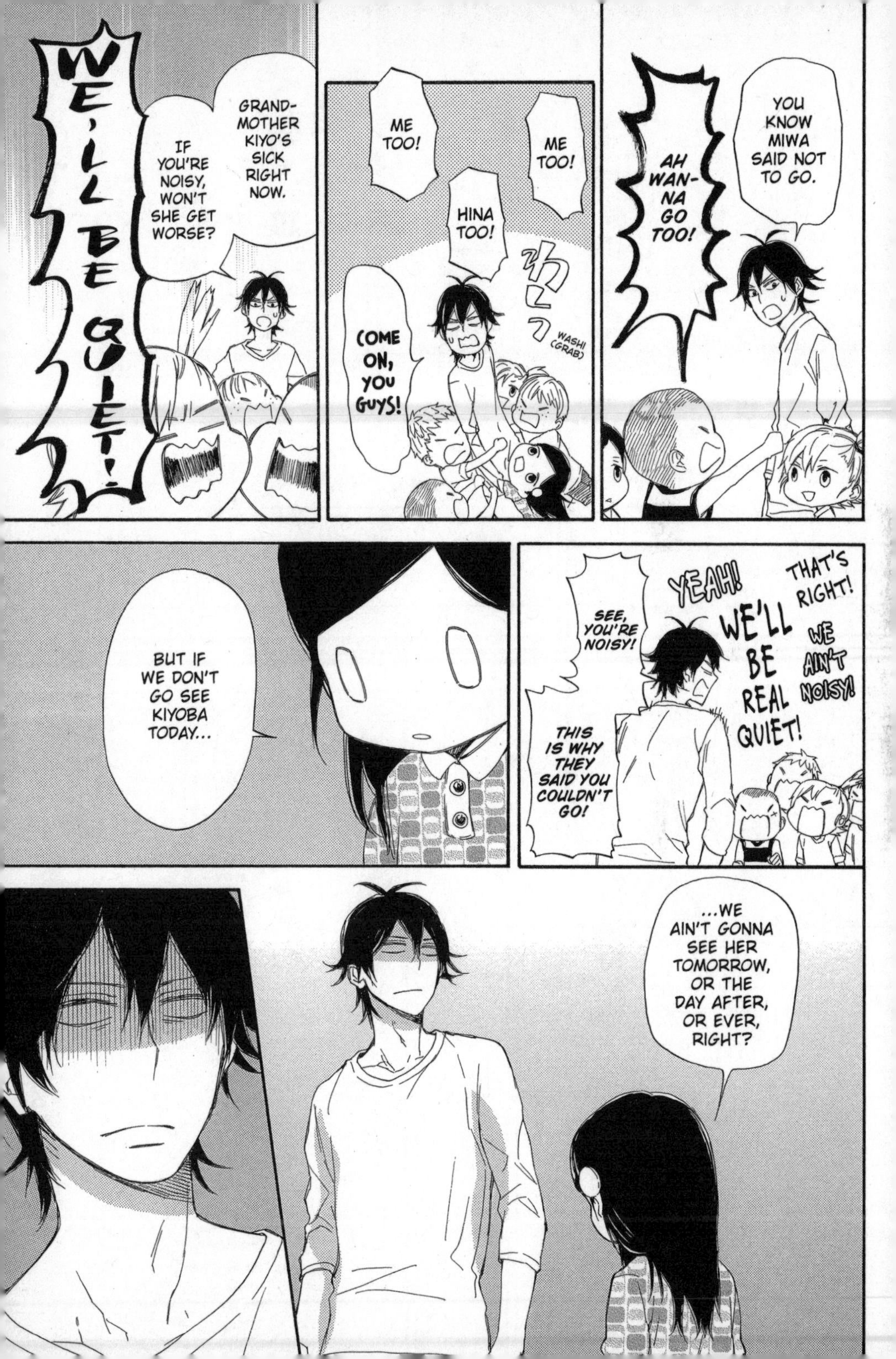
YOU KNOW MIWA SAID NOT TO GO.
AH WANNA GO TOO!
ME TOO!
ME TOO!
HINA TOO!
WASHI (GRAB)
COME ON, YOU GUYS!
GRANDMOTHER KIYO'S SICK RIGHT NOW.
IF YOU'RE NOISY, WON'T SHE GET WORSE?
WE-LL BE QUIET!
THAT'S RIGHT!
YEAH!
WE AIN'T NOISY!
WE'LL BE REAL QUIET!
SEE, YOU'RE NOISY!
THIS IS WHY THEY SAID YOU COULDN'T GO!
BUT IF WE DON'T GO SEE KIYOBA TODAY...
...WE AIN'T GONNA SEE HER TOMORROW, OR THE DAY AFTER, OR EVER, RIGHT?

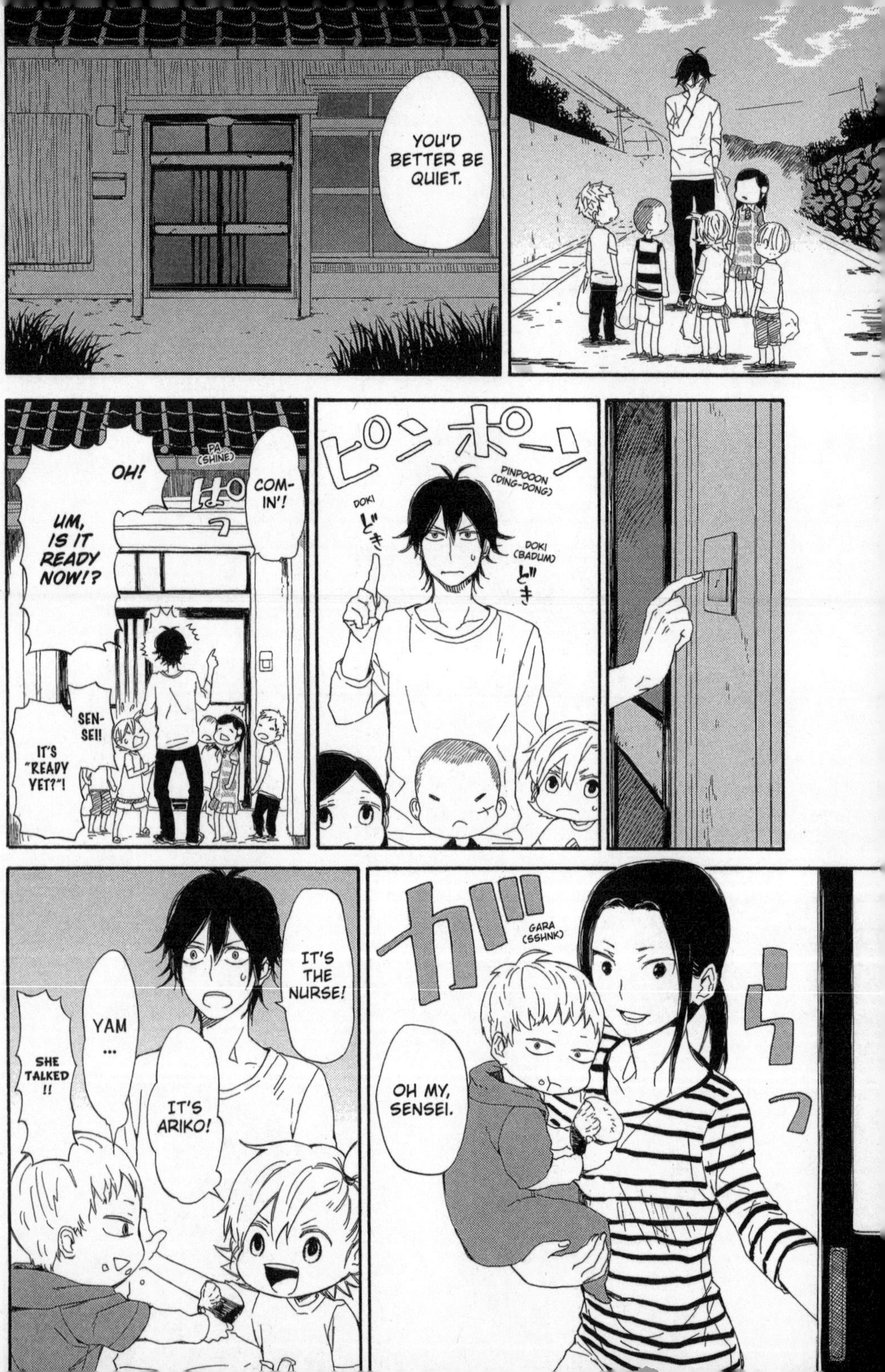

YOU'D BETTER BE QUIET.
PINPOOON (DING-DONG)
DOKI
DOKI (BADUM)
COM-IN'!
PA (SHINE)
OH!
UM, IS IT READY NOW!?
SEN-SEI!
IT'S "READY YET?"!
GARA (SSHNK)
OH MY, SENSEI.
IT'S THE NURSE!
YAM...
IT'S ARIKO!
SHE TALKED!!

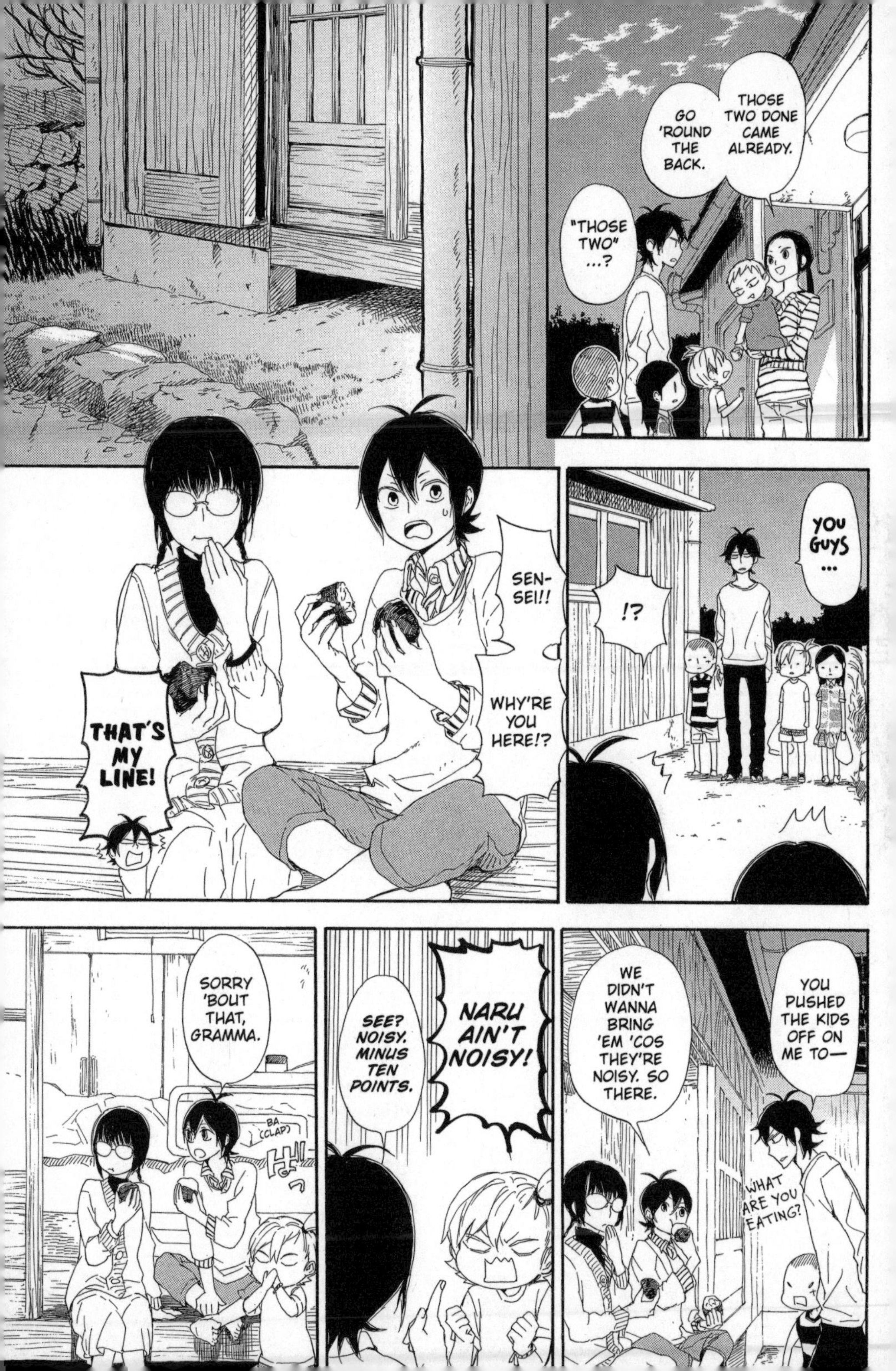
THOSE TWO DONE CAME ALREADY.
GO 'ROUND THE BACK.
"THOSE TWO" ...?
YOU GUYS ...
!?
SEN-SEI!!
WHY'RE YOU HERE!?
THAT'S MY LINE!
YOU PUSHED THE KIDS OFF ON ME TO—
WHAT ARE YOU EATING?
WE DIDN'T WANNA BRING 'EM 'COS THEY'RE NOISY. SO THERE.
NARU AIN'T NOISY!
SEE? NOISY. MINUS TEN POINTS.
SORRY 'BOUT THAT, GRAMMA.
BA (CLAP)

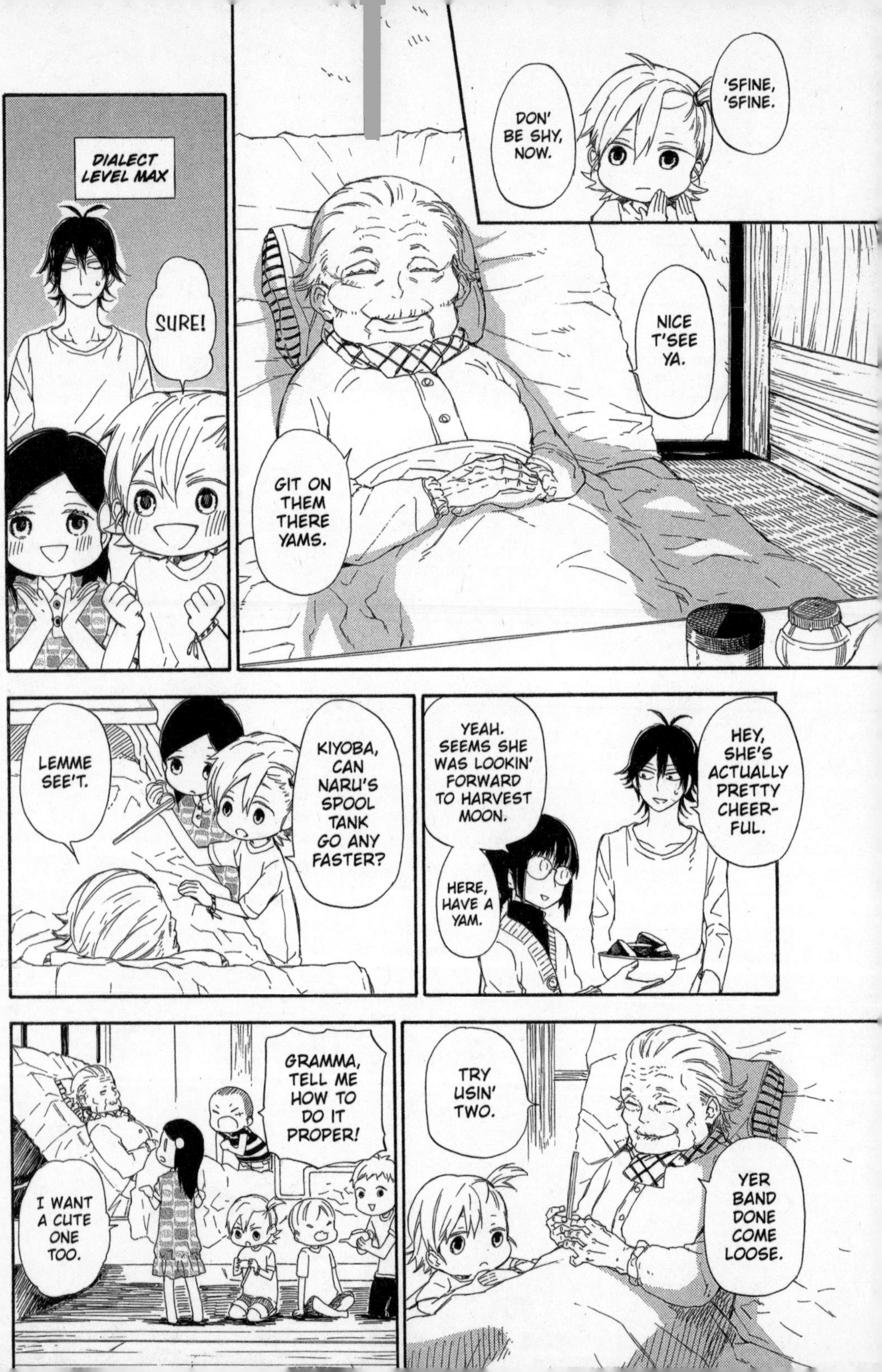
'SFINE, 'SFINE.
DON' BE SHY, NOW.
NICE T'SEE YA.
GIT ON THEM THERE YAMS.
DIALECT LEVEL MAX
SURE!
HEY, SHE'S ACTUALLY PRETTY CHEERFUL.
YEAH. SEEMS SHE WAS LOOKIN' FORWARD TO HARVEST MOON.
HERE, HAVE A YAM.
KIYOBA, CAN NARU'S SPOOL TANK GO ANY FASTER?
LEMME SEE'T.
TRY USIN' TWO.
YER BAND DONE COME LOOSE.
GRAMMA, TELL ME HOW TO DO IT PROPER!
I WANT A CUTE ONE TOO.

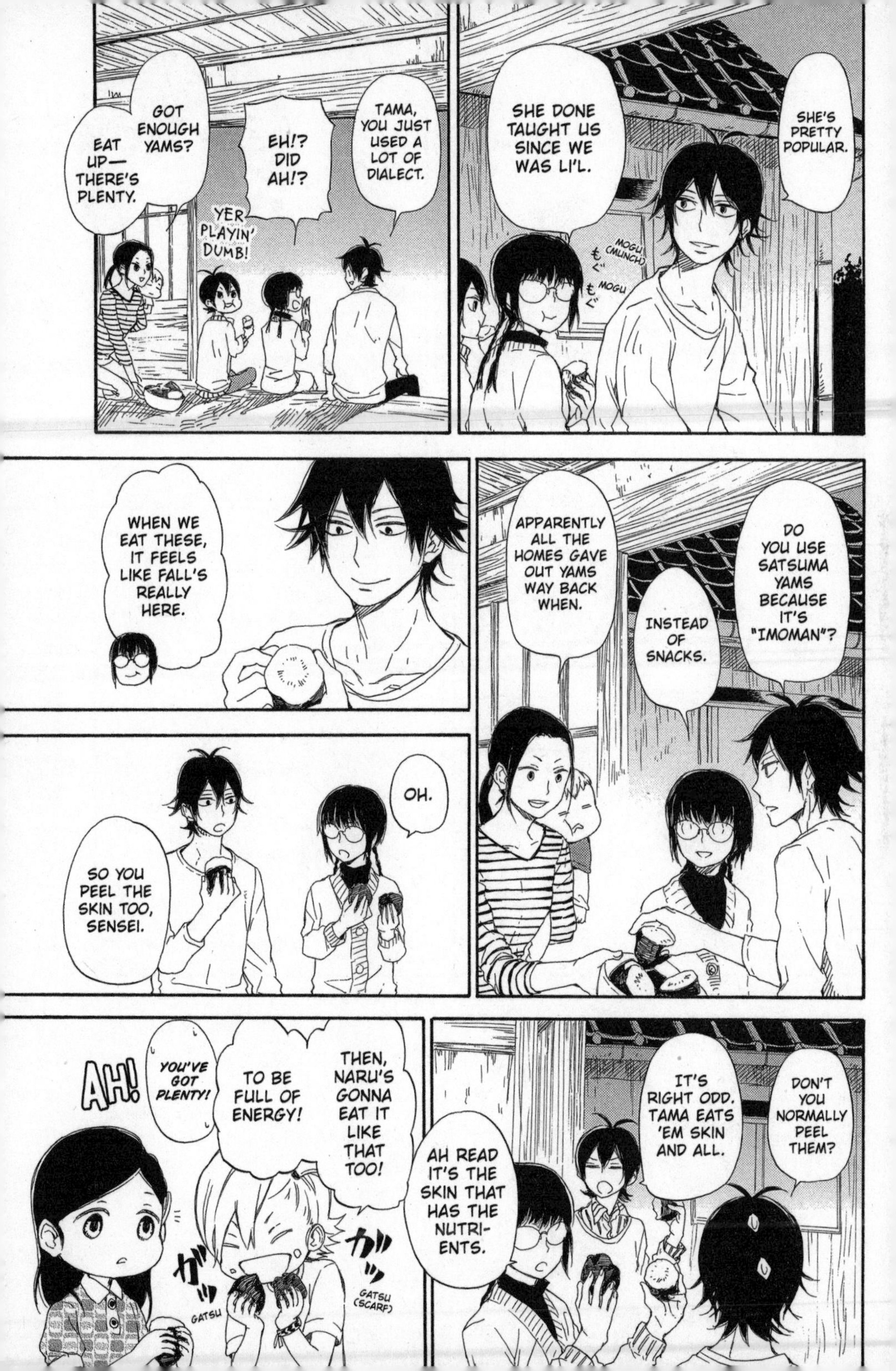
SHE'S PRETTY POPULAR.
SHE DONE TAUGHT US SINCE WE WAS LI'L.
MOGU (MUNCH)
MOGU
TAMA, YOU JUST USED A LOT OF DIALECT.
EH!? DID AH!?
YER PLAYIN' DUMB!
GOT ENOUGH YAMS?
EAT UP— THERE'S PLENTY.
DO YOU USE SATSUMA YAMS BECAUSE IT'S "IMOMAN"?
APPARENTLY ALL THE HOMES GAVE OUT YAMS WAY BACK WHEN.
INSTEAD OF SNACKS.
WHEN WE EAT THESE, IT FEELS LIKE FALL'S REALLY HERE.
OH.
SO YOU PEEL THE SKIN TOO, SENSEI.
DON'T YOU NORMALLY PEEL THEM?
IT'S RIGHT ODD. TAMA EATS 'EM SKIN AND ALL.
AH READ IT'S THE SKIN THAT HAS THE NUTRI-ENTS.
THEN, NARU'S GONNA EAT IT LIKE THAT TOO!
TO BE FULL OF ENERGY!
YOU'VE GOT PLENTY!
AH!
GATSU (SCARF)
GATSU

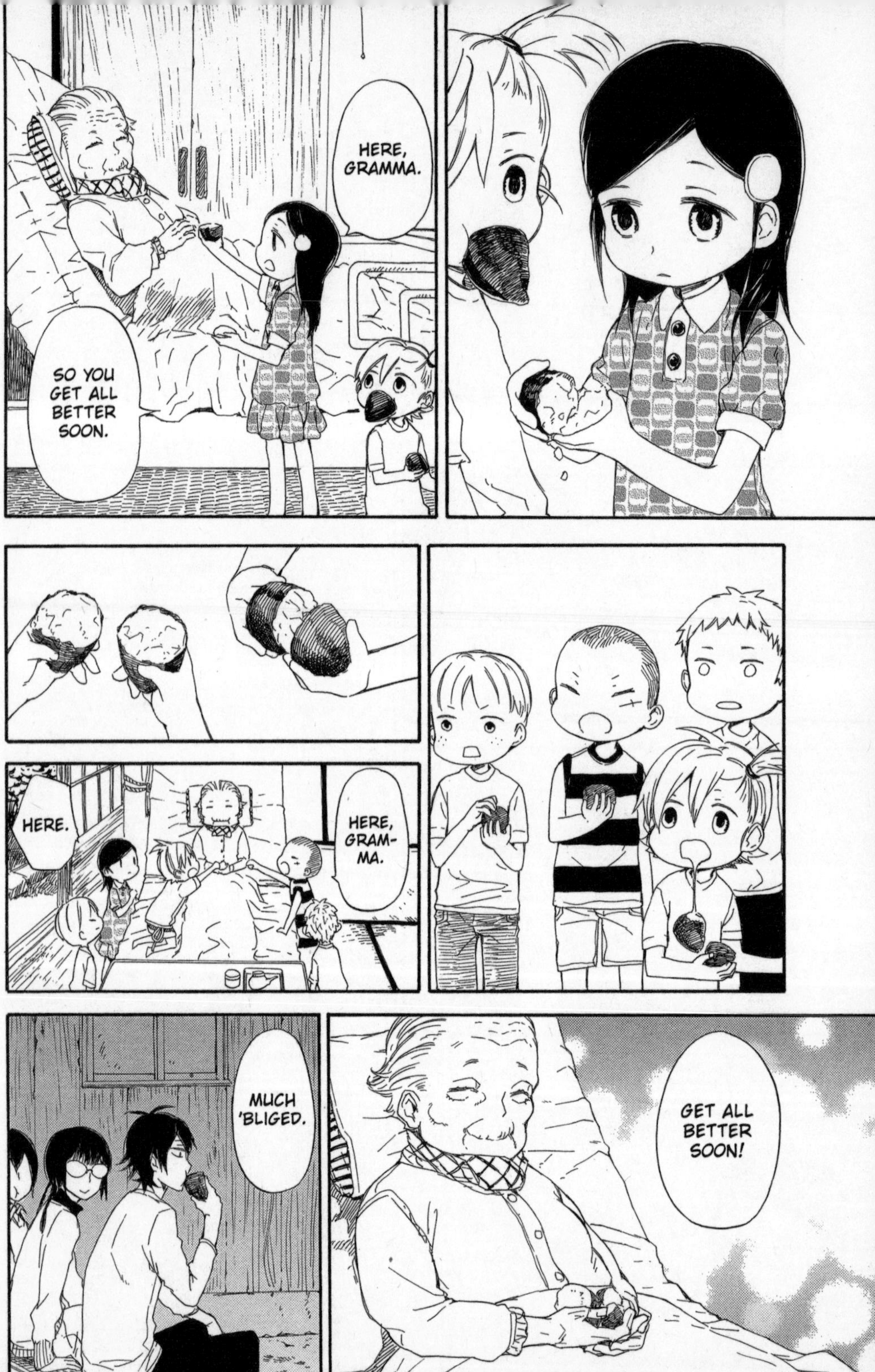
HERE, GRAMMA.
SO YOU GET ALL BETTER SOON.
HERE, GRAM-MA.
HERE.
GET ALL BETTER SOON!
MUCH 'BLIGED.

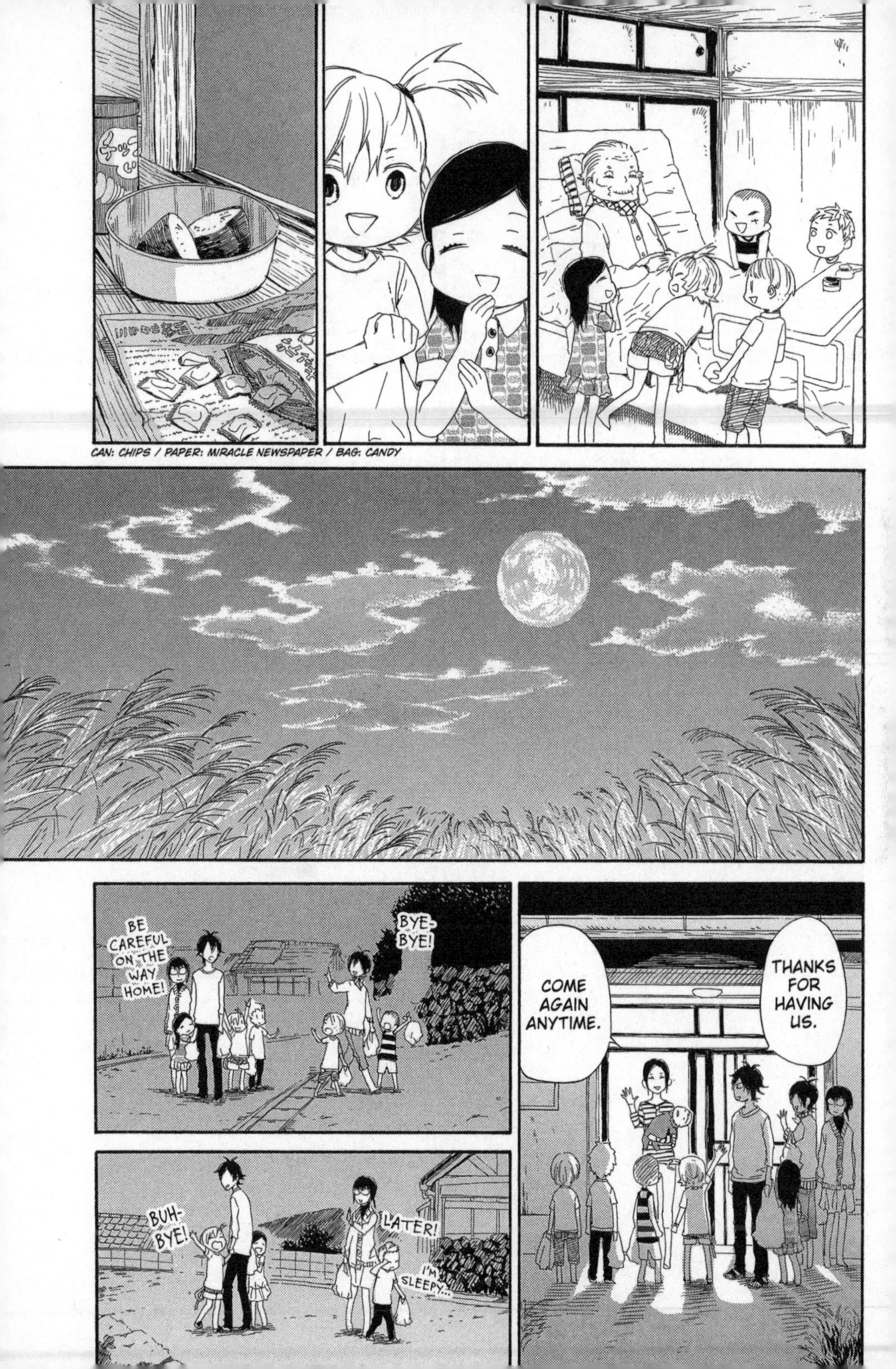
CAN: CHIPS / PAPER: MIRACLE NEWSPAPER / BAG: CANDY
THANKS FOR HAVING US.
COME AGAIN ANYTIME.
BYE-BYE!
BE CAREFUL ON THE WAY HOME!
I'M SLEEPY...
LATER!
BUH-BYE!

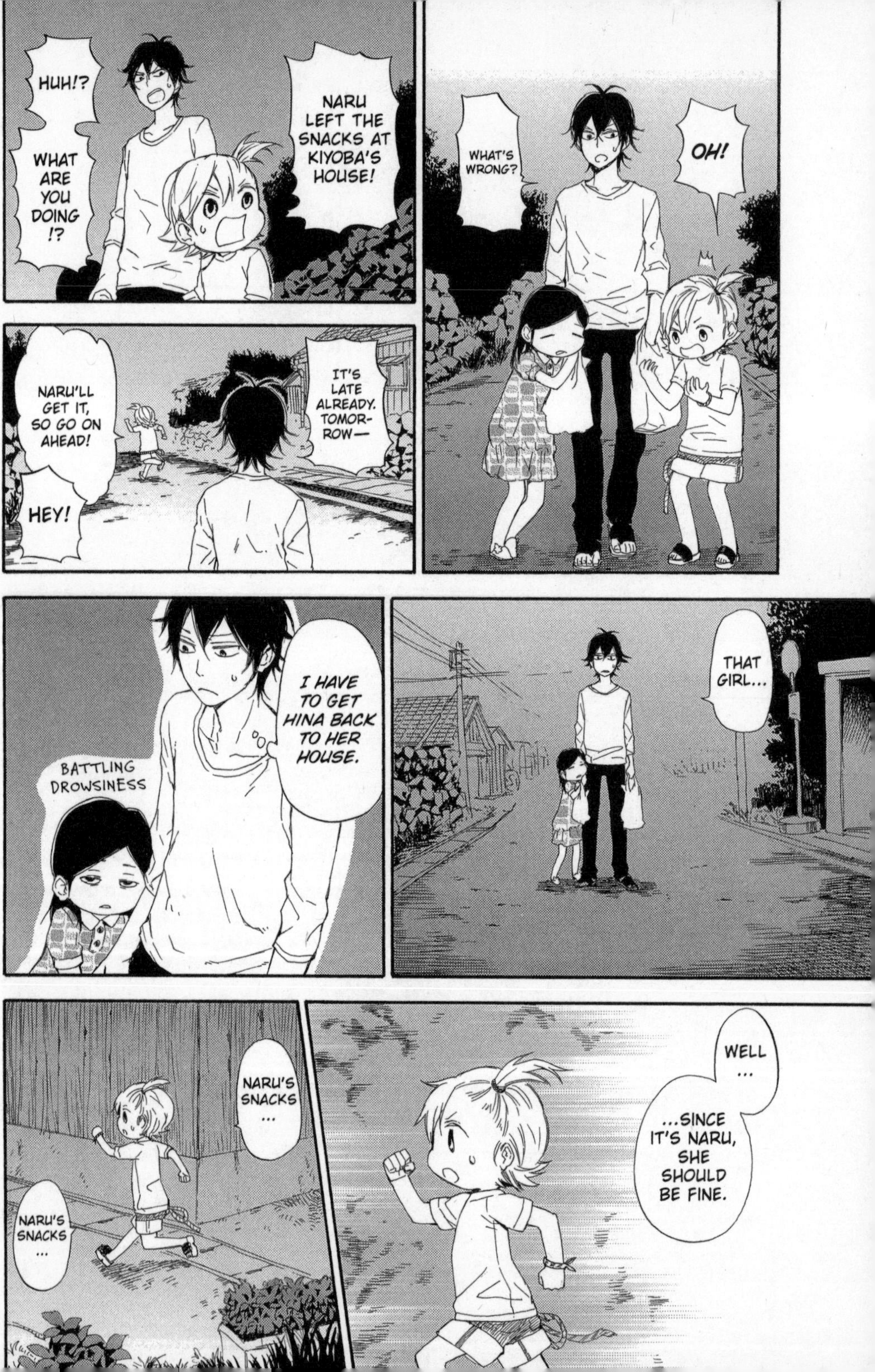
OH!
WHAT'S WRONG?
NARU LEFT THE SNACKS AT KIYOBA'S HOUSE!
HUH!?
WHAT ARE YOU DOING!?
IT'S LATE ALREADY. TOMORROW—
NARU'LL GET IT, SO GO ON AHEAD!
HEY!
THAT GIRL...
I HAVE TO GET HINA BACK TO HER HOUSE.
BATTLING DROWSINESS
WELL...
...SINCE IT'S NARU, SHE SHOULD BE FINE.
NARU'S SNACKS...
NARU'S SNACKS...

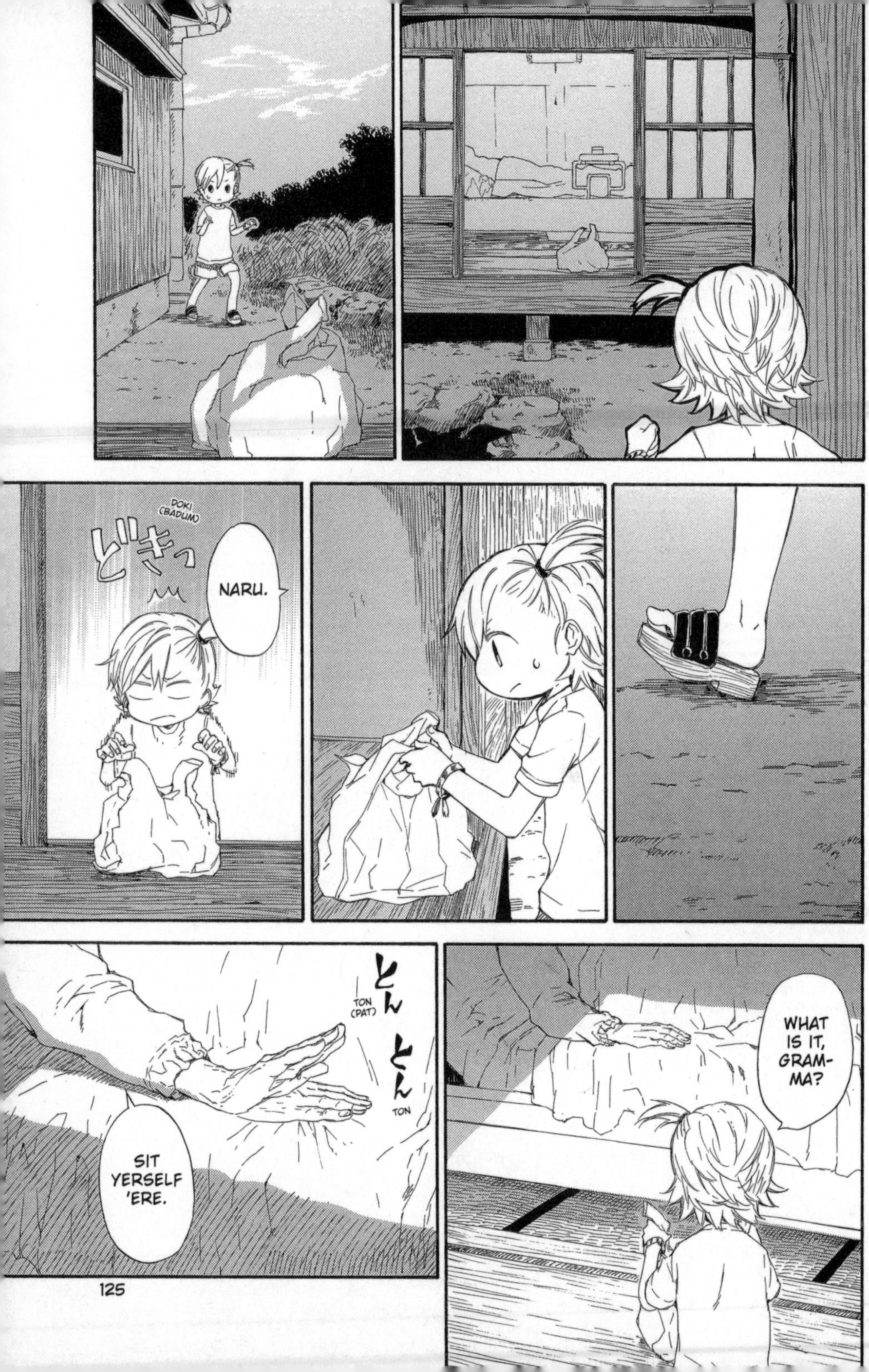

どきっ
DOKI (BADUM)
NARU.
WHAT IS IT, GRAMMA?
とん
TON (PAT)
とん
TON
SIT YERSELF 'ERE.

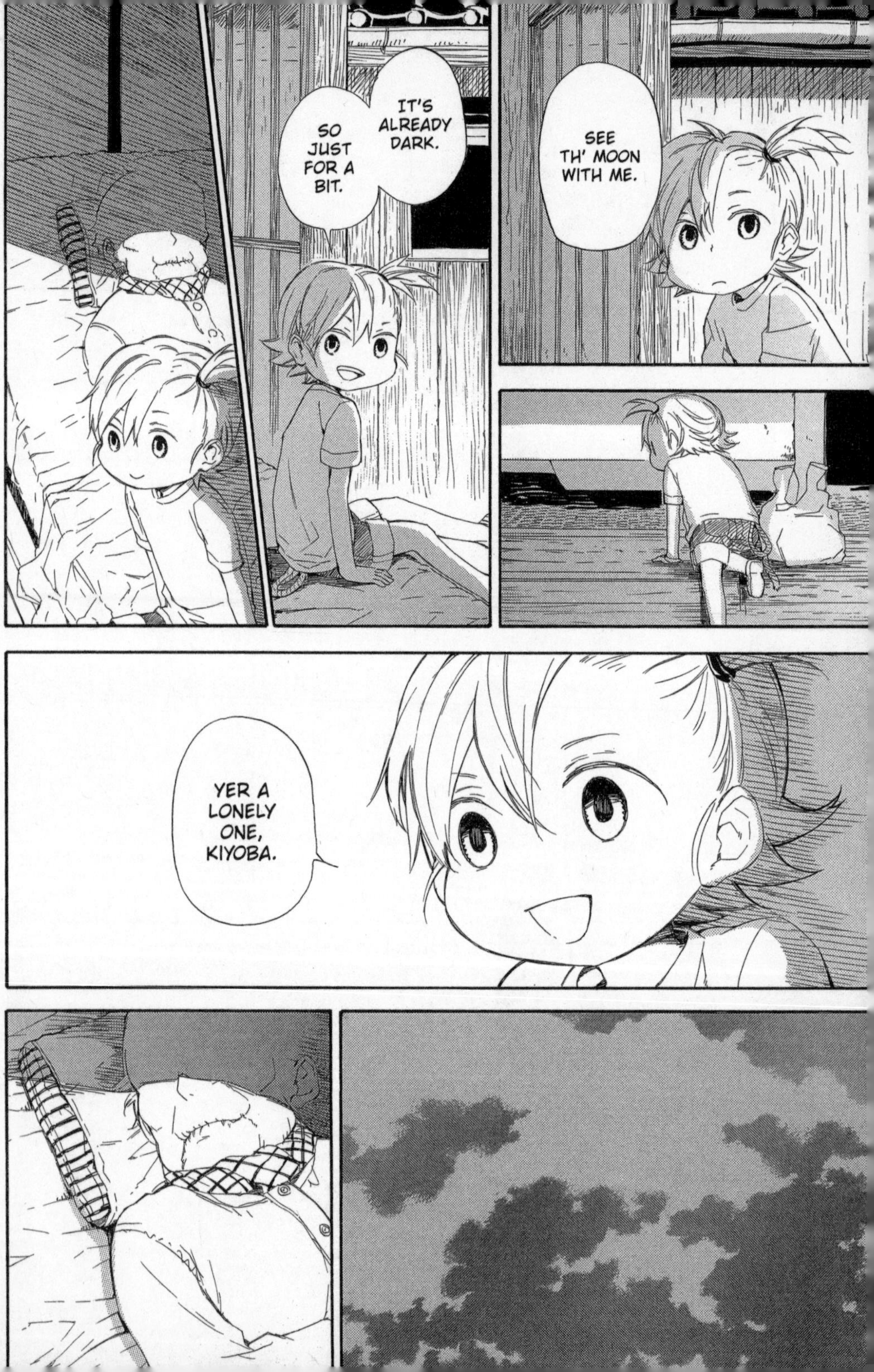
SEE TH' MOON WITH ME.
IT'S ALREADY DARK.
SO JUST FOR A BIT.
YER A LONELY ONE, KIYOBA.

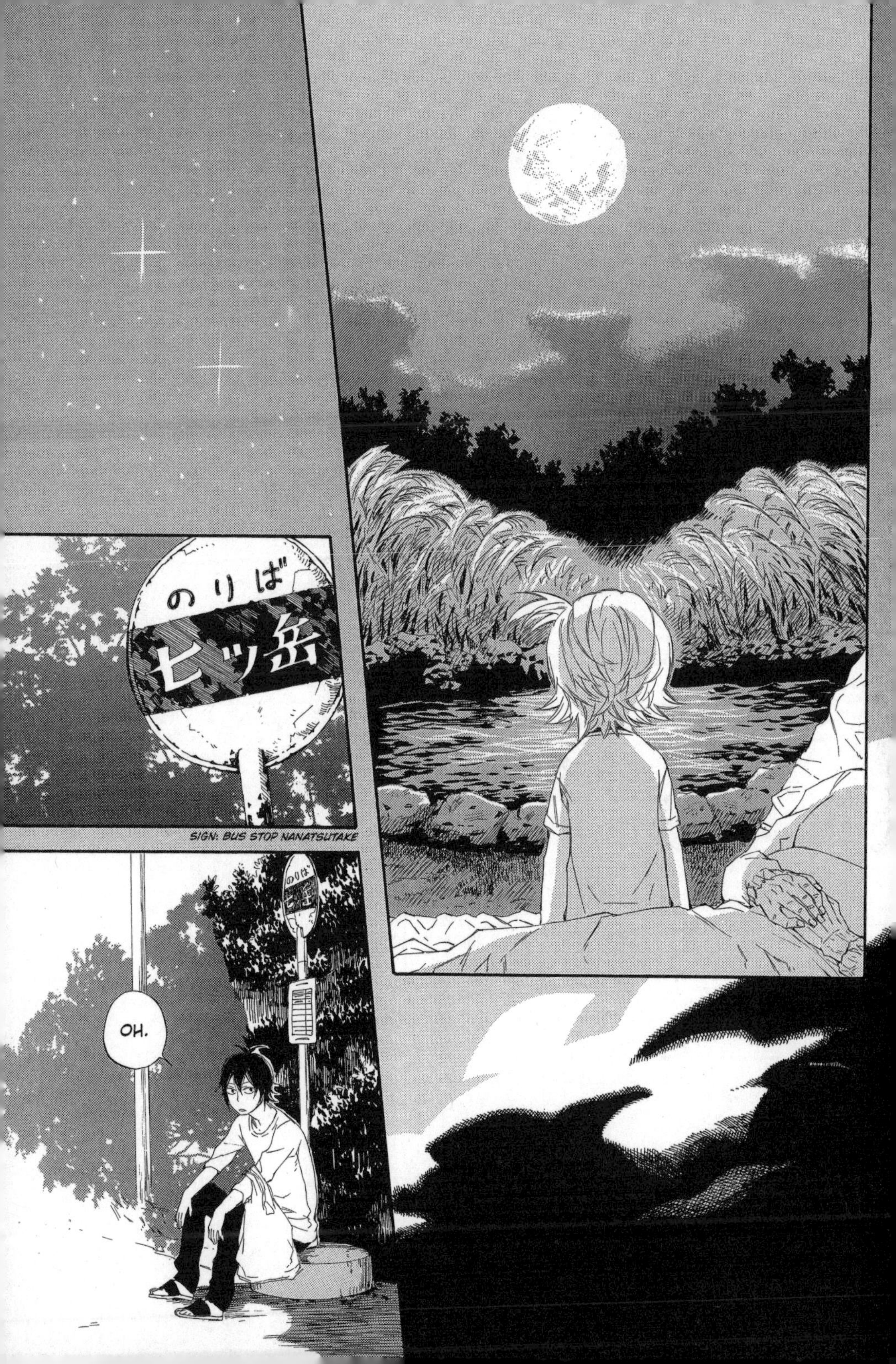
のりば
七ッ岳
SIGN: BUS STOP NANATSUTAKE
OH.

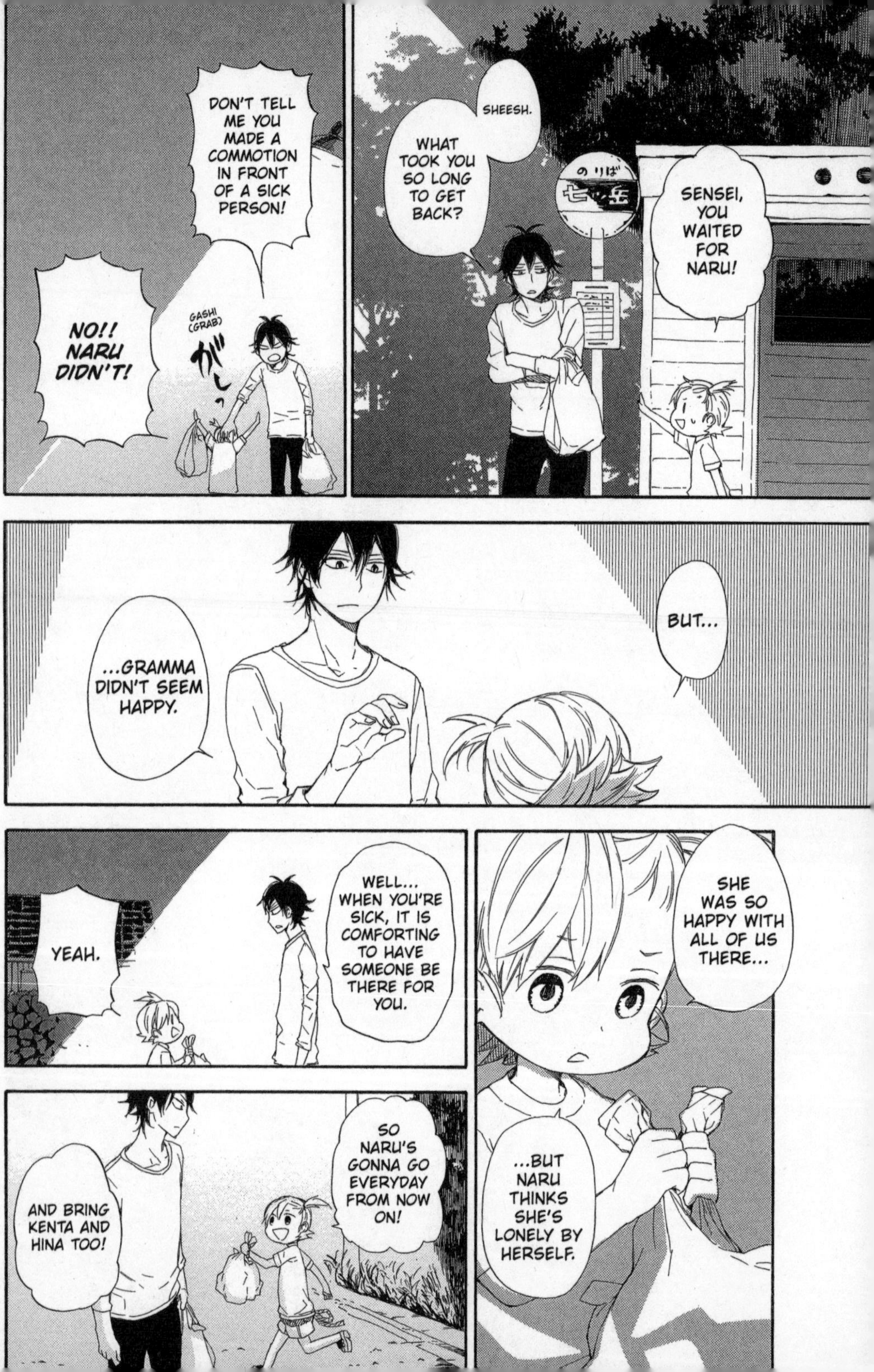
SENSEI, YOU WAITED FOR NARU!
SHEESH.
WHAT TOOK YOU SO LONG TO GET BACK?
DON'T TELL ME YOU MADE A COMMOTION IN FRONT OF A SICK PERSON!
GASHI (GRAB)
がしっ
NO!! NARU DIDN'T!
BUT...
...GRAMMA DIDN'T SEEM HAPPY.
SHE WAS SO HAPPY WITH ALL OF US THERE...
...BUT NARU THINKS SHE'S LONELY BY HERSELF.
WELL... WHEN YOU'RE SICK, IT IS COMFORTING TO HAVE SOMEONE BE THERE FOR YOU.
YEAH.
SO NARU'S GONNA GO EVERYDAY FROM NOW ON!
AND BRING KENTA AND HINA TOO!

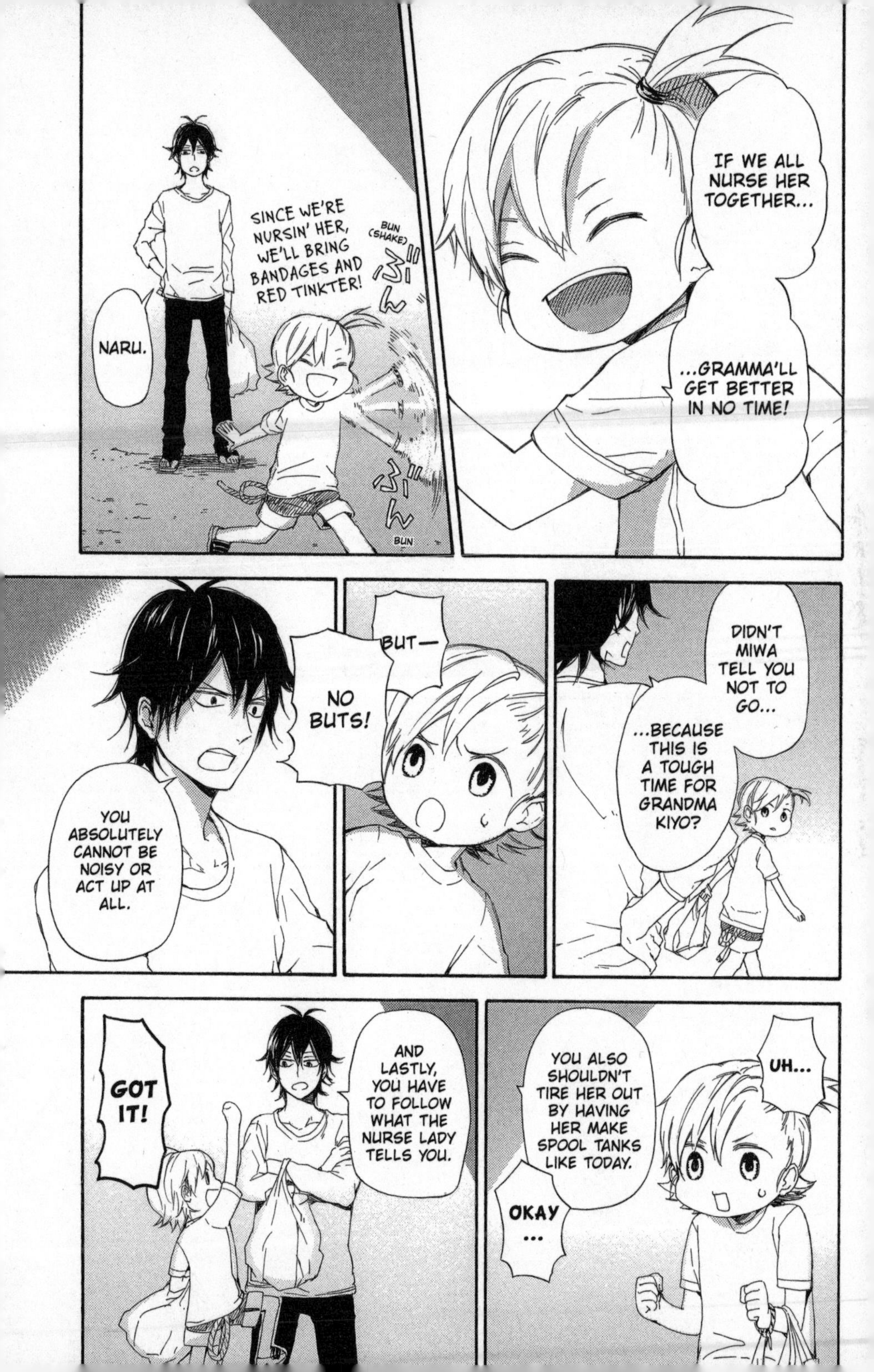
IF WE ALL NURSE HER TOGETHER...
...GRAMMA'LL GET BETTER IN NO TIME!
SINCE WE'RE NURSIN' HER, WE'LL BRING BANDAGES AND RED TINKTER!
ぶん
BUN (SHAKE)
ぶん
BUN
NARU.
DIDN'T MIWA TELL YOU NOT TO GO...
...BECAUSE THIS IS A TOUGH TIME FOR GRANDMA KIYO?
BUT—
NO BUTS!
YOU ABSOLUTELY CANNOT BE NOISY OR ACT UP AT ALL.
UH...
YOU ALSO SHOULDN'T TIRE HER OUT BY HAVING HER MAKE SPOOL TANKS LIKE TODAY.
OKAY...
AND LASTLY, YOU HAVE TO FOLLOW WHAT THE NURSE LADY TELLS YOU.
GOT IT!

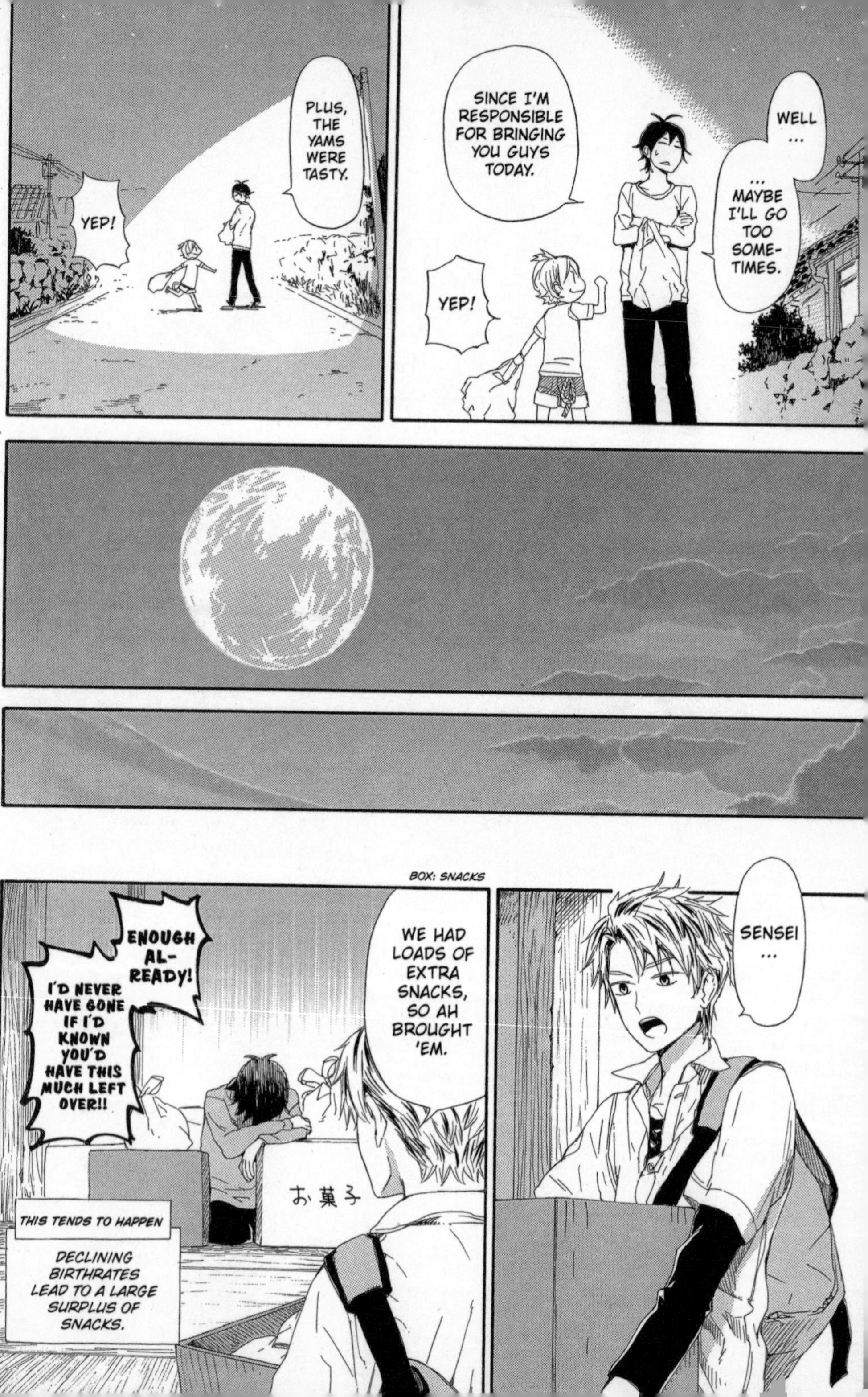
WELL ...
... MAYBE I'LL GO TOO SOME-TIMES.
SINCE I'M RESPONSIBLE FOR BRINGING YOU GUYS TODAY.
YEP!
PLUS, THE YAMS WERE TASTY.
YEP!
SENSEI ...
BOX: SNACKS
WE HAD LOADS OF EXTRA SNACKS, SO AH BROUGHT 'EM.
ENOUGH AL-READY!
I'D NEVER HAVE GONE IF I'D KNOWN YOU'D HAVE THIS MUCH LEFT OVER!!
お菓子
THIS TENDS TO HAPPEN
DECLINING BIRTHRATES LEAD TO A LARGE SURPLUS OF SNACKS.

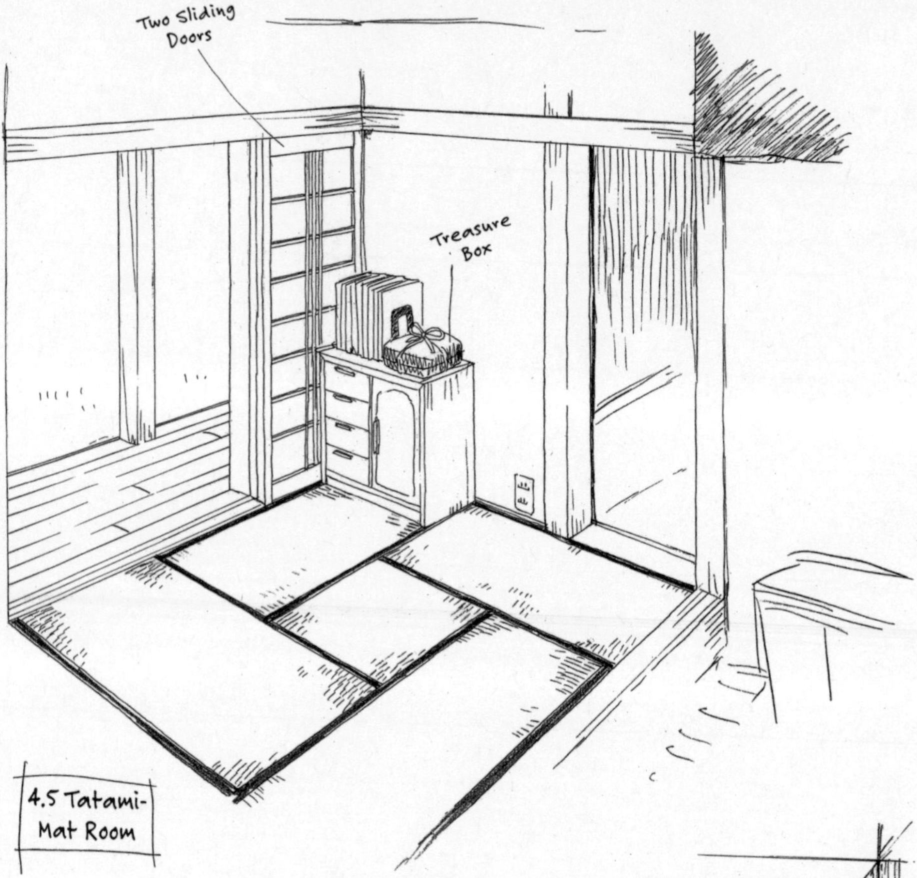
Two Sliding Doors
Treasure Box
4.5 Tatami-Mat Room

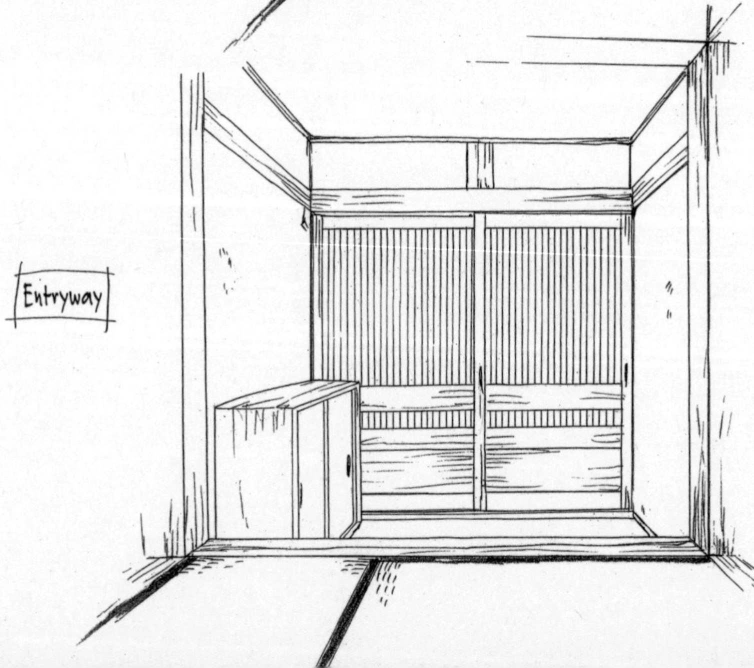
Entryway

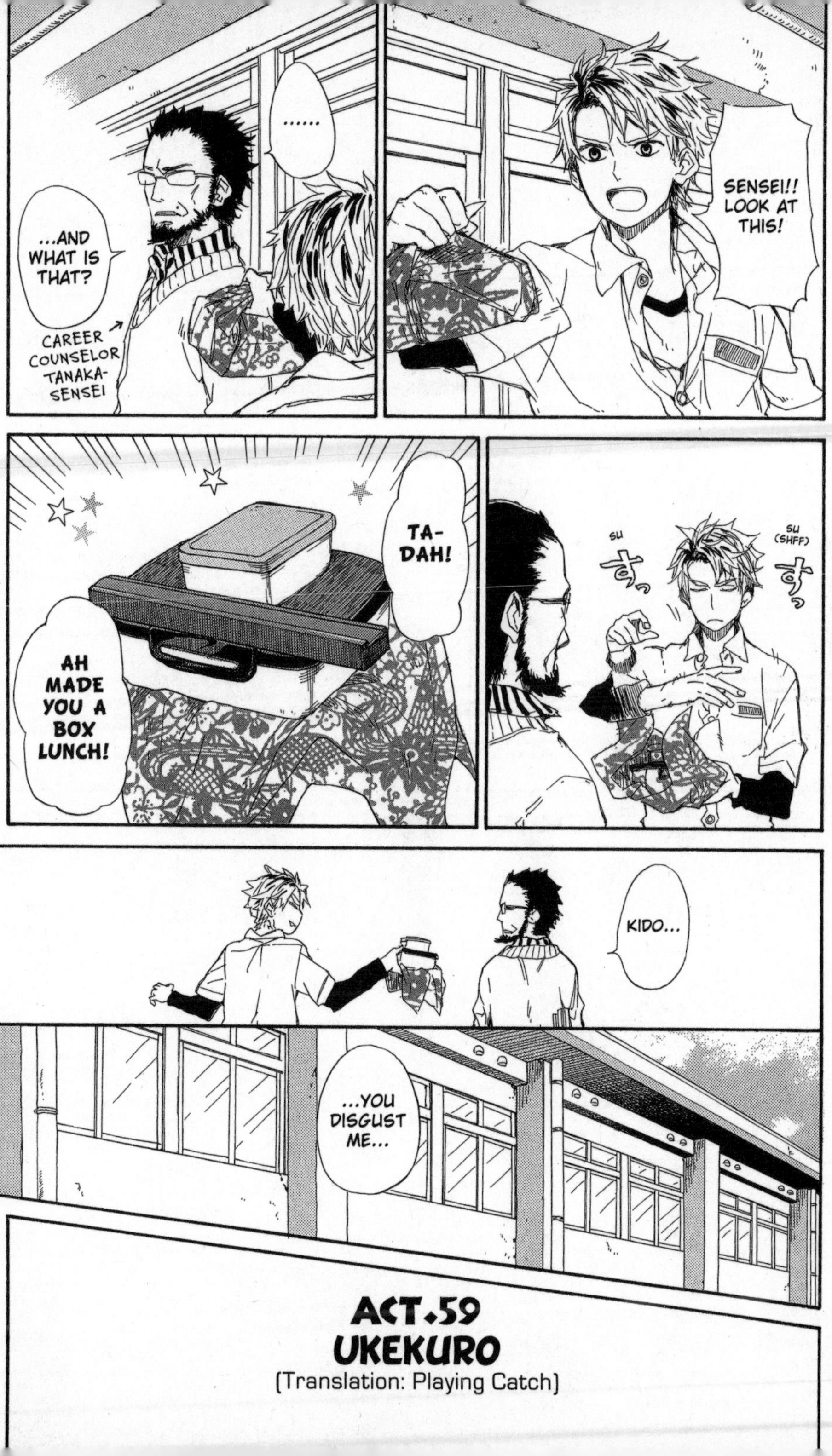
SENSEI!! LOOK AT THIS!
......
...AND WHAT IS THAT?
CAREER COUNSELOR TANAKA-SENSEI
SU (SHFF)
すっ
SU
すっ
TA-DAH!
AH MADE YOU A BOX LUNCH!
KIDO...
...YOU DISGUST ME...
ACT.59
UKEKURO
(Translation: Playing Catch)

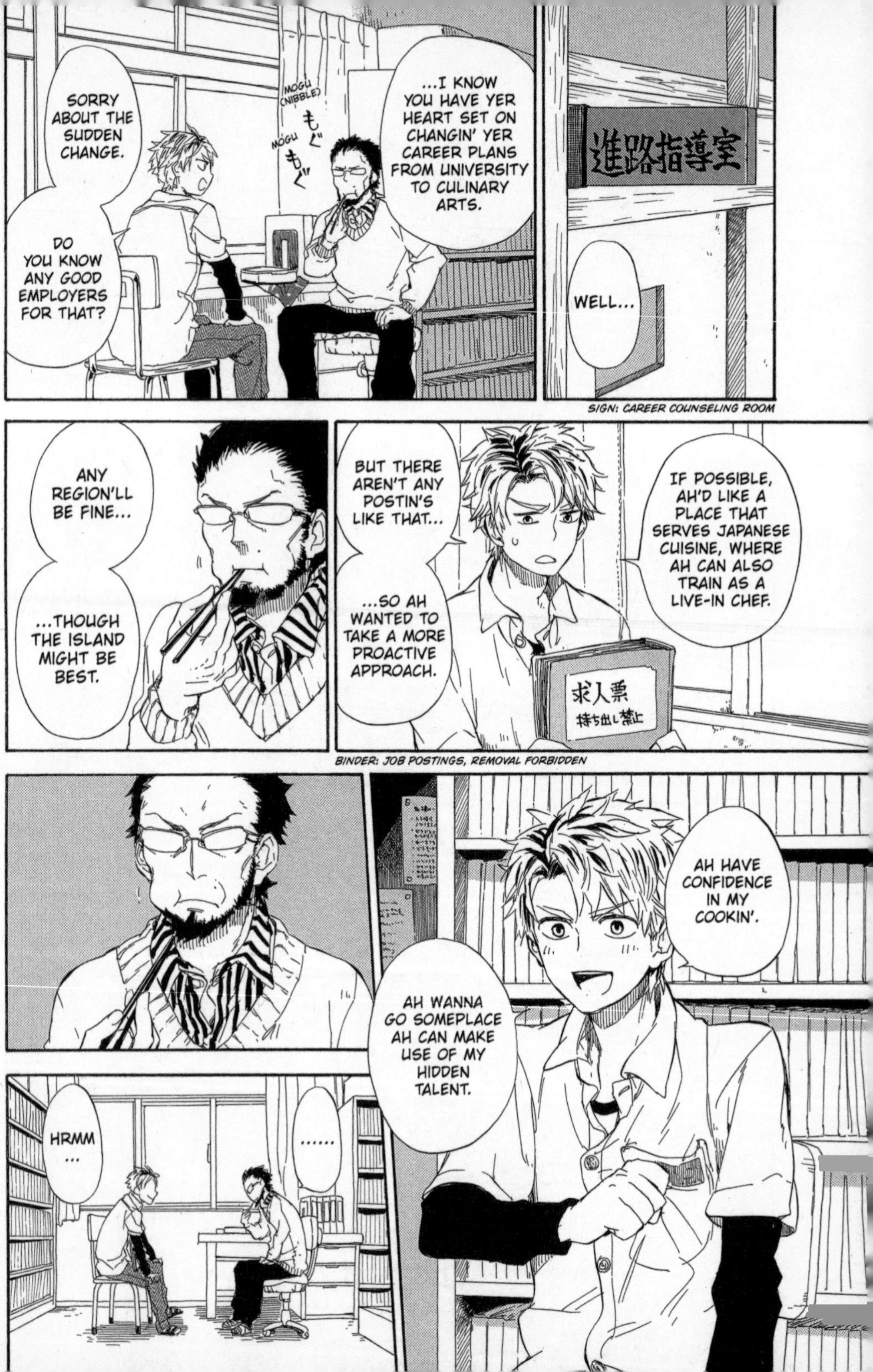
WELL...
進路指導室
SIGN: CAREER COUNSELING ROOM
...I KNOW YOU HAVE YER HEART SET ON CHANGIN' YER CAREER PLANS FROM UNIVERSITY TO CULINARY ARTS.
MOGU (NIBBLE)
もぐ
MOGU
もぐ
SORRY ABOUT THE SUDDEN CHANGE.
DO YOU KNOW ANY GOOD EMPLOYERS FOR THAT?
IF POSSIBLE, AH'D LIKE A PLACE THAT SERVES JAPANESE CUISINE, WHERE AH CAN ALSO TRAIN AS A LIVE-IN CHEF.
BUT THERE AREN'T ANY POSTIN'S LIKE THAT...
...SO AH WANTED TO TAKE A MORE PROACTIVE APPROACH.
求人票
持ち出し禁止
BINDER: JOB POSTINGS, REMOVAL FORBIDDEN
ANY REGION'LL BE FINE...
...THOUGH THE ISLAND MIGHT BE BEST.
AH HAVE CONFIDENCE IN MY COOKIN'.
AH WANNA GO SOMEPLACE AH CAN MAKE USE OF MY HIDDEN TALENT.
......
HRMM ...

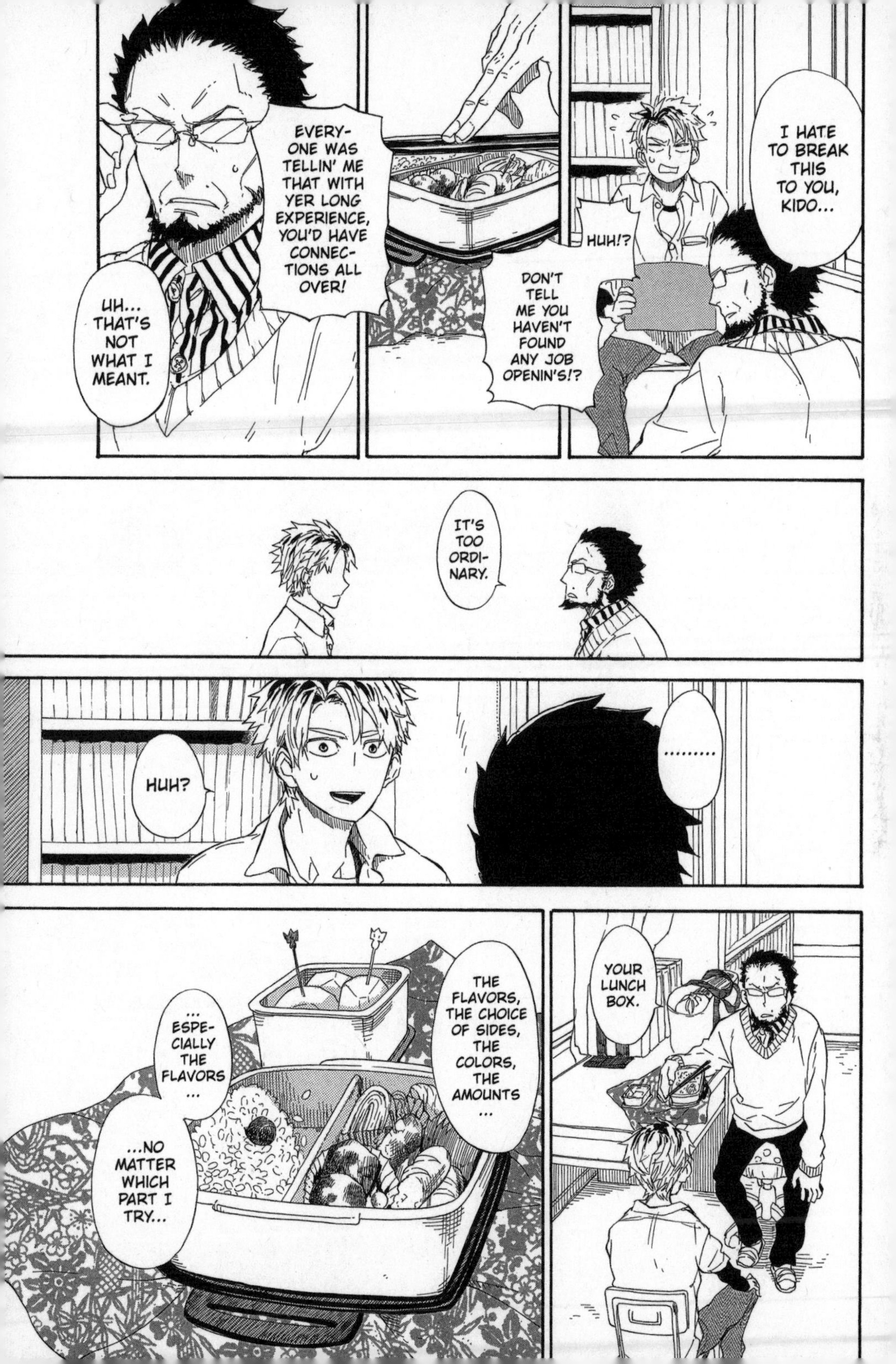
I HATE TO BREAK THIS TO YOU, KIDO...
HUH!?
DON'T TELL ME YOU HAVEN'T FOUND ANY JOB OPENIN'S!?
EVERYONE WAS TELLIN' ME THAT WITH YER LONG EXPERIENCE, YOU'D HAVE CONNECTIONS ALL OVER!
UH... THAT'S NOT WHAT I MEANT.
IT'S TOO ORDINARY.
....
HUH?
YOUR LUNCH BOX.
THE FLAVORS, THE CHOICE OF SIDES, THE COLORS, THE AMOUNTS ...
... ESPECIALLY THE FLAVORS ...
...NO MATTER WHICH PART I TRY...

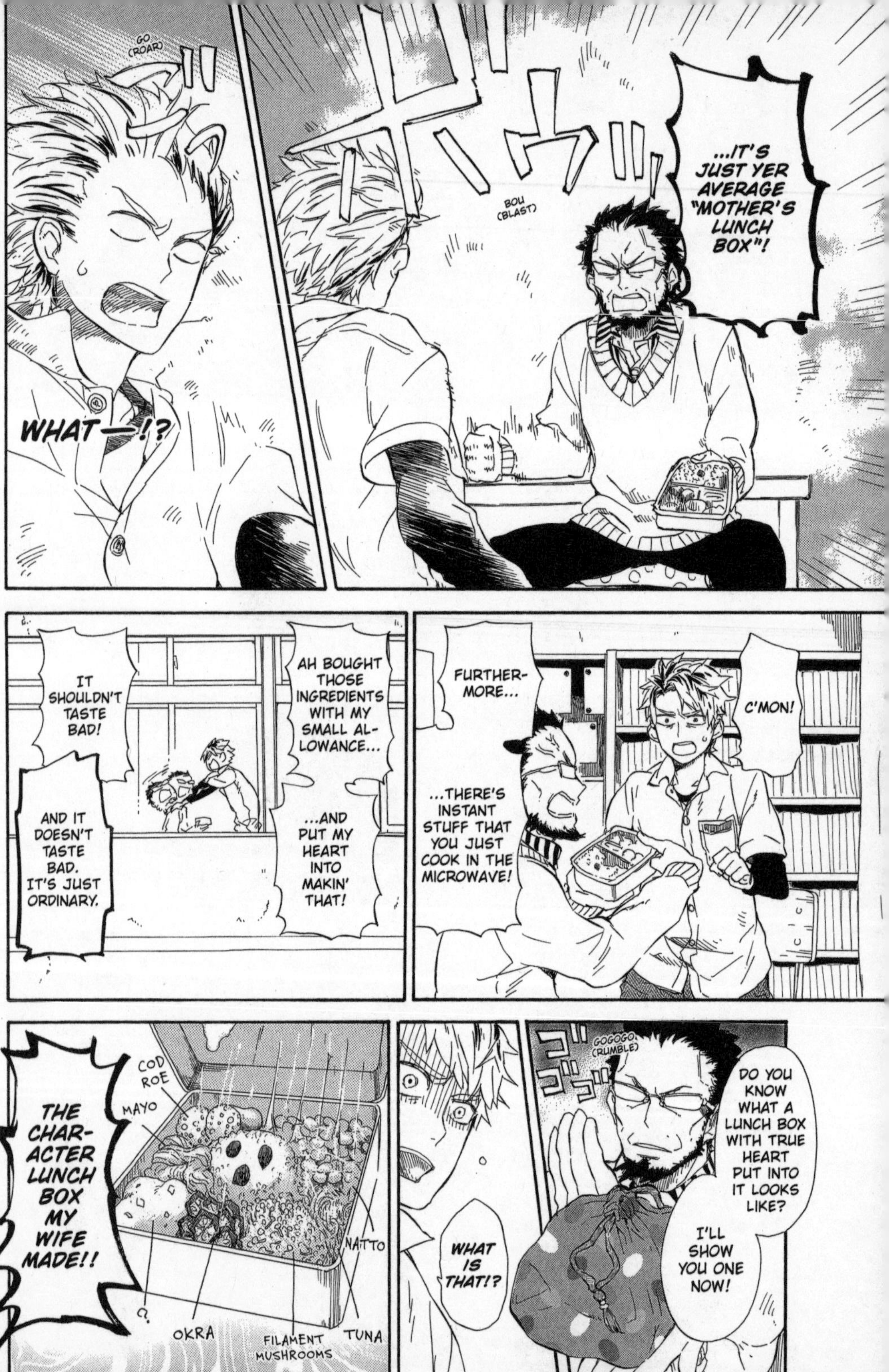

BOU (BLAST)
...IT'S JUST YER AVERAGE "MOTHER'S LUNCH BOX"!
GO (ROAR)
WHAT—!?
FURTHER-MORE...
C'MON!
...THERE'S INSTANT STUFF THAT YOU JUST COOK IN THE MICROWAVE!
AH BOUGHT THOSE INGREDIENTS WITH MY SMALL AL-LOWANCE...
...AND PUT MY HEART INTO MAKIN' THAT!
IT SHOULDN'T TASTE BAD!
AND IT DOESN'T TASTE BAD. IT'S JUST ORDINARY.
GOGOGO (RUMBLE)
DO YOU KNOW WHAT A LUNCH BOX WITH TRUE HEART PUT INTO IT LOOKS LIKE?
I'LL SHOW YOU ONE NOW!
WHAT IS THAT!?
THE CHAR-ACTER LUNCH BOX MY WIFE MADE!!
COD ROE
MAYO
NATTO
?
OKRA
FILAMENT MUSHROOMS
TUNA

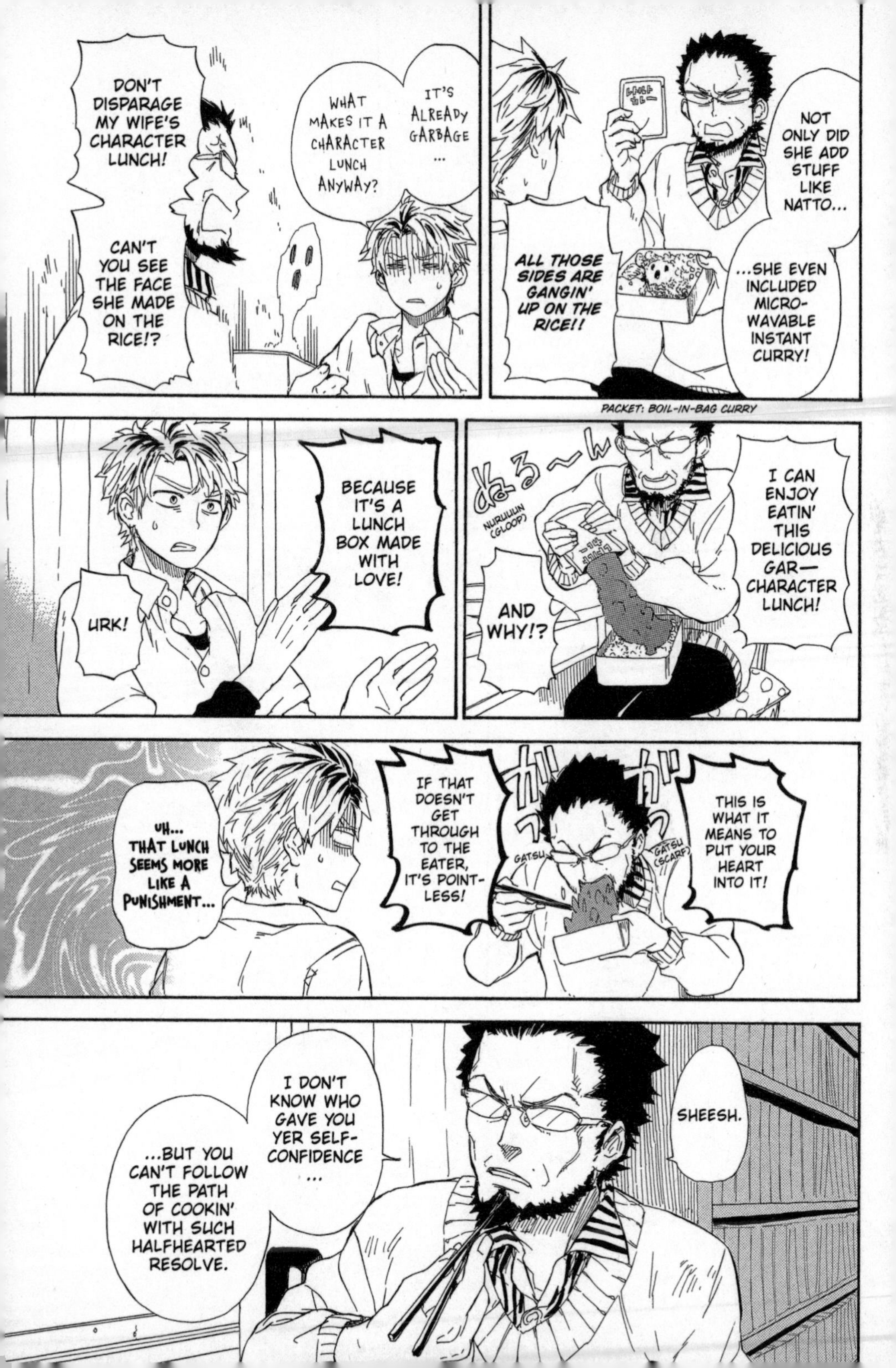
NOT ONLY DID SHE ADD STUFF LIKE NATTO...
...SHE EVEN INCLUDED MICRO-WAVABLE INSTANT CURRY!
ALL THOSE SIDES ARE GANGIN' UP ON THE RICE!!
PACKET: BOIL-IN-BAG CURRY
IT'S ALREADY GARBAGE ...
WHAT MAKES IT A CHARACTER LUNCH ANYWAY?
DON'T DISPARAGE MY WIFE'S CHARACTER LUNCH!
CAN'T YOU SEE THE FACE SHE MADE ON THE RICE!?
I CAN ENJOY EATIN' THIS DELICIOUS GAR— CHARACTER LUNCH!
ぬる〜ん
NURUUUN (GLOOP)
AND WHY!?
BECAUSE IT'S A LUNCH BOX MADE WITH LOVE!
URK!
THIS IS WHAT IT MEANS TO PUT YOUR HEART INTO IT!
がつ がつ
GATSU
GATSU (SCARF)
IF THAT DOESN'T GET THROUGH TO THE EATER, IT'S POINTLESS!
UH... THAT LUNCH SEEMS MORE LIKE A PUNISHMENT...
SHEESH.
I DON'T KNOW WHO GAVE YOU YER SELF-CONFIDENCE ...
...BUT YOU CAN'T FOLLOW THE PATH OF COOKIN' WITH SUCH HALFHEARTED RESOLVE.

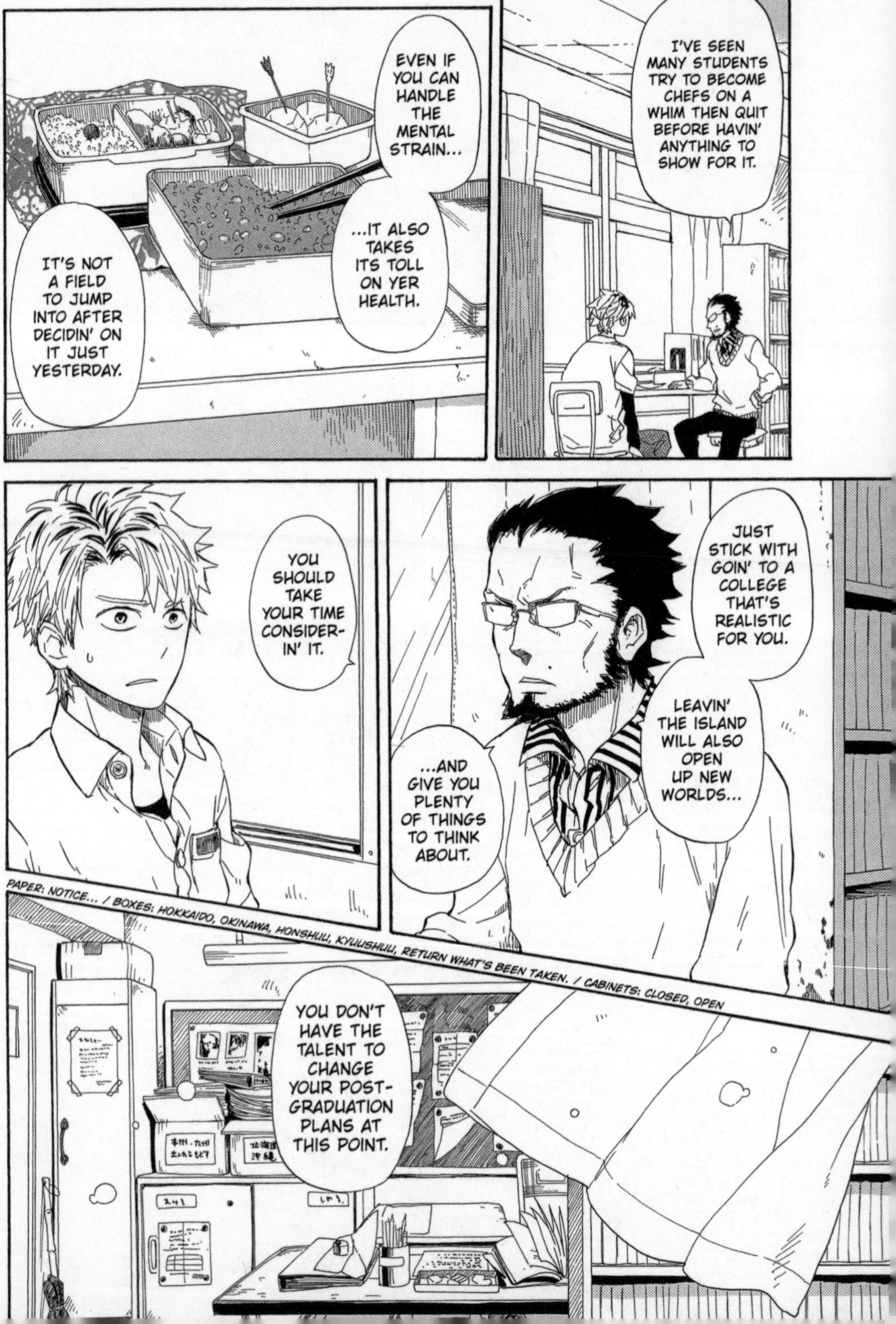
I'VE SEEN MANY STUDENTS TRY TO BECOME CHEFS ON A WHIM THEN QUIT BEFORE HAVIN' ANYTHING TO SHOW FOR IT.
EVEN IF YOU CAN HANDLE THE MENTAL STRAIN...
...IT ALSO TAKES ITS TOLL ON YER HEALTH.
IT'S NOT A FIELD TO JUMP INTO AFTER DECIDIN' ON IT JUST YESTERDAY.
JUST STICK WITH GOIN' TO A COLLEGE THAT'S REALISTIC FOR YOU.
LEAVIN' THE ISLAND WILL ALSO OPEN UP NEW WORLDS...
...AND GIVE YOU PLENTY OF THINGS TO THINK ABOUT.
YOU SHOULD TAKE YOUR TIME CONSIDERIN' IT.
PAPER: NOTICE... / BOXES: HOKKAIDO, OKINAWA, HONSHUU, KYUUSHUU, RETURN WHAT'S BEEN TAKEN. / CABINETS: CLOSED, OPEN
YOU DON'T HAVE THE TALENT TO CHANGE YOUR POST-GRADUATION PLANS AT THIS POINT.

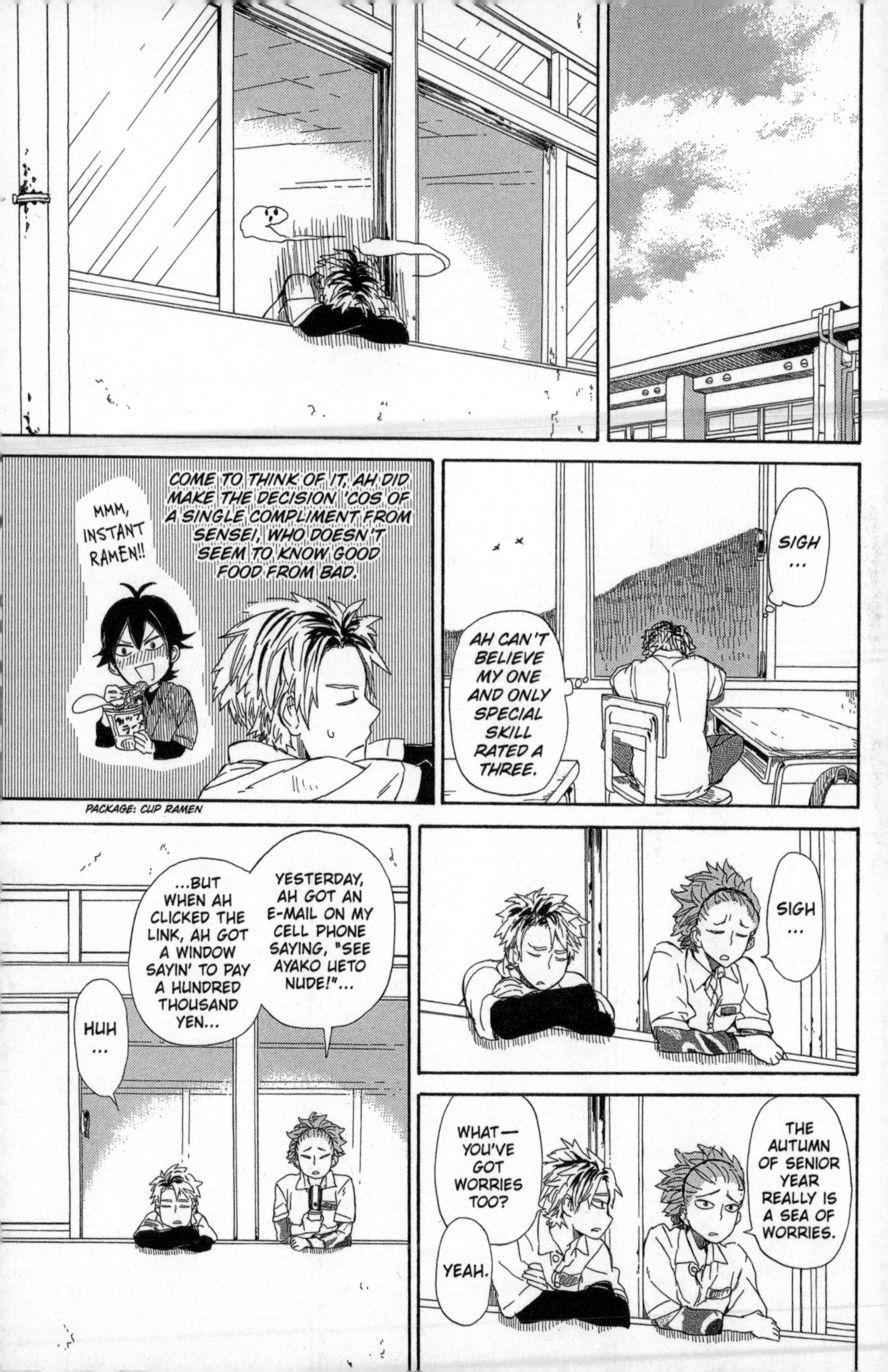
SIGH ...
AH CAN'T BELIEVE MY ONE AND ONLY SPECIAL SKILL RATED A THREE.
COME TO THINK OF IT, AH DID MAKE THE DECISION 'COS OF A SINGLE COMPLIMENT FROM SENSEI, WHO DOESN'T SEEM TO KNOW GOOD FOOD FROM BAD.
MMM, INSTANT RAMEN!!
PACKAGE: CUP RAMEN
SIGH ...
THE AUTUMN OF SENIOR YEAR REALLY IS A SEA OF WORRIES.
WHAT— YOU'VE GOT WORRIES TOO?
YEAH.
YESTERDAY, AH GOT AN E-MAIL ON MY CELL PHONE SAYING, "SEE AYAKO UETO NUDE!"...
...BUT WHEN AH CLICKED THE LINK, AH GOT A WINDOW SAYIN' TO PAY A HUNDRED THOUSAND YEN...
HUH ...

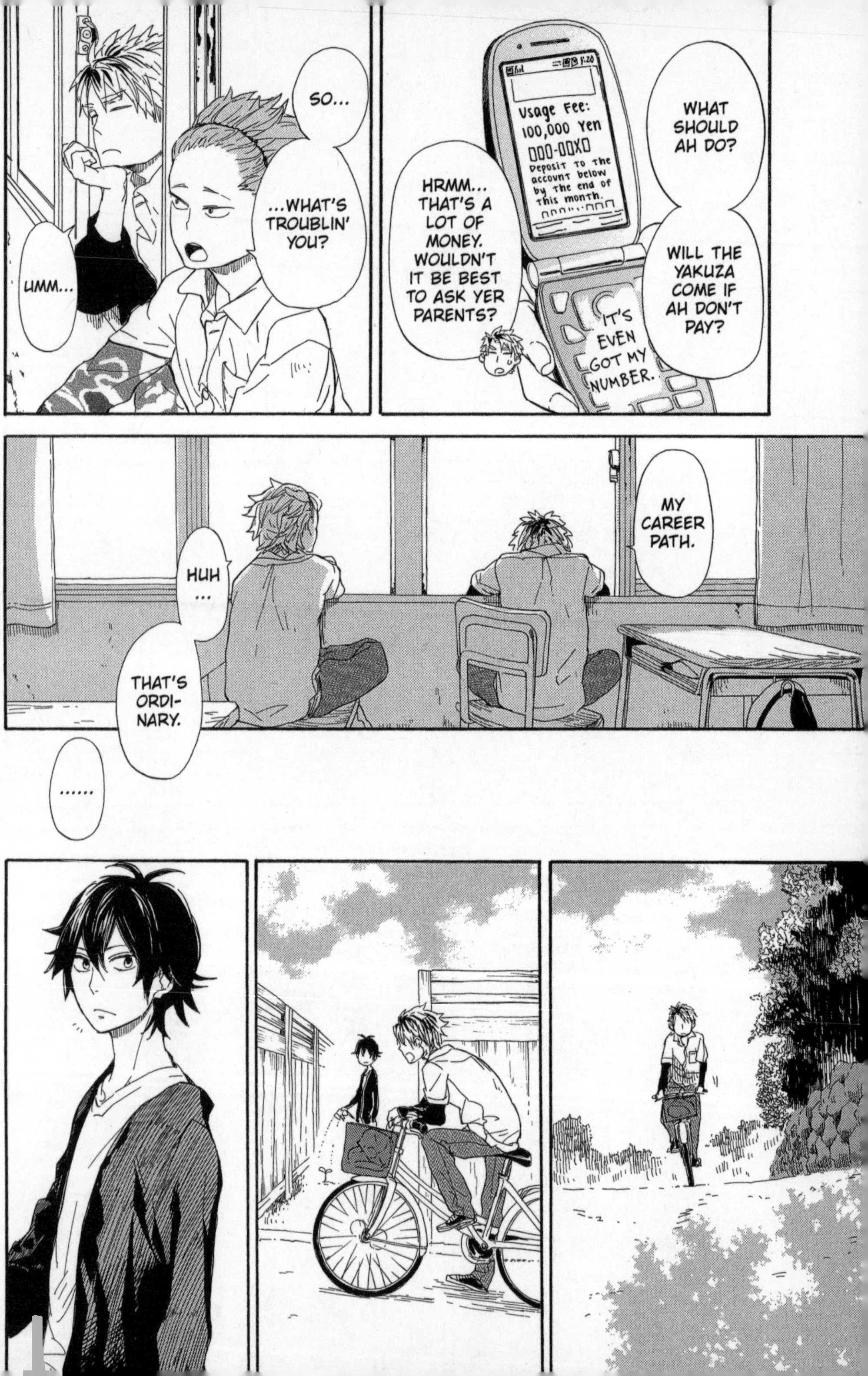
Usage Fee:
100,000 Yen
Deposit to the account below by the end of this month.
WHAT SHOULD AH DO?
WILL THE YAKUZA COME IF AH DON'T PAY?
IT'S EVEN GOT MY NUMBER.
HRMM... THAT'S A LOT OF MONEY. WOULDN'T IT BE BEST TO ASK YER PARENTS?
SO...
...WHAT'S TROUBLIN' YOU?
UMM...
MY CAREER PATH.
HUH ...
THAT'S ORDINARY.
......

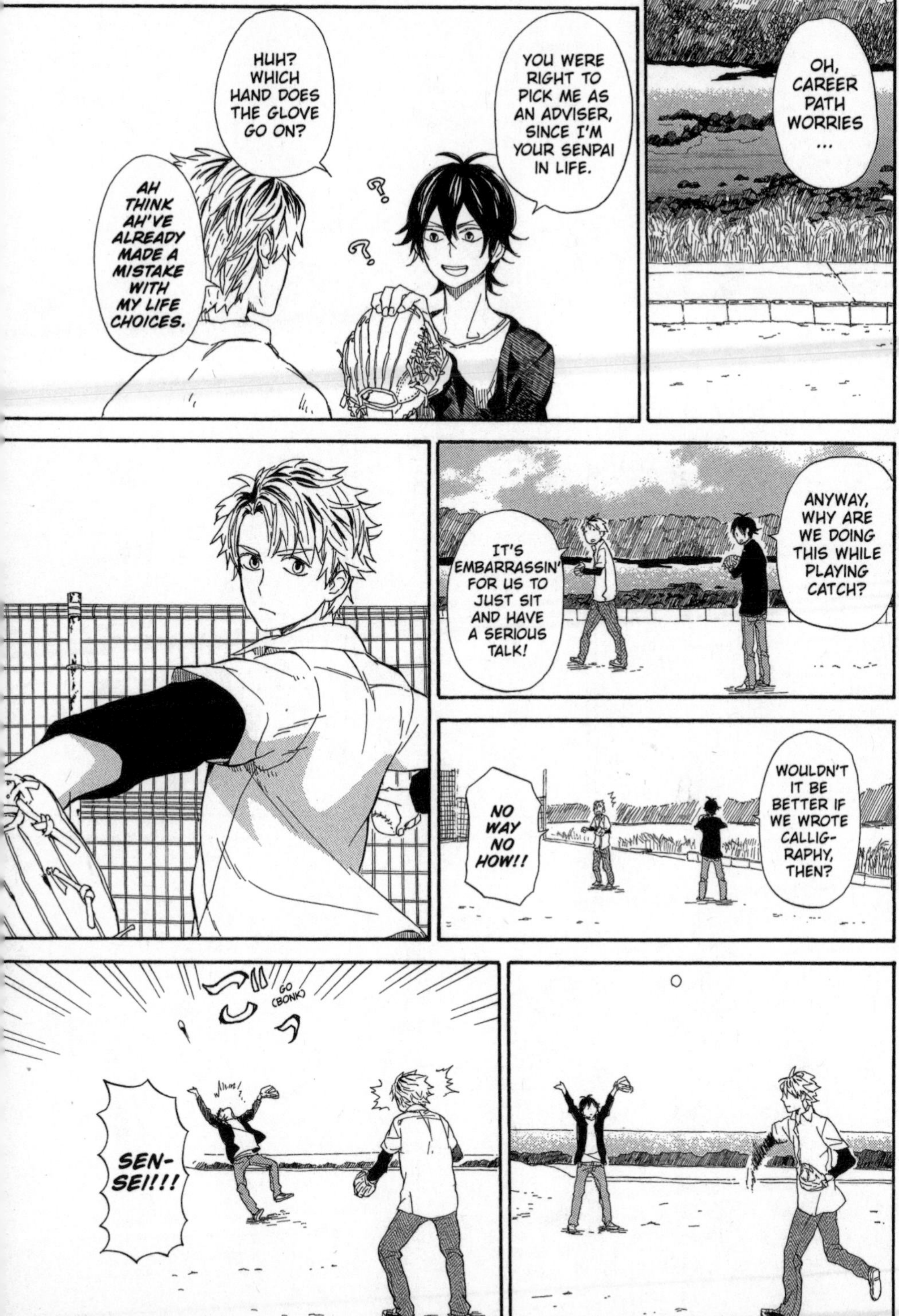

OH, CAREER PATH WORRIES ...
YOU WERE RIGHT TO PICK ME AS AN ADVISER, SINCE I'M YOUR SENPAI IN LIFE.
HUH? WHICH HAND DOES THE GLOVE GO ON?
AH THINK AH'VE ALREADY MADE A MISTAKE WITH MY LIFE CHOICES.
ANYWAY, WHY ARE WE DOING THIS WHILE PLAYING CATCH?
IT'S EMBARRASSIN' FOR US TO JUST SIT AND HAVE A SERIOUS TALK!
WOULDN'T IT BE BETTER IF WE WROTE CALLIG-RAPHY, THEN?
NO WAY NO HOW!!
GO (BONK)
SEN-SEI!!!

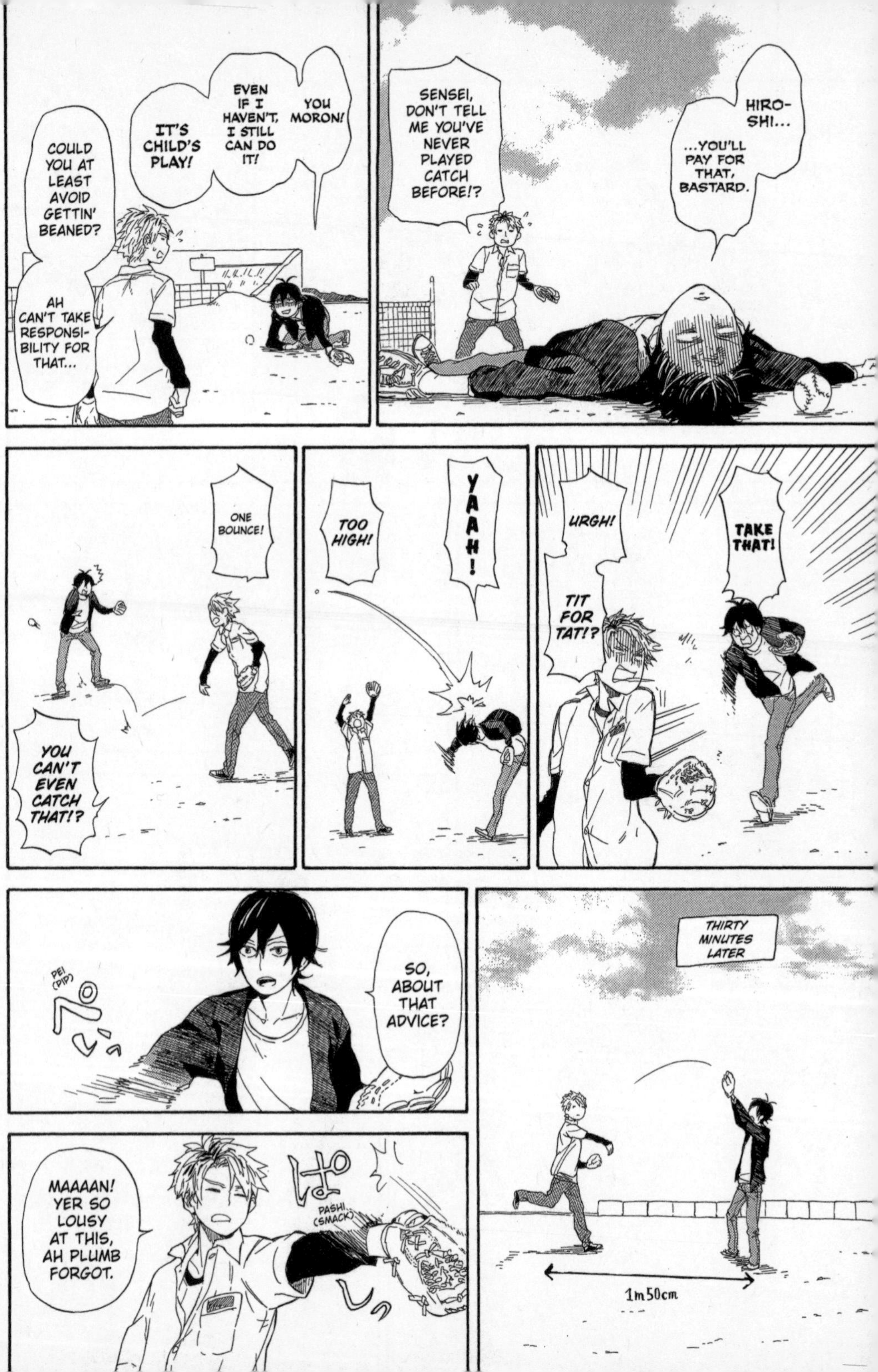
HIRO-SHI...
...YOU'LL PAY FOR THAT, BASTARD.
SENSEI, DON'T TELL ME YOU'VE NEVER PLAYED CATCH BEFORE!?
YOU MORON!
EVEN IF I HAVEN'T, I STILL CAN DO IT!
IT'S CHILD'S PLAY!
COULD YOU AT LEAST AVOID GETTIN' BEANED?
AH CAN'T TAKE RESPONSI-BILITY FOR THAT...
TAKE THAT!
URGH!
TIT FOR TAT!?
YAAAH!
TOO HIGH!
ONE BOUNCE!
YOU CAN'T EVEN CATCH THAT!?
THIRTY MINUTES LATER
1m50cm
SO, ABOUT THAT ADVICE?
PEI (PIP)
ぺいっ
MAAAAN! YER SO LOUSY AT THIS, AH PLUMB FORGOT.
ぱしっ
PASHI (SMACK)

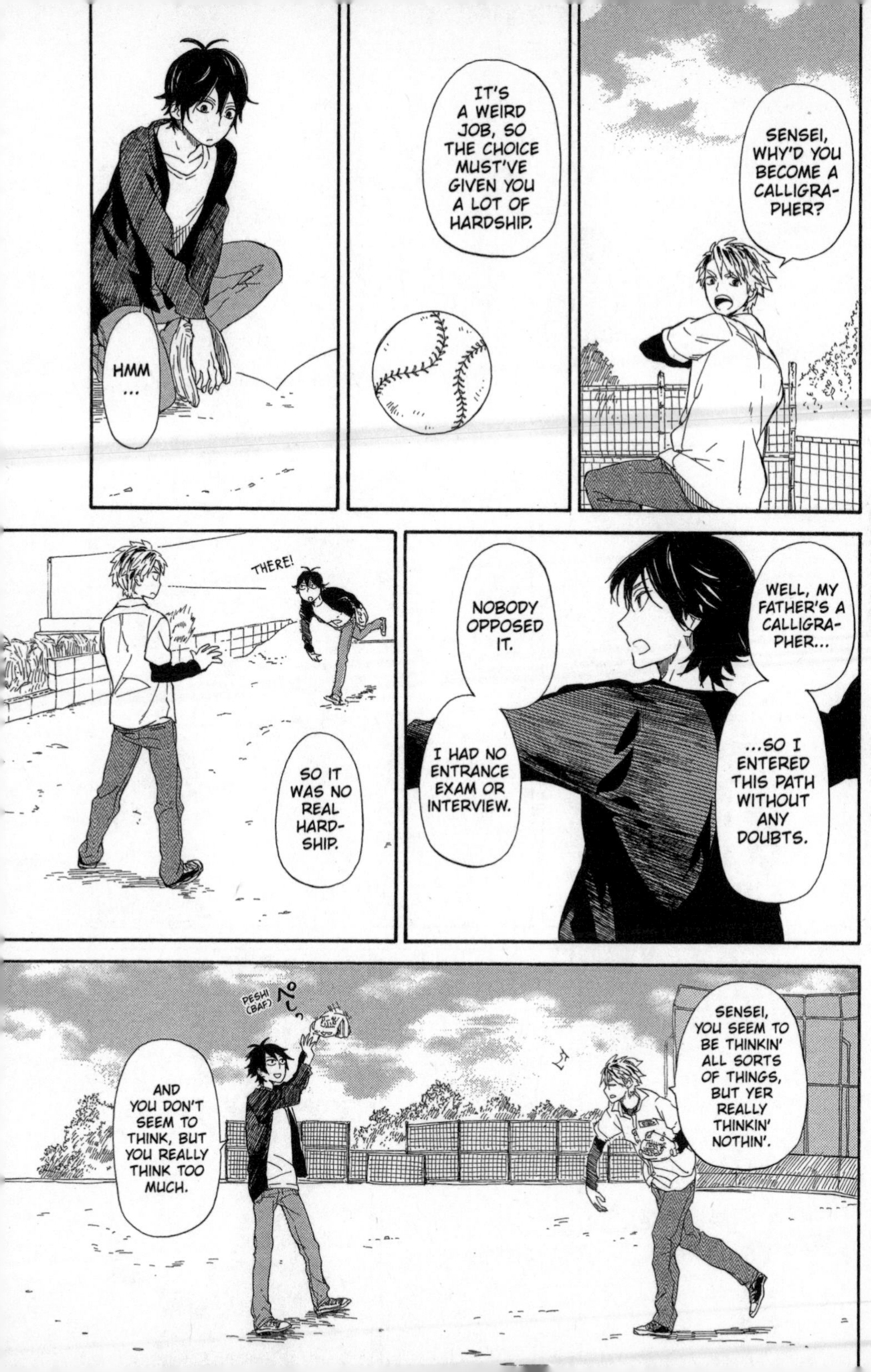
SENSEI, WHY'D YOU BECOME A CALLIGRAPHER?
IT'S A WEIRD JOB, SO THE CHOICE MUST'VE GIVEN YOU A LOT OF HARDSHIP.
HMM...
WELL, MY FATHER'S A CALLIGRAPHER...
NOBODY OPPOSED IT.
...SO I ENTERED THIS PATH WITHOUT ANY DOUBTS.
I HAD NO ENTRANCE EXAM OR INTERVIEW.
THERE!
SO IT WAS NO REAL HARDSHIP.
SENSEI, YOU SEEM TO BE THINKIN' ALL SORTS OF THINGS, BUT YER REALLY THINKIN' NOTHIN'.
ぺしっ
PESHI (BAF)
AND YOU DON'T SEEM TO THINK, BUT YOU REALLY THINK TOO MUCH.

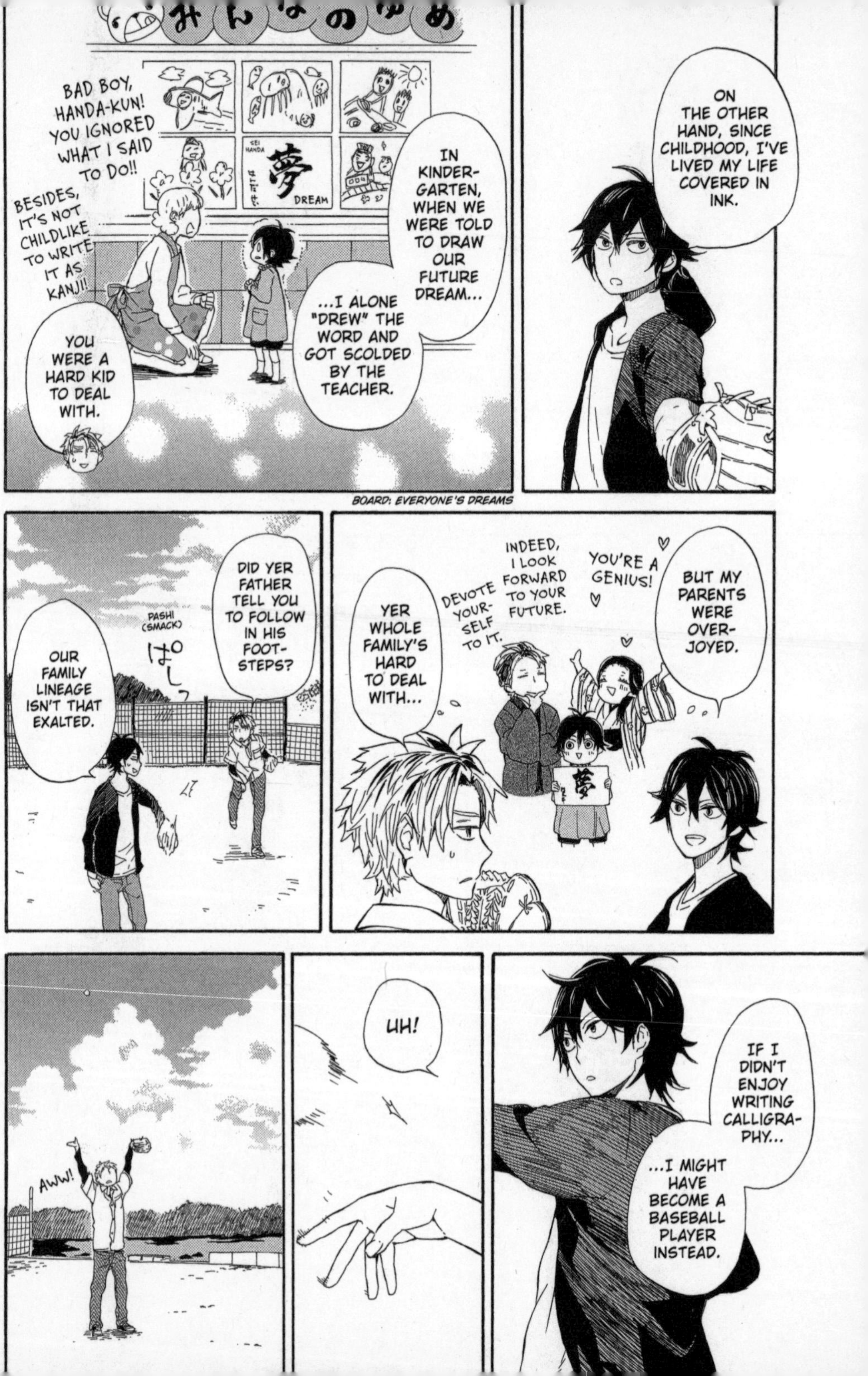

ON THE OTHER HAND, SINCE CHILDHOOD, I'VE LIVED MY LIFE COVERED IN INK.
みんなのゆめ
SEI HANDA
夢
DREAM
IN KINDERGARTEN, WHEN WE WERE TOLD TO DRAW OUR FUTURE DREAM...
...I ALONE "DREW" THE WORD AND GOT SCOLDED BY THE TEACHER.
BAD BOY, HANDA-KUN! YOU IGNORED WHAT I SAID TO DO!!
BESIDES, IT'S NOT CHILDLIKE TO WRITE IT AS KANJI!!
YOU WERE A HARD KID TO DEAL WITH.
BOARD: EVERYONE'S DREAMS
BUT MY PARENTS WERE OVERJOYED.
YOU'RE A GENIUS!
INDEED, I LOOK FORWARD TO YOUR FUTURE.
DEVOTE YOURSELF TO IT.
YER WHOLE FAMILY'S HARD TO DEAL WITH...
DID YER FATHER TELL YOU TO FOLLOW IN HIS FOOTSTEPS?
PASHI (SMACK)
ぱしっ
OUR FAMILY LINEAGE ISN'T THAT EXALTED.
IF I DIDN'T ENJOY WRITING CALLIGRAPHY...
...I MIGHT HAVE BECOME A BASEBALL PLAYER INSTEAD.
UH!
AWW!

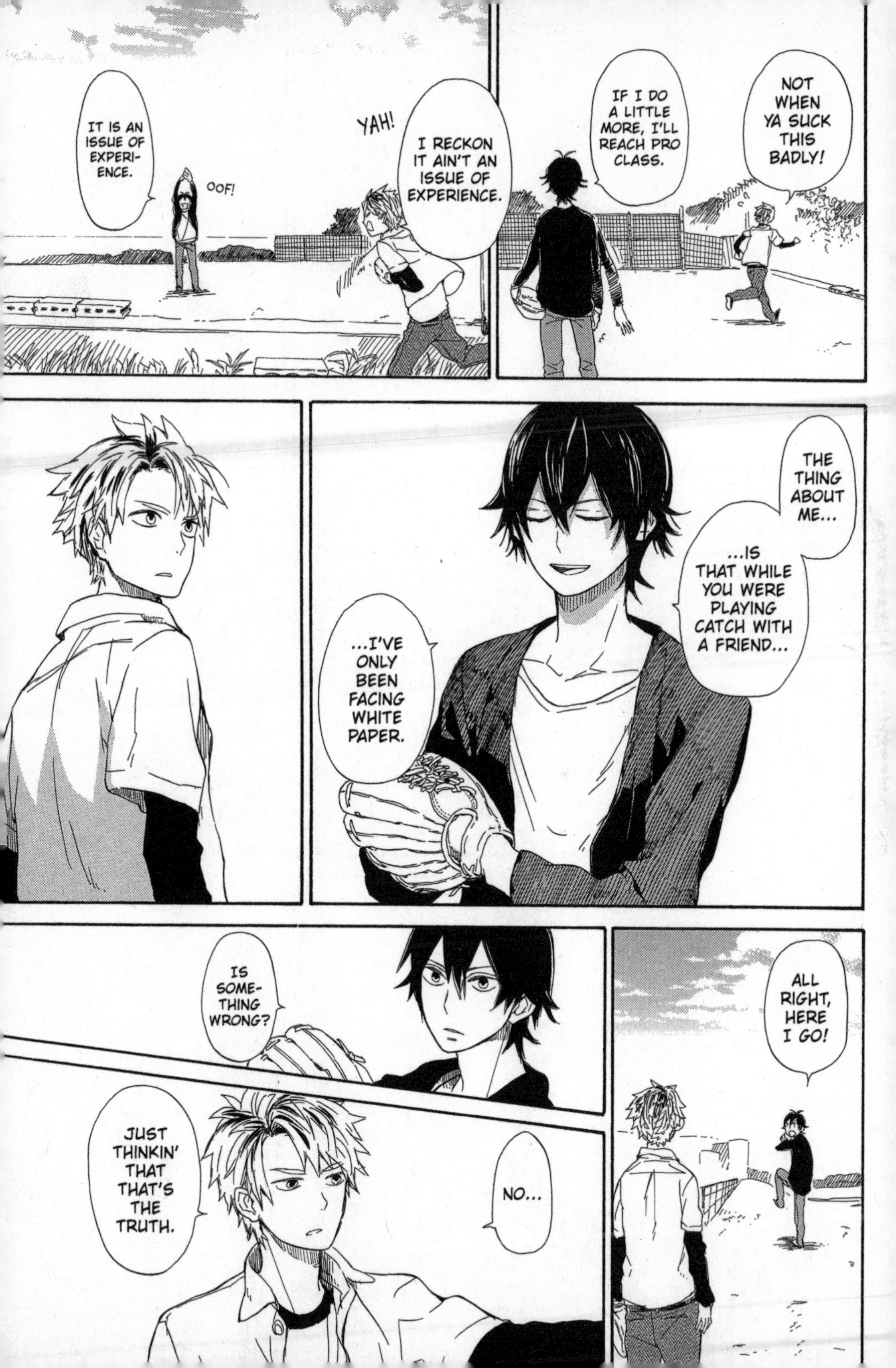
NOT WHEN YA SUCK THIS BADLY!
IF I DO A LITTLE MORE, I'LL REACH PRO CLASS.
YAH!
I RECKON IT AIN'T AN ISSUE OF EXPERIENCE.
OOF!
IT IS AN ISSUE OF EXPERI-ENCE.
THE THING ABOUT ME...
...IS THAT WHILE YOU WERE PLAYING CATCH WITH A FRIEND...
...I'VE ONLY BEEN FACING WHITE PAPER.
ALL RIGHT, HERE I GO!
IS SOME-THING WRONG?
NO...
JUST THINKIN' THAT THAT'S THE TRUTH.

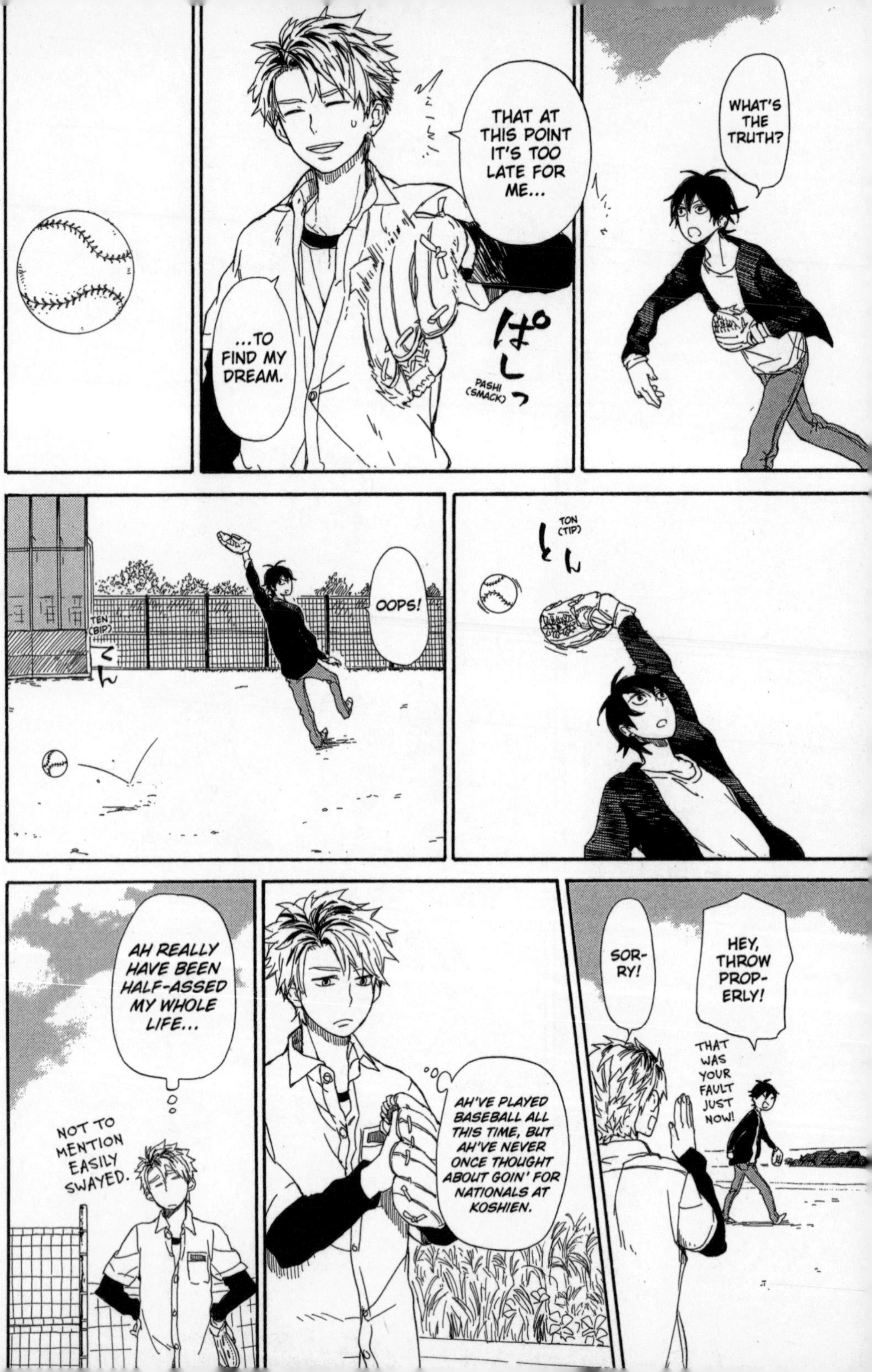
WHAT'S THE TRUTH?
THAT AT THIS POINT IT'S TOO LATE FOR ME...
...TO FIND MY DREAM.
ぱしっ
PASHI (SMACK)
とん
TON (TIP)
OOPS!
TEN (BIP)
HEY, THROW PROP-ERLY!
SOR-RY!
THAT WAS YOUR FAULT JUST NOW!
AH'VE PLAYED BASEBALL ALL THIS TIME, BUT AH'VE NEVER ONCE THOUGHT ABOUT GOIN' FOR NATIONALS AT KOSHIEN.
AH REALLY HAVE BEEN HALF-ASSED MY WHOLE LIFE...
NOT TO MENTION EASILY SWAYED.

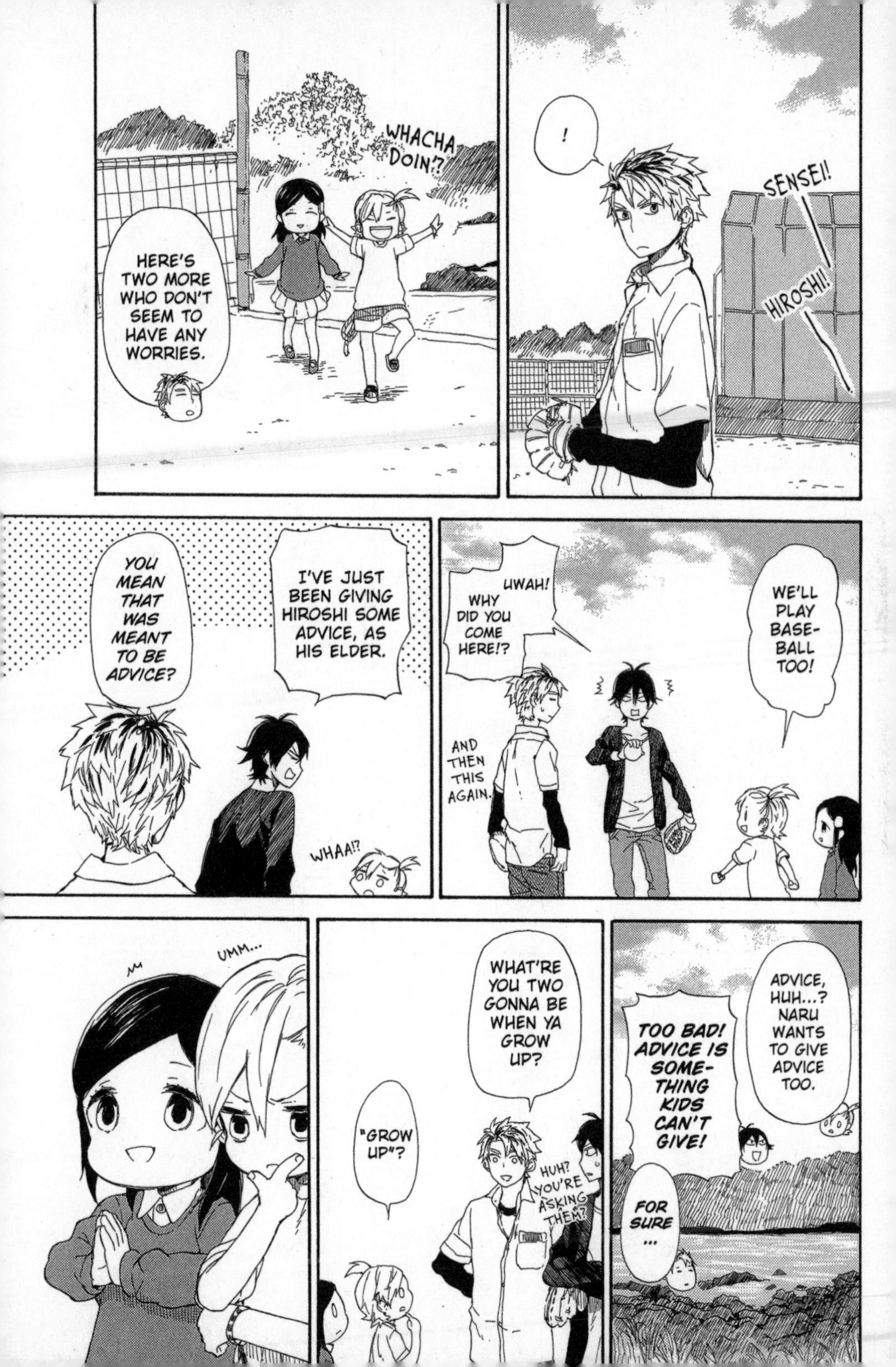
!
SENSEI!
HIROSHI!
WHACHA DOIN'!?
HERE'S TWO MORE WHO DON'T SEEM TO HAVE ANY WORRIES.
WE'LL PLAY BASE-BALL TOO!
UWAH! WHY DID YOU COME HERE!?
AND THEN THIS AGAIN.
I'VE JUST BEEN GIVING HIROSHI SOME ADVICE, AS HIS ELDER.
YOU MEAN THAT WAS MEANT TO BE ADVICE?
WHAA!?
ADVICE, HUH...? NARU WANTS TO GIVE ADVICE TOO.
TOO BAD! ADVICE IS SOME-THING KIDS CAN'T GIVE!
FOR SURE ...
WHAT'RE YOU TWO GONNA BE WHEN YA GROW UP?
HUH? YOU'RE ASKING THEM?
"GROW UP"?
UMM...

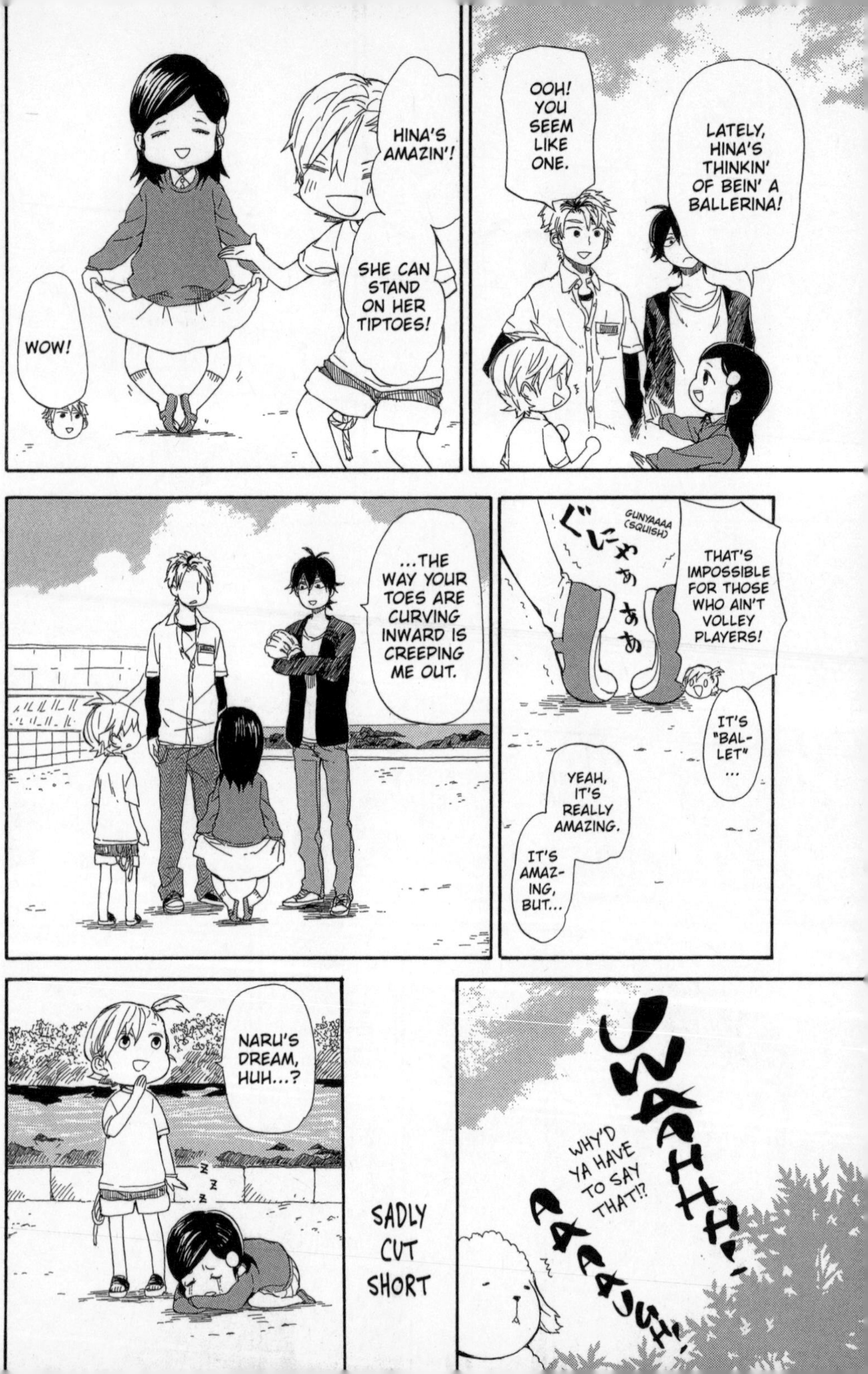

LATELY, HINA'S THINKIN' OF BEIN' A BALLERINA!
OOH! YOU SEEM LIKE ONE.
HINA'S AMAZIN'!
SHE CAN STAND ON HER TIPTOES!
WOW!
ぐにゃあああ
GUNYAAAA (SQUISH)
THAT'S IMPOSSIBLE FOR THOSE WHO AIN'T VOLLEY PLAYERS!
IT'S "BAL-LET"...
YEAH, IT'S REALLY AMAZING.
IT'S AMAZ-ING, BUT...
...THE WAY YOUR TOES ARE CURVING INWARD IS CREEPING ME OUT.
WAAHHH-AAAAUH!
WHY'D YA HAVE TO SAY THAT!?
NARU'S DREAM, HUH...?
Z Z Z
SADLY CUT SHORT

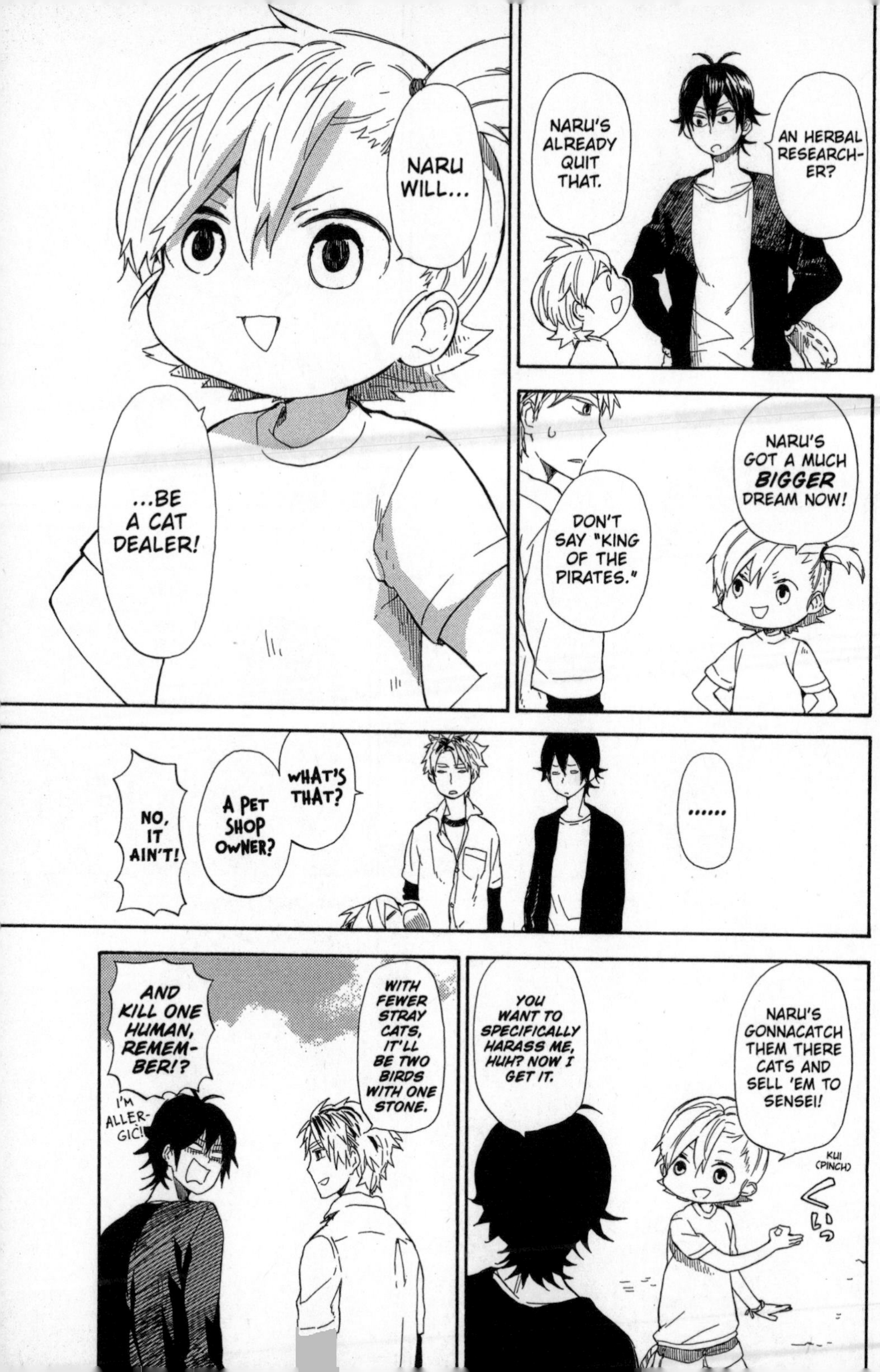

AN HERBAL RESEARCHER?
NARU'S ALREADY QUIT THAT.
NARU'S GOT A MUCH **BIGGER** DREAM NOW!
DON'T SAY "KING OF THE PIRATES."
NARU WILL...
...BE A CAT DEALER!
......
WHAT'S THAT?
A PET SHOP OWNER?
NO, IT AIN'T!
NARU'S GONNACATCH THEM THERE CATS AND SELL 'EM TO SENSEI!
KUI (PINCH)
YOU WANT TO SPECIFICALLY HARASS ME, HUH? NOW I GET IT.
WITH FEWER STRAY CATS, IT'LL BE TWO BIRDS WITH ONE STONE.
AND KILL ONE HUMAN, REMEMBER!?
I'M ALLERGIC!

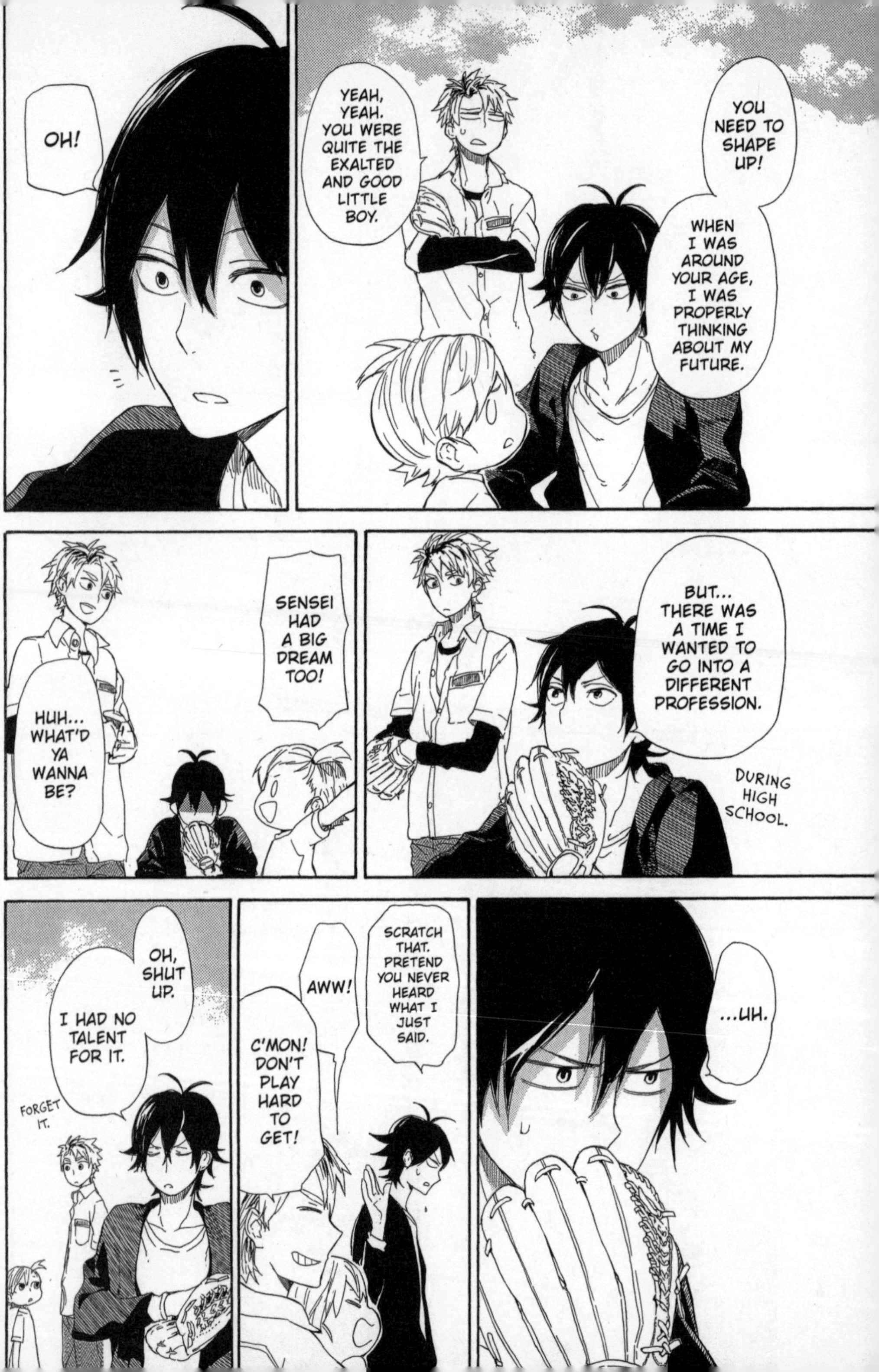
YOU NEED TO SHAPE UP!
WHEN I WAS AROUND YOUR AGE, I WAS PROPERLY THINKING ABOUT MY FUTURE.
YEAH, YEAH. YOU WERE QUITE THE EXALTED AND GOOD LITTLE BOY.
OH!
BUT... THERE WAS A TIME I WANTED TO GO INTO A DIFFERENT PROFESSION.
DURING HIGH SCHOOL.
SENSEI HAD A BIG DREAM TOO!
HUH... WHAT'D YA WANNA BE?
...UH.
SCRATCH THAT. PRETEND YOU NEVER HEARD WHAT I JUST SAID.
AWW!
C'MON! DON'T PLAY HARD TO GET!
OH, SHUT UP.
I HAD NO TALENT FOR IT.
FORGET IT.

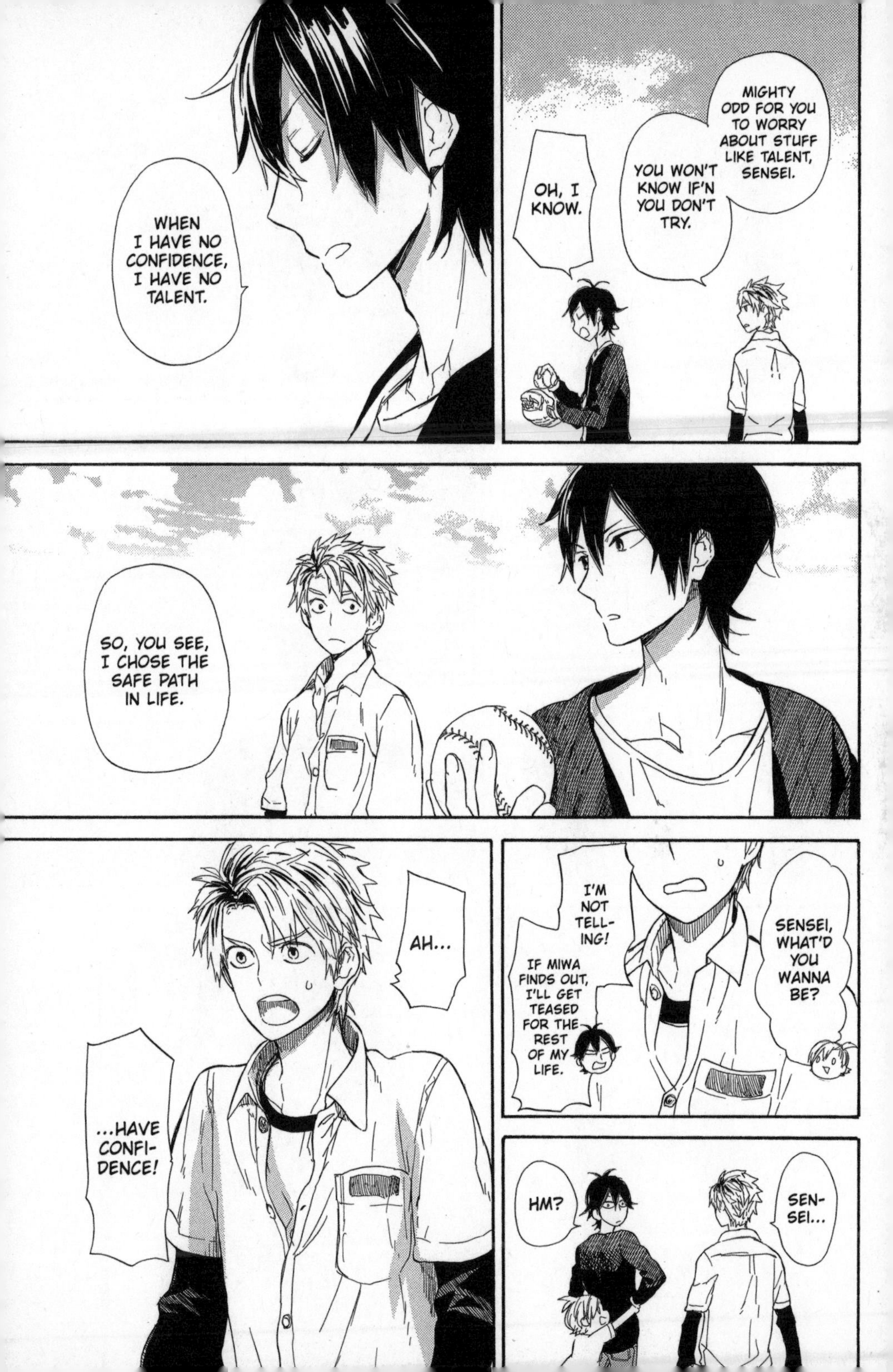

MIGHTY ODD FOR YOU TO WORRY ABOUT STUFF LIKE TALENT, SENSEI.
YOU WON'T KNOW IF'N YOU DON'T TRY.
OH, I KNOW.
WHEN I HAVE NO CONFIDENCE, I HAVE NO TALENT.
SO, YOU SEE, I CHOSE THE SAFE PATH IN LIFE.
SENSEI, WHAT'D YOU WANNA BE?
I'M NOT TELL-ING!
IF MIWA FINDS OUT, I'LL GET TEASED FOR THE REST OF MY LIFE.
SEN-SEI...
HM?
AH...
...HAVE CONFI-DENCE!

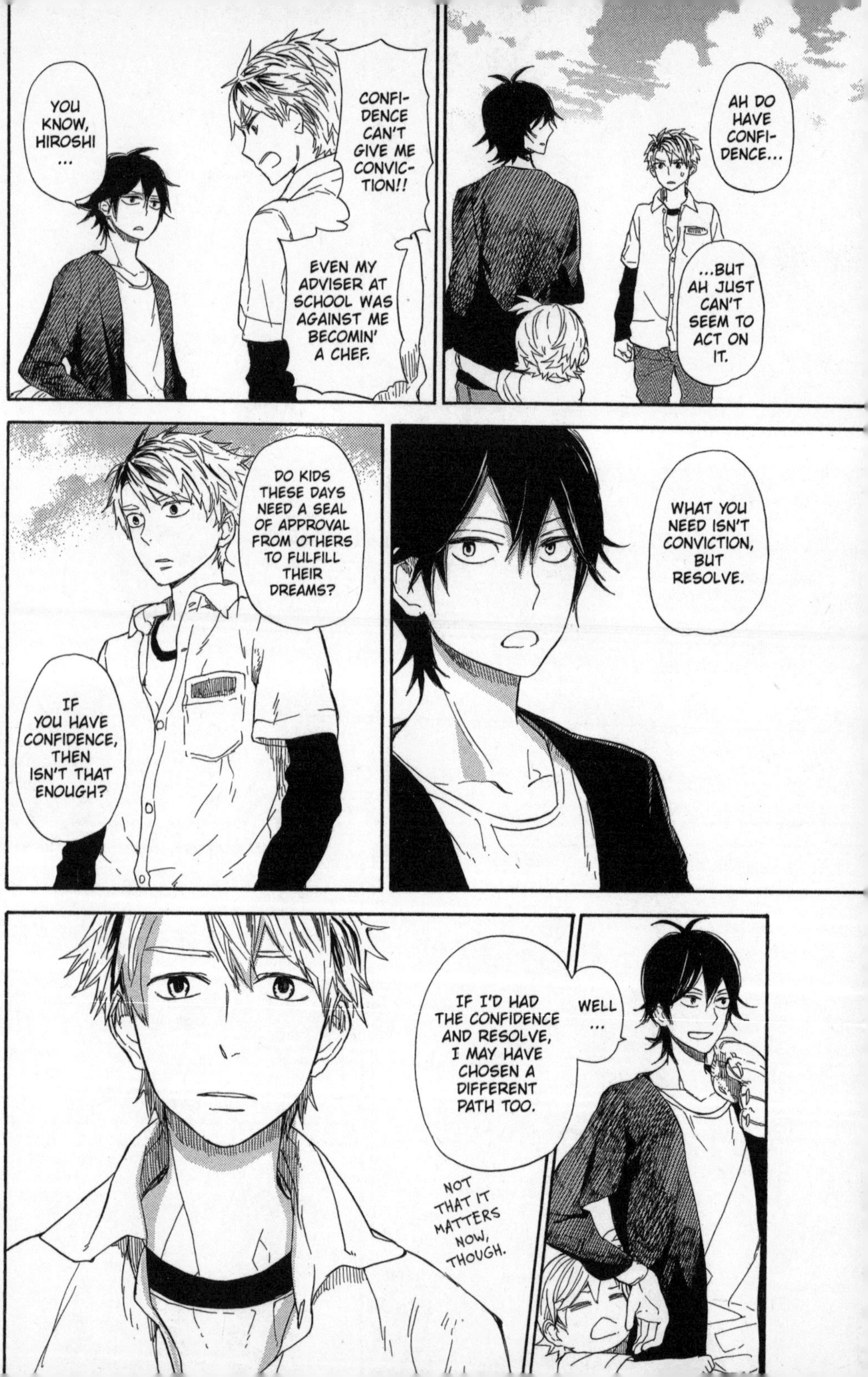
AH DO HAVE CONFIDENCE...
...BUT AH JUST CAN'T SEEM TO ACT ON IT.
CONFIDENCE CAN'T GIVE ME CONVICTION!!
EVEN MY ADVISER AT SCHOOL WAS AGAINST ME BECOMIN' A CHEF.
YOU KNOW, HIROSHI...
WHAT YOU NEED ISN'T CONVICTION, BUT RESOLVE.
DO KIDS THESE DAYS NEED A SEAL OF APPROVAL FROM OTHERS TO FULFILL THEIR DREAMS?
IF YOU HAVE CONFIDENCE, THEN ISN'T THAT ENOUGH?
WELL...
IF I'D HAD THE CONFIDENCE AND RESOLVE, I MAY HAVE CHOSEN A DIFFERENT PATH TOO.
NOT THAT IT MATTERS NOW, THOUGH.

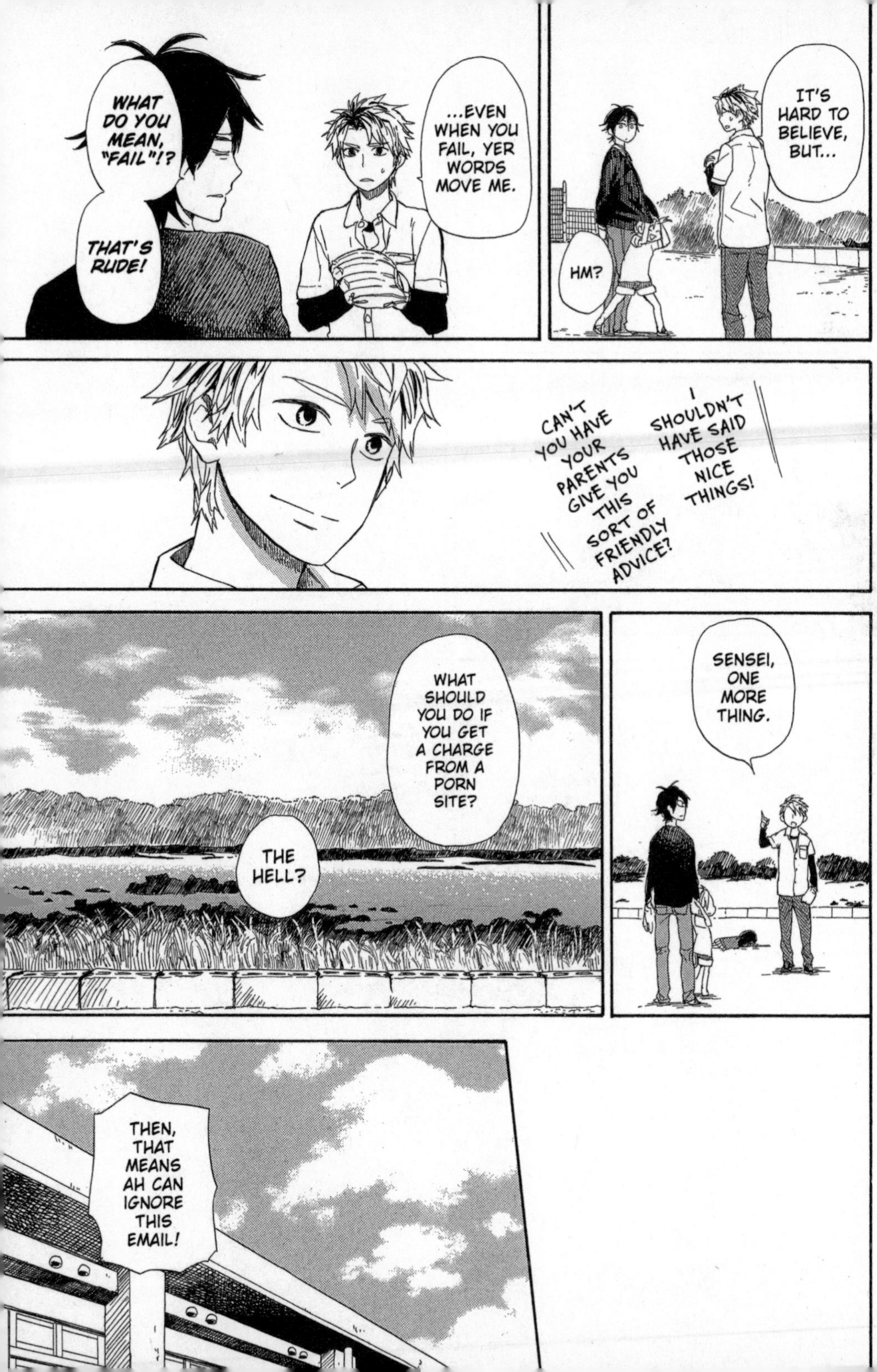
IT'S HARD TO BELIEVE, BUT...
HM?
...EVEN WHEN YOU FAIL, YER WORDS MOVE ME.
WHAT DO YOU MEAN, "FAIL"!?
THAT'S RUDE!
I SHOULDN'T HAVE SAID THOSE NICE THINGS!
CAN'T YOU HAVE YOUR PARENTS GIVE YOU THIS SORT OF FRIENDLY ADVICE?
SENSEI, ONE MORE THING.
WHAT SHOULD YOU DO IF YOU GET A CHARGE FROM A PORN SITE?
THE HELL?
THEN, THAT MEANS AH CAN IGNORE THIS EMAIL!

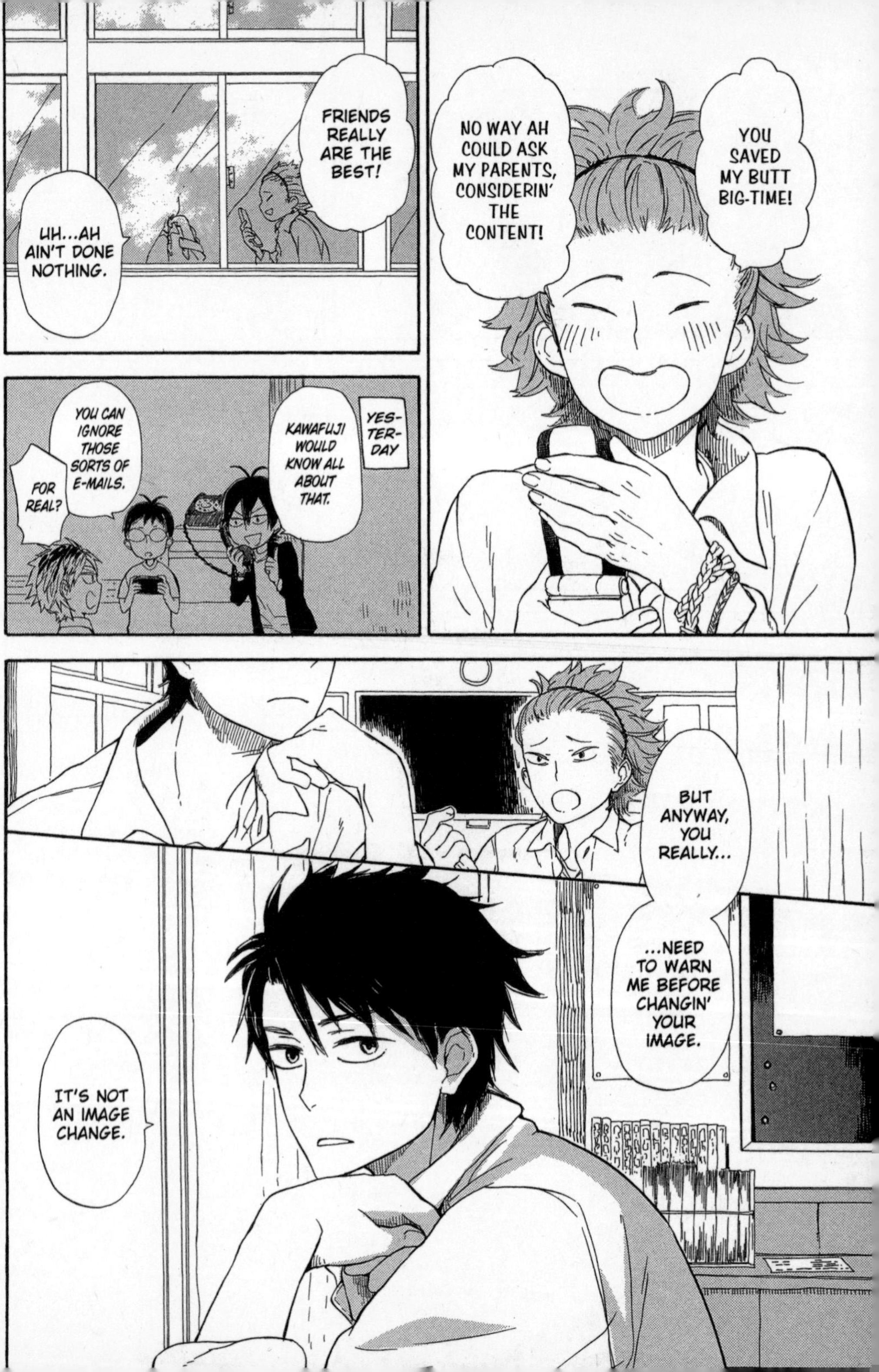
YOU SAVED MY BUTT BIG-TIME!
NO WAY AH COULD ASK MY PARENTS, CONSIDERIN' THE CONTENT!
FRIENDS REALLY ARE THE BEST!
UH...AH AIN'T DONE NOTHING.
YES-TER-DAY
KAWAFUJI WOULD KNOW ALL ABOUT THAT.
YOU CAN IGNORE THOSE SORTS OF E-MAILS.
FOR REAL?
BUT ANYWAY, YOU REALLY...
...NEED TO WARN ME BEFORE CHANGIN' YOUR IMAGE.
IT'S NOT AN IMAGE CHANGE.

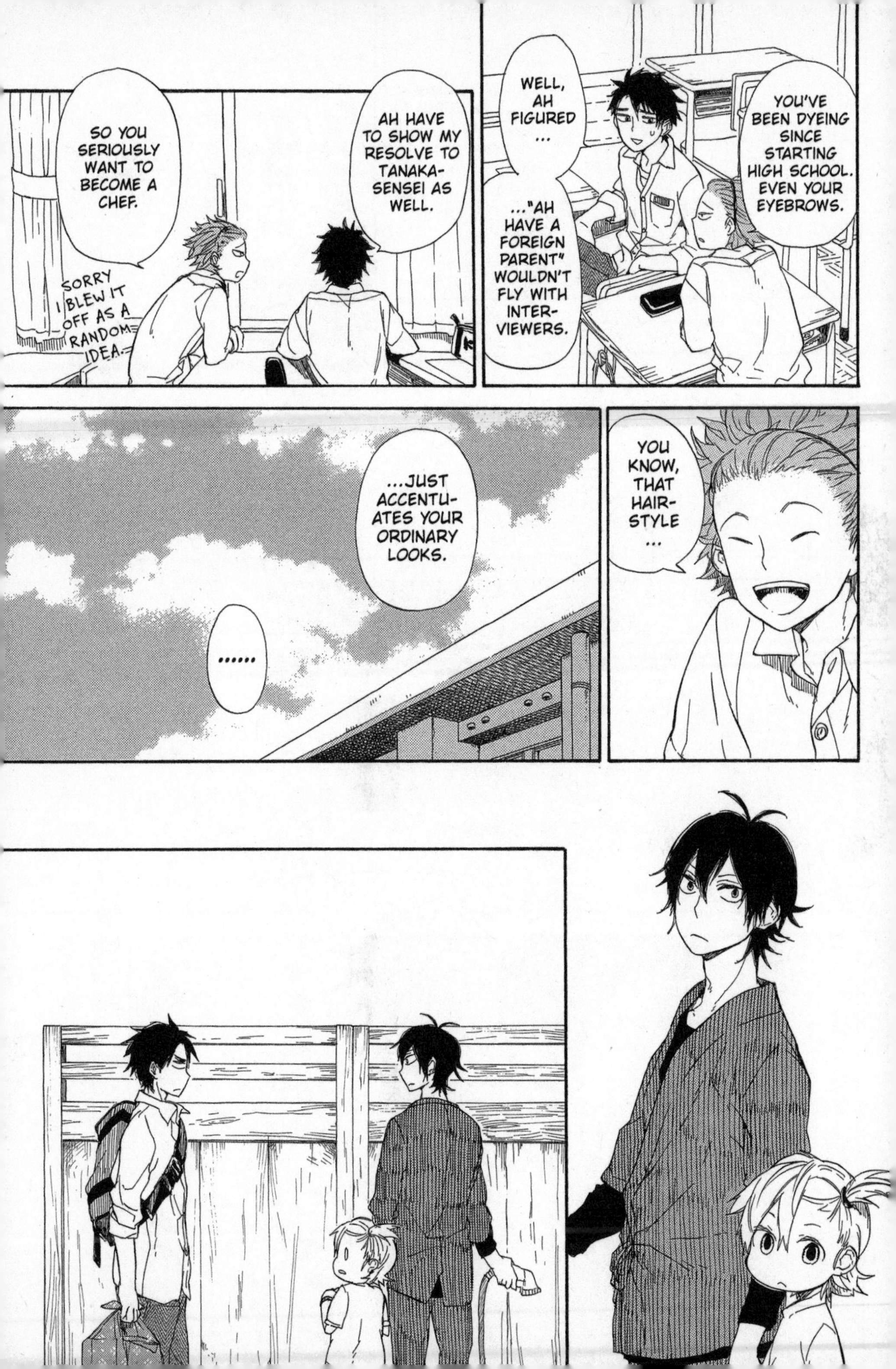
YOU'VE BEEN DYEING SINCE STARTING HIGH SCHOOL. EVEN YOUR EYEBROWS.
WELL, AH FIGURED ...
..."AH HAVE A FOREIGN PARENT" WOULDN'T FLY WITH INTER-VIEWERS.
AH HAVE TO SHOW MY RESOLVE TO TANAKA-SENSEI AS WELL.
SO YOU SERIOUSLY WANT TO BECOME A CHEF.
SORRY I BLEW IT OFF AS A RANDOM IDEA.
YOU KNOW, THAT HAIR-STYLE ...
...JUST ACCENTUATES YOUR ORDINARY LOOKS.
......

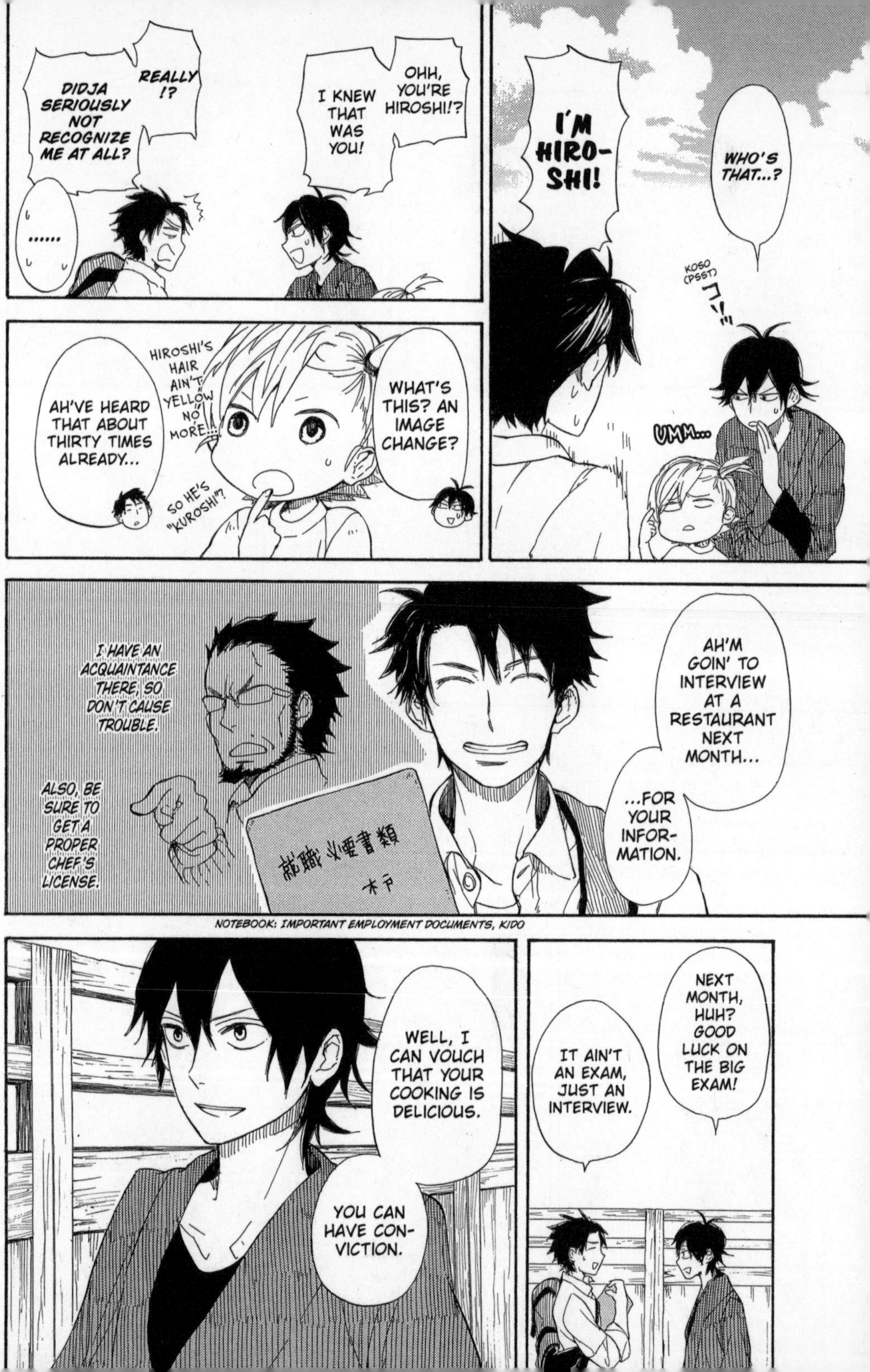
WHO'S THAT...?
I'M HIROSHI!
KOSO (PSST)
UMM...
OHH, YOU'RE HIROSHI!?
I KNEW THAT WAS YOU!
REALLY!?
DIDJA SERIOUSLY NOT RECOGNIZE ME AT ALL?
......
WHAT'S THIS? AN IMAGE CHANGE?
HIROSHI'S HAIR AIN'T YELLOW NO MORE...
SO HE'S "KUROSHI"?
AH'VE HEARD THAT ABOUT THIRTY TIMES ALREADY...
AH'M GOIN' TO INTERVIEW AT A RESTAURANT NEXT MONTH...
...FOR YOUR INFORMATION.
就職必要書類
木戸
I HAVE AN ACQUAINTANCE THERE, SO DON'T CAUSE TROUBLE.
ALSO, BE SURE TO GET A PROPER CHEF'S LICENSE.
NOTEBOOK: IMPORTANT EMPLOYMENT DOCUMENTS, KIDO
NEXT MONTH, HUH? GOOD LUCK ON THE BIG EXAM!
IT AIN'T AN EXAM, JUST AN INTERVIEW.
WELL, I CAN VOUCH THAT YOUR COOKING IS DELICIOUS.
YOU CAN HAVE CONVICTION.

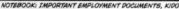

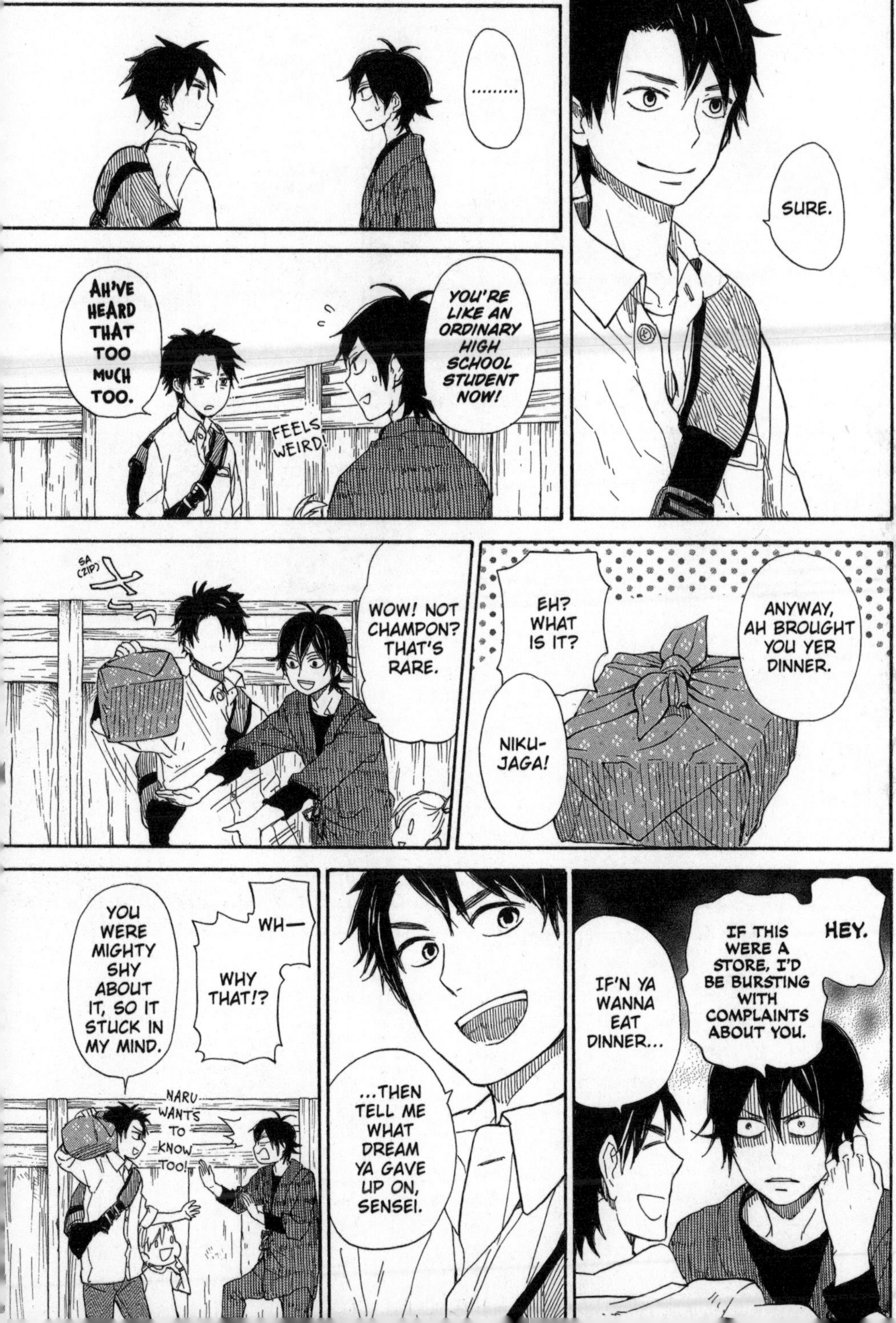
SURE.
....
YOU'RE LIKE AN ORDINARY HIGH SCHOOL STUDENT NOW!
FEELS WEIRD!
AH'VE HEARD THAT TOO MUCH TOO.
ANYWAY, AH BROUGHT YOU YER DINNER.
EH? WHAT IS IT?
NIKU-JAGA!
WOW! NOT CHAMPON? THAT'S RARE.
SA (ZIP)
HEY.
IF THIS WERE A STORE, I'D BE BURSTING WITH COMPLAINTS ABOUT YOU.
IF'N YA WANNA EAT DINNER...
...THEN TELL ME WHAT DREAM YA GAVE UP ON, SENSEI.
WH—
WHY THAT!?
YOU WERE MIGHTY SHY ABOUT IT, SO IT STUCK IN MY MIND.
NARU WANTS TO KNOW TOO!

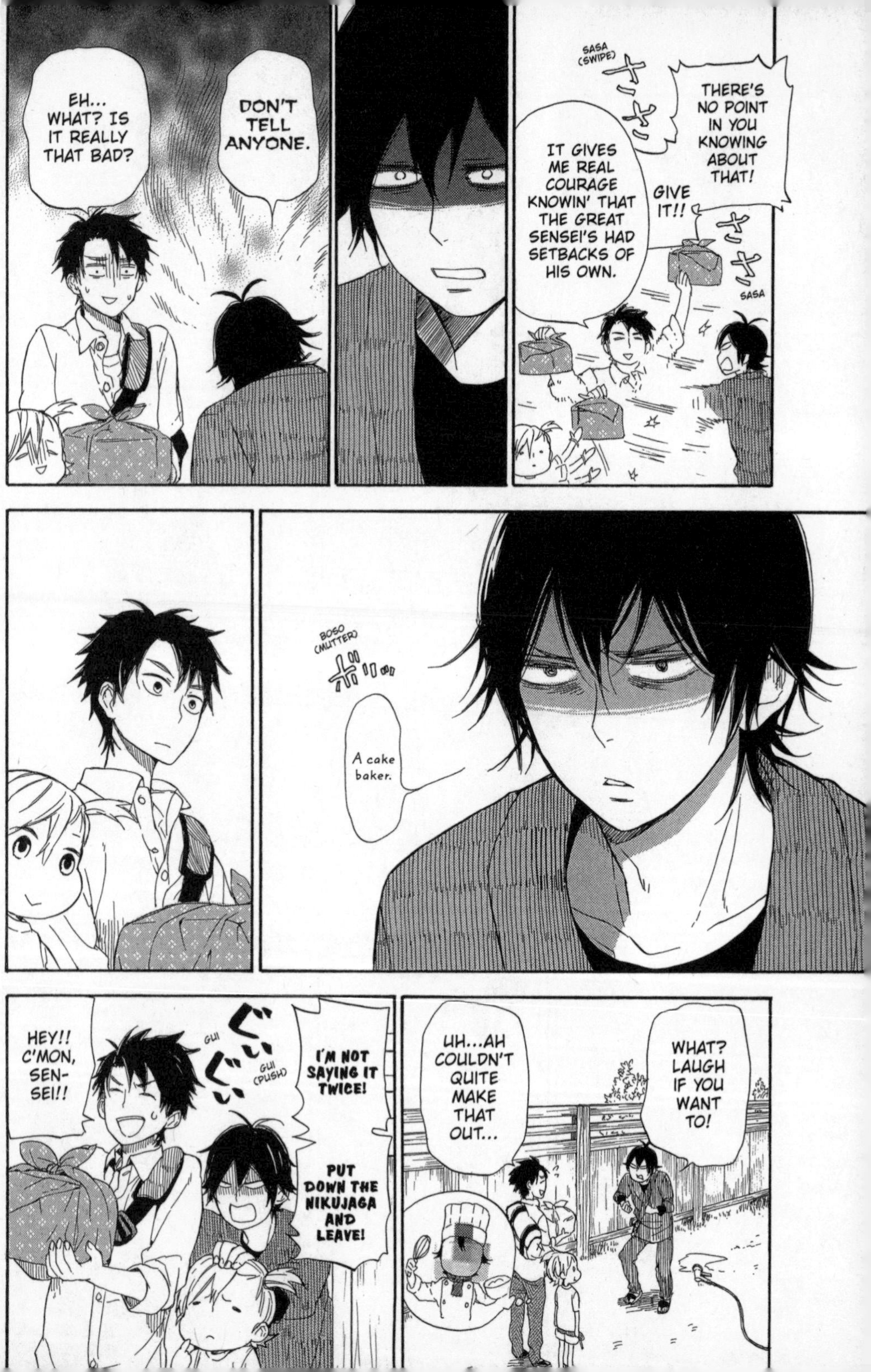
THERE'S NO POINT IN YOU KNOWING ABOUT THAT!
SASA (SWIPE)
GIVE IT!!
IT GIVES ME REAL COURAGE KNOWIN' THAT THE GREAT SENSEI'S HAD SETBACKS OF HIS OWN.
SASA
DON'T TELL ANYONE.
EH... WHAT? IS IT REALLY THAT BAD?
BOSO (MUTTER)
A cake baker.
WHAT? LAUGH IF YOU WANT TO!
UH...AH COULDN'T QUITE MAKE THAT OUT...
I'M NOT SAYING IT TWICE!
PUT DOWN THE NIKUJAGA AND LEAVE!
GUI
GUI (PUSH)
HEY!! C'MON, SEN-SEI!!

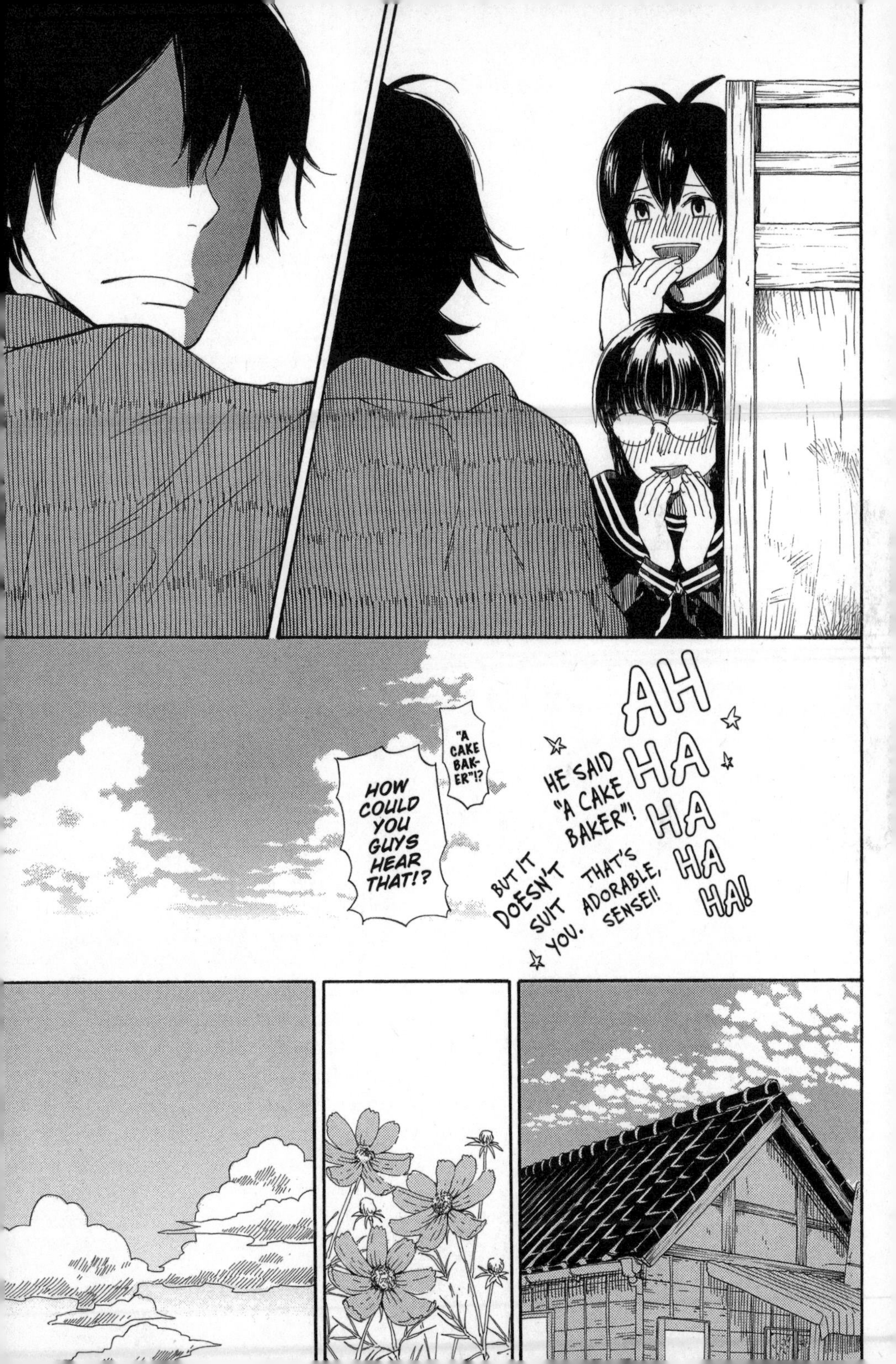
AH HA HA HA HA HA!
HE SAID "A CAKE BAKER"!
THAT'S ADORABLE, SENSEI!
BUT IT DOESN'T SUIT YOU.
"A CAKE BAKER"!?
HOW COULD YOU GUYS HEAR THAT!?

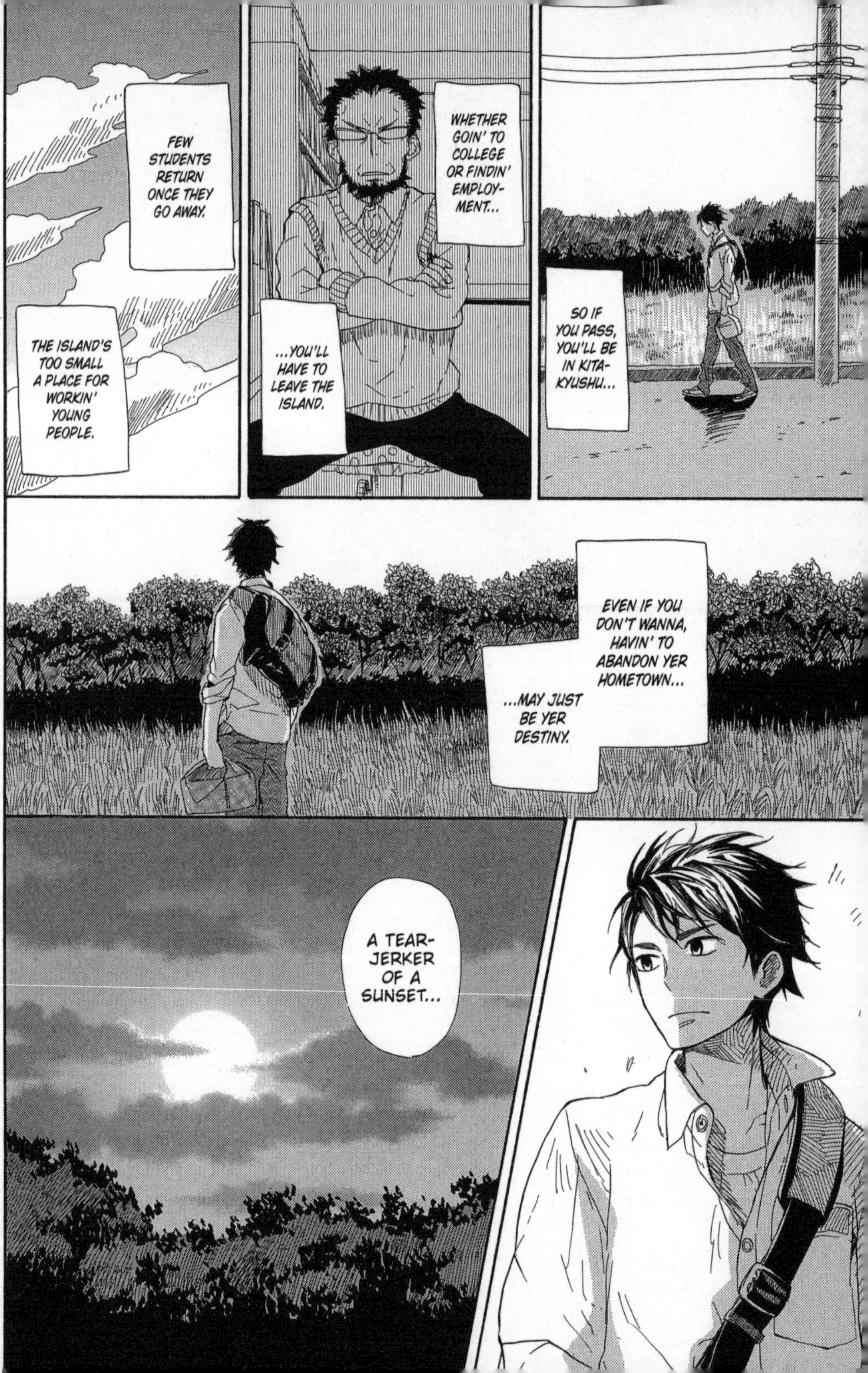
SO IF YOU PASS, YOU'LL BE IN KITA-KYUSHU...
WHETHER GOIN' TO COLLEGE OR FINDIN' EMPLOYMENT...
...YOU'LL HAVE TO LEAVE THE ISLAND.
FEW STUDENTS RETURN ONCE THEY GO AWAY.
THE ISLAND'S TOO SMALL A PLACE FOR WORKIN' YOUNG PEOPLE.
EVEN IF YOU DON'T WANNA, HAVIN' TO ABANDON YER HOMETOWN...
...MAY JUST BE YER DESTINY.
A TEAR-JERKER OF A SUNSET...

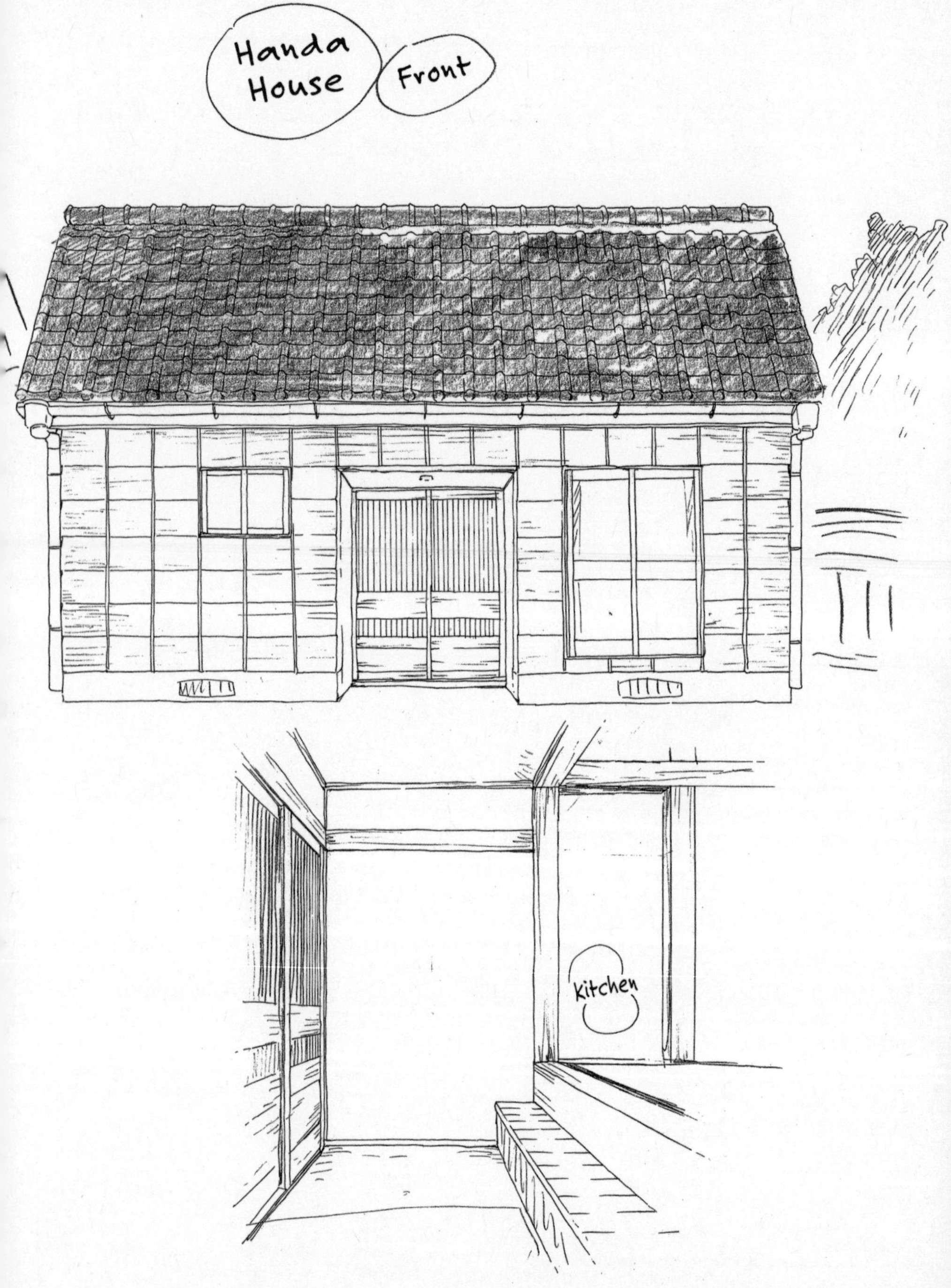

Handa House
Front
Kitchen

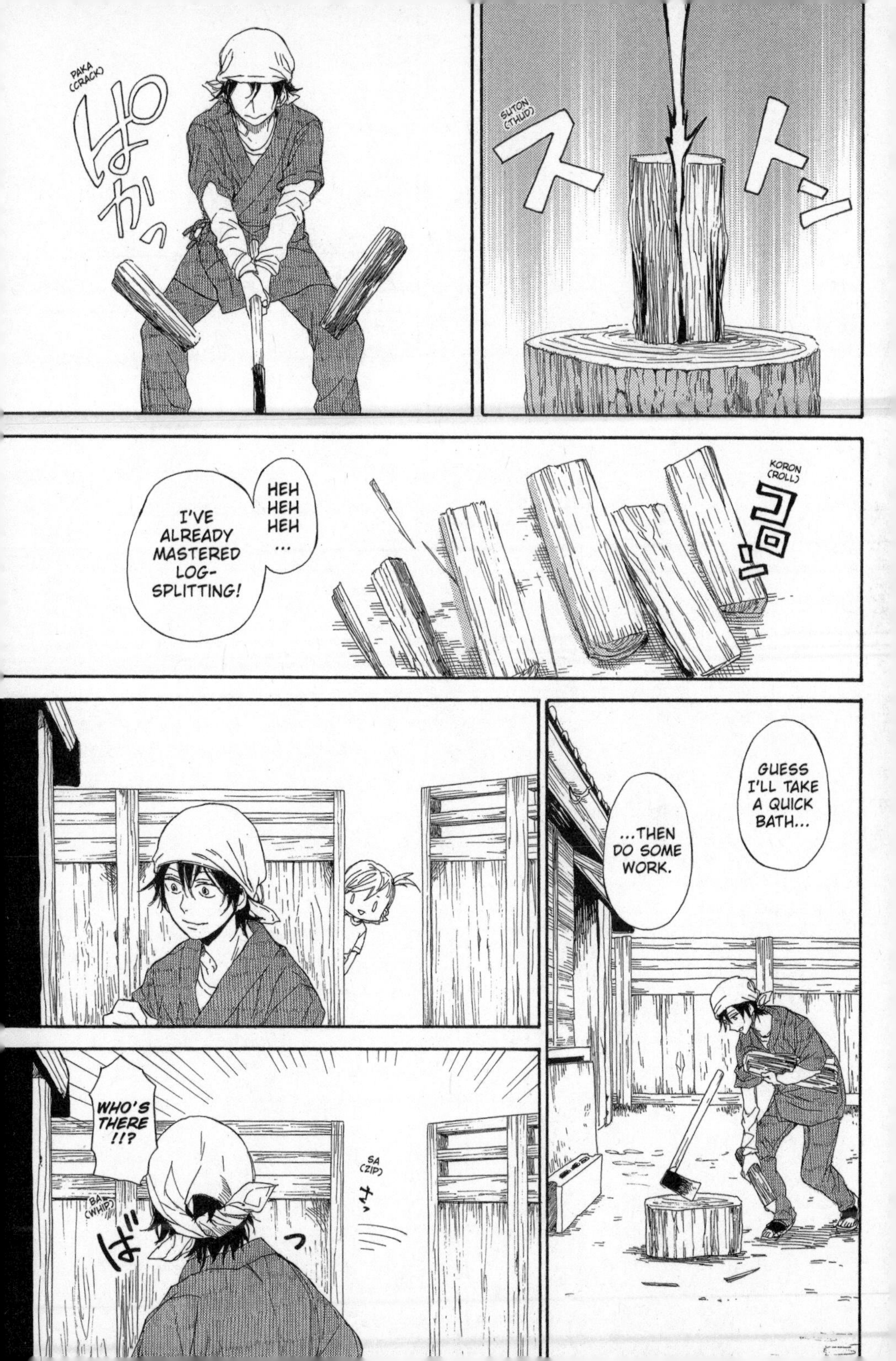
SUTON (THUD)
PAKA (CRACK)
KORON (ROLL)
HEH HEH HEH ... I'VE ALREADY MASTERED LOG-SPLITTING!
GUESS I'LL TAKE A QUICK BATH...
...THEN DO SOME WORK.
WHO'S THERE !!?
SA (ZIP)
BA (WHIP)

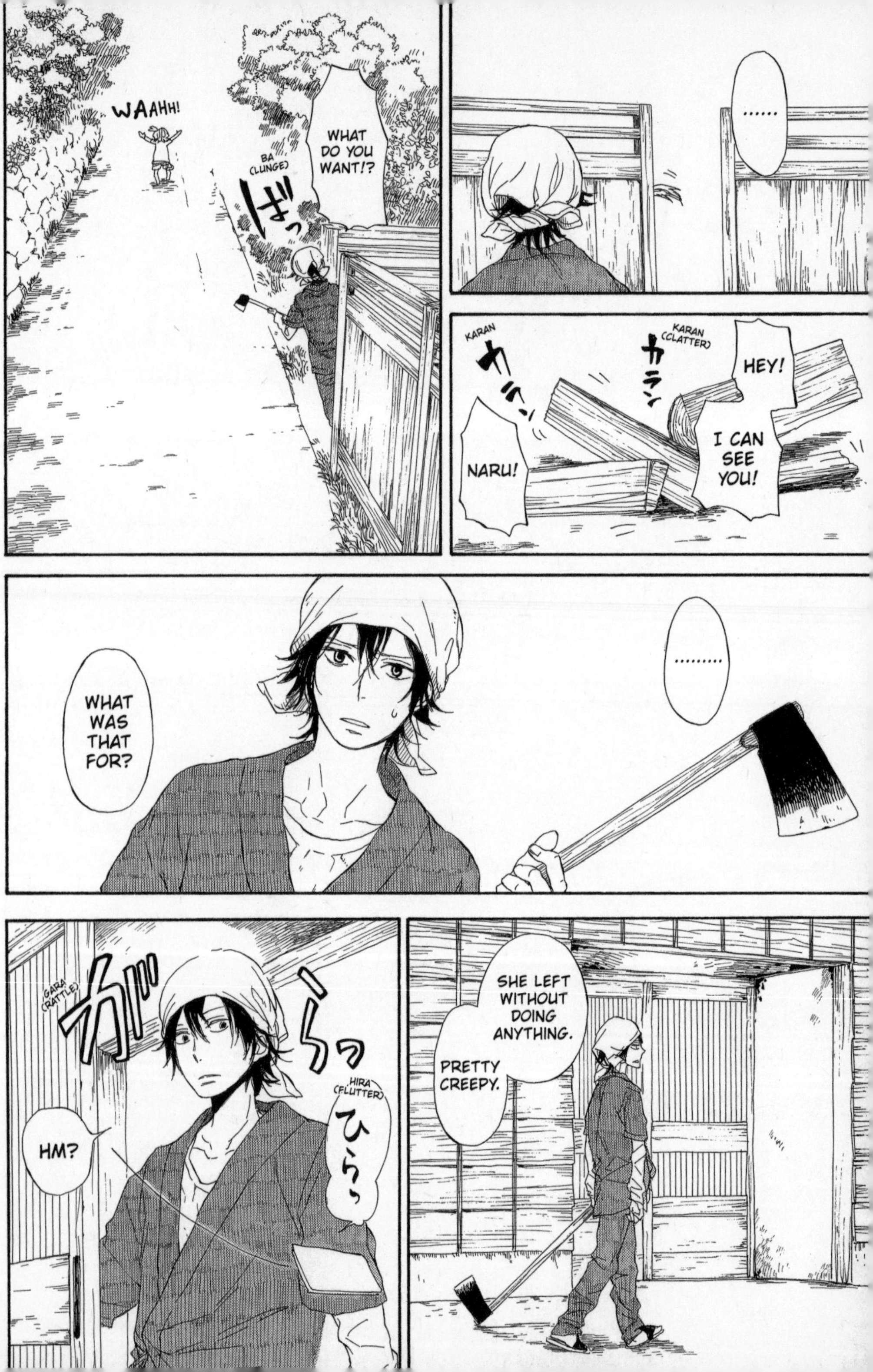
......
KARAN (CLATTER)
カラン
HEY!
I CAN SEE YOU!
KARAN
カラン
NARU!
WHAT DO YOU WANT!?
BA (LUNGE)
ばっ
WAAHH!
....
WHAT WAS THAT FOR?
SHE LEFT WITHOUT DOING ANYTHING.
PRETTY CREEPY.
GARA (RATTLE)
がらっ
HIRA (FLUTTER)
ひらっ
HM?

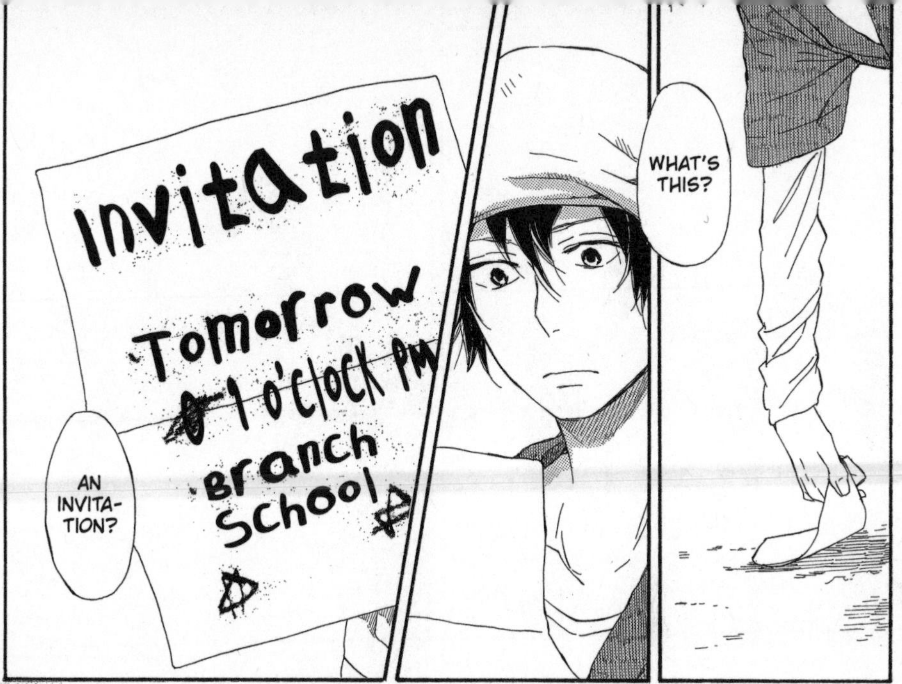
WHAT'S THIS?
AN INVITATION?
Invitation
Tomorrow
1 o'clock PM
Branch School

ACT.60
TONDARU UTOTARU ODOTTARU
(Translation: Jumping, Singing, Dancing)

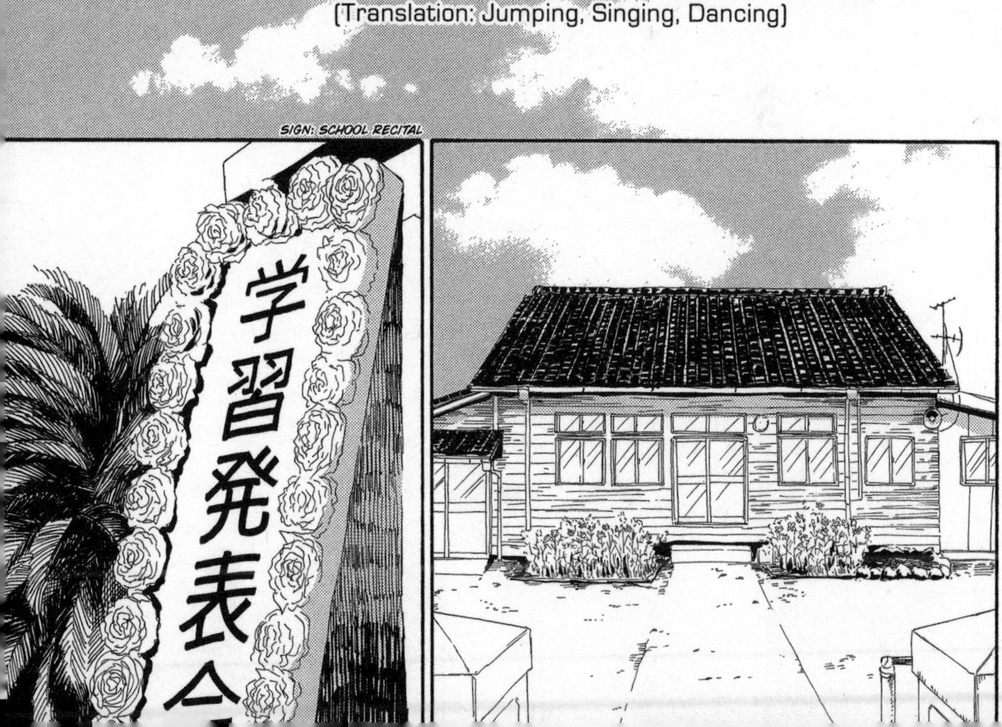
SIGN: SCHOOL RECITAL
学習発表会

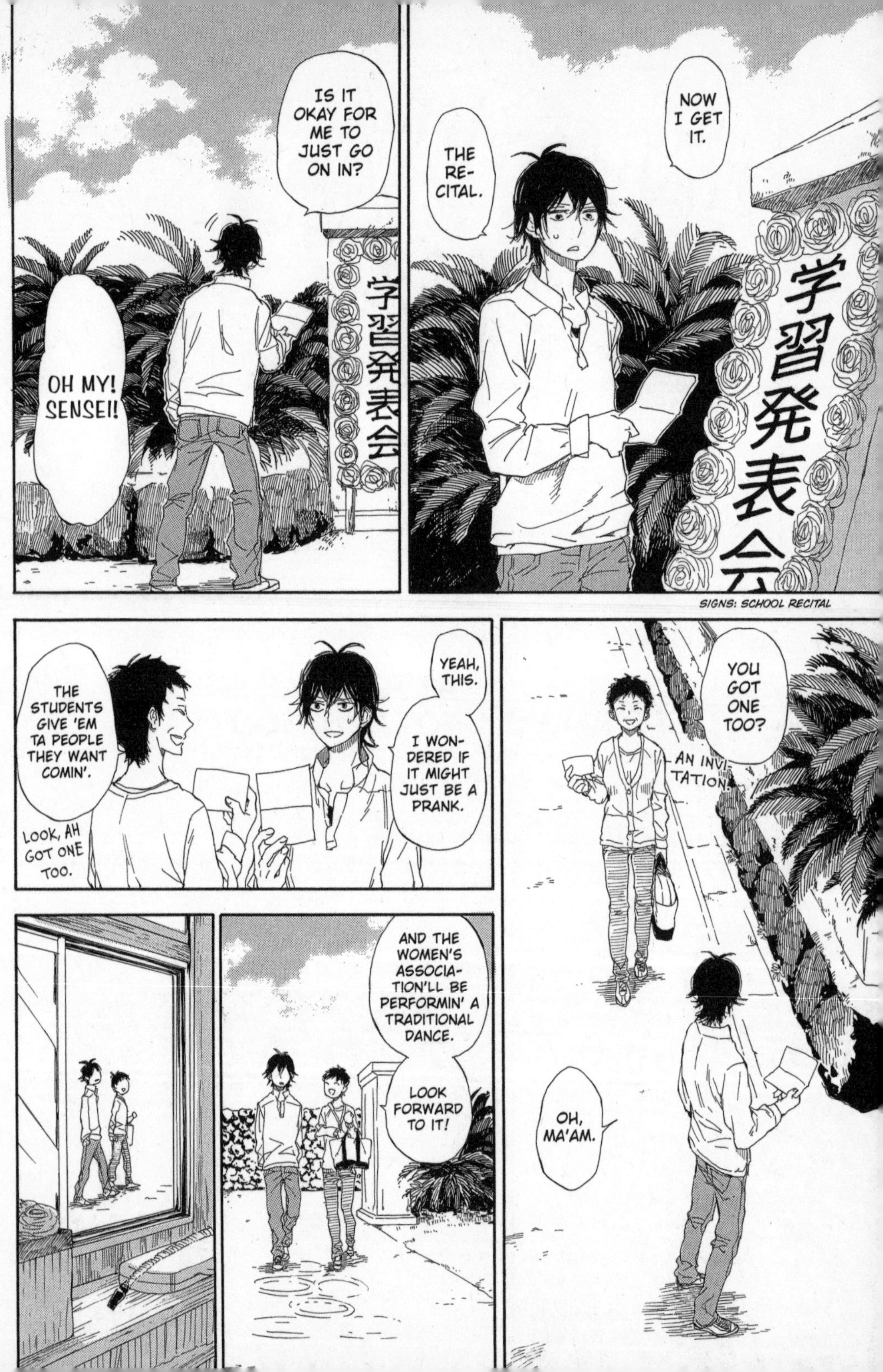
NOW I GET IT.
THE RE-CITAL.
学習発表会
IS IT OKAY FOR ME TO JUST GO ON IN?
学習発表会
OH MY! SENSEI!!
SIGNS: SCHOOL RECITAL
YOU GOT ONE TOO?
AN INVITATION.
OH, MA'AM.
YEAH, THIS.
I WONDERED IF IT MIGHT JUST BE A PRANK.
THE STUDENTS GIVE 'EM TA PEOPLE THEY WANT COMIN'.
LOOK, AH GOT ONE TOO.
AND THE WOMEN'S ASSOCIATION'LL BE PERFORMIN' A TRADITIONAL DANCE.
LOOK FORWARD TO IT!

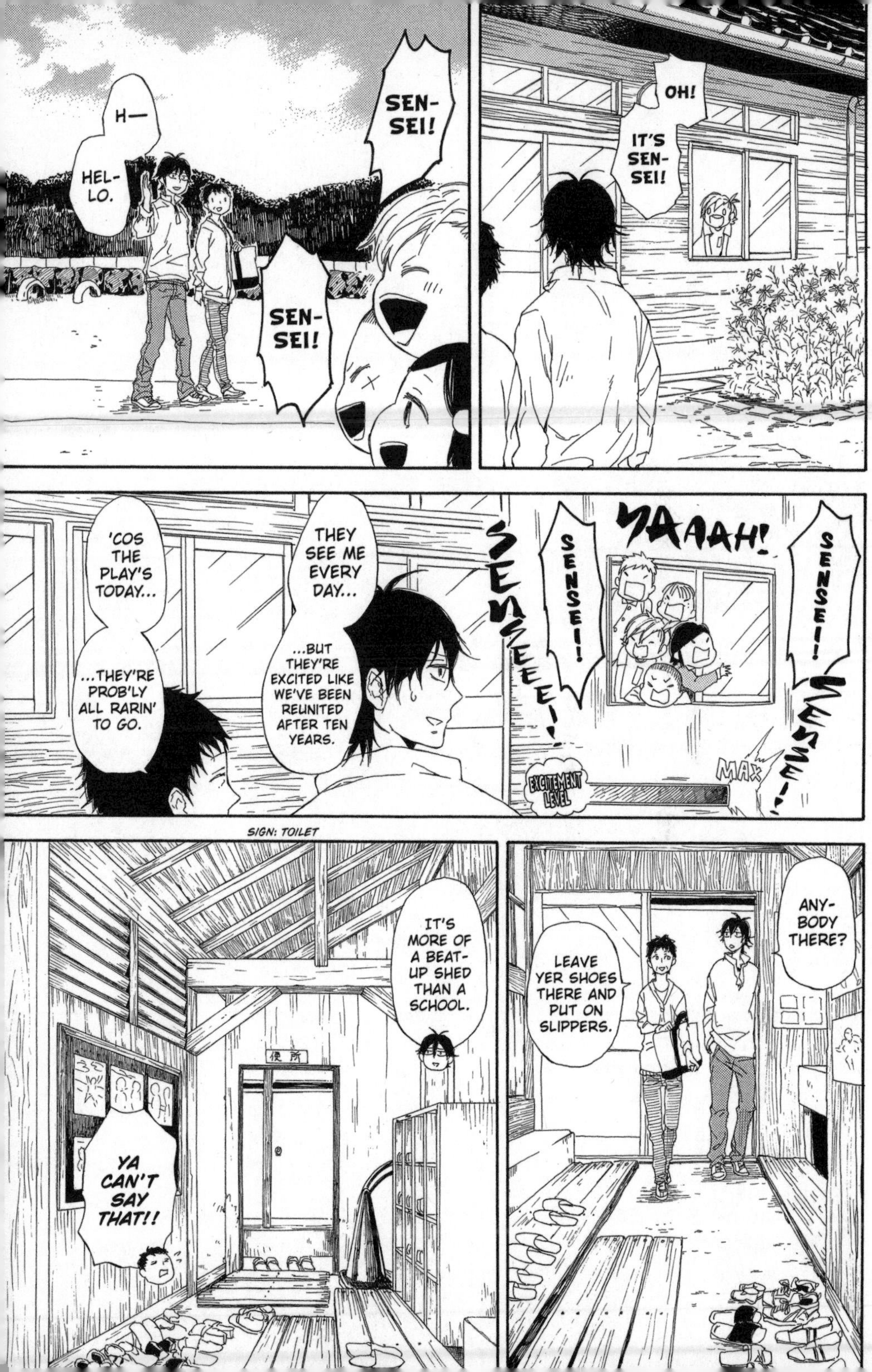
OH!
IT'S SEN-SEI!
SEN-SEI!
H—
HEL-LO.
SEN-SEI!
YAAAH!
SENSEI!
SENSEI!
SENSEEEI!
SENSEI!
EXCITEMENT LEVEL
MAX
THEY SEE ME EVERY DAY...
...BUT THEY'RE EXCITED LIKE WE'VE BEEN REUNITED AFTER TEN YEARS.
'COS THE PLAY'S TODAY...
...THEY'RE PROB'LY ALL RARIN' TO GO.
ANY-BODY THERE?
LEAVE YER SHOES THERE AND PUT ON SLIPPERS.
SIGN: TOILET
便所
IT'S MORE OF A BEAT-UP SHED THAN A SCHOOL.
YA CAN'T SAY THAT!!

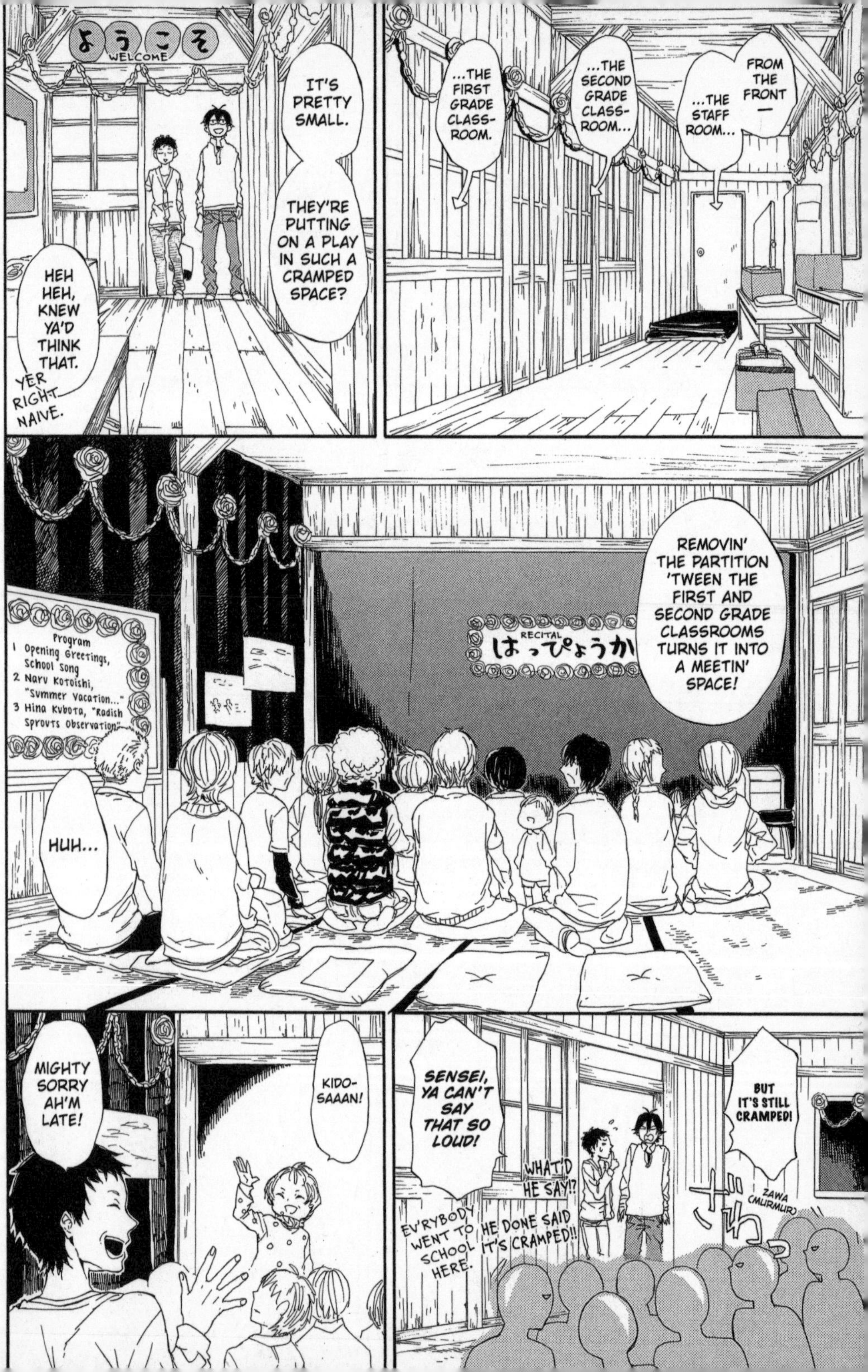
FROM THE FRONT—
...THE STAFF ROOM...
...THE SECOND GRADE CLASSROOM...
...THE FIRST GRADE CLASSROOM.
ようこそ
WELCOME
IT'S PRETTY SMALL.
THEY'RE PUTTING ON A PLAY IN SUCH A CRAMPED SPACE?
HEH HEH, KNEW YA'D THINK THAT.
YER RIGHT NAIVE.
REMOVIN' THE PARTITION 'TWEEN THE FIRST AND SECOND GRADE CLASSROOMS TURNS IT INTO A MEETIN' SPACE!
RECITAL
はっぴょうか
Program
1 Opening Greetings, School Song
2 Naru Kotoishi, "Summer Vacation..."
3 Hina Kubota, "Radish Sprouts Observation"
HUH...
BUT IT'S STILL CRAMPED!
ざわっ
ZAWA (MURMUR)
SENSEI, YA CAN'T SAY THAT SO LOUD!
WHAT'D HE SAY!?
HE DONE SAID IT'S CRAMPED!!
EV'RYBODY WENT TO SCHOOL HERE.
KIDO-SAAAN!
MIGHTY SORRY AH'M LATE!

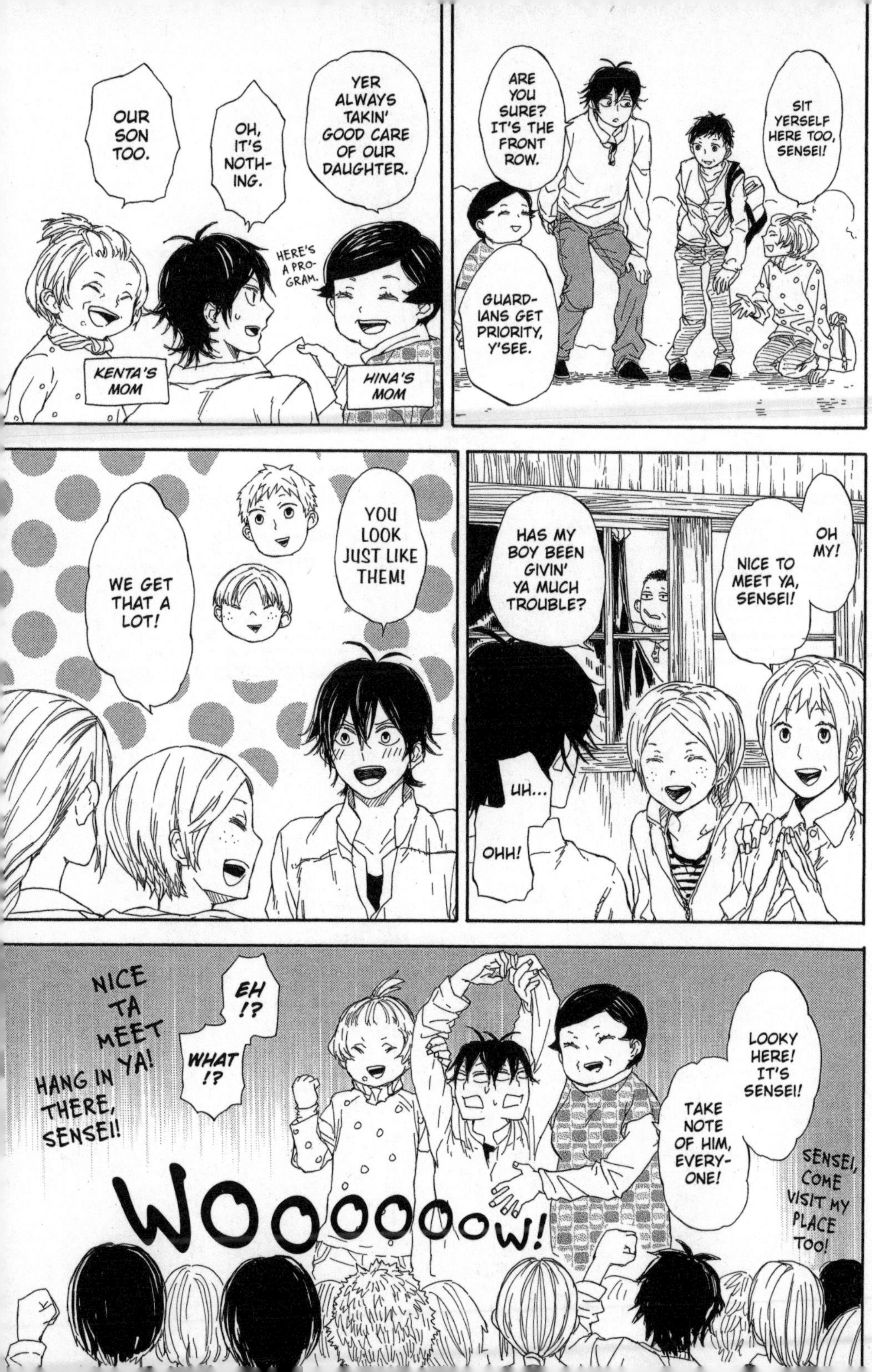
SIT YERSELF HERE TOO, SENSEI!
ARE YOU SURE? IT'S THE FRONT ROW.
GUARDIANS GET PRIORITY, Y'SEE.
YER ALWAYS TAKIN' GOOD CARE OF OUR DAUGHTER.
HERE'S A PROGRAM.
OH, IT'S NOTHING.
OUR SON TOO.
HINA'S MOM
KENTA'S MOM
OH MY!
NICE TO MEET YA, SENSEI!
HAS MY BOY BEEN GIVIN' YA MUCH TROUBLE?
UH...
OHH!
YOU LOOK JUST LIKE THEM!
WE GET THAT A LOT!
LOOKY HERE! IT'S SENSEI!
SENSEI, COME VISIT MY PLACE TOO!
TAKE NOTE OF HIM, EVERYONE!
EH!?
WHAT!?
NICE TA MEET YA!
HANG IN THERE, SENSEI!
WOOOOOOW!

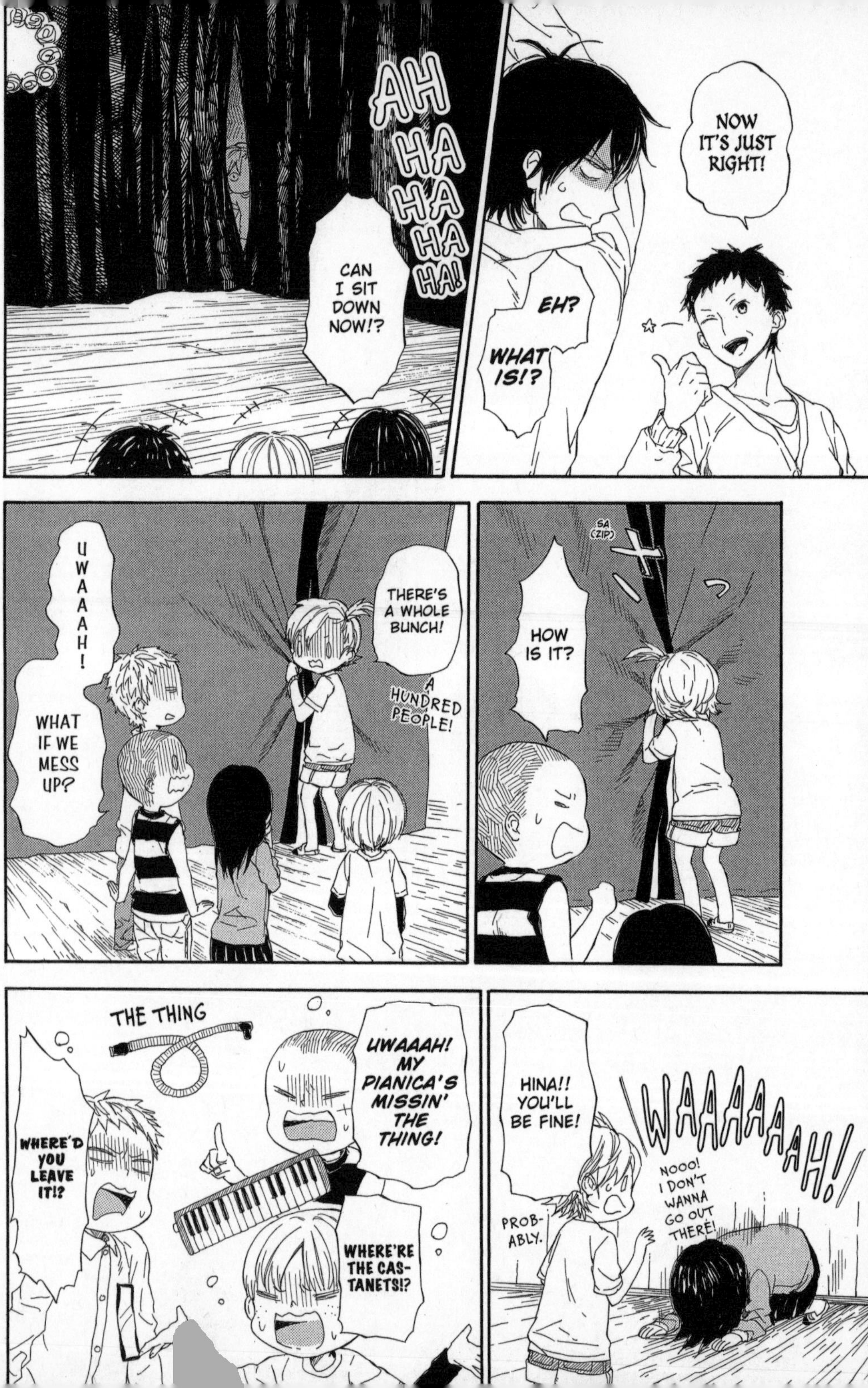
NOW IT'S JUST RIGHT!
EH?
WHAT IS!?
AH HA HA HA HA HA!
CAN I SIT DOWN NOW!?
SA (ZIP)
HOW IS IT?
THERE'S A WHOLE BUNCH!
A HUNDRED PEOPLE!
UWAAAAH!
WHAT IF WE MESS UP?
WAAAAAAAH!
NOOO! I DON'T WANNA GO OUT THERE!
HINA!! YOU'LL BE FINE!
PROB-ABLY.
UWAAAH! MY PIANICA'S MISSIN' THE THING!
THE THING
WHERE'D YOU LEAVE IT!?
WHERE'RE THE CAS-TANETS!?

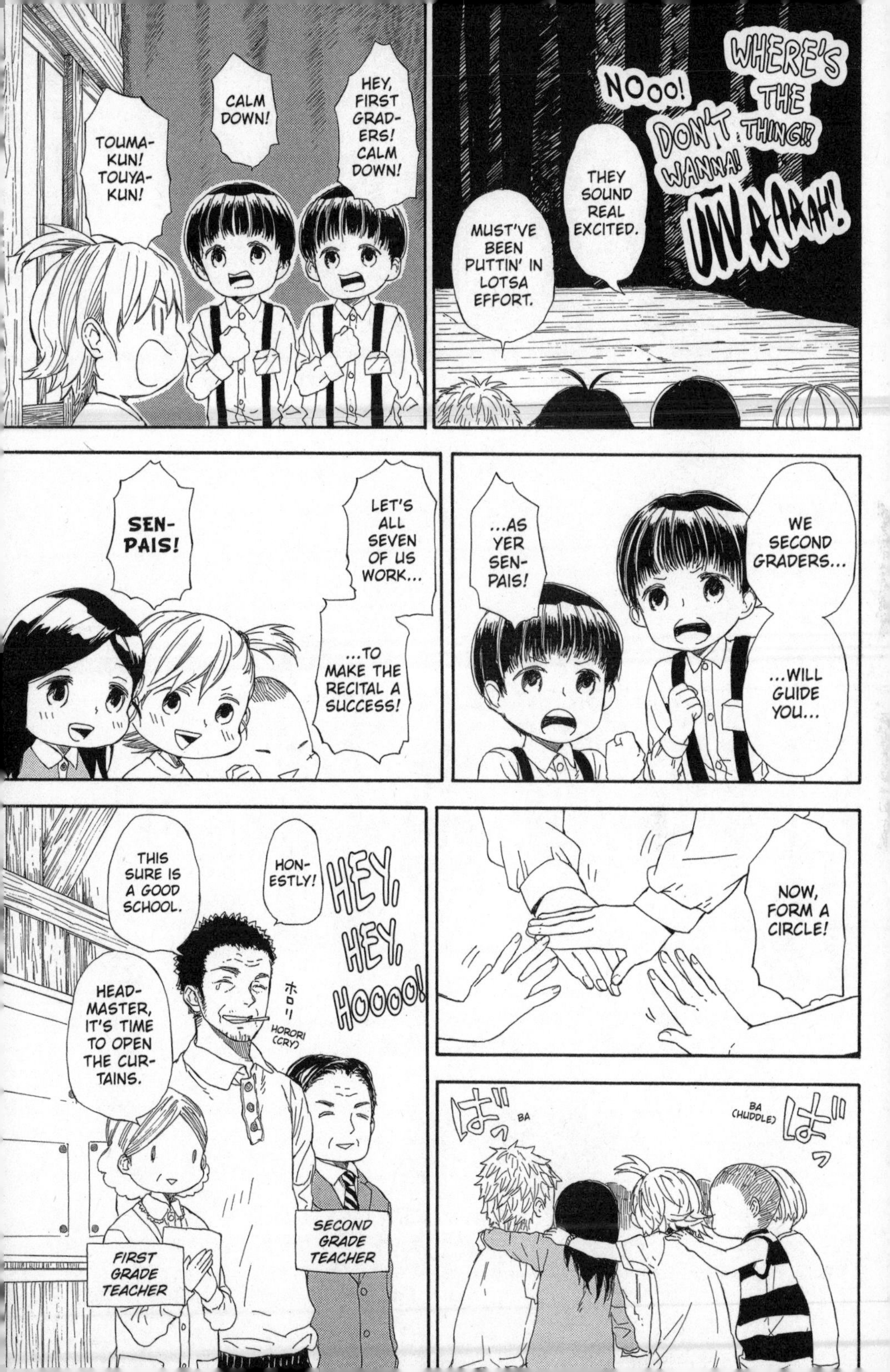
WHERE'S THE THING!?
NOOo!
DON'T WANNA!
UWAAAAH!
THEY SOUND REAL EXCITED.
MUST'VE BEEN PUTTIN' IN LOTSA EFFORT.
HEY, FIRST GRADERS! CALM DOWN!
CALM DOWN!
TOUMA-KUN! TOUYA-KUN!
WE SECOND GRADERS...
...WILL GUIDE YOU...
...AS YER SENPAIS!
SENPAIS!
LET'S ALL SEVEN OF US WORK...
...TO MAKE THE RECITAL A SUCCESS!
NOW, FORM A CIRCLE!
ばっ
BA (HUDDLE)
ばっ
BA
HEY, HEY, HOOOO!
HONESTLY!
THIS SURE IS A GOOD SCHOOL.
ホロリ
HORORI (CRY)
HEADMASTER, IT'S TIME TO OPEN THE CURTAINS.
SECOND GRADE TEACHER
FIRST GRADE TEACHER

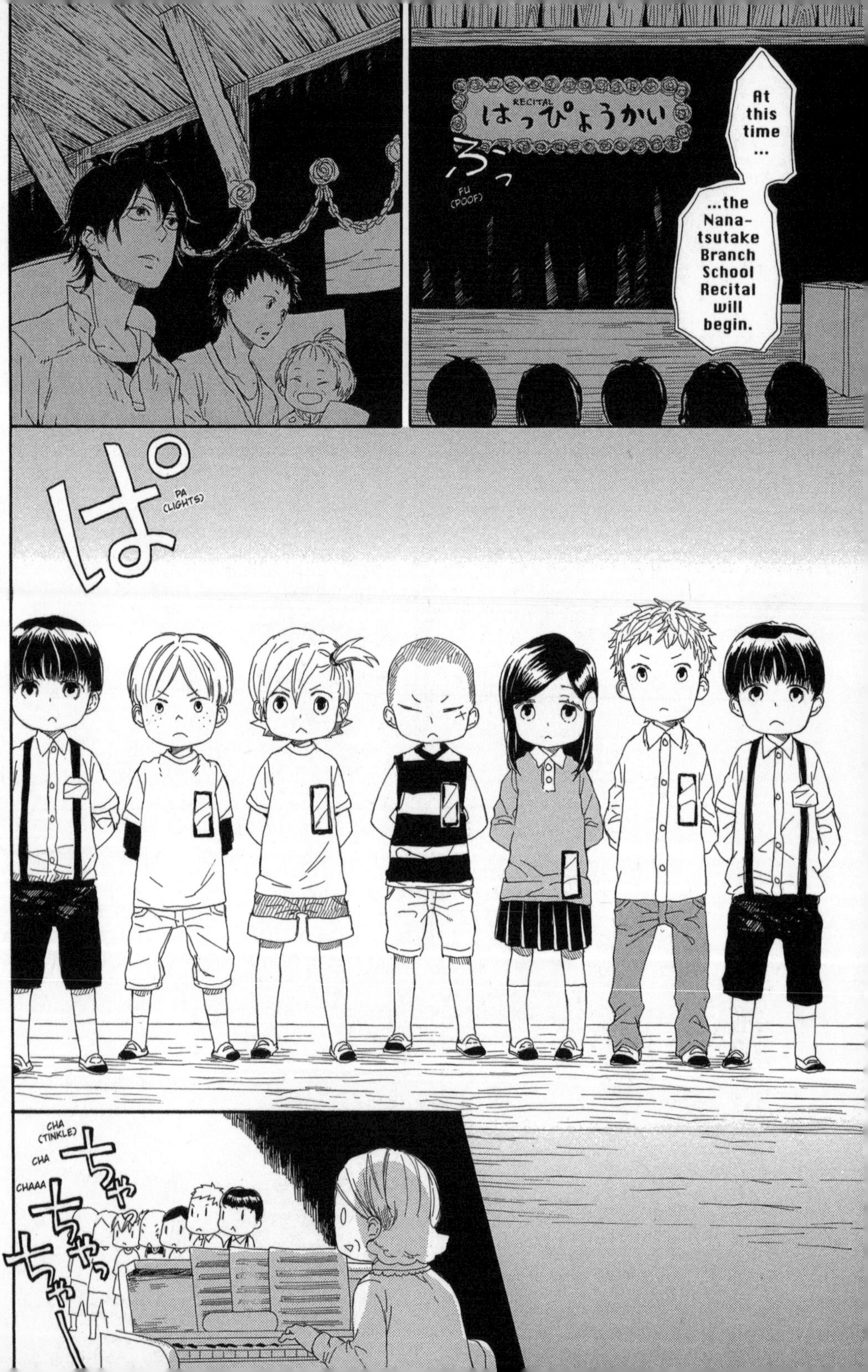
At this time...
...the Nana-tsutake Branch School Recital will begin.
RECITAL
はっぴょうかい
ふっ
FU (POOF)
ぱ
PA (LIGHTS)
ちゃ
CHA (TINKLE)
ちゃっ
CHA
ちゃー
CHAAA

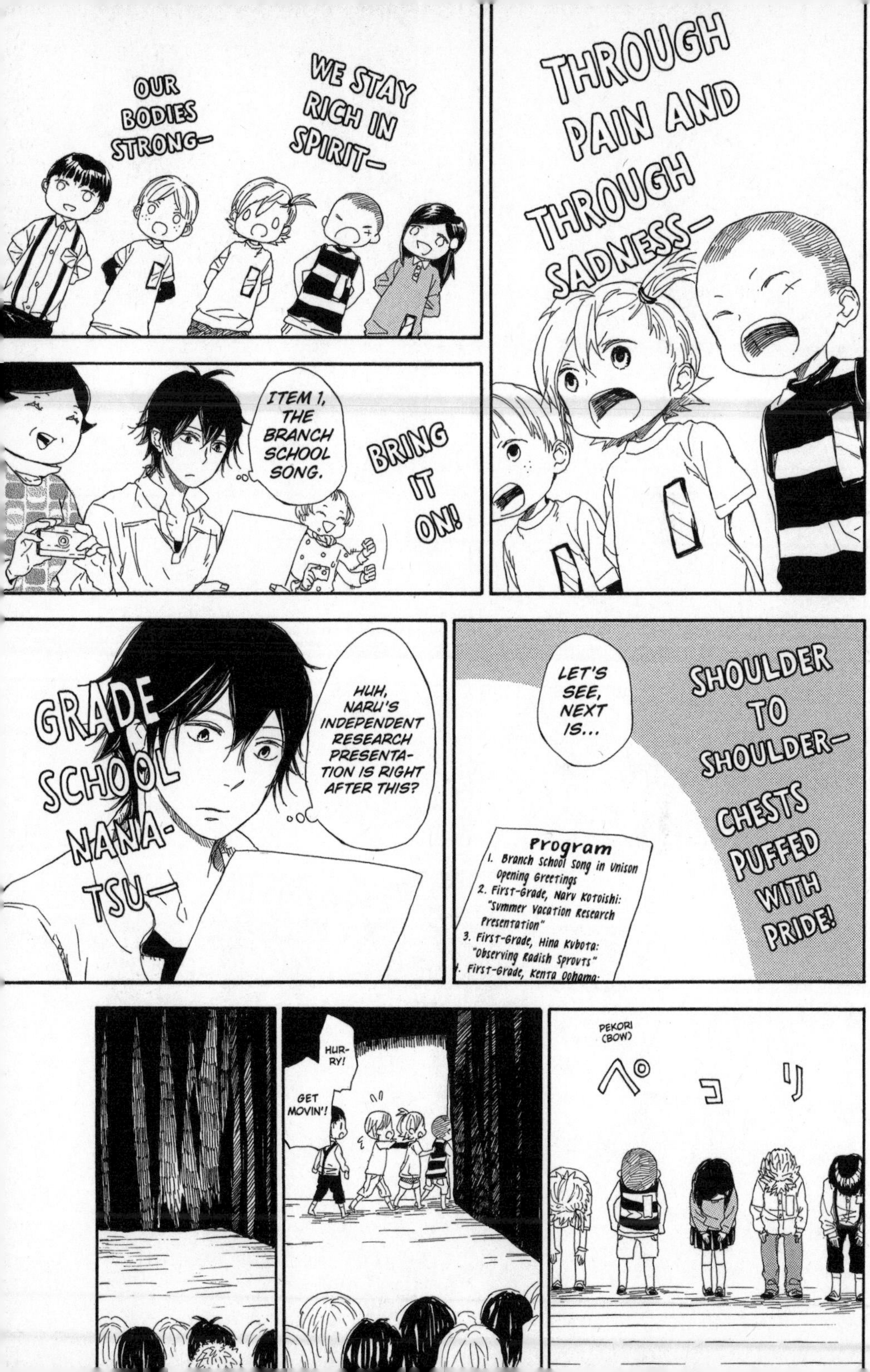
THROUGH PAIN AND THROUGH SADNESS—
WE STAY RICH IN SPIRIT—
OUR BODIES STRONG—
BRING IT ON!
ITEM 1, THE BRANCH SCHOOL SONG.
SHOULDER TO SHOULDER— CHESTS PUFFED WITH PRIDE!
LET'S SEE, NEXT IS...
Program
1. Branch School Song in Unison
Opening Greetings
2. First-Grade, Naru Kotoishi: "Summer Vacation Research Presentation"
3. First-Grade, Hina Kubota: "Observing Radish Sprouts"
4. First-Grade, Kenta Oohama:
HUH, NARU'S INDEPENDENT RESEARCH PRESENTATION IS RIGHT AFTER THIS?
GRADE SCHOOL NANA-TSU—
PEKORI (BOW)
ペコリ
HURRY!
GET MOVIN'!

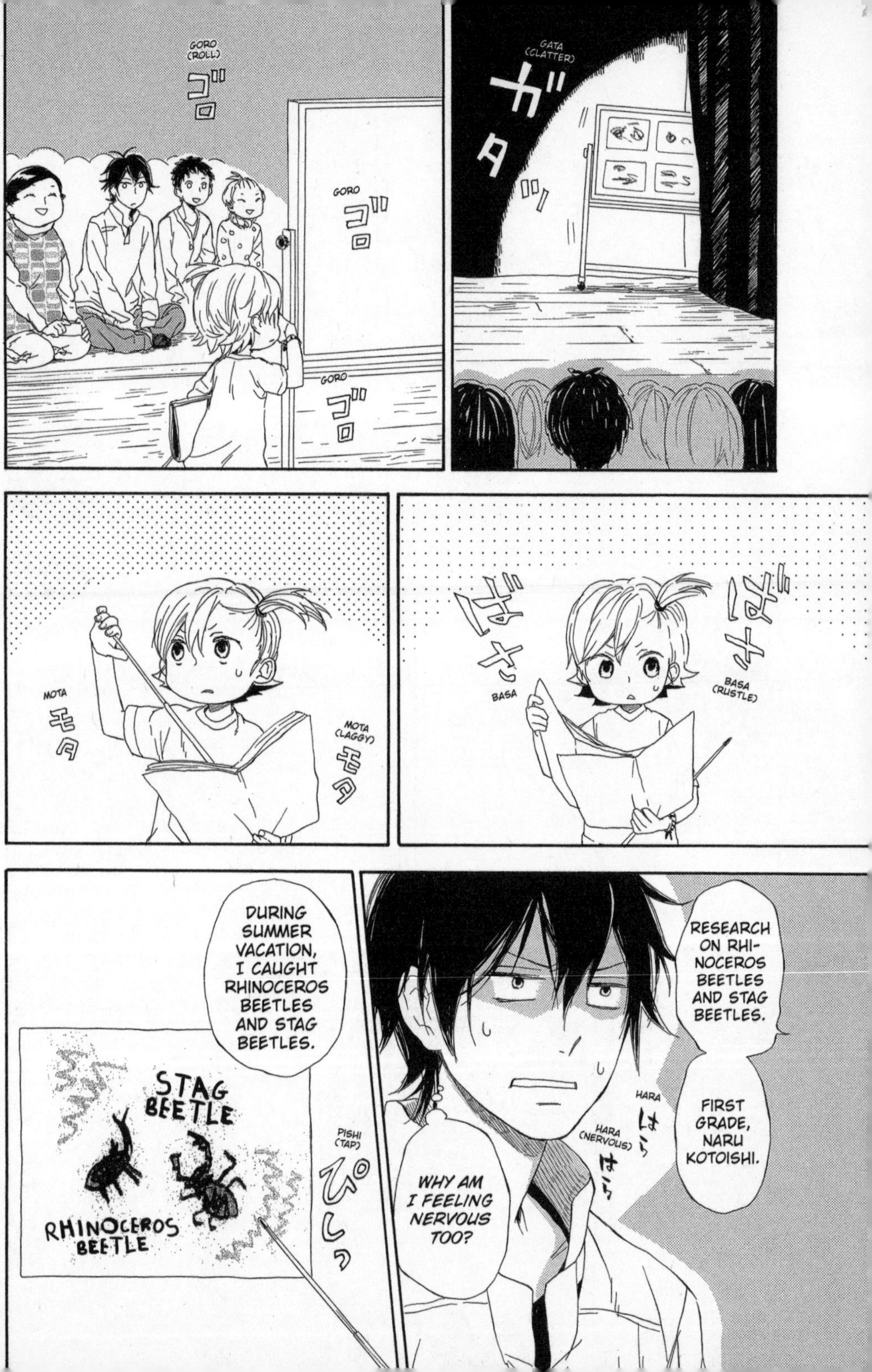
GATA (CLATTER)
ガタッ
GORO (ROLL)
ゴロ
GORO
ゴロ
GORO
ゴロ
BASA (RUSTLE)
ばさ
BASA
ばさ
MOTA (LAGGY)
モタ
MOTA
モタ
RESEARCH ON RHINOCEROS BEETLES AND STAG BEETLES.
FIRST GRADE, NARU KOTOISHI.
HARA
はら
HARA (NERVOUS)
はら
WHY AM I FEELING NERVOUS TOO?
DURING SUMMER VACATION, I CAUGHT RHINOCEROS BEETLES AND STAG BEETLES.
STAG BEETLE
RHINOCEROS BEETLE
PISHI (TAP)
ぴしっ

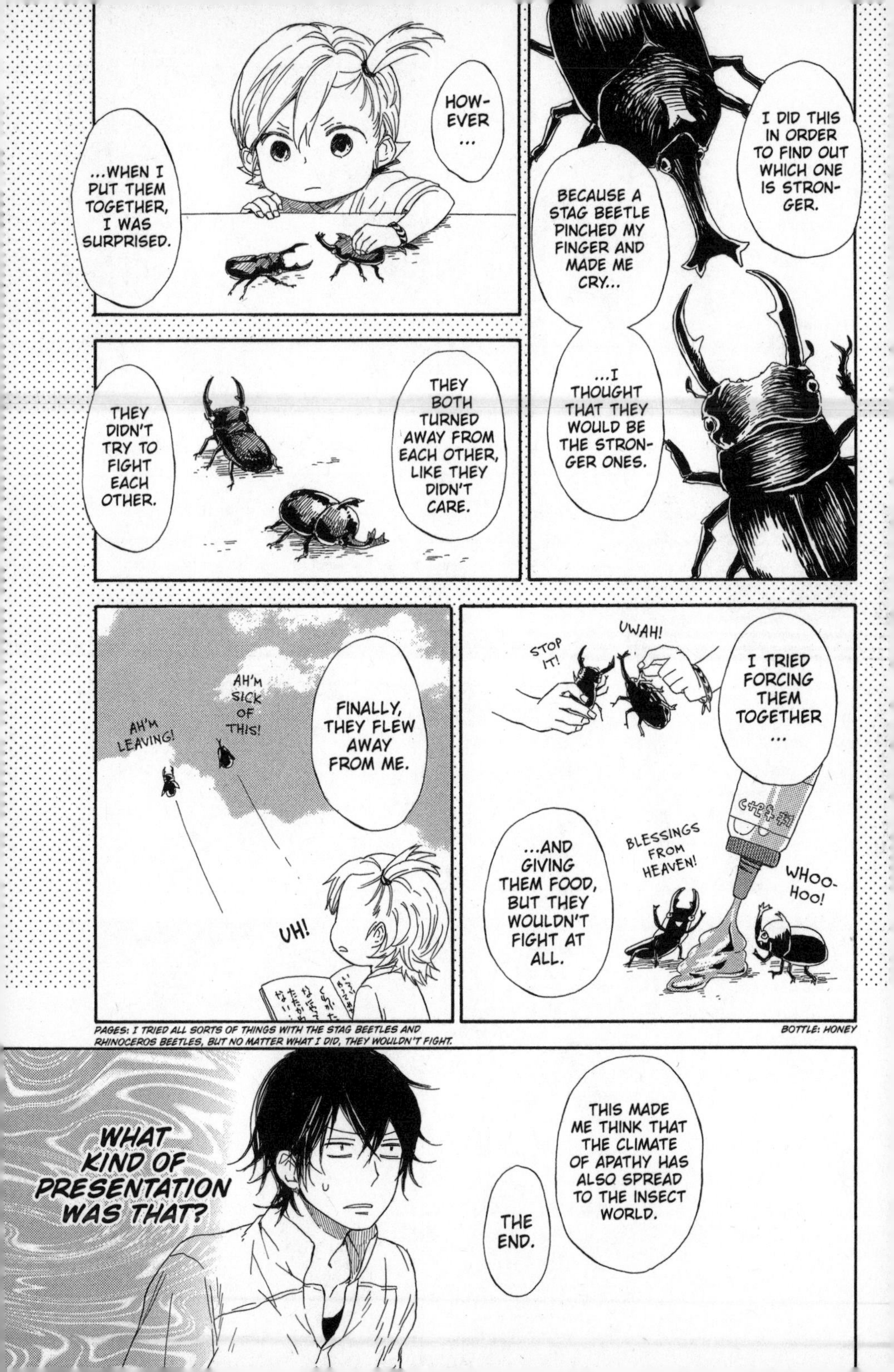

I DID THIS IN ORDER TO FIND OUT WHICH ONE IS STRONGER.
BECAUSE A STAG BEETLE PINCHED MY FINGER AND MADE ME CRY...
...I THOUGHT THAT THEY WOULD BE THE STRONGER ONES.
HOW-EVER ...
...WHEN I PUT THEM TOGETHER, I WAS SURPRISED.
THEY BOTH TURNED AWAY FROM EACH OTHER, LIKE THEY DIDN'T CARE.
THEY DIDN'T TRY TO FIGHT EACH OTHER.
I TRIED FORCING THEM TOGETHER ...
UWAH!
STOP IT!
...AND GIVING THEM FOOD, BUT THEY WOULDN'T FIGHT AT ALL.
WHOO-HOO!
BLESSINGS FROM HEAVEN!
BOTTLE: HONEY
FINALLY, THEY FLEW AWAY FROM ME.
AH'M SICK OF THIS!
AH'M LEAVING!
UH!
PAGES: I TRIED ALL SORTS OF THINGS WITH THE STAG BEETLES AND RHINOCEROS BEETLES, BUT NO MATTER WHAT I DID, THEY WOULDN'T FIGHT.
THIS MADE ME THINK THAT THE CLIMATE OF APATHY HAS ALSO SPREAD TO THE INSECT WORLD.
THE END.
WHAT KIND OF PRESENTATION WAS THAT?

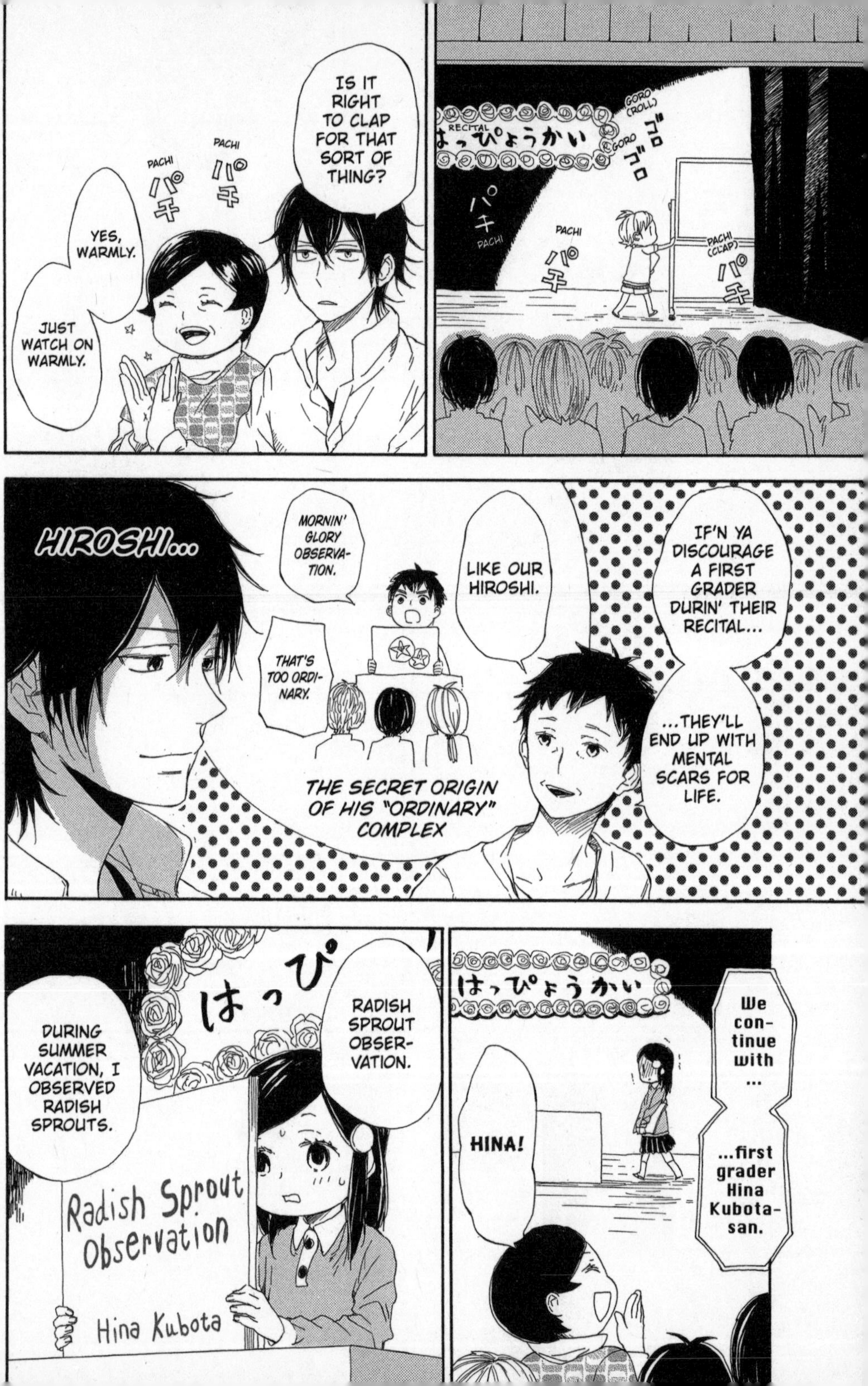
RECITAL
はっぴょうかい
GORO (ROLL)
ゴロ
GORO
ゴロ
パチ
PACHI
PACHI
パチ
PACHI (CLAP)
パチ
IS IT RIGHT TO CLAP FOR THAT SORT OF THING?
PACHI
パチ
PACHI
パチ
YES, WARMLY.
JUST WATCH ON WARMLY.
IF'N YA DISCOURAGE A FIRST GRADER DURIN' THEIR RECITAL...
...THEY'LL END UP WITH MENTAL SCARS FOR LIFE.
LIKE OUR HIROSHI.
MORNIN' GLORY OBSERVATION.
THAT'S TOO ORDINARY.
THE SECRET ORIGIN OF HIS "ORDINARY" COMPLEX
HIROSHI...
はっぴょうかい
We continue with...
...first grader Hina Kubota-san.
HINA!
RADISH SPROUT OBSERVATION.
DURING SUMMER VACATION, I OBSERVED RADISH SPROUTS.
はっぴ
Radish Sprout Observation
Hina Kubota

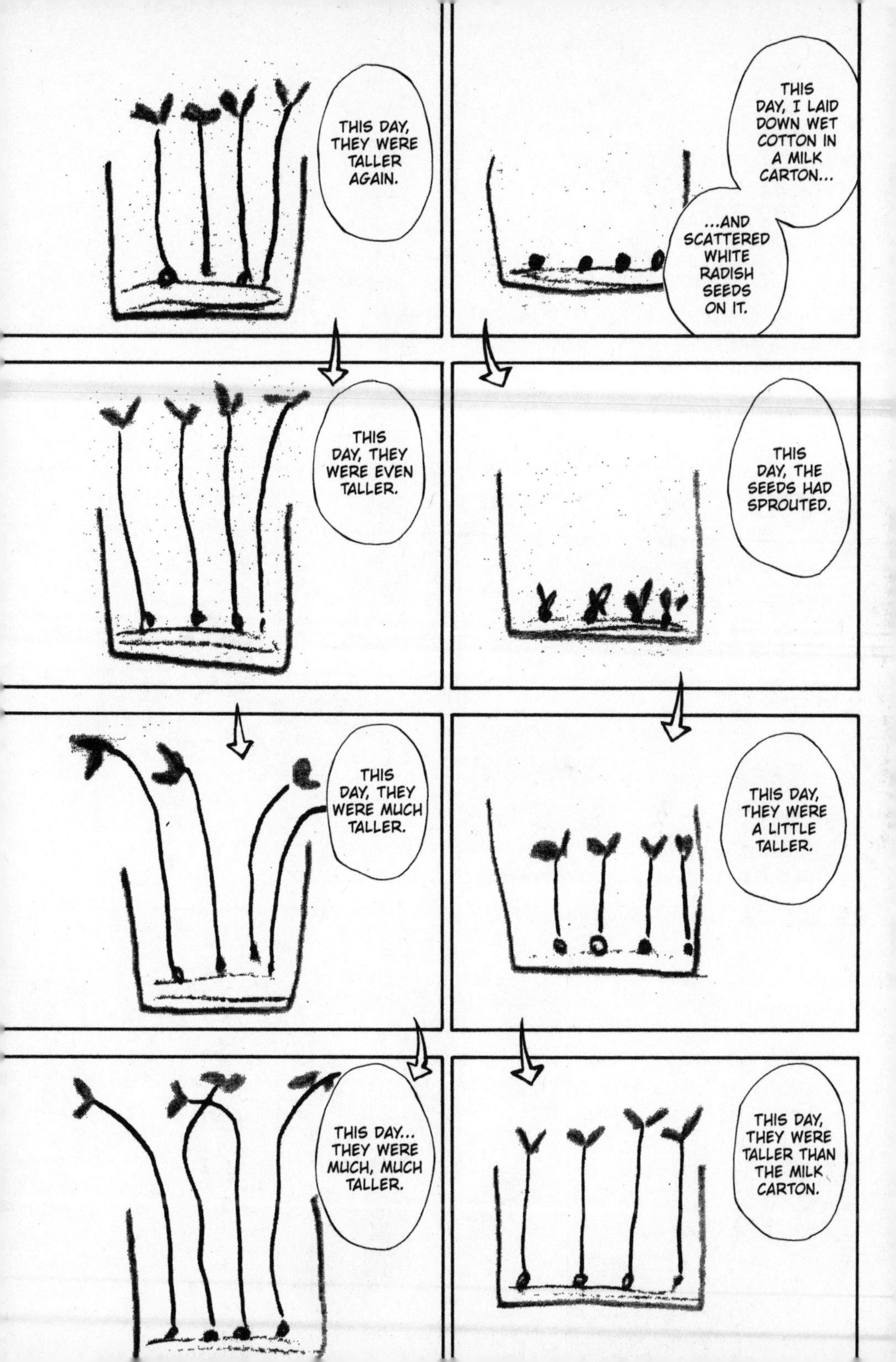
THIS DAY, I LAID DOWN WET COTTON IN A MILK CARTON...
...AND SCATTERED WHITE RADISH SEEDS ON IT.
THIS DAY, THE SEEDS HAD SPROUTED.
THIS DAY, THEY WERE A LITTLE TALLER.
THIS DAY, THEY WERE TALLER THAN THE MILK CARTON.
THIS DAY, THEY WERE TALLER AGAIN.
THIS DAY, THEY WERE EVEN TALLER.
THIS DAY, THEY WERE MUCH TALLER.
THIS DAY... THEY WERE MUCH, MUCH TALLER.

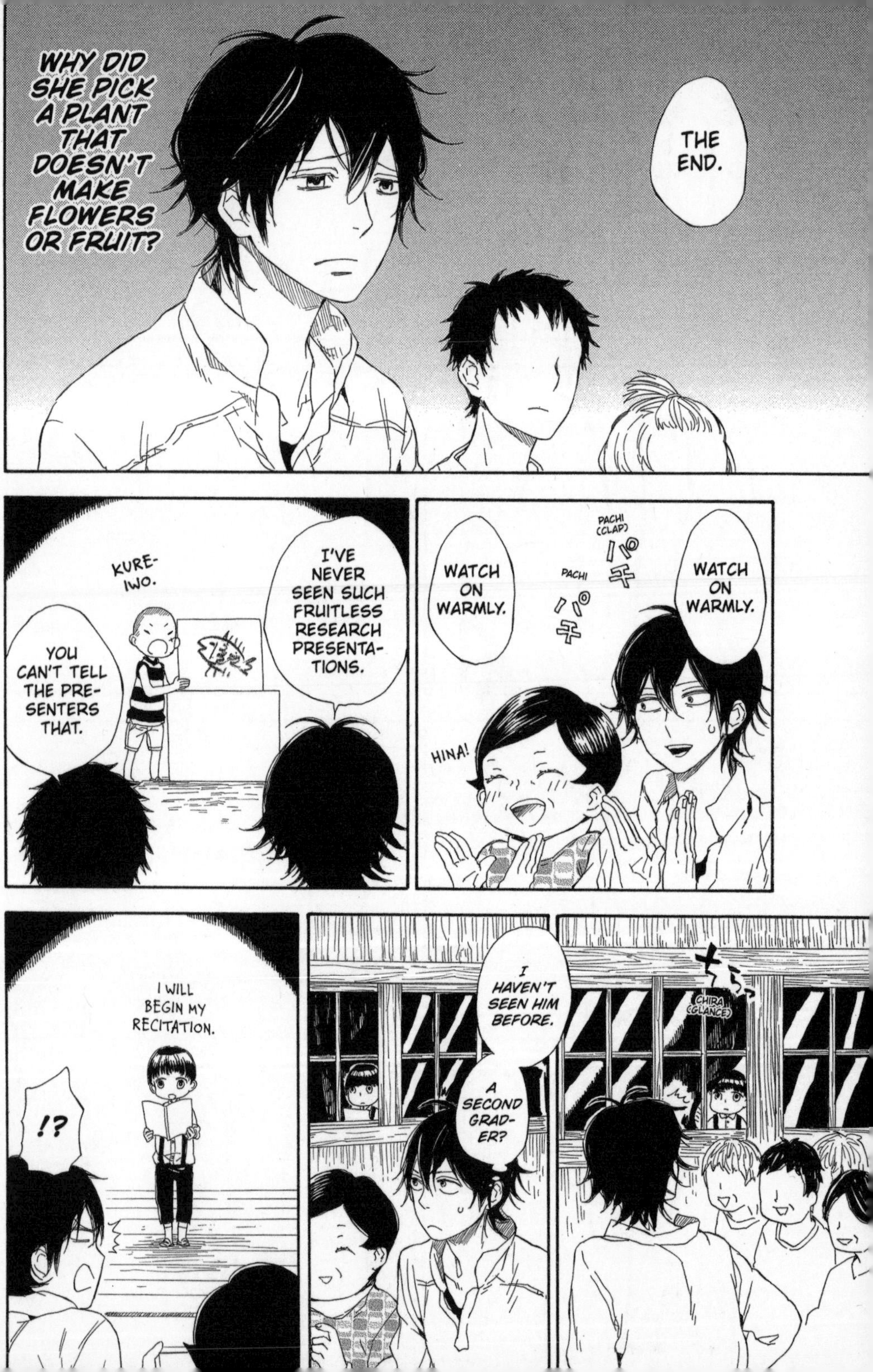
THE END.
WHY DID SHE PICK A PLANT THAT DOESN'T MAKE FLOWERS OR FRUIT?
WATCH ON WARMLY.
PACHI (CLAP)
PACHI
WATCH ON WARMLY.
HINA!
I'VE NEVER SEEN SUCH FRUITLESS RESEARCH PRESENTATIONS.
KURE-IWO.
YOU CAN'T TELL THE PRESENTERS THAT.
CHIRA (GLANCE)
I HAVEN'T SEEN HIM BEFORE.
A SECOND GRADER?
I WILL BEGIN MY RECITATION.
!?

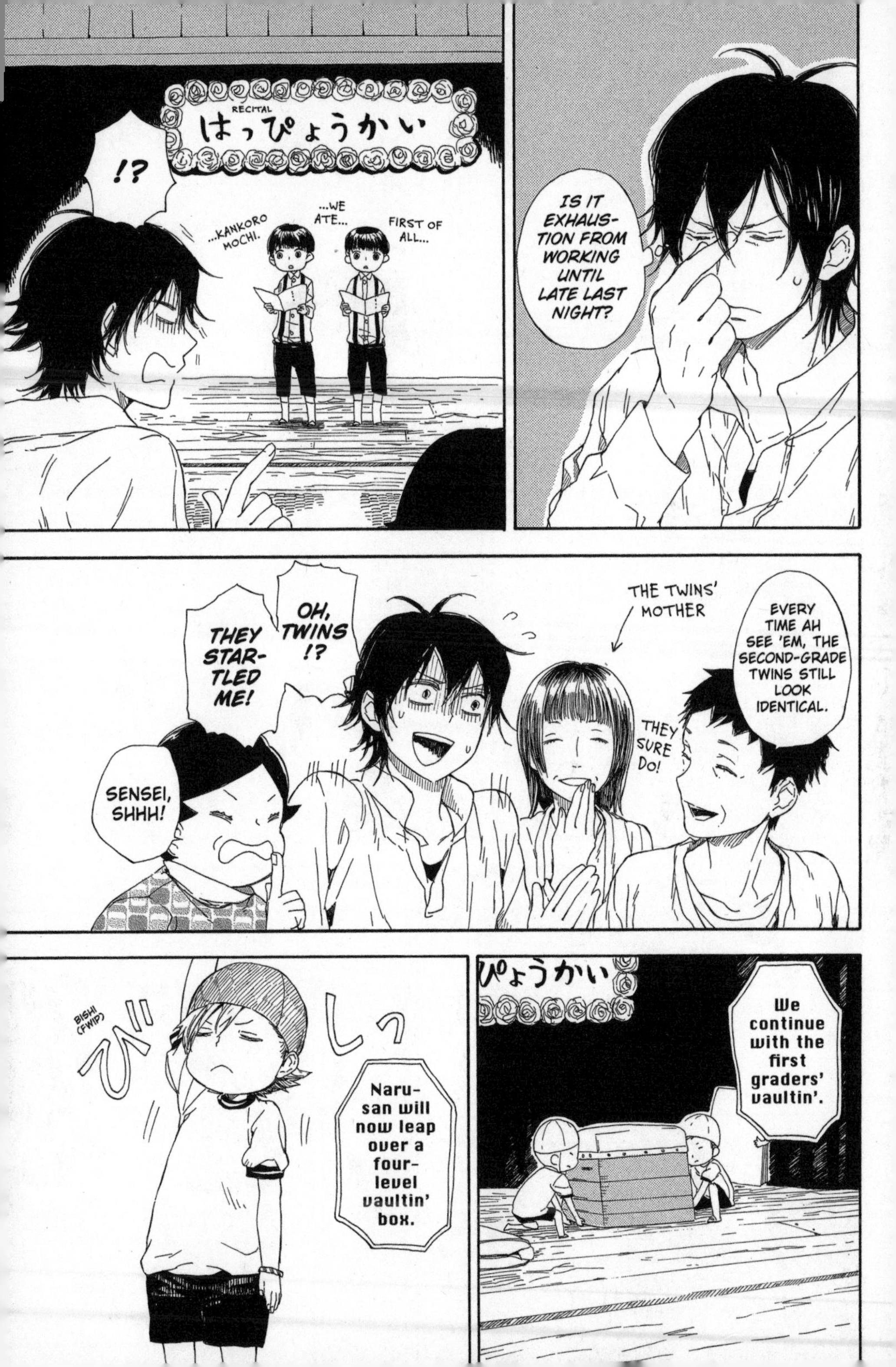
IS IT EXHAUSTION FROM WORKING UNTIL LATE LAST NIGHT?
!?
RECITAL
はっぴょうかい
FIRST OF ALL...
...WE ATE...
...KANKORO MOCHI.
EVERY TIME AH SEE 'EM, THE SECOND-GRADE TWINS STILL LOOK IDENTICAL.
THEY SURE DO!
THE TWINS' MOTHER
OH, TWINS!?
THEY STARTLED ME!
SENSEI, SHHH!
ぴょうかい
We continue with the first graders' vaultin'.
Naru-san will now leap over a four-level vaultin' box.
びしっ
BISHI (FWIP)

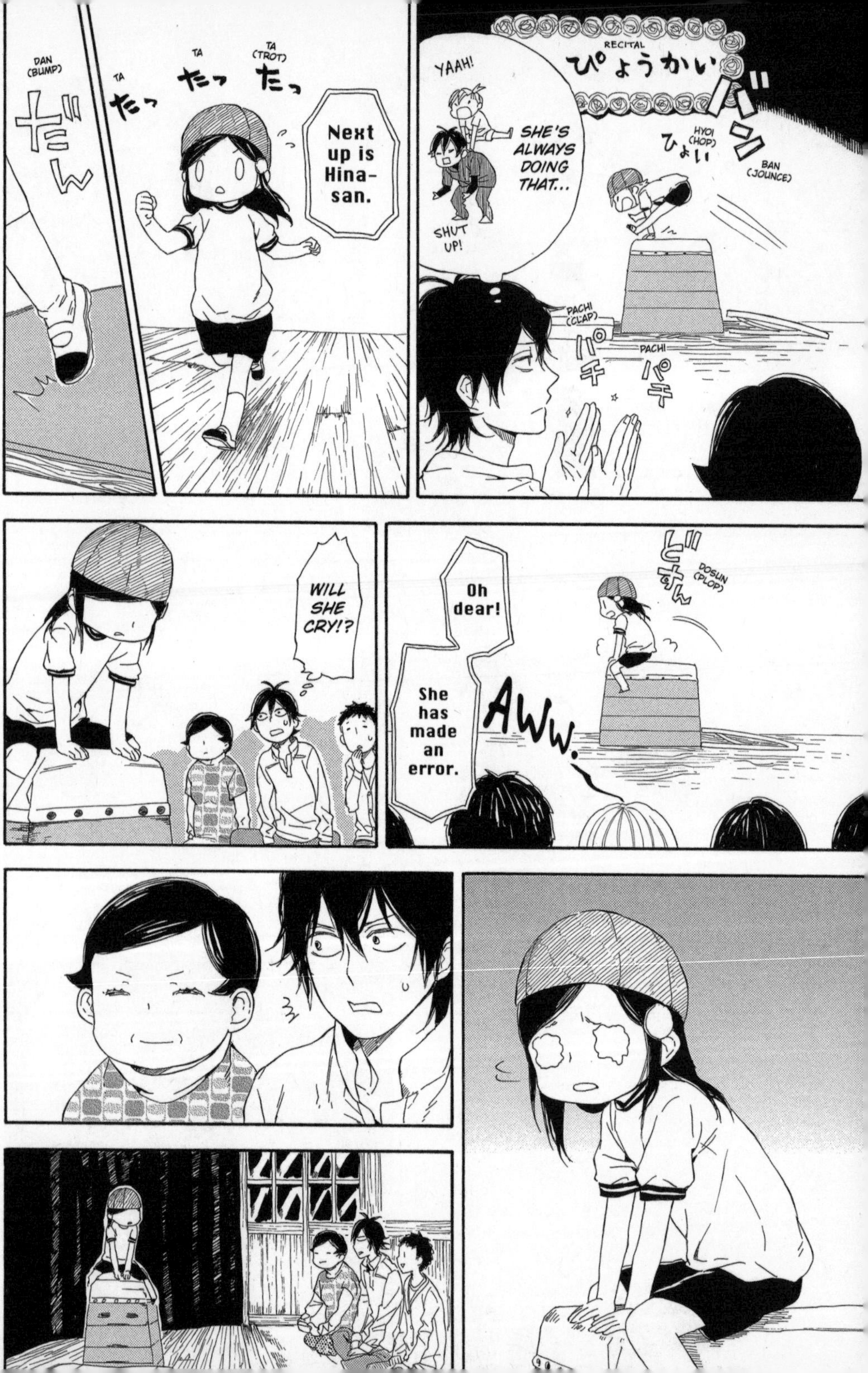
RECITAL
ぴょうかい
バン
YAAH!
SHE'S ALWAYS DOING THAT...
SHUT UP!
HYOI (HOP) ひょい
BAN (JOUNCE)
PACHI (CLAP) パチ
PACHI パチ
TA (TROT) たっ
TA たっ
TA たっ
Next up is Hina-san.
DAN (BUMP) だん
DOSUN (PLOP) どすん
Oh dear!
She has made an error.
AWW.
WILL SHE CRY!?

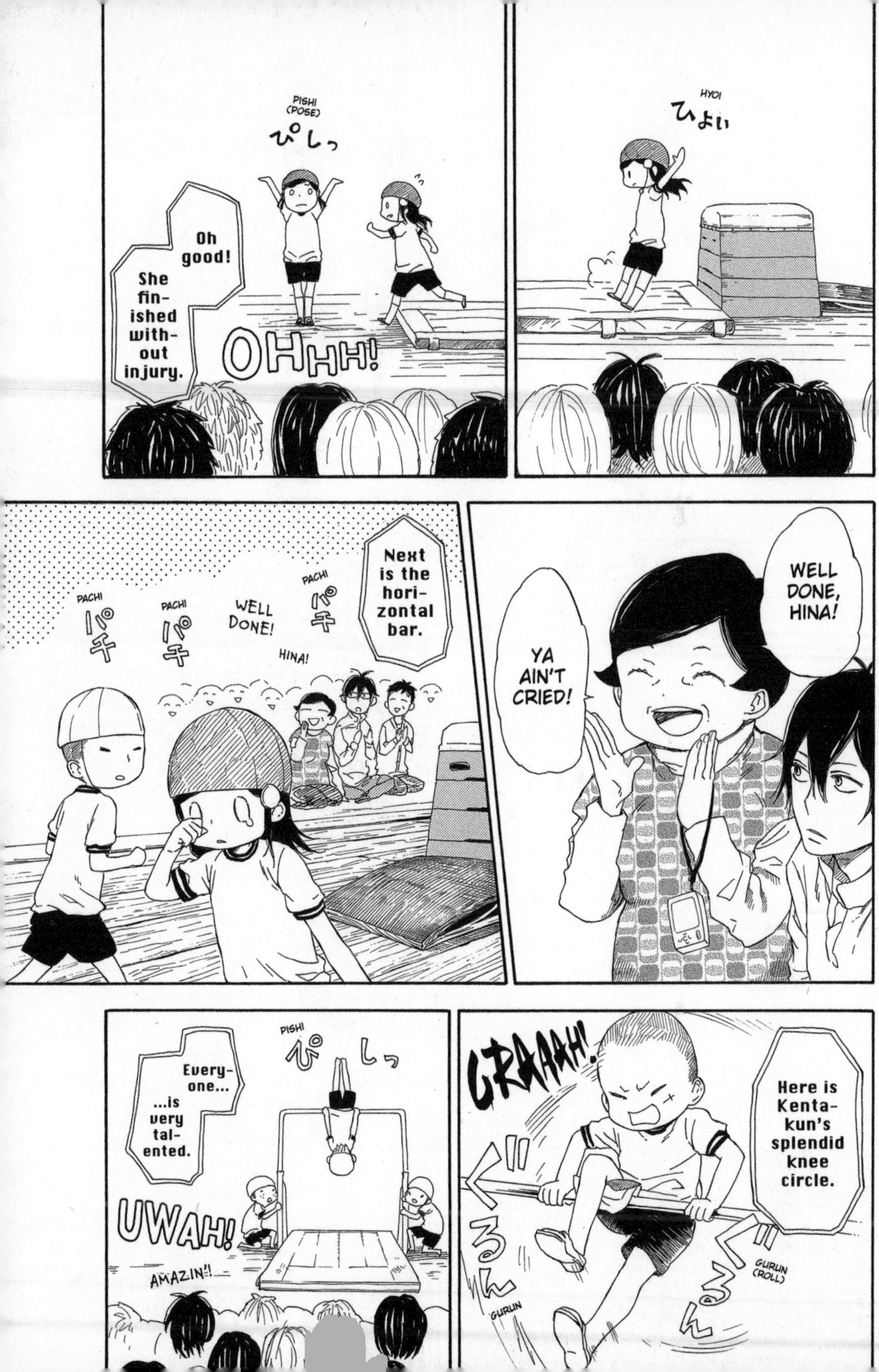
HYOI
ひよい
PISHI (POSE)
ぴしっ
Oh good!
She finished without injury.
OHHH!
WELL DONE, HINA!
YA AIN'T CRIED!
Next is the horizontal bar.
PACHI
パチ
WELL DONE!
HINA!
PACHI
パチ
PACHI
パチ
Here is Kenta-kun's splendid knee circle.
GRAAAH!
GURUN (ROLL)
ぐるん
GURUN
ぐるん
PISHI
ぴしっ
Everyone... ...is very talented.
UWAH!
AMAZIN'!

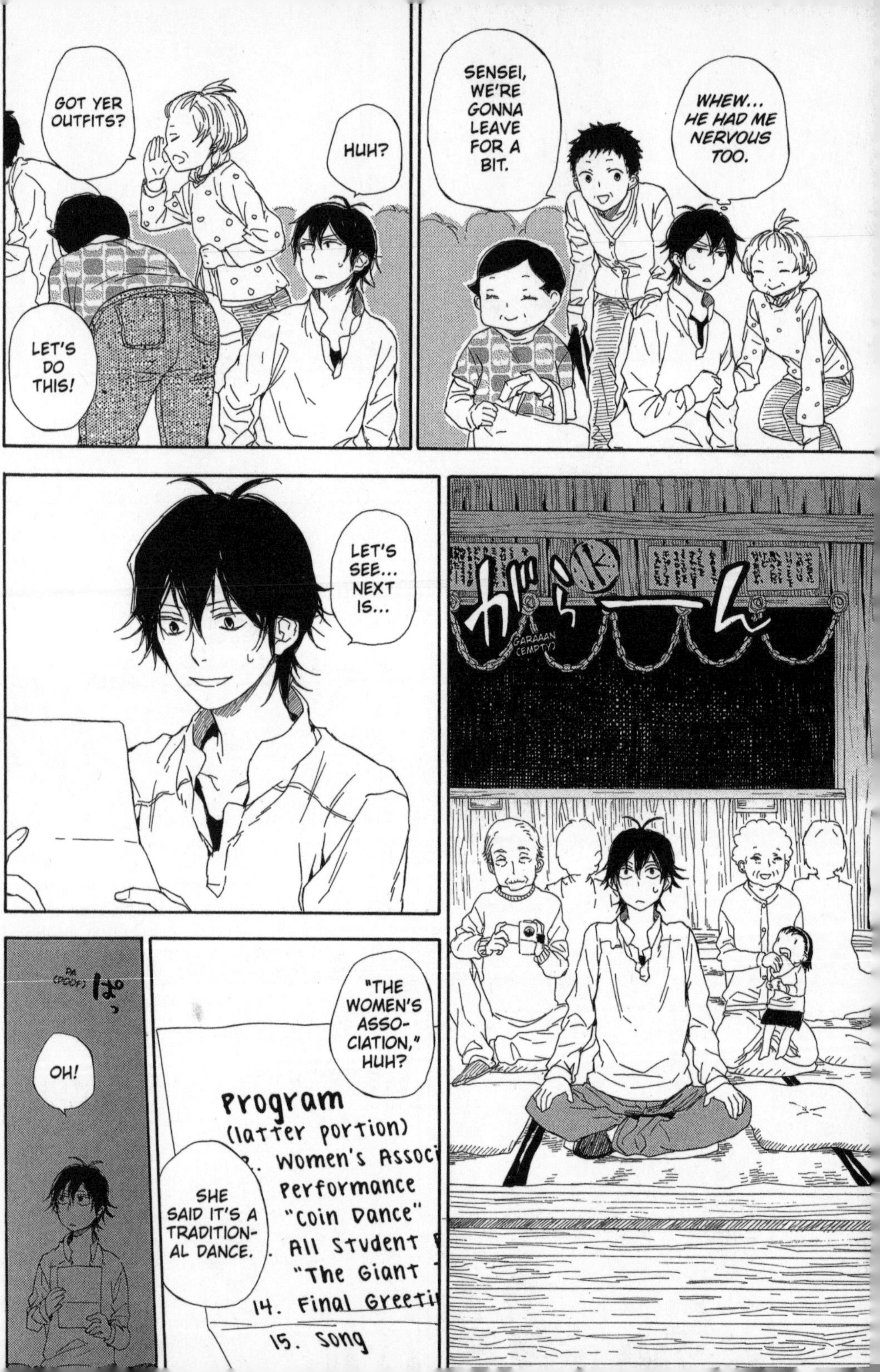
SENSEI, WE'RE GONNA LEAVE FOR A BIT.
WHEW... HE HAD ME NERVOUS TOO.
GOT YER OUTFITS?
HUH?
LET'S DO THIS!
がら〜ん
GARAAAN (EMPTY)
LET'S SEE... NEXT IS...
"THE WOMEN'S ASSOCIATION," HUH?
Program
(latter portion)
. Women's Associ
Performance
"Coin Dance"
. All Student
"The Giant
14. Final Greeti
15. Song
SHE SAID IT'S A TRADITIONAL DANCE.
ぱっ
PA (POOF)
OH!

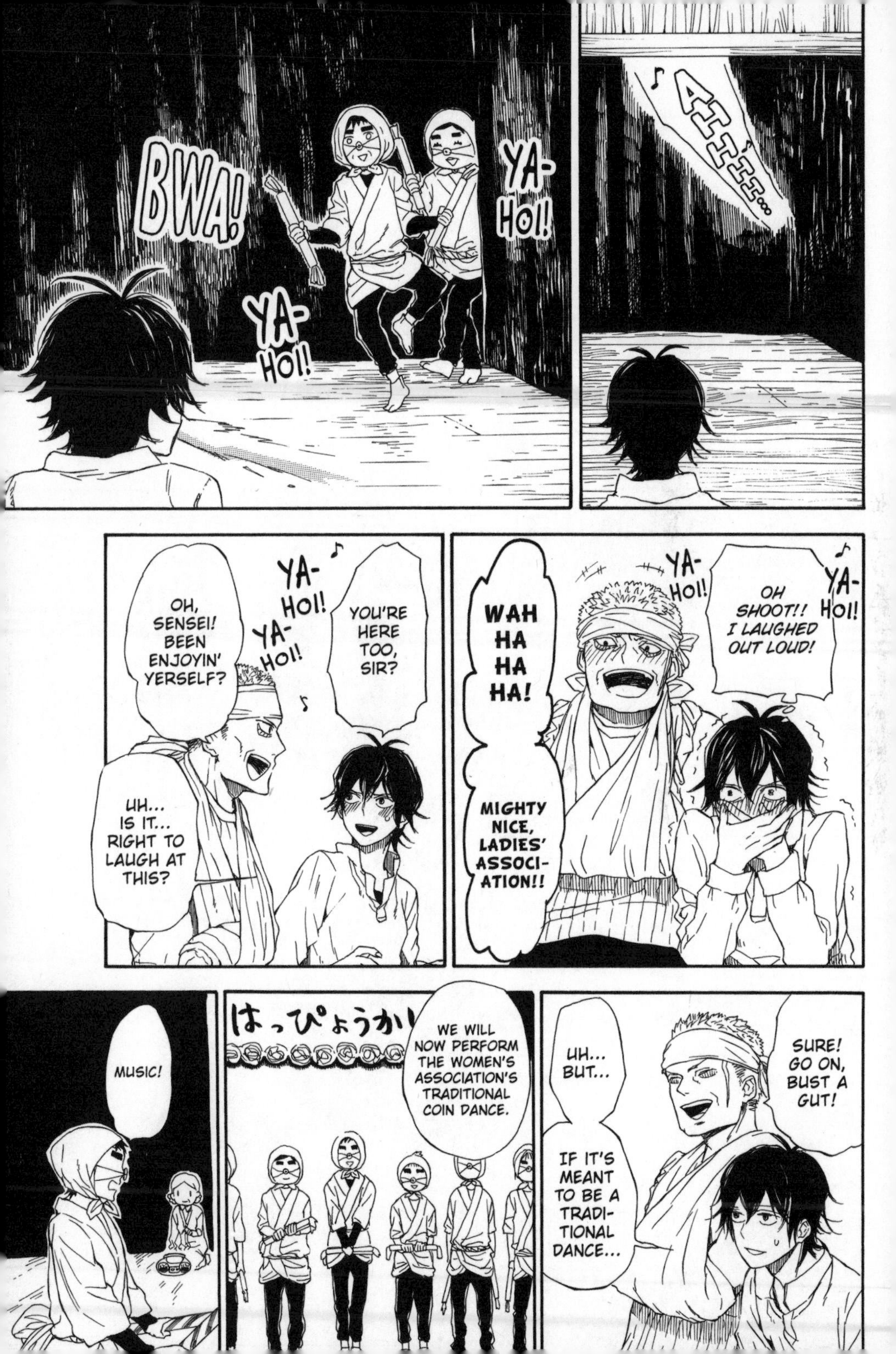
♪ AHHHHH... ♪
BWA!
YA-HOI!
YA-HOI!
YA-HOI!
OH SHOOT!! I LAUGHED OUT LOUD!
YA-HOI!
WAH HA HA HA!
MIGHTY NICE, LADIES' ASSOCIATION!!
YOU'RE HERE TOO, SIR?
YA-HOI!
YA-HOI!
OH, SENSEI! BEEN ENJOYIN' YERSELF?
UH... IS IT... RIGHT TO LAUGH AT THIS?
SURE! GO ON, BUST A GUT!
UH... BUT...
IF IT'S MEANT TO BE A TRADITIONAL DANCE...
はっぴょうかい
WE WILL NOW PERFORM THE WOMEN'S ASSOCIATION'S TRADITIONAL COIN DANCE.
MUSIC!

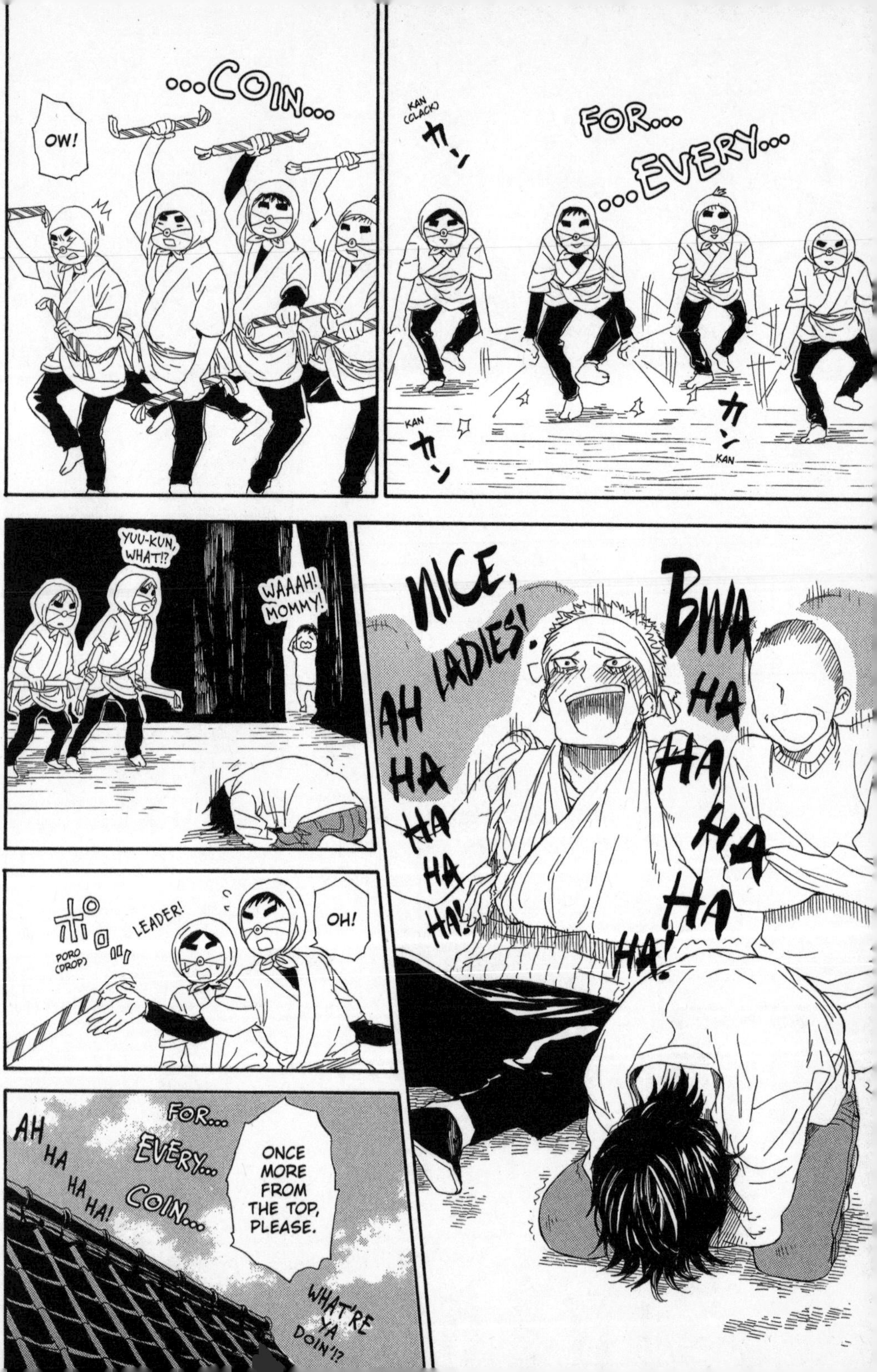
KAN (CLACK)
カン
FOR...
...EVERY...
KAN
カン
カン
KAN
...COIN...
OW!
NICE, LADIES!
BWA HA HA HA HA HA HA!
AH HA HA HA HA HA!
YUU-KUN, WHAT!?
WAAAH! MOMMY!
OH!
LEADER!
ポロ
PORO (DROP)
FOR... EVERY... COIN...
ONCE MORE FROM THE TOP, PLEASE.
AH HA HA HA!
WHAT'RE YA DOIN'!?

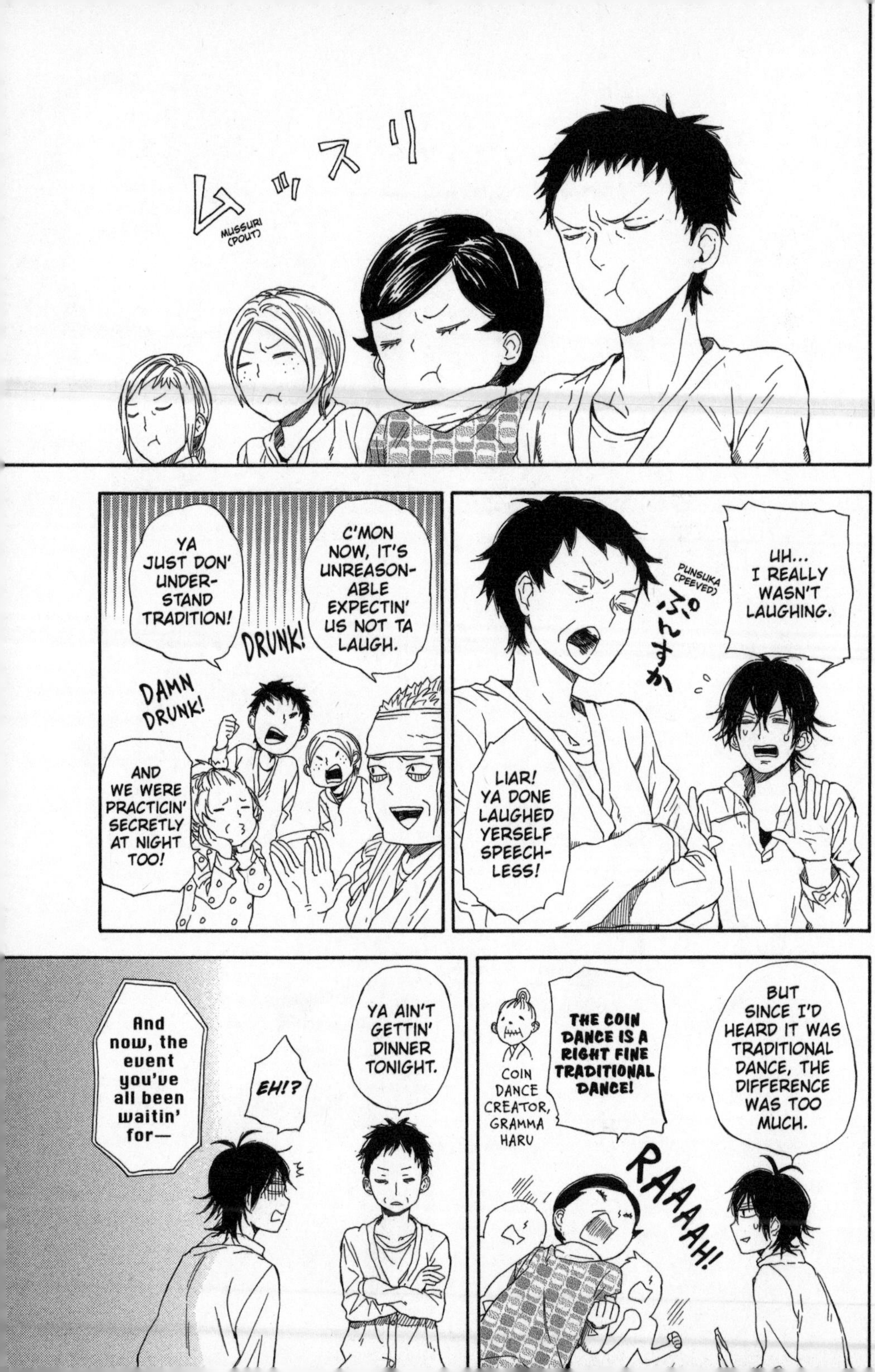
ムッスリ
MUSSURI (POUT)
UH... I REALLY WASN'T LAUGHING.
ぷんすか
PUNSUKA (PEEVED)
LIAR! YA DONE LAUGHED YERSELF SPEECHLESS!
C'MON NOW, IT'S UNREASONABLE EXPECTIN' US NOT TA LAUGH.
YA JUST DON' UNDERSTAND TRADITION!
DRUNK!
DAMN DRUNK!
AND WE WERE PRACTICIN' SECRETLY AT NIGHT TOO!
BUT SINCE I'D HEARD IT WAS TRADITIONAL DANCE, THE DIFFERENCE WAS TOO MUCH.
THE COIN DANCE IS A RIGHT FINE TRADITIONAL DANCE!
COIN DANCE CREATOR, GRAMMA HARU
RAAAAH!
YA AIN'T GETTIN' DINNER TONIGHT.
EH!?
And now, the event you've all been waitin' for—

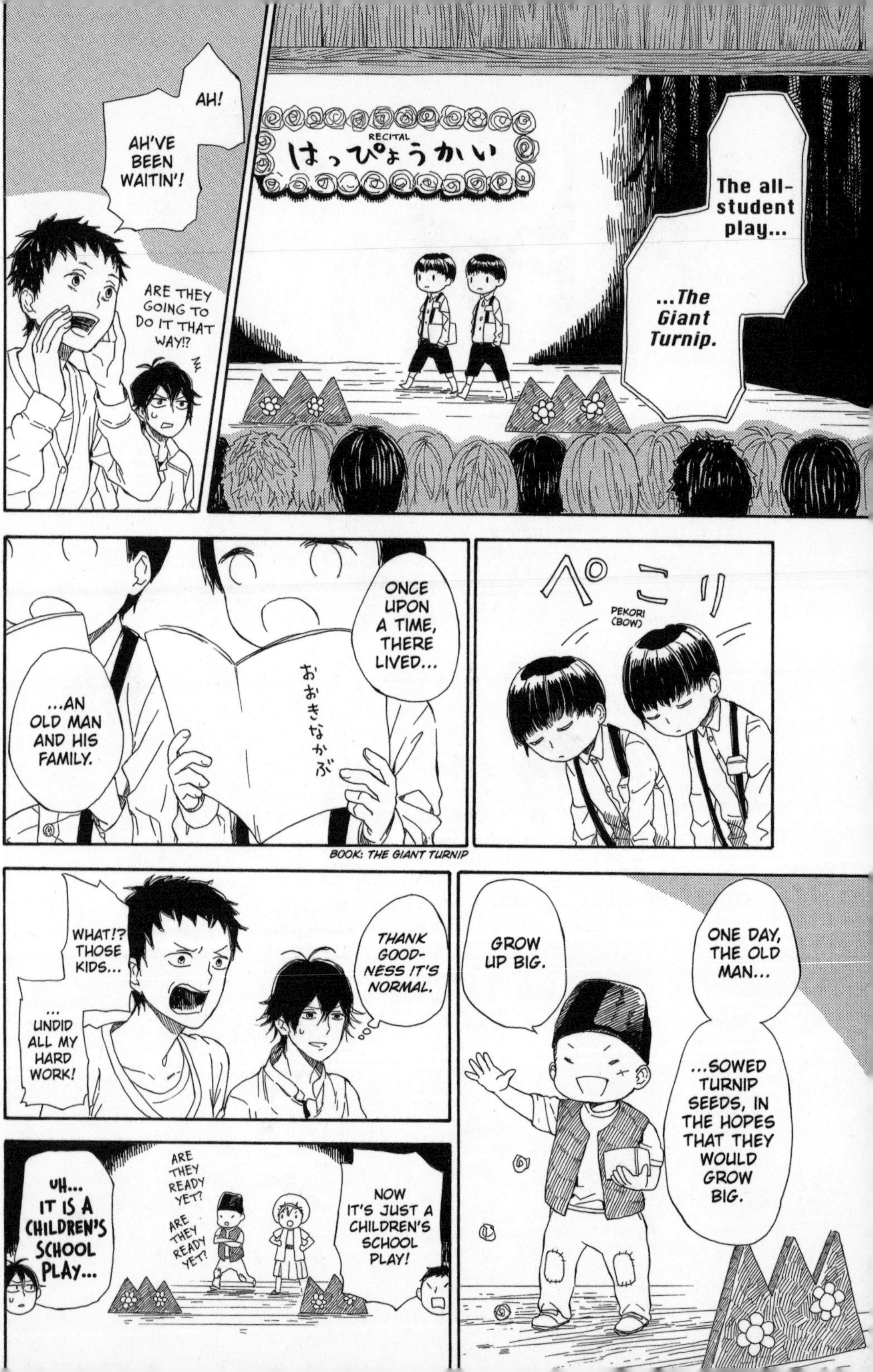

RECITAL
はっぴょうかい
The all-student play...
...The Giant Turnip.
AH!
AH'VE BEEN WAITIN'!
ARE THEY GOING TO DO IT THAT WAY!?
ペこり
PEKORI (BOW)
ONCE UPON A TIME, THERE LIVED...
おおきなかぶ
...AN OLD MAN AND HIS FAMILY.
BOOK: THE GIANT TURNIP
ONE DAY, THE OLD MAN...
...SOWED TURNIP SEEDS, IN THE HOPES THAT THEY WOULD GROW BIG.
GROW UP BIG.
THANK GOODNESS IT'S NORMAL.
WHAT!? THOSE KIDS...
...UNDID ALL MY HARD WORK!
NOW IT'S JUST A CHILDREN'S SCHOOL PLAY!
ARE THEY READY YET?
ARE THEY READY YET?
UH... IT IS A CHILDREN'S SCHOOL PLAY...

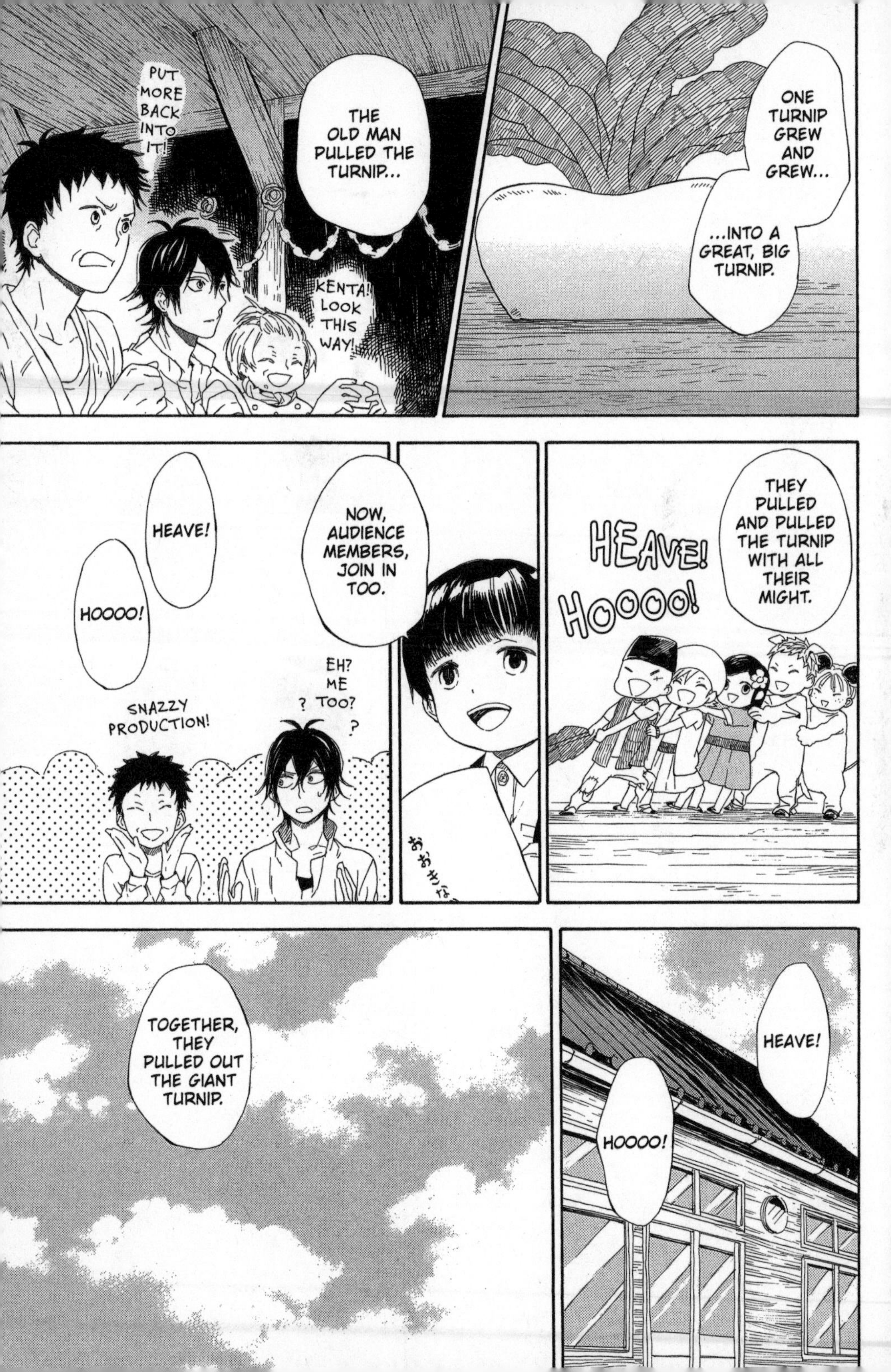
ONE TURNIP GREW AND GREW...
...INTO A GREAT, BIG TURNIP.
THE OLD MAN PULLED THE TURNIP...
PUT MORE BACK INTO IT!
KENTA! LOOK THIS WAY!
THEY PULLED AND PULLED THE TURNIP WITH ALL THEIR MIGHT.
HEAVE!
HOOOO!
NOW, AUDIENCE MEMBERS, JOIN IN TOO.
おおきな
HEAVE!
HOOOO!
EH? ME TOO?
? ?
SNAZZY PRODUCTION!
HEAVE!
HOOOO!
TOGETHER, THEY PULLED OUT THE GIANT TURNIP.

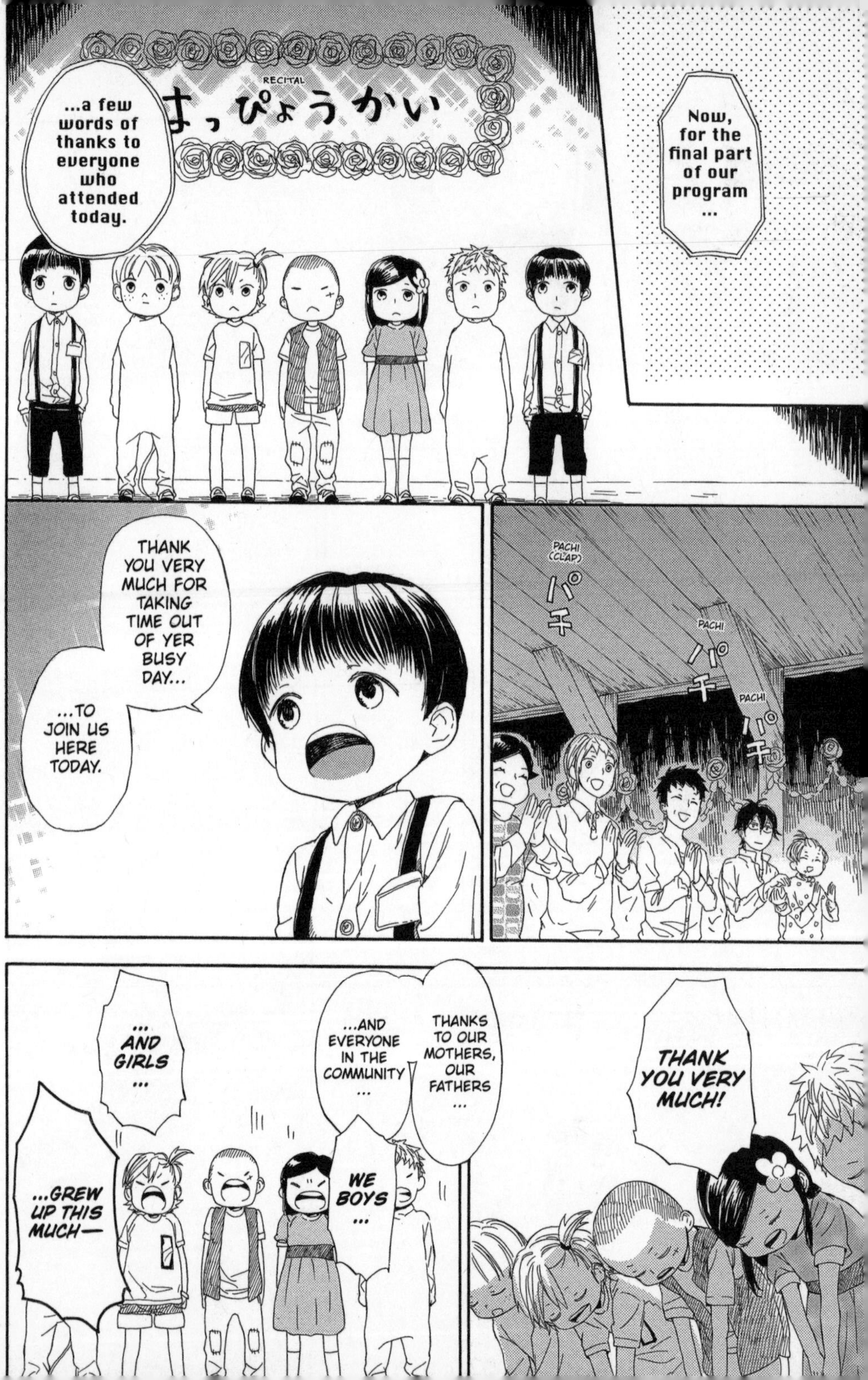

Now, for the final part of our program ...
RECITAL
はっぴょうかい
...a few words of thanks to everyone who attended today.
PACHI (CLAP)
パチ
PACHI
パチ
PACHI
パチ
THANK YOU VERY MUCH FOR TAKING TIME OUT OF YER BUSY DAY...
...TO JOIN US HERE TODAY.
THANK YOU VERY MUCH!
THANKS TO OUR MOTHERS, OUR FATHERS ...
...AND EVERYONE IN THE COMMUNITY ...
WE BOYS ...
... AND GIRLS ...
...GREW UP THIS MUCH—

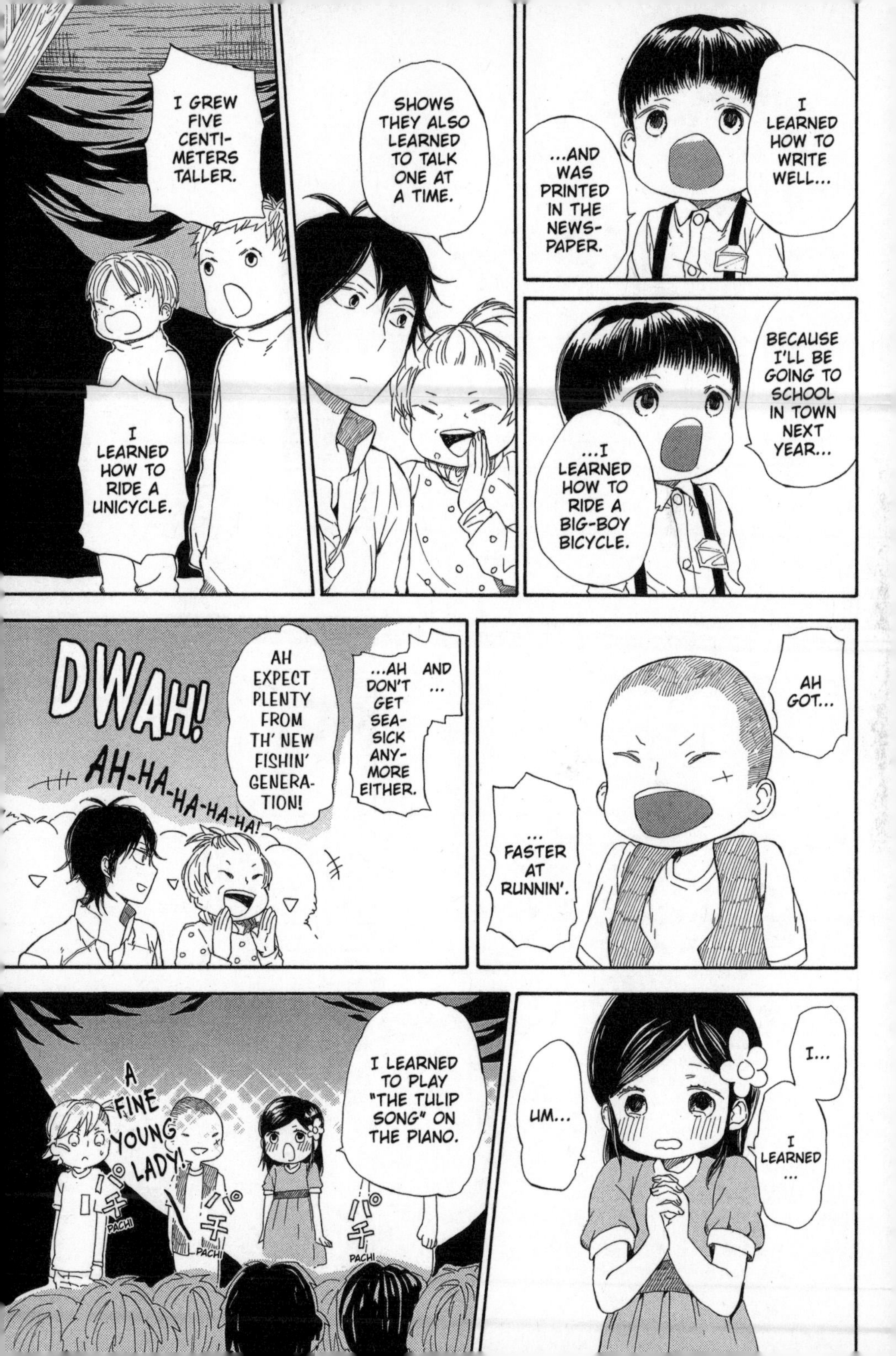
I LEARNED HOW TO WRITE WELL...
...AND WAS PRINTED IN THE NEWSPAPER.
BECAUSE I'LL BE GOING TO SCHOOL IN TOWN NEXT YEAR...
...I LEARNED HOW TO RIDE A BIG-BOY BICYCLE.
SHOWS THEY ALSO LEARNED TO TALK ONE AT A TIME.
I GREW FIVE CENTIMETERS TALLER.
I LEARNED HOW TO RIDE A UNICYCLE.
AH GOT...
...FASTER AT RUNNIN'.
AND ...
...AH DON'T GET SEASICK ANYMORE EITHER.
AH EXPECT PLENTY FROM TH' NEW FISHIN' GENERATION!
DWAH!
AH-HA-HA-HA-HA!
I...
UM...
I LEARNED ...
I LEARNED TO PLAY "THE TULIP SONG" ON THE PIANO.
A FINE YOUNG LADY!
PACHI
PACHI
PACHI

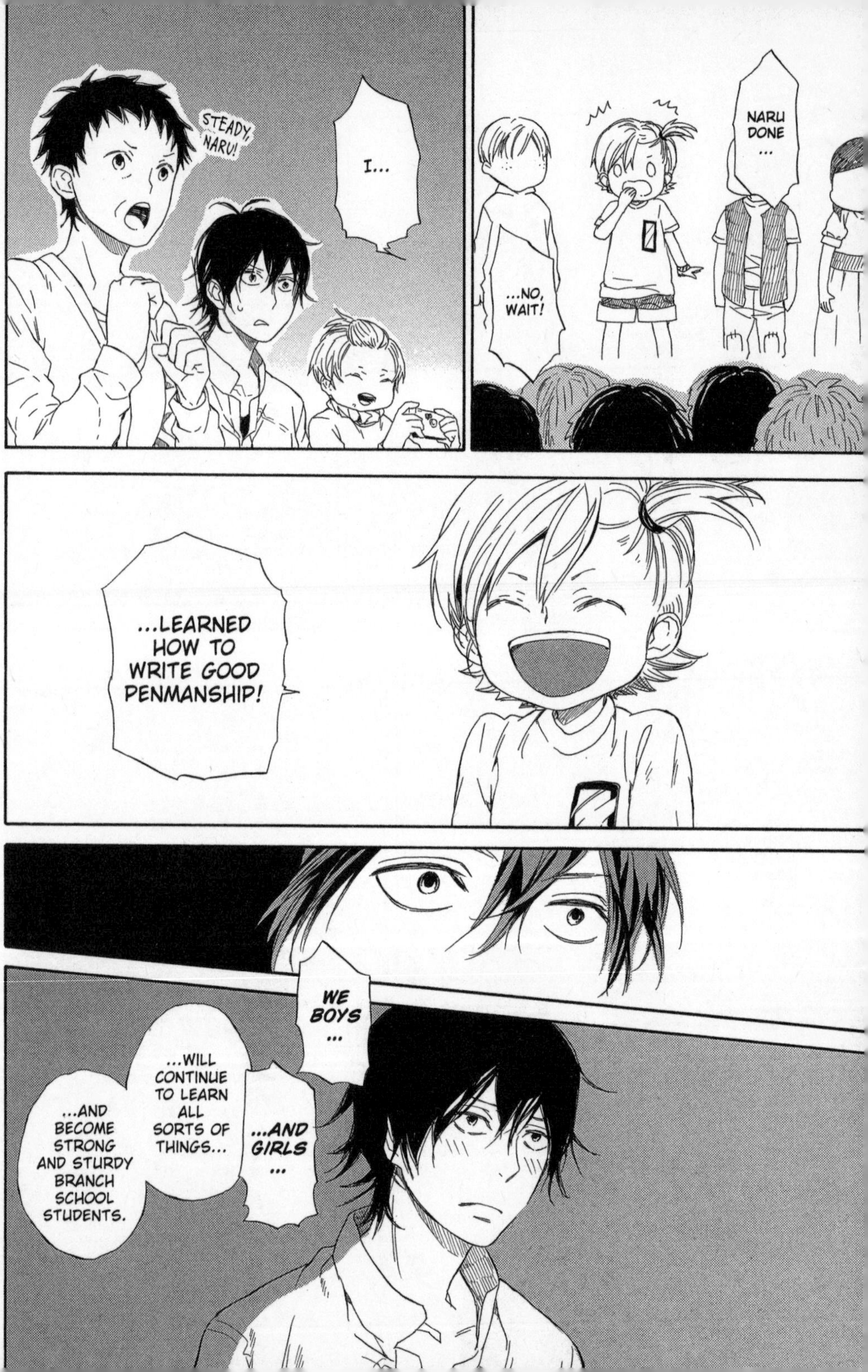
NARU DONE ...
...NO, WAIT!
I...
STEADY, NARU!
...LEARNED HOW TO WRITE GOOD PENMANSHIP!
WE BOYS ...
...AND GIRLS ...
...WILL CONTINUE TO LEARN ALL SORTS OF THINGS...
...AND BECOME STRONG AND STURDY BRANCH SCHOOL STUDENTS.

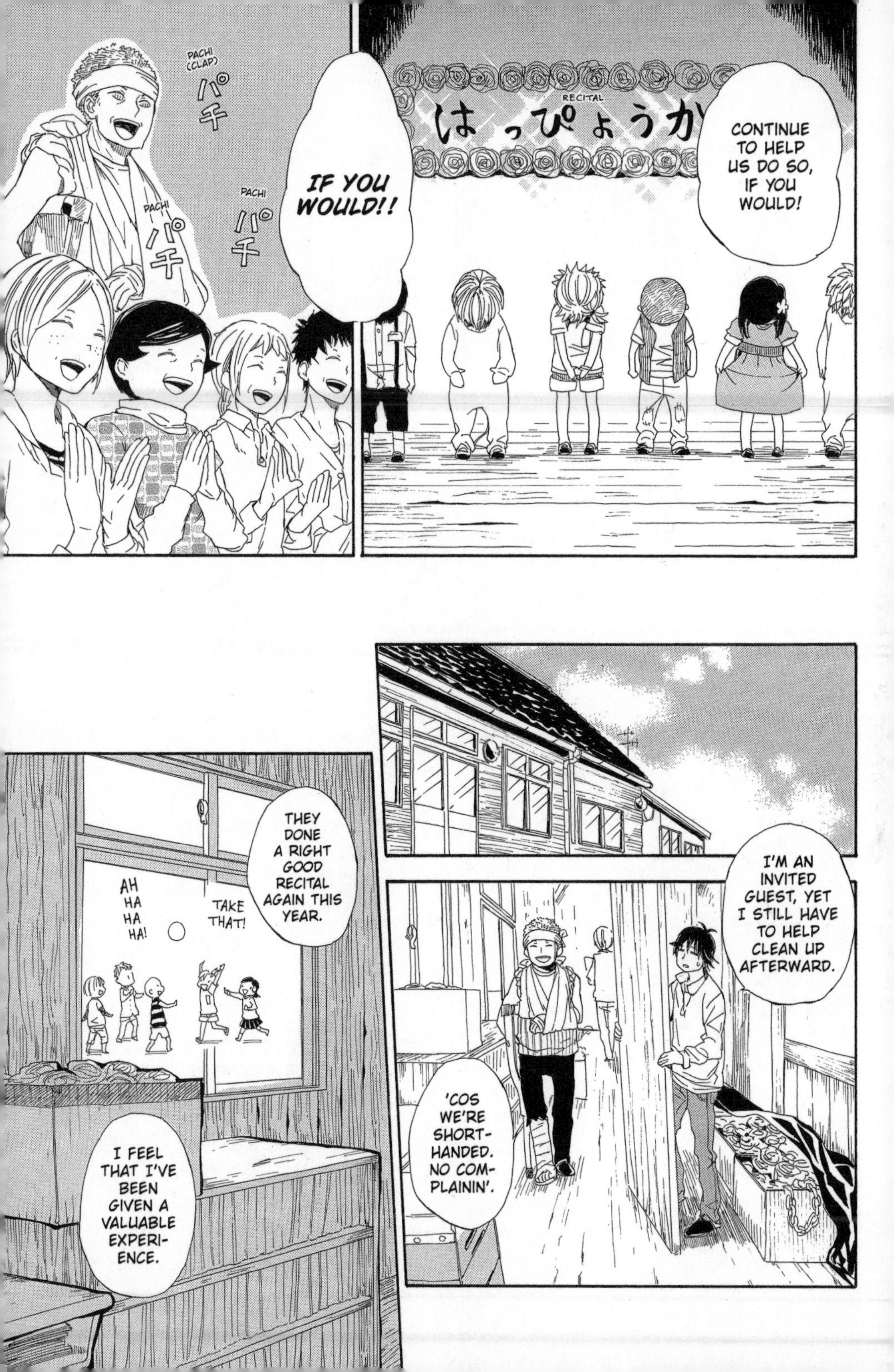
RECITAL
はっぴょうか
CONTINUE TO HELP US DO SO, IF YOU WOULD!
IF YOU WOULD!!
PACHI (CLAP)
パチ
PACHI
パチ
PACHI!
パチ
I'M AN INVITED GUEST, YET I STILL HAVE TO HELP CLEAN UP AFTERWARD.
'COS WE'RE SHORT-HANDED. NO COMPLAININ'.
THEY DONE A RIGHT GOOD RECITAL AGAIN THIS YEAR.
TAKE THAT!
AH HA HA HA!
I FEEL THAT I'VE BEEN GIVEN A VALUABLE EXPERIENCE.

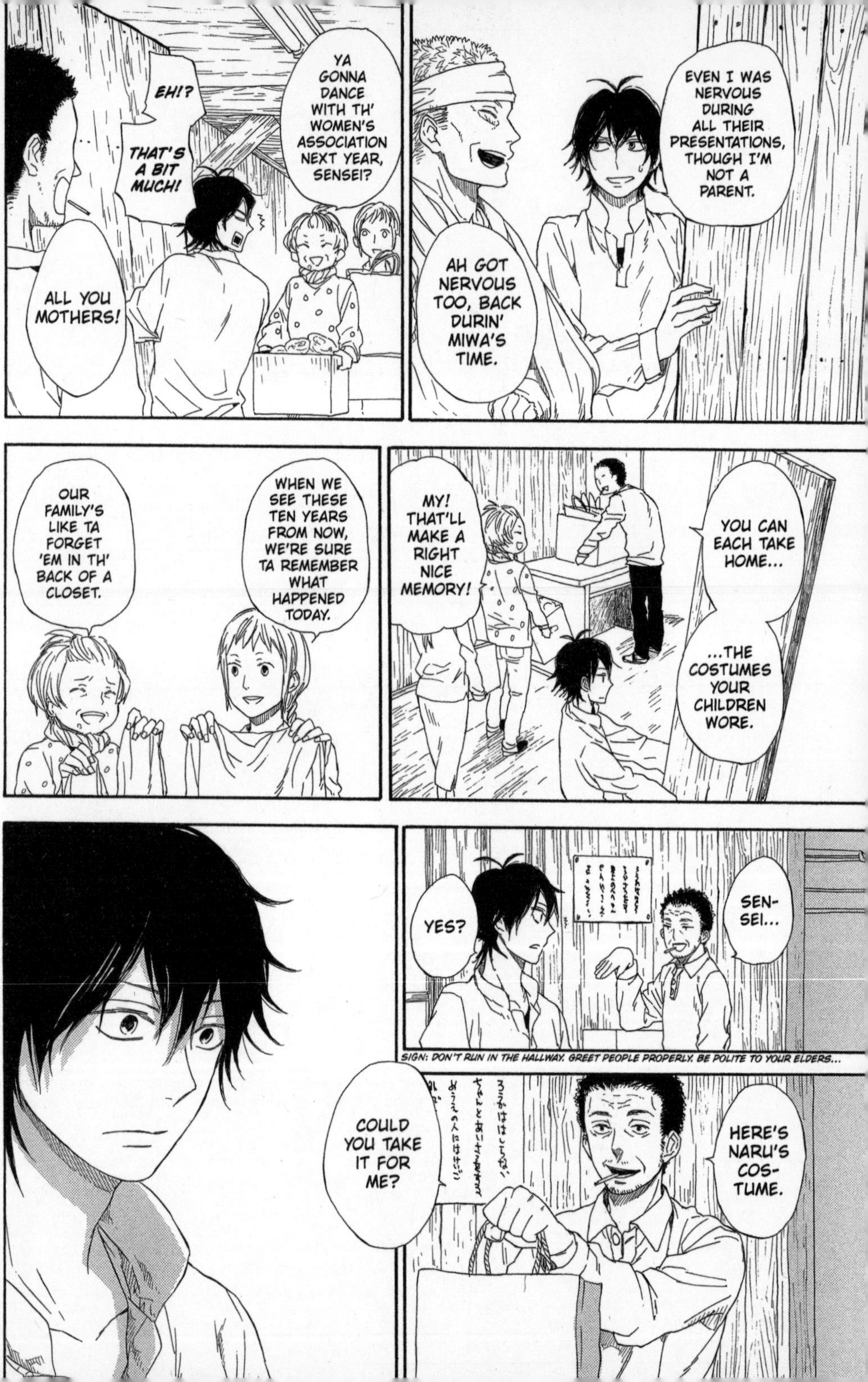
EVEN I WAS NERVOUS DURING ALL THEIR PRESENTATIONS, THOUGH I'M NOT A PARENT.
AH GOT NERVOUS TOO, BACK DURIN' MIWA'S TIME.
YA GONNA DANCE WITH TH' WOMEN'S ASSOCIATION NEXT YEAR, SENSEI?
EH!?
THAT'S A BIT MUCH!
...
ALL YOU MOTHERS!
YOU CAN EACH TAKE HOME...
...THE COSTUMES YOUR CHILDREN WORE.
MY! THAT'LL MAKE A RIGHT NICE MEMORY!
WHEN WE SEE THESE TEN YEARS FROM NOW, WE'RE SURE TA REMEMBER WHAT HAPPENED TODAY.
OUR FAMILY'S LIKE TA FORGET 'EM IN TH' BACK OF A CLOSET.
SEN-SEI...
YES?
SIGN: DON'T RUN IN THE HALLWAY. GREET PEOPLE PROPERLY. BE POLITE TO YOUR ELDERS...
HERE'S NARU'S COS-TUME.
COULD YOU TAKE IT FOR ME?

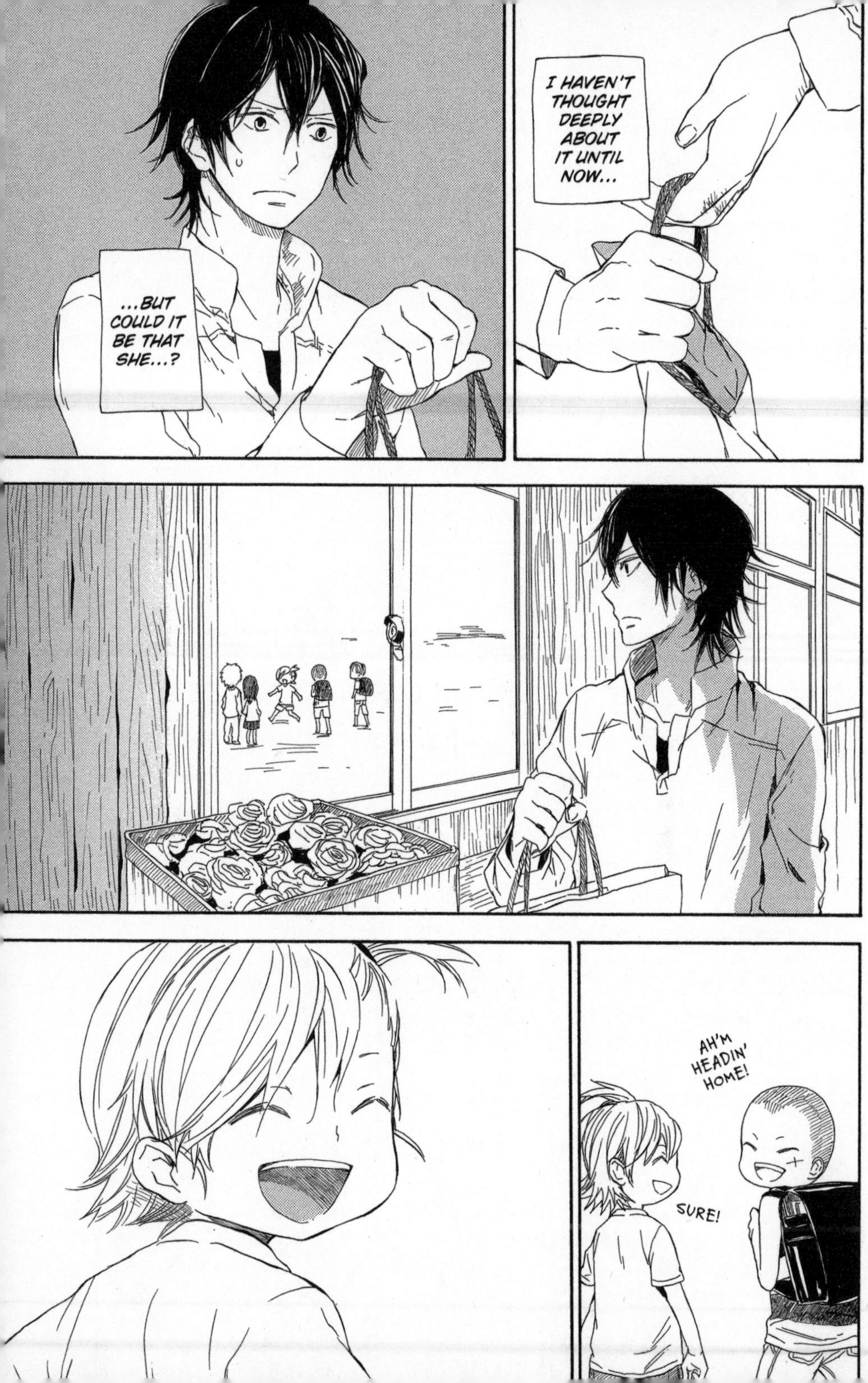
I HAVEN'T THOUGHT DEEPLY ABOUT IT UNTIL NOW...
...BUT COULD IT BE THAT SHE...?
AH'M HEADIN' HOME!
SURE!

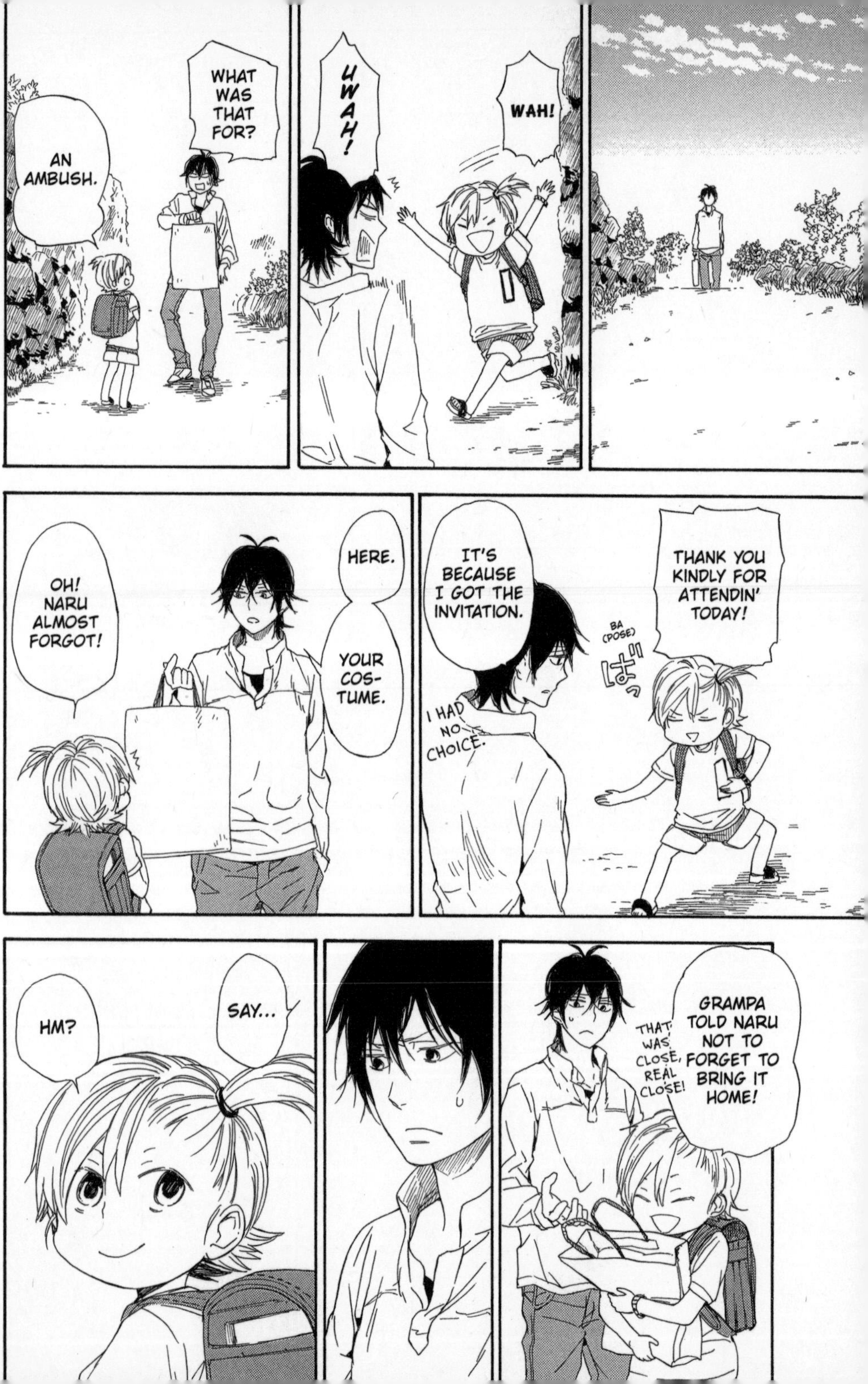
WAH!
UWAH!
WHAT WAS THAT FOR?
AN AMBUSH.
THANK YOU KINDLY FOR ATTENDIN' TODAY!
BA (POSE)
ばっ
IT'S BECAUSE I GOT THE INVITATION.
I HAD NO CHOICE.
HERE.
YOUR COS-TUME.
OH! NARU ALMOST FORGOT!
GRAMPA TOLD NARU NOT TO FORGET TO BRING IT HOME!
THAT WAS CLOSE, REAL CLOSE!
SAY...
HM?

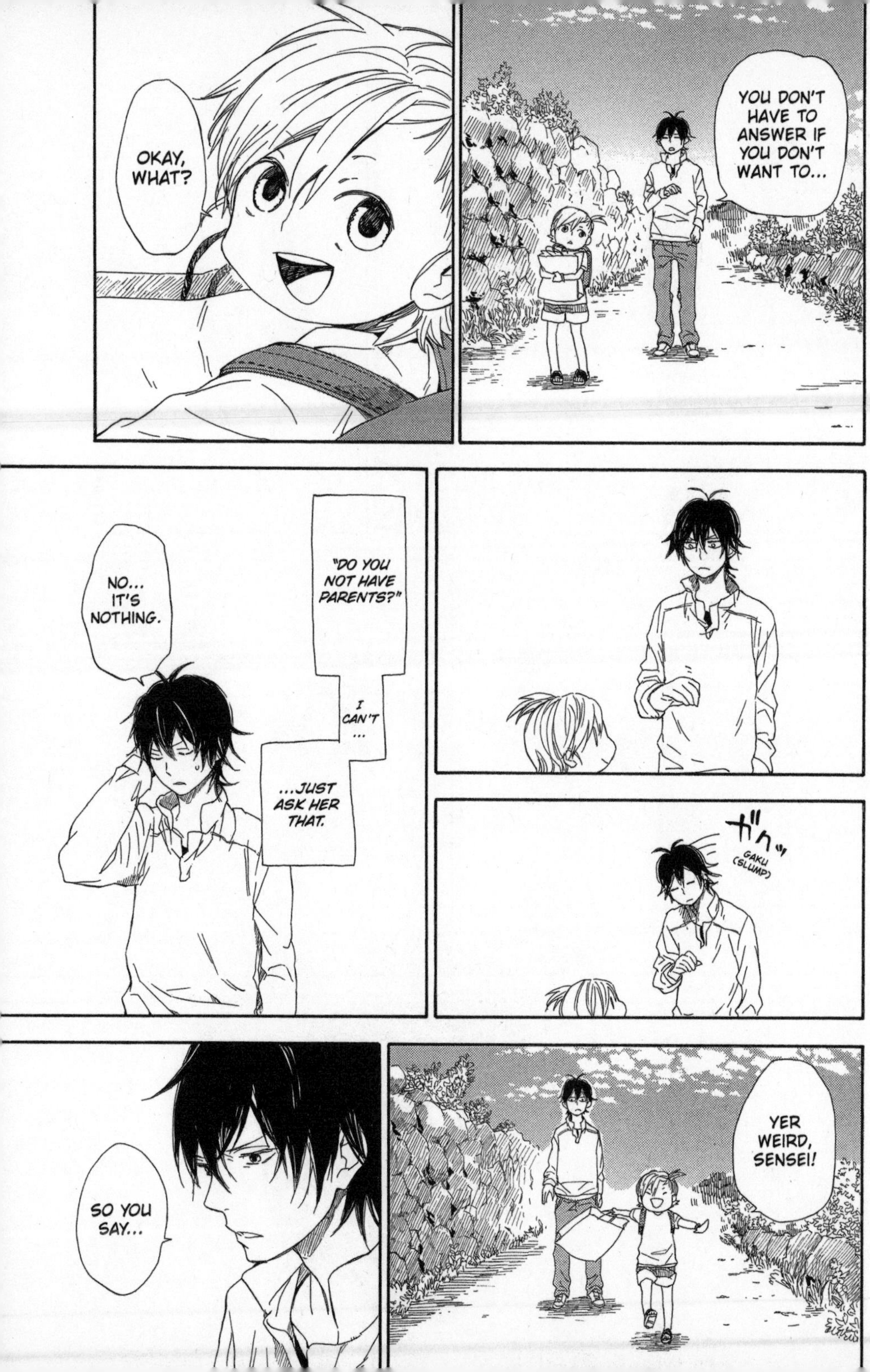
YOU DON'T HAVE TO ANSWER IF YOU DON'T WANT TO...
OKAY, WHAT?
ガクッ
GAKU (SLUMP)
"DO YOU NOT HAVE PARENTS?"
I CAN'T ...
...JUST ASK HER THAT.
NO... IT'S NOTHING.
YER WEIRD, SENSEI!
SO YOU SAY...

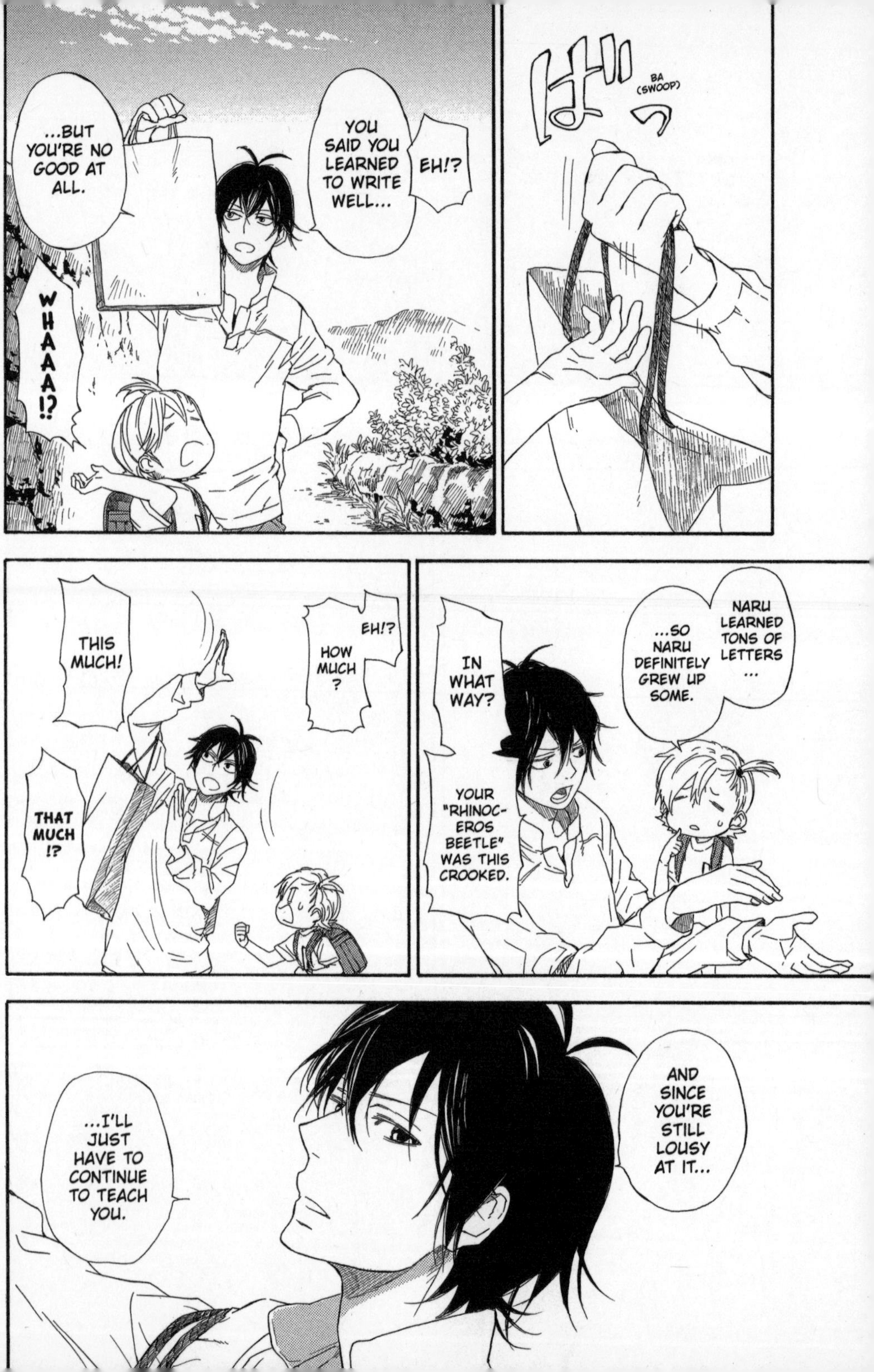
ばっ
BA (SWOOP)
EH!?
YOU SAID YOU LEARNED TO WRITE WELL...
...BUT YOU'RE NO GOOD AT ALL.
WHAAAA!?
NARU LEARNED TONS OF LETTERS...
...SO NARU DEFINITELY GREW UP SOME.
IN WHAT WAY?
YOUR "RHINOCEROS BEETLE" WAS THIS CROOKED.
EH!? HOW MUCH?
THIS MUCH!
THAT MUCH!?
AND SINCE YOU'RE STILL LOUSY AT IT...
...I'LL JUST HAVE TO CONTINUE TO TEACH YOU.

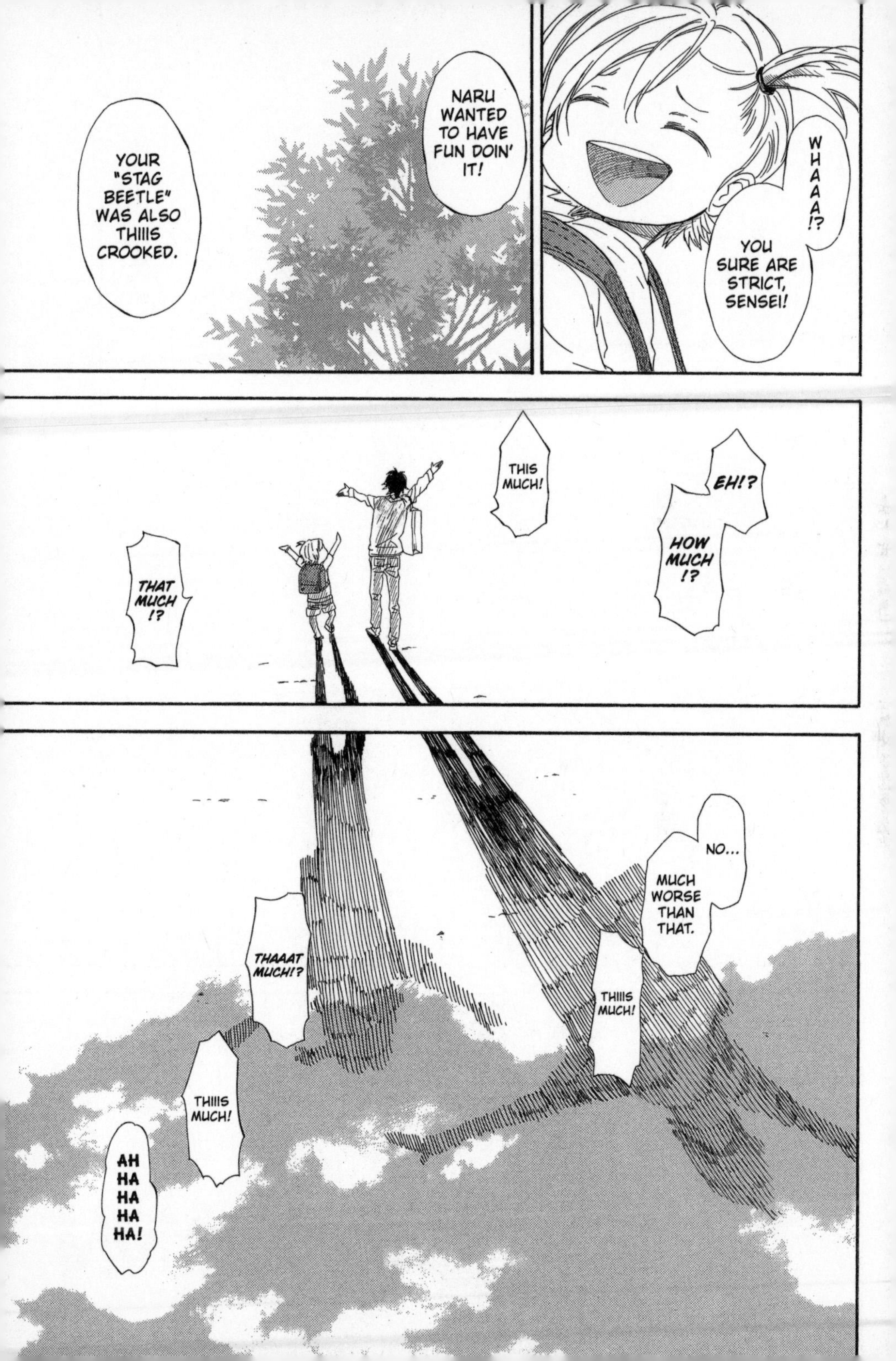
WHAAAA!?
YOU SURE ARE STRICT, SENSEI!
NARU WANTED TO HAVE FUN DOIN' IT!
YOUR "STAG BEETLE" WAS ALSO THIIIS CROOKED.
EH!?
HOW MUCH!?
THIS MUCH!
THAT MUCH!?
NO...
MUCH WORSE THAN THAT.
THIIIS MUCH!
THAAAT MUCH!?
THIIIS MUCH!
AH HA HA HA HA!

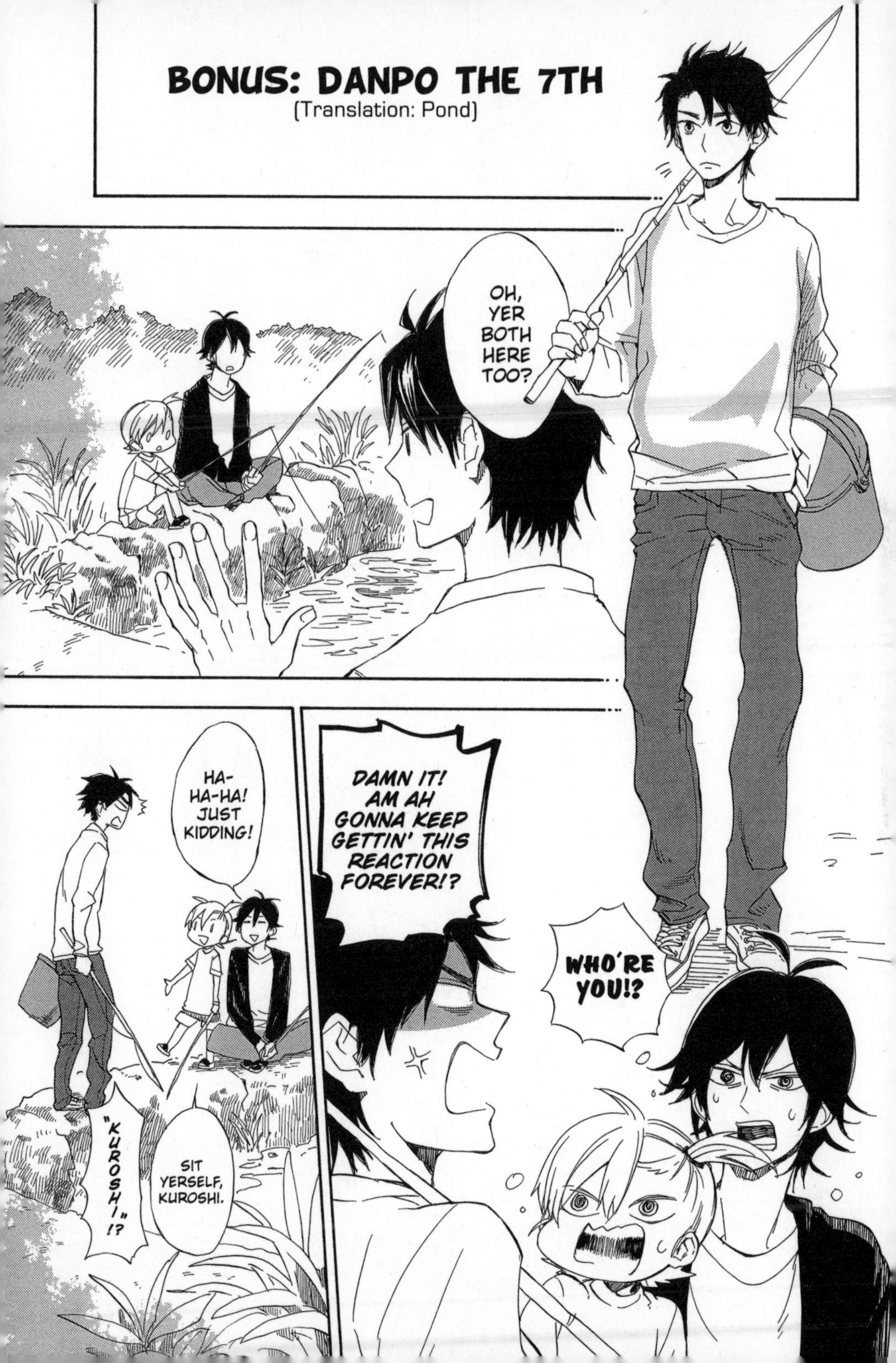
BONUS: DANPO THE 7TH
(Translation: Pond)
OH, YER BOTH HERE TOO?
WHO'RE YOU!?
DAMN IT! AM AH GONNA KEEP GETTIN' THIS REACTION FOREVER!?
HA-HA-HA! JUST KIDDING!
SIT YERSELF, KUROSHI.
"KUROSHI"!?

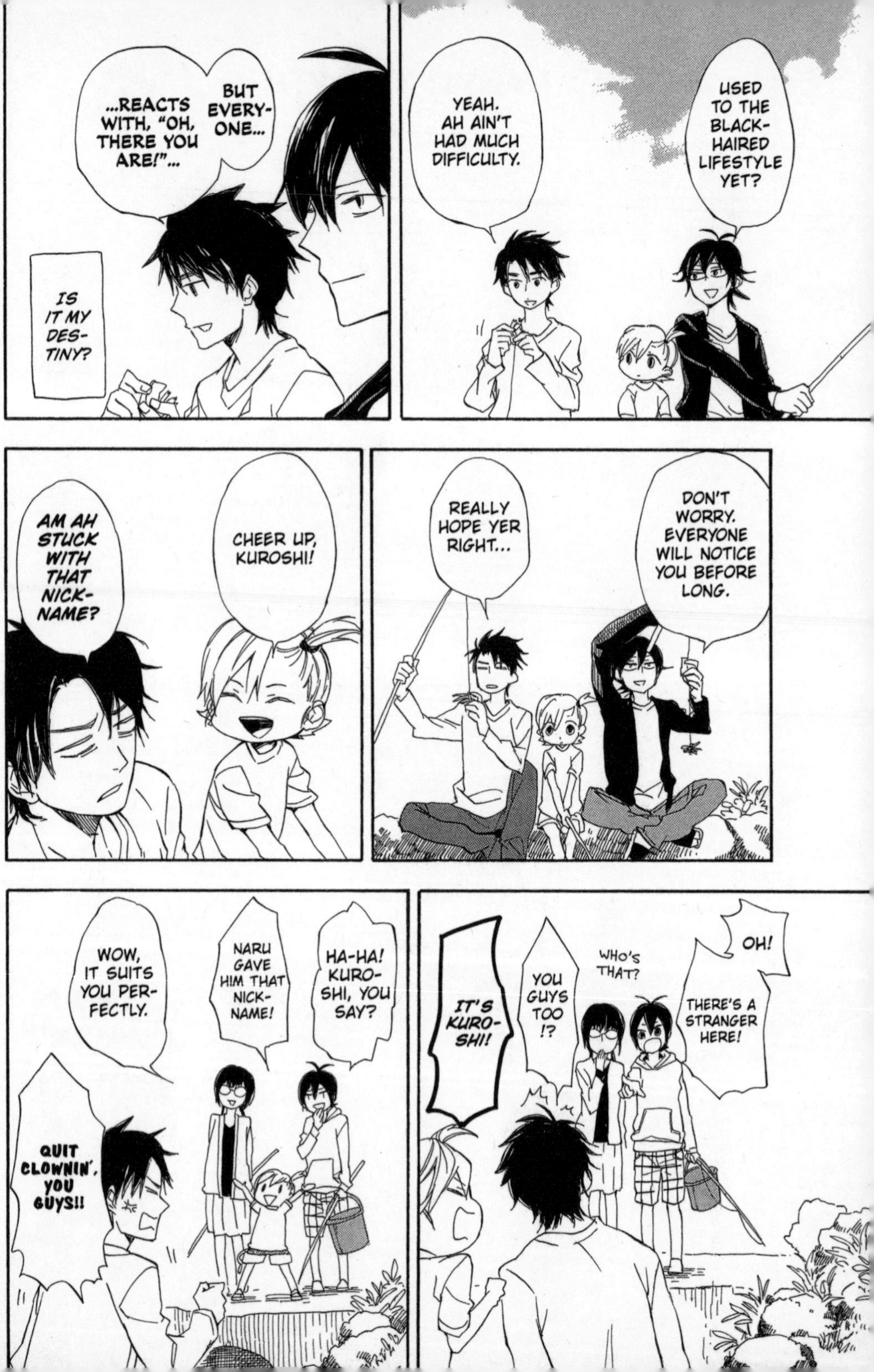
USED TO THE BLACK-HAIRED LIFESTYLE YET?
YEAH. AH AIN'T HAD MUCH DIFFICULTY.
BUT EVERY-ONE...
...REACTS WITH, "OH, THERE YOU ARE!"...
IS IT MY DES-TINY?
DON'T WORRY. EVERYONE WILL NOTICE YOU BEFORE LONG.
REALLY HOPE YER RIGHT...
CHEER UP, KUROSHI!
AM AH STUCK WITH THAT NICK-NAME?
OH!
THERE'S A STRANGER HERE!
WHO'S THAT?
YOU GUYS TOO!?
IT'S KURO-SHI!
HA-HA! KURO-SHI, YOU SAY?
NARU GAVE HIM THAT NICK-NAME!
WOW, IT SUITS YOU PER-FECTLY.
QUIT CLOWNIN', YOU GUYS!!

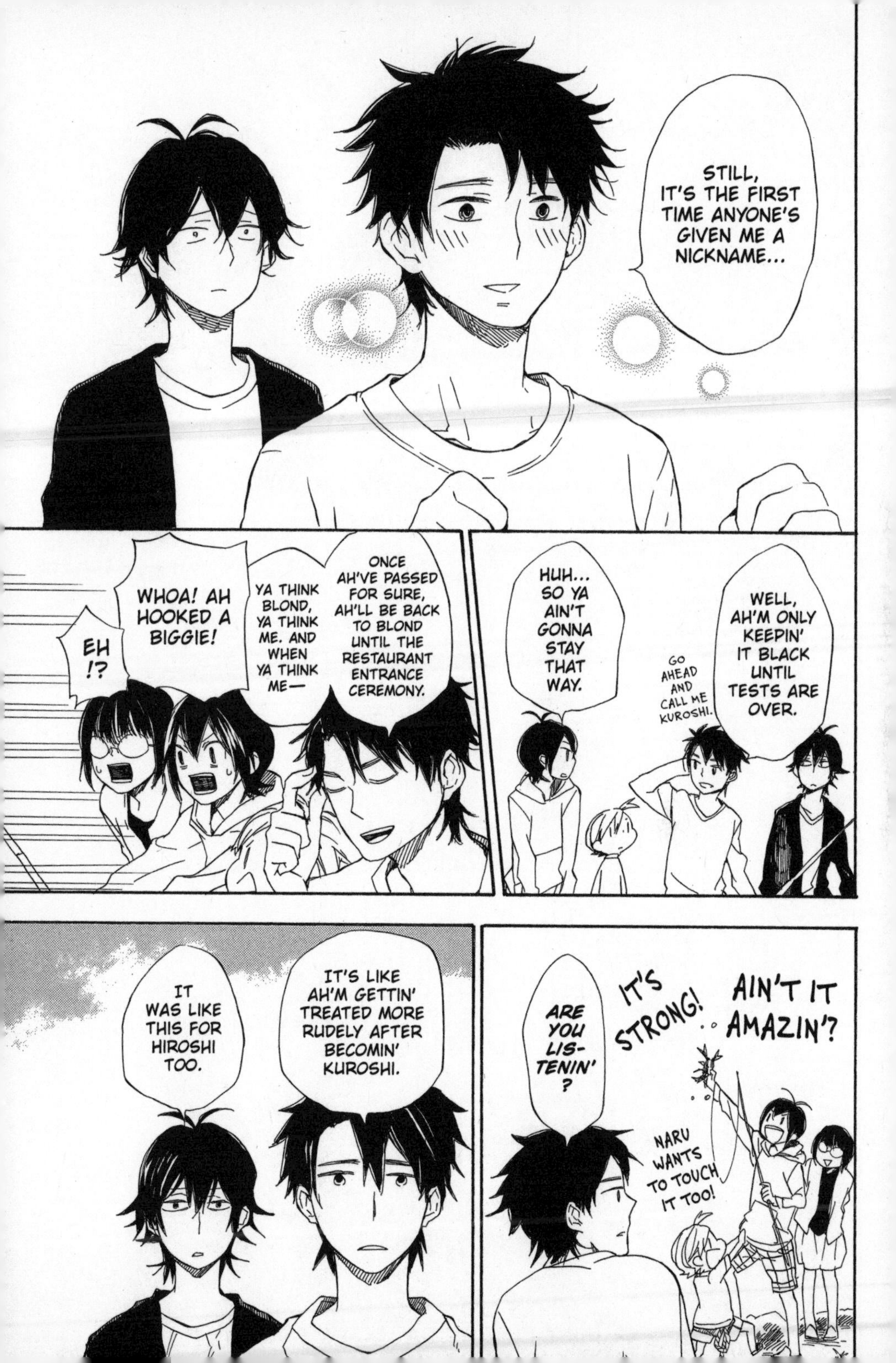
STILL, IT'S THE FIRST TIME ANYONE'S GIVEN ME A NICKNAME...
WELL, AH'M ONLY KEEPIN' IT BLACK UNTIL TESTS ARE OVER.
GO AHEAD AND CALL ME KUROSHI.
HUH... SO YA AIN'T GONNA STAY THAT WAY.
ONCE AH'VE PASSED FOR SURE, AH'LL BE BACK TO BLOND UNTIL THE RESTAURANT ENTRANCE CEREMONY.
YA THINK BLOND, YA THINK ME. AND WHEN YA THINK ME—
WHOA! AH HOOKED A BIGGIE!
EH !?
AIN'T IT AMAZIN'?
IT'S STRONG!
NARU WANTS TO TOUCH IT TOO!
ARE YOU LIS-TENIN' ?
IT'S LIKE AH'M GETTIN' TREATED MORE RUDELY AFTER BECOMIN' KUROSHI.
IT WAS LIKE THIS FOR HIROSHI TOO.

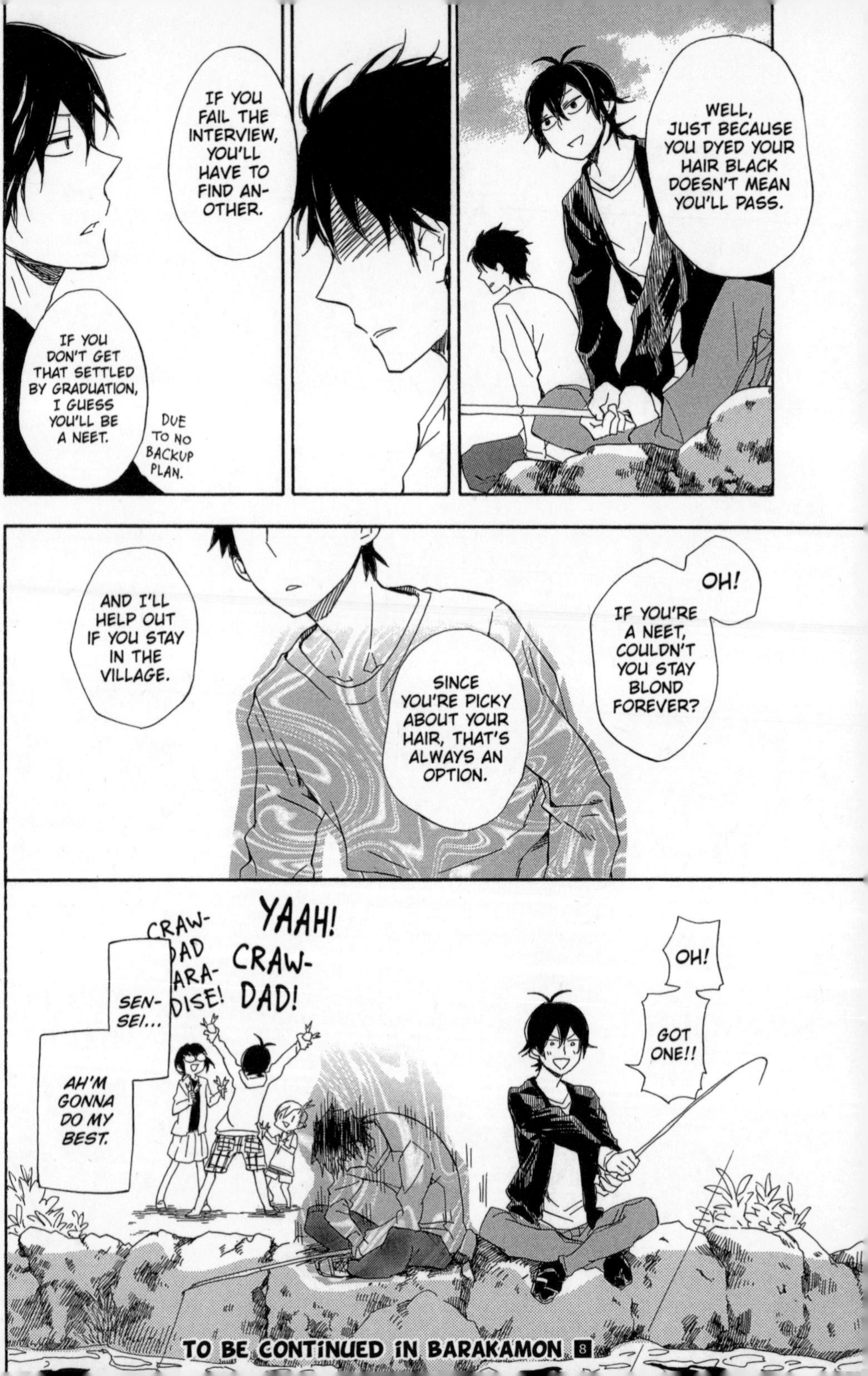
WELL, JUST BECAUSE YOU DYED YOUR HAIR BLACK DOESN'T MEAN YOU'LL PASS.
IF YOU FAIL THE INTERVIEW, YOU'LL HAVE TO FIND AN-OTHER.
IF YOU DON'T GET THAT SETTLED BY GRADUATION, I GUESS YOU'LL BE A NEET.
DUE TO NO BACKUP PLAN.
OH!
IF YOU'RE A NEET, COULDN'T YOU STAY BLOND FOREVER?
SINCE YOU'RE PICKY ABOUT YOUR HAIR, THAT'S ALWAYS AN OPTION.
AND I'LL HELP OUT IF YOU STAY IN THE VILLAGE.
OH!
GOT ONE!!
YAAH! CRAW-DAD!
CRAW- AD ARA- DISE!
SEN-SEI...
AH'M GONNA DO MY BEST.
TO BE CONTINUED IN BARAKAMON 8

BARAKAMON

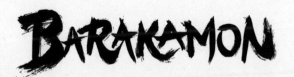

TRANSLATION NOTES

COMMON HONORIFICS

no honorific: Indicates familiarity or closeness; if used without permission or reason, addressing someone in this manner would constitute an insult.

-san: The Japanese equivalent of Mr./Mrs./Miss. If a situation calls for politeness, this is the fail-safe honorific.

-sama: Conveys great respect; may also indicate that the social status of the speaker is lower than that of the addressee.

-kun: Used most often when referring to boys, this indicates affection or familiarity. Occasionally used by older men among their peers, but it may also be used by anyone referring to a person of lower standing.

-chan: An affectionate honorific indicating familiarity used mostly in reference to girls; also used in reference to cute persons or animals of either gender.

-sensei: A Japanese term of respect commonly used for teachers, but can also refer to doctors, writers, and artists. Hence, Village Chief is not implying that Handa is a teacher when he calls him "sensei."

Calligraphy: Japanese calligraphy has a long history and tradition, with roots stemming from ancient China. One of the traditions carried over was the Chinese expression of the "Four Treasures," which refers to the brush, ink, paper, and inkstone used in calligraphy. Traditionally, an inkstick—solidified ink—is ground against an inkstone filled with water in order to produce ink with which to write. This time-consuming process helped to teach patience, which is important in the art of calligraphy. However, modern advances have developed a bottled liquid ink, commonly used by beginners and within the Japanese school system.

Gotou Dialect: Many of the villagers, especially the elderly ones, are actually speaking the local Gotou dialect in the original Japanese. This dialect is reflected in the English translation with some of the grammar elements of older Southern American English to give it a more rustic, rural coastal feel without making it too hard to read (it's not meant to replicate any particular American accent exactly). This approach is similar to how dialect is made accessible in Japanese media, including *Barakamon*, because a complete dialect with all of its different vocabulary would be practically incomprehensible to most Tokyo residents.

PAGE 18
demon instructor: This is used the same way "drill sergeant" might be used in English.

PAGE 24
"Fight on! One shot!": "*Faito! Ippatsu!*" is the catchphrase for the vitamin drink Lipovitan D and has been used in commercials since 1977.

PAGE 32
The Giant Turnip: Репка (Repka) is a Russian fairy tale that has been translated into a variety of languages, including English and Japanese. In the original Russian, all the character names rhyme by ending with the diminutive "ka," making the "X pulled Y, Y pulled Z" lines even funnier.

PAGE 39
Pompoko: "*Pompoko*" means to thump one's belly like a drum and/or have a very full stomach. It's commonly used with the Japanese native mammal called a "*tanuki*," or "raccoon dog."

PAGE 61
The Gorgeous Family: This is likely modeled after the early 1970s serial novel *The Grand Family* by Toyoko Yamasaki, which is about a powerful banking and manufacturing family in the 1960s with a dark secret and was adapted into a TV drama in 2007. With the company strife, politics, and family drama in the story, Sensei is right to worry about conflicting that by writing the title prettily!

PAGE 71
Rampo Edogawa: A famous Japanese mystery writer. His stories written in the 1930s had a fair amount of abnormal sexuality, which he called "ero (erotic)-guro (grotesque)-nonsense."

PAGE 77
"Han't kelp it.": In Japanese, Miwa said the pun, "*Wake wakame*," which substitutes *wakame* seaweed into the phrase "*Wake wakannai* (Makes no sense)."

PAGE 103
yams: Japanese sweet potatoes are different varieties than those grown in the U.S., with the most common satsuma variety having purple skin and sweet, light-yellow flesh.

PAGE 105
imoman: Short for "*Imo wa Manda ka na?*" I.e., "Ready yet, yams?"

PAGE 107
okaki: Snack made from mochi cut into thin strips, then baked or fried.

PAGE 113
Akki the Demon: One of the Japanese words for "demon" is actually pronounced *akki*.

PAGE 114
choosing chant: Japanese has a child's chant used for choosing one of multiple items, "*Dochira ni shiyou ka na*," much like the English chant "Eenie meenie miney mo."

"God in Hea-then": What Naru said in Japanese, "*ura no kami-sama* (god of the other side)," is actually a replacement for the more common phrase "*ten no kami-sama* (god in heaven)" in some regional variations of the "*Dochira ni shiyou ka na*" chant.

"Shouldn't you stop at three?": Sometimes the chant uses a count, and it's usually up to three, but there's at least one variation that goes up to ten.

PAGE 136
natto: Soybeans fermented until they become stringy; a common item to eat on rice for breakfast in eastern Japan.

Filament mushrooms: "*Nametake*" is the common name for mushrooms that have a very thin, elongated shape, and include *nameko* mushrooms.

character lunch: A lunch box made using food items specially assembled to look like a cartoon character (or something marginally resembling one in this case).

PAGE 138
Honshuu: The largest island in Japan, which contains most of the well-known cities such as Tokyo, Kyoto, and Hiroshima.
Hokkaido: The large northern island of Japan, containing the city of Sapporo.
Kyuushuu: The southwestern large island of Japan, containing the cities of Nagasaki and Fukuoka, is also the closest one to the villagers' home island of Gotou.
Okinawa: A chain of islands stretching far to the south and west, leading toward the island of Taiwan.

PAGE 139
Ayako Ueto: possibly a reference to a Japanese former adult-video actress.

PAGE 144
"drew" the word: The word "*kaku*," meaning "to write," can also be used for the verb "to draw"—"*egaku*" is a less ambiguous verb for "draw."

PAGE 148
volley? ballet?: These two words are easily confused in Japanese, since they both have the same pronunciation of "*baree*."

PAGE 149
King of the Pirates: Reference to the future dream of Monkey D. Luffy, the main character of the anime and manga series *One Piece*.

PAGE 156
kuro: Means "black," hence Naru's joke that Hiroshi should now be called "Kuroshi."

PAGE 157
nikujaga: A beef and potato stew made using Japanese seasonings.

PAGE 160
Kitakyushu: A large city at the northern tip of the island of Kyuushuu, just across a narrow strait from the main Japanese island, Honshuu.

PAGE 170
pianica: Aka "melodica," a wind instrument that's like a reed harmonica with a small piano keyboard.

PAGE 179
kankoro mochi: A type of soft rice cake with sweet potato mixed in.

PAGE 181
knee circle: A gymnastics horizontal bar move, where the person makes a complete circle around the bar, gripping it by one or both knees (just one in Kenta's case).

PAGE 182-185
Coin Dance: The *zeni-odori* is a folk dance from southwestern Japan, where the dancers use *zeni-daiko* (coin drums), a percussion instrument which is traditionally made by stringing old coins inside a stick of bamboo, to make a jangling sound by striking their body or the ground. However, the creator of this particular version of the dance appears to have included costume elements from a humorous folk dance called "*Dojosukui* (Loach Scooping)," where the dancers wear *ichimon* coin on their noses, scarves around their heads, and carry bamboo baskets to mimic fishing for loach. No wonder Handa wasn't sure if it was meant to be serious or funny...

PAGE 189
"The Tulip Song": Hina actually called it "*Saita Saita*," from the first full line of the Japanese children's song: "*Saita saita, tulip no hana ga* (bloomed, bloomed, tulips have bloomed)."

PAGE 202
NEET: Acronym for "Not engaged in Employment, Education, or Training."

BARAKAMON NEWS

Vol.510

We're including another figure.

SHIP ME BACK TO THE ISLAND...

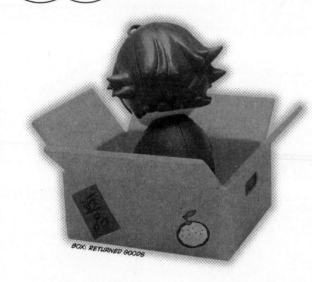

BOX: RETURNED GOODS

Satsuki Yoshino

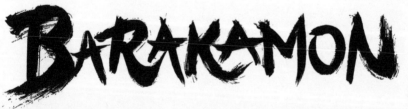

BARAKAMON

Volume 8

Regular Edition & First-Press Limited Special Edition

※ Figure images are all from during development.

ENGLISH REGULAR EDITION on sale December 2015!

Now a Series of Hapless Figures!!

Here's that scene!! His haplessness is even too much for his friend!!

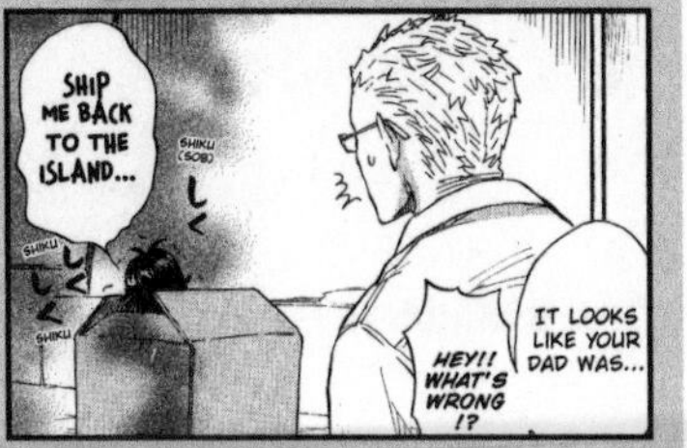
IT LOOKS LIKE YOUR DAD WAS...
HEY!! WHAT'S WRONG !?
SHIKU (SOB)
SHIP ME BACK TO THE ISLAND...
SHIKU
SHIKU

Everyone, thank you very much for buying Volume 7 of *BARAKAMON*! Due to unbelievable, popular demand, we are set to release a second first-press limited special edition that includes a "Hapless Handa-sensei Figure"! This figure depicts the too-hapless scene where the suit-wearing Handa-sensei gets into a cardboard box, wishing to get shipped back to the island! It's the reappearance of the panel from Act. 46 "I Am In Tokyo," from Volume 6!

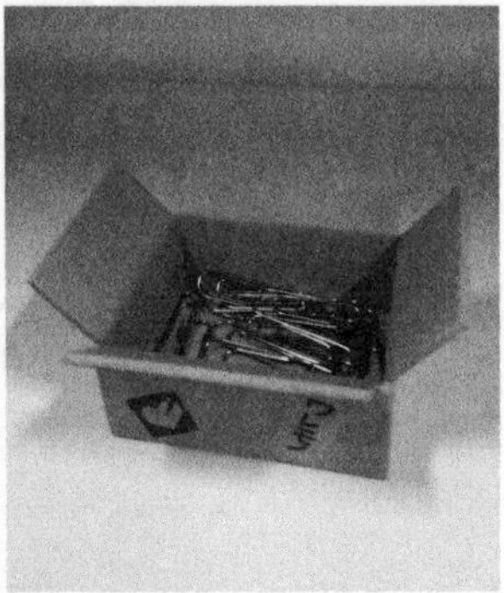

⬆ Because the box and Handa-sensei are separate, at worst you could use it as an accessory case for other trifles—very handy.☆ Volume 8 plus the figure will cost 1500 yen (including tax)!

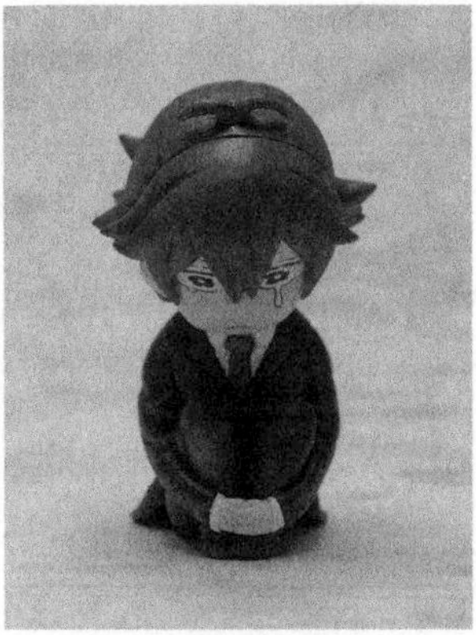

⬆ Out of the box, he's twice as sorry-looking. A full-grown man stubbornly hugging his knees is just begging for pathos. So hapless.

BOX: FRAGILE

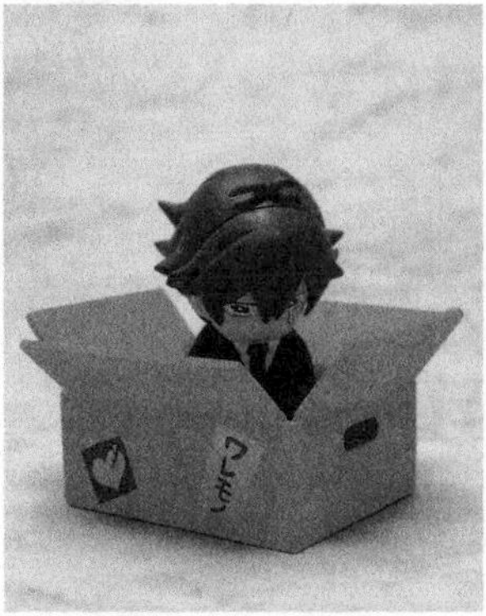

⬆ Has there ever been such a pathetic man in a suit? He really is like an abandoned puppy all alone in the city. Truly hapless.

This Limited Edition is Made-to-order!!

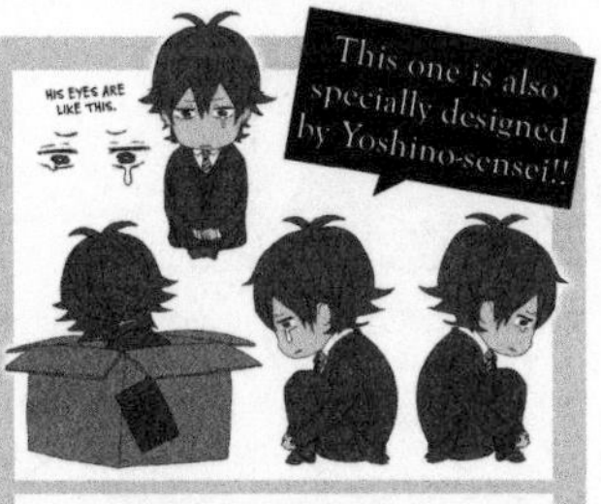
HIS EYES ARE LIKE THIS.
This one is also specially designed by Yoshino-sensei!!

NOTE FROM YEN PRESS

As with the previous volume, the limited edition figure was only available in Japan. Still, we hope you enjoyed the *BARAKAMON* news and photos from the original Volume 7!

Of course, the "regular edition" with just the comic will go on sale the same day, so please look forward to it!

Well then, I sincerely hope to see you all again in Volume 8!!

The first-press limited special edition is a "made-to-order" product that will only be made for the quantity of preorders received, so those who wish to have one should be sure to reserve a copy. Please check the details on how to preorder a copy at Gangan ONLINE.

MON 7

SATSUKI YOSHINO

WITHDRAWN

Translation/Adaptation: Krista Shipley, Karie Shipley
Lettering: Lys Blakeslee

This book is a work of fiction. Names, characters, places, and incidents
are the product of the author's imagination or are used fictitiously.
Any resemblance to actual events, locales, or persons, living or dead, is
coincidental.

Barakamon vol. 7 © 2013 Satsuki Yoshino / SQUARE ENIX CO., LTD. First
published in Japan in 2013 by SQUARE ENIX CO., LTD. English translation
rights arranged with SQUARE ENIX CO., LTD. and Hachette Book Group
through Tuttle-Mori Agency, Inc.

Translation © 2015 by SQUARE ENIX CO., LTD.

Yen Press
Hachette Book Group
1290 Avenue of the Americas
New York, NY 10104

www.HachetteBookGroup.com
www.YenPress.com

Yen Press is an imprint of Hachette Book Group, Inc.
The Yen Press name and logo are
trademarks of Hachette Book Group, Inc.

The publisher is not responsible for websites
(or their content) that are not owned by the publisher.

First Yen Press Edition: October 2015

ISBN: 978-0-316-34035-9

10 9 8 7 6 5 4 3 2 1

BVG

Printed in the United States of America